Philology and Confrontation

Philology and Confrontation

Paul Hacker on Traditional and Modern Vedānta

Edited by
Wilhelm Halbfass

STATE UNIVERSITY OF NEW YORK PRESS

Published by Ruth Fisher
Marketing by Bernadette LaManna

Published by
State University of New York Press, Albany

Printed in the United States of America

For information, address the State University of New York Press, State University Plaza, Albany NY 12246

Library of Congress Cataloging-in-Publication Data

Hacker, Paul, 1913–
Philology and confrontation : Paul Hacker on traditional and modern vedanta / edited by Wilhelm Halbfass.
p. cm.
Includes index.
ISBN 0-7914-2582-7 (PB : acid free). — ISBN 0-7914-2581-9 (CH : acid free)
I. Halbfass, Wilhelm.
B132.V3H28 1995
181'.48—dc20 95-19393
CIP

10 9 8 7 6 5 4 3 2 1

Contents

Foreword

Lambert Schmithausen

Paul Hacker (1913–1979) was one of the most important and influential German Indologists. To be sure, there were more prolific scholars; poor health prevented him from completing much of what he had begun. Nonetheless, his work has been truly pioneering in various areas of Indian studies.

At the beginning of his Indological career, Hacker studied the works ascribed to Śaṅkara and was intrigued by the problem of authenticity. To solve it, he developed a method based primarily on internal criteria, such as terminology. He counterchecked this method against the works of other representatives of Advaita Vedānta, especially those of Śaṅkara's personal disciples, on whose ideas he published an important monograph. He was, however, unable to complete the book on the earlier Upaniṣads he had been planning for many years. Some of his basic ideas on this subject, as recorded in his classes, were published posthumously by his pupil Klaus Rüping.[1] Paul Hacker also initiated new ways of exploring what he called the anonymous literature of Hinduism, especially the Epics and Purāṇas. He developed Willibald Kirfel's text-historical method into an instrument for the discovery not only of textual changes and developments, but also of the motives and ideas behind these changes. In this way, he was able to contribute to a more differentiated picture of the various currents of what we call medieval Hinduism.

For Hacker, Indology was not a merely antiquarian subject; it was also concerned with present-day India. He made substantial contributions to the study of Hindi syntax, and showed new ways for understanding and questioning what he used to call "Neo-Hinduism" (in contradistinction to contemporary traditional Hinduism).

Paul Hacker's scholarship was, moreover, characterized by a high level of reflection on the methods and concepts he used. Several of his articles are dedicated to questions of methodology or to the clarification of concepts. He was particularly interested in such Indian religious or philosophical concepts for which there is no Western equivalent, and he tried to identify specifically Indian ways of thinking (among these, what he called "inclusivism" turned out to be most challenging).

Paul Hacker's work has a very sound scholarly and philological basis; but it is certainly not uncommitted scholarship. His personal religious and philosophical background is revealed in his theological writings. As the editor of the present volume has put it, Hacker is "also a personally and systematically committed participant in the continuing encounter and dialogue between India and Europe."[2] The articles on traditional and modern Vedānta translated and compiled in this volume provide ample evidence for this. The volume itself is a timely and welcome effort to make Hacker's contributions more universally accessible through the medium of English.

Notes

1. See Paul Hacker, *Grundlagen indischer Dichtung und indischen Denkens.* Ed. by Klaus Rüping (Vienna, 1985).

2. See Wilhelm Halbfass, *India and Europe. An Essay in Understanding* (Albany, 1988), p. 418.

Introduction
An Uncommon Orientalist: Paul Hacker's Passage to India

Wilhelm Halbfass

I. Paul Hacker's biography does not require much space.[1] He was born on January 6, 1913, in Seelscheid near Cologne in Germany. From 1932 he studied Indology and various other philological disciplines (Romance languages, English, and Russian) at the universities of Bonn, Heidelberg, Frankfurt, and Berlin. In addition to his philological studies, he attended lectures in Indo-European linguistics, theology, and philosophy. In 1940 he submitted his doctoral dissertation on the "realism" of the Russian novelist I. S. Turgenev at the University of Berlin *(Studien zum Realismus I. S. Turgenevs).* After World War II, during which he was drafted into military service, and various interim jobs, including a brief period of work for the Allied "German News Service," he resumed his academic career in 1946 at the University of Bonn, where he had the support of Willibald Kirfel, the well-known Purāṇa scholar. In 1949 he submitted his "habilitation" thesis on the early history of Advaita Vedānta *(Untersuchungen zur Geschichte des frühen Advaita).* Major parts of this thesis were published in 1951 under the title *Untersuchungen über Texte des frühen Advaitavāda. 1: Die Schüler Śaṅkaras* (Ak. Wiss. Lit. Mainz, 1950). A section on Vimuktātman's *Iṣṭasiddhi,* which had been part of the thesis, was omitted from the published version.

In 1950 Hacker started teaching at the University of Münster. In 1954 he accepted a professorship at the Mithila Postgraduate Research Institute in Darbhanga, India, where he spent a little more than a year. In 1955 he returned to Germany to become W. Kirfel's successor and occupy the chair for Indology at the University of Bonn. This was Germany's oldest chair for Indian studies, founded in 1818 and first held by A. W. von Schlegel. In 1963 he moved to Münster as director of the newly established Institute of Indology (Indologisches Seminar), a position he held until his retirement in 1978. In 1971 he taught Indian philosophy as a visiting professor at the University of Pennsylvania in Philadelphia. A major event in Hacker's life that was not part of his academic career took place in 1962: his conversion from Lutheran Protestantism to Roman Catholicism.

Paul Hacker died on March 18, 1979, less than a year after his retirement from the University of Münster.

II. On the occasion of Paul Hacker's sixty-fifth birthday, most of his articles and some major book reviews were collected and reprinted under the title *Kleine Schriften* (ed. by L. Schmithausen. Wiesbaden, 1978). This volume also contains an elaborate and almost complete list of Hacker's publications, including his book reviews.[2] Various additional materials were published after the appearance of the *Kleine Schriften* and after Hacker's death in 1979. These include an article on "inclusivism" (1983),[3] the text of Hacker's last lecture course at the University of Münster (*Grundlagen indischer Dichtung und indischen Denkens,* ed. by K. Rüping. Vienna, 1985; i.e., "Foundations of Indian Poetry and Thought"), and his doctoral dissertation of 1940 on I. S. Turgenev's realism.[4]

We do not have to enumerate and discuss Hacker's publications in detail. Some general observations and references to a few exemplary pieces will be sufficient. Lambert Schmithausen, editor of the *Kleine Schriften,* has divided Hacker's articles into the following categories: a) methods and tasks of Indian studies; b) Indian philosophy, especially Advaita Vedānta; c) comparative studies; d) the religious history of Hinduism; e) Neo-Hinduism; f) modern Indo-Aryan languages; g) theology. Apart from his early work on Turgenev, these categories apply also to Hacker's monographs. Among these, the most significant ones deal with Advaita Vedānta, especially Śaṅkara and his disciples (*Untersuchungen über Texte des frühen Advaitavāda. 1: Die Schüler Śaṅkaras.* Ak.Wiss.Lit.Mainz, 1950; see also *Vivarta.* Ak.Wiss.Lit.Mainz, 1953), and with Purāṇic mythology (*Prahlāda. Werden und Wandlungen einer Idealgestalt.* Ak.Wiss.Lit.Mainz, 1959). Another exemplary study deals with the function of auxiliary verbs in Hindi (*Zur Funktion einiger Hilfsverben im modernen Hindi.* Ak.Wiss.Lit.Mainz, 1958). In the field of theology, Hacker published a critical and controversial account of Luther's notion of faith (*Das Ich im Glauben bei Martin Luther*. Graz, 1966). An abbreviated version of this book appeared in English (*The Ego in Faith: Martin Luther and the Origin of Anthropocentric Religion*. Chicago, 1970).[5]

A chronological overview of Hacker's writings reveals some general trends and developments. For more than a decade, the philological exploration of Advaita Vedānta, in particular the works of Śaṅkara and his disciples, is clearly predominant. Excursions into other areas of Indian philosophy are relatively rare. The series of publications in this area begins with the article "Śaṅkarācārya and Śaṅkarabhagavatpāda" (1947); the topic of this article, which concerns Śaṅkara's personal development and the authenticity of much of the literature associated with his name, is resumed in the article "Śaṅkara der Yogin und Śaṅkara der Advaitin" (1968). The two monographs mentioned earlier and the important article "Eigentümlichkeiten der Lehre und Terminologie Śaṅkaras" (1950) constitute further highlights in this series.[6] The philological approach to Advaita Vedānta is supplemented by comparative studies which correlate and contrast Advaita Vedānta with Western, primarily Christian, philosophy and theology; as an example, we may mention the article "Sein und Geist im Vedānta" (1969) which compares and contrasts Śaṅkara with Thomas Aquinas.[7]

Beginning in the late fifties, Purāṇic mythology, the general development of Hindu religious thought, and Neo-Hinduism play an increasingly conspicuous role in Hacker's research and publications. We have already mentioned the classic study of *Prahlāda* (1959). To this, we may add a study of the concept of *vrata* (Ak.Wiss.Lit. Göttingen, 1973) and important articles on the development of the *avatāra* doctrine ("Zur Entwicklung der Avatāralehre," 1960), the concept of *śraddhā* or faith ("Śraddhā," 1963), and related topics.[8] Neo-Hinduism, or Hindu modernism of the nineteenth and twentieth centuries, emerges as an area of provocative research and interpretation in articles on the modern reinterpretation of the concept of *dharma* ("Der Dharmabegriff des Neuhinduismus," 1958), the influence of Schopenhauer's thought on the idea of "practical Vedānta" ("Schopenhauer und die Ethik des Hinduism," 1961), Vivekananda's religious nationalism ("Der religiöse Nationalismus Vivekanandas," 1971), etc.[9] Concerning Hacker's research on the Hindi language, we may note that, in addition to his linguistic studies, he also showed a special interest in its historical role as a national language and the problems concerning its semantic adjustment to the modern Westernized world ("Probleme der indischen Nationalsprache," 1966).

Theological interests and preoccupations became more conspicuous in Hacker's later years. A remarkable personal statement, "Today's India and We Christians" ("Das heutige Indien und wir Christen") was published in 1962, the year of his conversion to Catholicism.[10] Numerous theological publications followed after his conversion. In addition to his book on Luther (1966; English version 1970), we may mention such articles as "Priestertum und Eucharistie heute" (1970) and "The Christian Attitude toward Non-Christian Religions" (1971).[11] In his last contributions to Indian studies, Hacker tried to sum up the most basic results of his previous work and to define some of the most general and distinctive features of the Indian religious and philosophical tradition. In particular, this applies to the lectures on the "Foundations of Indian Poetry and Thought" published after his death.[12]

III. In his later years, Hacker liked to present himself as an outsider, and even as an outcaste, among German Indologists; at the very least, we may agree that he was a somewhat unusual figure among his colleagues. But he also distanced himself from much of what was going on in contemporary theology, philosophy, and religious studies. There was overt confrontation not only with the objects of his research, i.e., the Indian religious and philosophical teachings, but also with the ideas and methods of his fellow-researchers.[13] In his methodological articles as well as in other (written and oral) statements, he criticized some of the leading figures of German Indology. His methodological critique of the work of Paul Thieme gained special significance and recognition, as well as a certain degree of notoriety. This critique found its most coherent expression in an article on the "method of philological concept research" ("Zur Methode der philologischen Begriffsforschung," 1965).[14] The article deals, above all, with the postulate of "consistent translating" ("konsequentes Übersetzen"), i.e., the idea that one and the same term and concept should be used to translate a foreign (specifically Sanskrit) word. The case in question is Heinrich Lüders' consistent rendering of *ṛta* as "truth" ("Wahrheit"), which Thieme defends against critics, such as Gonda and Renou, and tries to justify in a more theoretical fashion. Hacker resumed and continued the debate in his later monograph on *vrata* (1973), in which he argues in detail against the attempt of Thieme's disciple, Hanns-Peter Schmidt, to render and explain the word *vrata* in all its occurrences invariably as "vow" ("Gelübde").[15] Hacker's sustained critique of the postulate of "consistent translation" has, of course, wider ramifications.

It implies some fundamental disagreements concerning the very nature of translation, interpretation, and philological research, as well as the role and relevance of methodological reflection and hermeneutic awareness.[16] It also shows that Hacker found such reflections either to be lacking or inadequate in the work of some of his most distinguished colleagues.

There is another major point of contention which Hacker saw, once again, exemplified in the work of Heinrich Lüders, specifically in Lüders' studies on the Ṛṣyaśṛṅga myth and its historical transformations.[17] What he found here was, in his view, a form of historical and philological positivism which was, nonetheless, committed to the Romantic ideal of the "origin," or the "original version," an obsession with "earlier stages" and *disiecta membra,* an attitude of reduction, dissection, and unrestrained objectification, and a corresponding disregard for organic historical growth and meaningful totalities. With some intended hyperbole, Hacker describes the results of Lüders' analysis as follows: "The scholar has won a total victory. The textual bodies are lying on the philological battlefield, smashed and lifeless, beautifully lined up with one another, side by side with a garbage pile of inner contradictions, misunderstandings and textual corruptions. But distantly above the bloody philological battleground, the romantic 'blue blossom' of the *origin* shines in positivistic abstractness."[18] Hacker proposes an idea of philology which is not restricted to dissection and the pursuit of origins or earlier versions. The positivistic method fails to realize that legends, myths, doctrines, etc., constitute meaningful structures ("Gestalten") and totalities, which undergo historical changes and remain meaningful through such changes. This means that "later versions" deserve as much attention as their earlier or "original" elements, and that the changes and transformations themselves have to be explored as meaningful historical processes.[19]

Of course, one might object at this point that Hacker's own philological contributions, in particular his investigations concerning Purāṇic mythology, apply the same methodological patterns which he denounced in his critique of Lüders. Didn't he follow the lead of Willibald Kirfel, his predecessor at the University of Bonn, who certainly was no less positivistic than Lüders? Isn't his *Prahlāda,* his *magnum opus* in the field of Purāṇic studies, dedicated to Kirfel? Indeed, Hacker did pay tribute to Kirfel's work, but he also distanced himself from it. In particular, he rejected the claim that the reduction of the Purāṇas to certain ultimate units, and thus the dissolution of the very form and structure of a Purāṇa, was the "final result" ("letztes Ergebnis") of Purāṇic philology.[20] Such dissection may be legitimate as a first step, but in the end it should contribute to a better understanding of the Purāṇas as "individual totalities" ("individuelle Ganzheiten") which combine the various parts and pieces in a historically and spiritually meaningful fashion. Philology itself not only permits but requires this step beyond the goals and methods of Kirfel.[21]

Hacker's own contributions as a philologist lie in two different areas: 1) in his exploration of anonymous Sanskrit literature, primarily the Purāṇas; 2) in his search for criteria of authorship and authenticity and for distinctive individual features in the literature of Advaita Vedānta, specifically the works of Śaṅkara and his disciples. In the second area, too, the first step has to be one of analysis and dissection of what is often presented as one unified school of thought. We have to determine what sets Śaṅkara's genuine works apart from those of Sureśvara or Vimuktātman, as well as from those countless works which were falsely ascribed to him; we may even try to distinguish between his own late and earlier works.[22] But in the end we also want to know what holds Śaṅkara's thought together; we want to understand its inner unity and its most fundamental philosophical and theological premises, as well as those of Advaita Vedānta in general. There can hardly be any doubt that, once again, Hacker was at least as committed to the second step as to the first.[23]

IV. This is not the place to discuss Hacker's philological achievements in detail, to review the specific results and problems of his treatment of anonymous Sanskrit literature, or to assess his arguments concerning the authorship and authenticity of particular Advaita Vedānta works. In any case, it would be safe to say that his contributions are both challenging and exemplary, and that they have had a considerable influence on the development of Indian philological studies. His *Prahlāda* has become a kind of classic in its field, even though its actual readership has remained rather limited because of linguistic and other reasons. His philological explorations of Advaita Vedānta, and specifically of the nature and authenticity of the literature associated with the name of Śaṅkara, have been continued by Sengaku Mayeda, Tilmann Vetter, and others.[24]

As we have seen, Hacker's notion of philology is wider and more open than that of other leading Indologists. But even in this extended sense of the word, Hacker's work was obviously not restricted to philology. With growing intensity, it crossed over into the areas of theology, philosophy, and cross-cultural and comparative studies.

In an article published in 1967/68, Hacker made some programmatic statements about "Indology between Past and Future" ("Die Indologie zwischen Vergangenheit und Zukunft"): "If Indology has a future, then this is possible only in the same manner in which it began: i.e., in a living interaction with European spiritual and intellectual life. . . . There ought to be a philosophizing which is based on an immediate knowledge of Indian *and* European sources."[25] In the following section, Hacker emphasizes the special affinity between Indian studies and theology (which had become his own major preoccupation by this time): "Today, the proximity of theology is greater than ever before. . . . But today as ever, India is the classical land for the study of source materials in the history of religion." Such study requires a clear perspective, a sense of direction, a "religious decision" ("religiöse Entscheidung"). A complete absence of preconceptions, a total freedom from any sense of commitment, pure objectivity, would be counterproductive. "Theological thought can open the religious scholar's eyes for realities which would otherwise remain hidden from him."[26] In conclusion, the article calls for scholars "who combine theology and philology in one and the same person, whose eyes have been opened for the essentials by theology, and who have learned through philological means to grasp the meaning of religious or theological notions of Hinduism in their own appropriate context, and then to contrast them in a precise manner with Christian thought, before venturing into speculations."[27] It is hardly necessary to emphasize that this may be read as an expression of Hacker's own self-understanding and as a programmatic statement of the goals and standards he had set for himself at this point in his career several years after his conversion to Catholicism.

It would certainly be wrong to view Hacker's earlier philological work as a deliberate preparation for his later attempts to combine Indology and theology. Nonetheless, there is an undeniable direction in his development. His philological dedication to the works of Śaṅkara and Advaita Vedānta reflects his intense personal fascination with the teachings of nondualism. His resolute resumption of a Christian standpoint and finally his conversion to the Catholic faith are certainly not unrelated to the challenge of Advaita Vedānta. The monograph *Vivarta* (1953), which concludes the series of his earlier philological Vedānta studies, indicates that Hacker was now moving toward a more confrontational approach.

At the end of this study, he deplores what he considers to be the ultimate failure of the concept of *vivarta* in the works of Vimuktātman and Prakāśānanda, and he speaks of an "attitude, which was no longer committed to an increase of knowledge, but only to the rigid redemption of monistic mysticism."[28] This element of confrontation becomes much more central and explicit in some of his later articles on Advaita Vedānta, such as "The Idea of the Person in the Thinking of Vedānta Philosophers" ("Die Idee der Person im Denken von Vedānta-Philosophen," 1963) and "Being and Spirit in Vedānta" ("Sein und Geist im Vedānta," first published in an Italian version in 1969).[29] Again and again, his arguments revolve around what he considered to be the great challenges, but also fatal flaws of radical nondualism; above all, the devaluation and, ultimately, elimination of the idea of the person, i.e., the human person as well as the personal God. Nonetheless, he continued to search for a fundamental rapport and the potential for a dialogue in this most crucial and problematic area of religious thought. He was convinced that he had found an implicit, unacknowledged anthropology, even a latent theory of personhood, in Śaṅkara's philosophy of the spirit. (See, for instance, "Śaṅkara's Conception of Man," 1970). Hacker's fascination with the Vedānta concept of *cit* or spirit is still evident in his last article on Advaita Vedānta, which compares the thought of Śaṅkara with that of Plotinus and other Neoplatonists ("Cit and Noûs, or the Concept of Spirit in Vedāntism and in Neoplatonism," 1976).[30]

V. Hacker's confrontational approach to Indian thought takes a somewhat different turn in his work on Neo-Vedānta, i.e., nontraditional, modern Vedānta, as exemplified by Swami Vivekananda or Sarvepalli Radhakrishnan. Here we are not simply dealing with a foreign, non-Christian, non-Western philosophy and religion, but with ways of thinking which are, more or less explicitly, responses to Western and Christian ideas. According to Hacker, they are no longer authentic expressions of the Indian tradition; they are, in a sense, hybrid formations. They require a different mode of access. 'Understanding,' as well as 'confrontation,' cannot have the same meaning in this case as in the case of classical Advaita Vedānta represented by Śaṅkara and his followers. Whatever Hacker's disagreements with classical, traditional Advaita Vedānta may be, he certainly respects it in its genuine, authentic otherness, as a challenge against which he has to rediscover and reaffirm his own identity. Such fundamental respect seems to be absent when he is dealing with what he calls Neo-

Hinduism. Here, the otherness has become questionable. Vivekananda, Radhakrishnan, and the other Neo-Vedāntins are treated as dialogue partners with a broken identity who cannot truly and authentically speak for themselves and for the Indian tradition. They have made too many concessions; they have blurred crucial lines of demarcation. Instead of confronting them directly as representatives of genuinely different religious and philosophical views, Hacker seems preoccupied with exposing what distinguishes their thought from that of the tradition. He may even present himself as an advocate of the tradition against its modern spokesmen and interpreters. He invokes, for instance, the "magnificent discipline" ("grossartige Zucht") of classical Indian thought against the propensity for an "undisciplined rambling of the spirit" ("regelloses Schweifen des Geistes") which he finds in the works of such Neo-Hindus or Neo-Vedāntins as Radhakrishnan.[31] We may note here that the term "Neo-Hinduism" ("Neuhinduismus"), which Hacker borrowed from the Jesuit scholar Robert Antoine (who may have adopted it from Brajendranath Seal, 1864–1938), is much more visible and significant in his writings than "Neo-Vedānta," which appears only sporadically.[32] "Neo-Vedānta" or "Neo-Vedāntism" and the corresponding Bengali expression *abhinava vedānta* had been used earlier by Christian missionaries as well as Hindu traditionalists against the innovations of Rammohan Roy.[33]

Nonetheless, there may be something vicarious and not entirely genuine in Hacker's own philological and historical denunciation of the inauthenticity of Neo-Vedānta. This is the impression one gets from a close reading of his article on "Schopenhauer and Hindu Ethics" ("Schopenhauer und die Ethik des Hinduismus," 1961), in which he deals with the idea of "practical Vedānta," i.e., the attempt to apply the "great saying" of radical nondualism, *tat tvam asi,* in a practical, ethical sense. Hacker describes the "*tat tvam asi* ethics" as a symptom of a generally hybrid, derivative, and inauthentic way of thinking, a reflection of the colonial situation, an apologetic response to foreign critique. Yet his article shows that, even in its Neo-Vedāntic reinterpretations and alleged adulterations, Vedāntic nondualism continues to be a challenge for him. Hacker presents himself as an "Indologist and historian";[34] the contents and methodology of his article seem to support this claim. Yet through all the textual documentation and historical analysis and the triumphant display of philological and chronological evidence, we also hear the voice of an advocate of the European tradition and, more specifically, of a Christian theologian. The historical analysis itself, in all its "objectivity," reflects but also conceals a very pronounced sense of religious and cultural identity and an uncompromising commitment to certain Christian and European premises and values. Of course, as we have seen elsewhere, Hacker himself rejects pure objectivity as an abstract and vacuous ideal.[35]

Hacker presents the historical argument that in traditional India, prior to the influence of Western (i.e., in this case, Schopenhauerian) thought, Vedāntic nondualism was not applied in an ethical sense. But he also claims that it could not possibly have been applied in this way. Nondualism, in particular the purely "cognitional" nondualism of classical Advaita Vedānta, is, in his view, simply incompatible with ethics: "Nondualistic ethics" is a "logical impossibility," a "monstrosity."[36] Nondualism leaves no room for the idea of the person. Without recognition of the existence of persons and interpersonal relations, ethical conduct, as understood by Hacker, would be impossible.[37] This is, of course, a premise which Vivekananda rejects. In his lecture on "Practical Vedānta," he is an eloquent advocate of an impersonalistic metaphysics and ethics, and of the compatibility of impersonalism and ethical commitment. As he sees it, only impersonalism gives us the necessary freedom from attachment, fear, and egoism which makes ethical behavior possible.[38]

Hacker's general diagnosis of modern Indian thought and of what he calls "Neo-Hinduism" which concludes his article on "Schopenhauer and Hindu Ethics" sounds very harsh indeed. Among the cases of Neo-Hindu reinterpretation and accommodation which he cites in this section, we find the concept of *dharma.* In several other studies, most explicitly in his article "The Concept of Dharma in Neo-Hinduism" ("Der Dharmabegriff des Neuhinduismus," 1958), which opens the series of his studies on Neo-Hinduism, he tried to demonstrate how this key-concept of traditional Hindu self-understanding assumed a fundamentally new meaning and function in modern Indian thought, beginning with Bankim Chandra Chatterjee in the nineteenth century. This process, in which *dharma* was presented as an equivalent of, but also a response to, the Western notion of "religion," reflects a fundamental change in the Hindu sense of identity and in the attitude toward other religious and cultural traditions. The foreign notions of "religion" and "nation" became tools of self-definition, and a new and precarious sense of the "unity of Hinduism" and of national as well as religious identity took root.[39]

VI. The sense of identity and otherness, the meaning of unity and plurality, and the potential for interaction and dialogue with other religious groups in both traditional and modern Hinduism emerge as an important complex of themes in Hacker's work. His interest in and commitment to these themes found a very visible and at the same time problematic and controversial expression in his propositions concerning the role of inclusivism in Indian thought.[40]

"Inclusivism" ("Inklusivismus") is the title of a posthumous article by Hacker, and it is a topic which accompanied his Indological research as well as his theological and philosophical reflection for several decades. It concerns his Christian self-understanding no less than his understanding of Hinduism and the Indian tradition in general. He presents numerous exemplifications from both traditional and modern Indian thought; he refers to the Purāṇas, the Bhagavadgītā, Tulsīdās, but also to Radhakrishnan and other Neo-Hindus. The central element in his definitions and exemplifications is the practice of "claiming for, and thus including in, one's own religion" or world view what belongs in reality to another, foreign or competing system.[41] It is a subordinating identification of other teachings with parts or preliminary stages of one's own religious system, which is thus presented as a superior structure, and an implicit anticipation of competing views.

Hacker first used the terms 'inclusivism,' 'inclusivistic,' etc., in a somewhat casual and tentative fashion, in his article "Religious Tolerance and Intolerance in Hinduism" ("Religiöse Toleranz und Intoleranz im Hinduismus," 1957). Here, he classifies various types of tolerance in the Indian tradition, focuses on what he calls "doctrinal tolerance" ("doktrinäre Toleranz"), and suggests that it amounts very often to an "inclusivistic attitude."[42] In conclusion, he questions the applicability of the terms 'tolerance' and 'intolerance' to the Indian religious situation. In a series of subsequent statements Hacker supplemented and modified his observations. In a review article published in 1964, his statements became more pronounced. He now described inclusivism as "typically Indian" and essentially different from tolerance, and suggested that its presentation, or rather misrepresentation, as tolerance was a device to maintain "the fiction of unity in Hinduism."[43] The topic became most conspicuous toward the end of Hacker's life, especially in his posthumous article "Inklusivismus." In another posthumous publication, *Grundlagen indischer Dichtung und indischen Denkens* (1985; based on his lecture course of 1978), he treats inclusivism as a case of "gradualism."[44]

A chronological review of Hacker's statements reveals a development in which his views became more sweeping and radical. In his earlier approach, he dealt with various modes of religious encounter and interaction in India and discussed the applicability of certain Western terms, especially 'tolerance,' to these phenomena. In his later statements, above all in his posthumous article, he presented inclusivism as a peculiar mental and spiritual attitude, genuinely different from tolerance, which was quintessentially, even exclusively, Indian and had no real equivalent outside of the Indian "cultural domain" ("Kulturkreis").[45] However, Hacker did not make any serious effort to demonstrate its general absence in all other religious and cultural traditions. What he is ultimately concerned about is its distinction from the Christian approach to other religions, which presupposes, in his view, a clear recognition of *others* in their *otherness.* More specifically, he contrasts the dynamic interaction of early Christianity with the Greco-Roman world, its active and deliberate "use" *(chrēsis)* of "heathen" concepts to articulate its own message, with the attitude of inclusivism.[46]

Once again, Hacker is asserting his Christian identity against what he considers to be an Indian form of self-assertion. He seems genuinely convinced that his notion of inclusivism is the result of Indological, i.e., historical and philological, research and thus an essentially empirical discovery. Yet it is obvious that it is also an expression of specific religious and philosophical premises and convictions. In his use of the idea of inclusivism, Hacker is not only making statements about India, but also about himself. He is a personally committed participant in the encounter between India and Europe, and in particular between Hinduism and Christianity. Here, as elsewhere in his work, philology and confrontation go hand in hand.[47] At this point, it is not necessary to discuss the more specific questions to which Hacker's treatment of inclusivism gives rise, or the criticism to which it has been subject.[48]

VII. More or less explicitly, Hacker reiterates his questions concerning the Hindu sense of identity and his critique of the idea of the "unity of Hinduism" in a number of different articles and book reviews. In his view, the unity of Hinduism is a modern postulate, a product of Neo-Hinduism. It is "essentially inspired by apologetics and nationalism,"[49] proclaimed by "the leaders of Neo-Hinduism" and adopted to a certain extent outside of India.[50] In reality, the unity of traditional Hinduism is not much more than a geographical unity; and Hinduism itself amounts basically to a group of religions which coexist in the same geographical region and display numerous common features, but even more signs of division and antagonism.[51] Medieval figures like Vidyāraṇya, who found themselves exposed to the challenge of Islam, may have been distant forerunners of Vivekananda and advocates of the inclusive superiority of Advaita Vedānta, but even they certainly did not promulgate the unity of Hinduism.[52] And the sense of unity and coherence which is associated with the traditional notion of *dharma* is obviously very different from the religious *and* national unity proclaimed by the Neo-Hindus.[53]

In the same review article in which he presents the leaders of Neo-Hinduism as the main propagators of the unity of Hinduism, Hacker also suggests that the concept of Hinduism as such is basically a Western creation. It is, in his words, a "collective label" ("Sammelbezeichnung"), which was produced by Western scholars of religion in order to have a common designation for "the innumerable, partly cognate, partly divergent religious phenomena of one geographical and historical region" ("die zahllosen, teils verwandten, teils divergenten religiösen Erscheinungen eines geographisch-geschichtlichen Raumes").[54] Hacker does not explain the correlation between this Western input and the Neo-Hindu propagation of Hinduism as a unitary entity. He does not discuss the specific Western share in the Neo-Hindu ideology of Hinduism, nor does he try to determine how or to what extent Neo-Hindu ideas were echoed in the West.[55]

Since Hacker made his observations, questions concerning the nature and the very existence of Hinduism have become much more familiar, and the critique of Western constructs and superimpositions has become far more sweeping and radical. More or less contemporaneously with Hacker, W. Cantwell Smith states: "There are Hindus, but there is no Hinduism."[56] H. von Stietencron describes Hinduism as a European invention, "an orchid bred by European scholarship. . . . In nature, it does not exist."[57] Other, even more radical denunciations of the concept of Hinduism are associated with the general critique of Orientalism, "Orientalist constructions," and Western "discourses of domination" which has gained popularity and momentum in recent years.[58] Indeed, Hacker's observations may appear trivial and obsolete after the intellectual and rhetorical fireworks displayed by Edward Said and Ronald Inden. Moreover, Hacker himself might be seen as just another, though somewhat idiosyncratic, instance of common Orientalism, and as a convenient target of criticism and deconstruction. Yet Hacker's position in relation to Orientalism itself (arguably just another "orchid bred by European scholarship"), on the one hand, and its latter-day critics, on the other, may not be quite as clear and unambiguous. His approach to India, awkward and offensive as it may appear in the present climate of debate, is perhaps less obsolete than it seems at first sight.

Critics of Orientalism and of Orientalist constructions, such as R. Inden, have complained that the West has tried to "represent" India as well as other non-Western traditions, and that Western scholarship, in an unholy alliance with the political and economic power of the West, has taken away the intellectual and epistemic sovereignty of the Indians, their own independent self-understanding, their ability to speak for themselves. The West should return the "capacity to have true knowledge," i.e., epistemic sovereignty, to India and other non-Western traditions by withdrawing its own superimpositions, its "Orientalist constructions."[59] Hacker would have agreed that modern Indian thought lacks in intellectual and spiritual sovereignty and authenticity, and that Westerners have imposed foreign and inappropriate categories upon the Indian self-understanding. In fact, he proposed his own elaborate and provocative diagnosis of this situation.[60] But he would not have agreed with any suggestion that it is up to the West to return "epistemic sovereignty" to the Indians and to restore the authenticity of their self-understanding. Such an act of restoration cannot come from Western self-abrogation or self-critique; it has to come from Indian initiative, from Indian self-assertion and self-critique. Indians and others can and must speak for themselves; they are responsible for themselves. In all its harshness, Hacker's critique of Neo-Hinduism and his disagreement with fundamental teachings of traditional Hinduism retains a fundamental respect for the ability and obligation of the other to speak for himself. Hacker's diagnosis of Neo-Hinduism addresses and challenges modern Indian thinkers and intellectuals; it does not try to please and accommodate them. What they deserve is not Western generosity and accommodation, but a respect which can very well be expressed in disagreement and critique. This should be kept in mind by those who will be offended by the (real or apparent) exaggerations and distortions which they may find in Hacker's statements.

Time and again Hacker presents himself as an advocate of clear boundaries, of open confrontation, of an honest recognition of otherness. Just as he criticizes the trend toward accommodation and assimilation in Neo-Hinduism, so he deplores the sense of compromise, assimilation, and accommodation which he finds in certain contemporary Christian approaches to India. This is expressed in numerous reviews of literature in the fields of comparative religion, theology, and the so-called "theology of religions." It may suffice to mention the names of R. Panikkar, K. Klostermaier, E. Cornelis, and, more indirectly, K. Rahner.[61]

VIII. Hacker responded strongly to what he found questionable and unacceptable in Indian thought, above all in Advaita Vedānta and its modern interpretations. But his most intense and passionate critique was reserved for certain developments within Western and Christian thought. After his intense and personally committed studies of Advaita Vedānta and after his return from India, he distanced himself increasingly from the Protestantism with which he had grown up. As we have noted in our brief biographical sketch, he converted to Catholicism in 1962 after years of inner conflict. His book on Luther, which appeared in 1966, gives us some of the reasons for this decision. What he found most threatening in Lutheranism was an excess of subjectivity, reflexivity, and anthropocentrism. According to Hacker, Luther's "ego in faith" tries to establish itself in its subjective "certitude of faith" ("Glaubensgewissheit") and to ascertain its salvation through an act of consciousness and reflection.[62] This self-proclamation of the autonomous subject of faith was then transferred into the epistemic and secular sphere by philosophers like Descartes, and it led to the grand subjectivistic schemes of German idealism which Hacker abhorred. For him, this was an even greater threat and provocation than Śaṅkara's radical nondualism and impersonalism, and it was something for which he did not have the deep and fundamental respect which he always retained with regard to Śaṅkara.

According to Hacker's own interpretation of his Catholic experience, he found a certain structured freedom in the Catholic dogma (and he used to emphasize the word 'freedom'). He also felt that he had gained a sense of identity within an objective framework.[63] Of course, over the years he also found much to disagree with concerning particular developments within Catholicism. As usual, he voiced his concerns and disagreements in an open and sometimes passionate fashion.[64]

This is not the place to discuss the specific and somewhat idiosyncratic nature of Hacker's Catholicism or the role it played in his personal life. But we may reflect, in a tentative and perhaps slightly speculative fashion, on the question of how his fascination with the Indian spiritual tradition and his encounter with and understanding of Śaṅkara's Advaita Vedānta may have affected his Christian faith in general and his movement toward Catholicism in particular, and how, on the other hand, his Christian and Catholic commitment may have informed his Indological work. We have already referred to Hacker's belief that the philosophical study of the Indian sources had to be guided by a sense of spiritual relevance, that there was a special affinity between Indology and theology, and that a "religious decision" was necessary to do justice to the Indian religious and philosophical texts. We have quoted his statement that "theological thought can open the religious scholar's eyes for realities which would otherwise remain hidden from him."[65] There is no reason for us to doubt the sincerity of Hacker's remarks and their applicability to his own situation. We may even go a step further: it seems that his desire to do justice to the Indian religious and philosophical teachings, to explore them not just historically, but to respond to them, was for him not only compatible with his commitment to the Catholic faith, but could even reinforce it by adding a sense of hermeneutic necessity to it. Such commitment seemed to provide him with an adequate vantage point, an antenna so to speak, in order to be truly receptive to teachings such as those of Śaṅkara, to be a potential dialogue partner for them, to agree or disagree with them in a meaningful manner, to face them at a commensurate level of discourse. The Indian religious tradition cannot speak to positivistic philology or to mere historicism. And it can, we may add, certainly not speak to the Hegelian subordination of all other traditions to modern European thought; nor can it speak to those who reduce religion to an object of anthropological or sociological study. Europeans who are confined to the secularity and modernity they have brought about will remain confined to a kind of monologue. To overcome this monologue of modernity with itself was one of Hacker's deepest aspirations. The choice of a firm religious and theological position was, paradoxically, a step toward dialogue. That Hacker was deeply committed to religious encounter and dialogue, and that he had great expectations as to the potential Indian contribution to such a dialogue, is made clear by a remarkable article published in 1962, the year of his conversion to Catholicism.[66] No doubt, Hacker speaks not only as a Christian, but also as an advocate of the active propagation and defense of Christianity. Once again, he denounces assimilation and accommodation and speaks in favor of *chrēsis,* the use of Indian terms and concepts to rearticulate the unadulterated Christian message. But this in itself is not a one-sided affair, and in Hacker's presentation it is not just a missionary device. It is also a vehicle of listening and learning.

Hacker says: "Yes, there is something to learn for us. We should be put to shame by the Indian openness for religion which is still very much alive in our days." He adds that, even in conversations with Westernized Indians who have become skeptical about religion but cannot get away from it, one can be reminded of "what it means to speak of God." "Then we will (it is to be hoped) notice that we have missed something—so much so that our speaking of God seems unauthentic . . . the very manner in which our theologians speak today reveals our lack of authenticity."[67] Once again, Hacker emphasizes that we should be "put to shame by the spiritual sensitivity which continues to be alive in many representatives of modern Indian spiritual and intellectual life, including such personalities as Radhakrishnan—alive to such a degree that we do not have standards to assess it; instead, we have to put up with being judged by it. We should, indeed, listen to the critique to which the sensitive Indian spirit subjects us." Christianity itself would benefit from any *chrēsis,* any successful use of Indian terms and concepts, or from Indians themselves presenting the Christian message in accordance with Indian ways of thinking. Europeans and Christians of all denominations bear part of the responsibility for the fact that this has not happened. They are incapable of a truly religious dialogue. Instead, they have been confined to an occidental monologue. The fascination with Indian religious discourse which we find today in the West is only an effect of this "sad situation of our monologue" ("unsere traurige Monologsituation").[68]

In general, Hacker credited traditional India with a sense of purpose and meaning which he found missing in the West. Throughout his teaching career, he reminded his students that in India knowledge was supposed to have a purpose *(prayojana).* Hacker thought that the Western notion of "pure," "value-free" knowledge and research was an abstraction and an aberration.[69]

IX. It should not be necessary at this point to emphasize that we are not trying to present Hacker's intensely personal and provocative passage to India as a repeatable and generally available method or hermeneutic strategy; nor are we trying to promote the hermeneutic virtues of a Catholic standpoint in Indian studies. Nevertheless, we have to respect Hacker's conviction that his commitment to Christianity and Catholicism had great significance for his scholarly work on Indian religion and philosophy. Indeed, it is inseparable from his fascination *and* confrontation with India. This distinguishes his case from another, more famous conversion to Catholicism which occurred at the very beginning of German Indology, i.e., the conversion of Friedrich Schlegel in 1808, after the publication of his pioneering work *Über die Sprache und Weisheit der Indier* ("On the Language and Wisdom of the Indians"). For Schlegel, his conversion marked the end of his serious commitment to Indian studies; for Hacker, it was a new beginning.[70]

The question may suggest itself whether Hacker's religious commitment has helped or hurt his Indological work. Has it helped him to discover realities which he would have overlooked otherwise? Has it interfered with his rigorous philological standards and the soundness of his historical judgment? Has it really opened his eyes *or* given him a false sense of discovery? We may, indeed, dispute the validity of Hacker's discovery of inclusivism and its description as a quintessentially or exclusively Indian phenomenon, or the soundness and historical accuracy of some of his statements on Neo-Hinduism and on the origin and nature of Practical Vedānta and the role of ethics in Indian thought.[71] In some specific instances, the voice of the *homo religiosus,* if not religious polemicist, seems to be louder and clearer than that of the philologist and historian. Yet it would be preposterous and counterproductive to balance Hacker's religious commitment and philological research against each other, and to try to determine the positive or negative impact of such commitment in a definitive and entirely impartial manner. It is precisely the combination and interaction of commitment and research, philology and confrontation, which makes Hacker's work unique and which accounts for the fact that even his errors and exaggerations provide fruitful and challenging perspectives.

Hacker himself described his work as a "field of rubble of unfinished projects" ("Trümmerfeld des Nichtfertiggewordenen"), and he expressed his hope that others might use these fragments for their own work, either in a positive way or through critique.[72] We may want to disagree with Hacker's characterization of his own work; there is probably more finished architecture in it than his own metaphor would seem to suggest. But at any rate, there can be little doubt that he has left us with a rich supply of precious building materials, as well as with some major, but equally precious, stumbling blocks.

The essays compiled in this book are representative of Hacker's work in general. They are important documents in the history of Indology, but they are also exemplary statements in the encounter between India and Europe. In more than one sense, they continue to be a living challenge.

Notes

1. For a somewhat more detailed biographical survey, see K. Rüping, "Paul Hacker (6.1.1913–18.3.1979)." *WZKS* 25 (1981), pp. 5–16 (p. 17: bibliographical appendix). For further pertinent observations, see L. Schmithausen, "Paul Hacker (1913–1979)." ZDMG 131 (1981), pp. 1–8.

2. *Kl. Schr.*, pp. ix–xxi.

3. In: *Inklusivismus. Eine indische Denkform,* ed. by G. Oberhammer (Vienna, 1983), pp. 11–28. This volume also contains contributions by W. Halbfass, A. Wezler, and G. Oberhammer.

4. *Studien zum Realismus I. S. Turgenevs,* ed. by P. Thiergen (Munich, 1988).

5. The American edition is Hacker's own "condensed recast" (p. IV) of the original. The preface to both editions is by J. Ratzinger.

6. See below, Chapters 3–5. Apart from Advaita Vedānta, the article "Ānvīkṣikī" (*WZKS* 2, 1958, pp. 54–83; *Kl. Schr.*, pp. 137–66) deserves special attention; in this article, Hacker deals with the problem of an Indian equivalent for the term and concept 'philosophy.' On this problem and its treatment by Hacker, see also *India and Europe,* Chapter 15.

7. See below, Chapter 9. Chapters 7 and 10 are also comparative studies.

8. Articles on the role of faith in Hindu religious thought ("Über den Glauben in der Religionsphilosophie des Hinduismus." *ZMR* 38, 1954, pp. 51–66; *Kl. Schr.*, pp. 360–75) and on the traditional Hindu concept of *dharma* ("Dharma im Hinduismus." *ZMR* 49, 1965, pp. 17–28; *Kl. Schr.*, pp. 484–95) may also be mentioned in this connection.

9. See below, Chapters 13–14; as well as Chapter 11 ("Aspects of Neo-Hinduism as Contrasted with Surviving Traditional Hinduism," first presented as a lecture in 1970).

10. See below, section VIII; the article appeared in *Radius* 2 (1962), cols. 30–39 (*Kl. Schr.*, pp. 732–37). Hacker characterizes the "success" of the Christian missionary activities in India as follows: "We have done missionary work among the Indians, and their educated class has become what our fathers have demonstrated to them: humanistic, secularistic, political—but not Christian."

11. These articles are not included in *Kl. Schr.* "The Christian Attitude toward Non-Christian Religions," together with two related articles from *ZMR* 54 (1970), was published separately in: P. Hacker, *Theological Foundations of Evangelization* (St. Augustin, 1980); see also Hacker's article "Das Katholische Christentum im Gegenüber zum Hinduismus" in: *Weltmission in der Weltkrise,* ed. by J. Dörmann (St. Augustin, n.d.), pp. 31–46. For additional references, *see Kl. Schr.*, pp. XIII f.; WZKS 25 (1981), p. 17.

12. *Grundlagen indischer Dichtung und indischen Denkens,* ed. by K. Rüping (Vienna, 1985). See especially pp. 105–41, where Hacker gives a survey of what he considers to be basic "schemes of thought" ("Denkschemata") in India, such as "anthropological-cosmological parallelism," "substantialism," "gradualism," and various forms of paradox (see p. 139).

13. In Hacker's view, debate and controversy are a natural ingredient of scholarly life; see the opening statement of the article referred to in n. 14 (*Kl.*

Schr., p. 18): "Diskussionen, bis hin zur Kontroverse, gehören zum Leben der Wissenschaft."

14. See *Kl. Schr.,* pp. 18–32.

15. See H. P. Schmidt, *Vedisch vratá und awestisch urvıta* (Hamburg, 1958); H. Lüders, *Varuṇa.* 2 vols. (Göttingen, 1951–59).

16. Cf. *Kl. Schr.,* p. 8, where Hacker notes the rarity of methodological reflection in the field of Indology: "Grundsätzliche, methodologische Reflexionen sind vielleicht in unserer Wissenschaft etwas ungewöhnlich." This is the first sentence of his article "Zur Methode der geschichtlichen Erforschung der anonymen Sanskritliteratur des Hinduismus" (1961).

17. See H. Lüders, *Philologica Indica* (Göttingen, 1940), pp. 1–43; 47–73; Lüders' Ṛṣyaśṛṅga studies were first published in 1897–99 (Ak.Wiss.Lit. Göttingen).

18. See *Kl. Schr.,* p. 10.

19. *Kl. Schr.,* pp. 10 f.

20. *Kl. Schr.,* pp. 2 f. (from the article "Purāṇen und Geschichte des Hinduismus," 1960).

21. See *Kl. Schr.,* pp. 13, 17.

22. See below, Chapter 5; also Hacker's preface to his monograph *Untersuchungen über Texte des frühen Advaitavāda. 1: Die Schüler Śaṅkaras* (Ak.Wiss.Lit.Mainz, 1950).

23. This is, of course, most obvious in Hacker's later comparative studies, and in the ways in which he contrasts Advaita Vedānta with Christian thought.

24. See, for instance, *Śaṅkara's Upadeśasāhasrī,* crit. ed. by S. Mayeda (Tokyo, 1973), pp. 22–64; T. Vetter, *Studien zur Lehre und Entwicklung Śaṅkaras* (Vienna, 1979). Cf. also my *Tradition and Reflection,* (Albany, 1991), Chapter 6, for some critical observations.

25. See *Kl. Schr.,* p. 38.

26. *Kl. Schr.,* pp. 38 f.

27. *Kl. Schr.,* p. 40.

28. See *Vivarta. Studien zur Geschichte der illusionistischen Kosmologie und Erkenntnistheorie der Inder.* (Ak.Wiss.Lit.Mainz, 1953), p. 54.

29. See below, Chapters 7 and 9. In "Die Idee der Person," Max Scheler's notion of personhood provides the (unquestioned) standard for a critical and sometimes polemical assessment of Advaita Vedānta.

30. See below, Chapter 10 (*Kl. Schr.,* pp. 320–37); the article was also published in: *Neoplatonism and Indian Thought,* ed. by R. B. Harris (Albany, 1982), pp. 161–80.

31. See *Kl. Schr.,* p. 529 (from: "Ein Prasthānatraya-Kommentar des Neuhinduismus," 1961).

32. See, for instance, *Kl. Schr.,* p. 584; and below, p. 233; also p. 526 (below, p. 339; Vivekananda as "Neo-Vedāntin"). On Antoine's use of "Neo-Hinduism," see Kl. Schr., p. 581; for Seal, see *Bankimchandra Chatterjee, Essays in Perspective,* ed. by B. Chatterjee (New Delhi, 1994), pp. 85ff.

33. See *India and Europe,* pp. 219 ff.; especially 222. The polemical undertone in these uses is obvious.

34. *Kl. Schr.,* p. 531; and below, p. 531. The following section is based on my article "Practical Vedānta," in *Hinduism. Self-Perception and Assessment of Tradition,* ed. by H. von Stietencron (Delhi, forthcoming); see also *India and Europe,* pp. 239 ff.

35. See above, n. 26.

36. See *Kl. Schr.,* pp. 561, 563; and below, p. 305 ff.

37. *Kl. Schr.,* p. 562.

38. Cf. the conclusion of my article "Practical Vedānta" (see above, n. 34).

39. Cf. *India and Europe,* Chapter 18; and below, Chapter 12.

40. Cf. *India and Europe,* Chapter 22, for a more detailed discussion.

41. *India and Europe,* pp. 404 f, 411.

42. See *Kl. Schr.,* pp. 384, 387.

43. *Kl. Schr.,* p. 480.

44. See *Grundlagen,* pp. 132 ff., especially 134.

45. See *Inklusivismus* (as above, n. 3), pp. 11, 28.

46. *Inklusivismus,* p. 28; see also the contribution by G. Oberhammer, pp. 105 ff.

47. Cf. *India and Europe,* pp. 417 ff. (with references to Hegel's notion of "substantialism" in relation to Hacker's "inclusivism").

48. See, for instance, the review by P. Olivelle in *Journal of the American Oriental Society* 106 (1986), pp. 867 f.

49. See *Kl. Schr.,* p. 802; cf. also p. 790.

50. *Kl. Schr.,* p. 482.

51. *Kl. Schr.,* p. 570; cf. also pp. 496, 790; and below, p. 324.

52. Cf. *Kl. Schr.,* p. 479.

53. *Kl. Schr.,* pp. 509, 482; cf. also *India and Europe,* Chapters 17–18.

54. *Kl. Schr.*, p. 480; cf. also p. 290, n. 43; and *Tradition and Reflection*, p. 8.

55. Occasionally, Hacker seems to suggest implicit Neo-Hindu influences in the work of Western Indologists, such as J. Gonda; see, for instance, *Kl. Schr.*, p. 479 (on Śaṅkara and "Hindu unity").

56. W. Cantwell Smith, *The Meaning and End of Religion* (New York, 1962), p. 65; according to Smith, "religion" is a fundamentally inadequate notion. Cf. also *Tradition and Reflection*, pp. 7 ff.

57. See H. von Stietencron in: H. Küng and H. von Stietencron, *Christentum und Weltreligionen. 2: Hinduismus* (Gütersloh, 1987), pp. 25 f.

58. Cf. *Tradition and Reflection*, pp. 9 ff.

59. See R. Inden, "Orientalist Constructions of India." *Modern Asian Studies* 29 (1986), pp. 401–46; especially 444 ff.; cf. also Inden's *Imagining India* (Oxford, 1990), pp. 127 ff.; and, of course, E. Said, *Orientalism* (New York, 1979); without specific reference to India and Hinduism.

60. Especially in his articles on "Schopenhauer and Hindu Ethics" (below, Chapter 13) and "Aspects of Neo-Hinduism as Contrasted with Surviving Traditional Hinduism" (Chapter 11).

61. See *Kl. Schr.*, pp. 793 ff., 798 ff., 811 ff., 805 ff., 815 ff.

62. See *Das Ich im Glauben bei Martin Luther* (Graz, 1966); especially pp. 1 ff., 35 ("Rückbeugung auf das eigene Ich").

63. Hacker made this clear in several personal communications, mostly during his visit to Philadelphia in 1976.

64. This included direct confrontations with Catholic clergymen and letters to high-ranking officials in the Vatican.

65. See above, n. 26.

66. We are referring to the article "Today's India and We Christians" ("Das heutige Indien und wir Christen"); see above, n. 10.

67. *Kl. Schr.*, p. 733.

68. *Kl. Schr.*, p. 734; in the same context, Hacker mentions the "purely materialistic" conception of "Entwicklungshilfe," i.e., economic aid to developing countries, as another symptom of the "occidental monologue."

69. See *Grundlagen indischer Dichtung und indischen Denkens*, pp. 14 ff., 48 ff., cf. also K. Rüping, "Paul Hacker" (see above, n. 1), p. 5.

70. On F. Schlegel's Indian studies, see *India and Europe*, pp. 74 ff.

71. See above, sections V and VI; we may also mention that Hacker's distinction between "Neo-Hinduism" and "surviving traditional Hinduism" may be in need of some qualifications; the Hindi tracts published by the Gītā Press in

Gorakhpur, which Hacker cites as documents of "traditional" Hinduism, are themselves products of a deliberate and commercially motivated program of revivalism initiated by the publishers of the Gītā Press, beginning with Hanumānprasād Poddār around 1920. Their "living continuity with the past" (*Kl. Schr.*, p. 583; and below, p. 232) should not simply be taken for granted. Hacker himself recognizes "cases of assimilation of foreign elements" (p. 235) in the tracts of the Gītā Press.

72. *Kl. Schr.*, p. vii (Hacker's preface, written in 1977).

PART 1

Śaṅkara and the Tradition of Advaita Vedānta: Philological Explorations

1

On Śaṅkara and Advaitism[1]

Śaṅkara's date is given by Gonda, p. 82,[2] as "presumably 788–820."[3] Since the publication of the *Brahmasiddhi* of Maṇḍanamiśra, however, it has emerged that Śaṅkara almost certainly lived before or about 700 A.D. For Śaṅkara quotes Dharmakīrti,[4] who lived about the middle of the seventh century; on the other hand Maṇḍana unmistakably makes reference to Śaṅkara's *Brahmasūtrabhāṣya.*[5]

Gonda talks about the "tradition" according to which Śaṅkara "was an incarnation of Śiva" (p. 83). This tradition, however, certainly does not go back to the life-time of Śaṅkara. His direct pupils Sureśvara and Padmapāda show no awareness of it.[6] Śaṅkara's *Brahmasūtrabhāṣya* and other works which are of undisputed authorship indicate that he came from a Vaiṣṇava background.[7] This is shown by the fact that whenever he refers to examples of cults of deities he chooses those belonging to the Viṣṇuite sphere, that he explains the name of *Sambuddha* mentioned by Gauḍapāda, *Māṇḍūkyakārikā* IV,1, as *Nārāyaṇa,* that he refers to Śiva not by the name Śiva but Rudra. Maṇḍanamiśra, on the other hand, who was Śaṅkara's rival and probably contemporary, came from a Śaivite background, as the last pages of his *Brahmasiddhi* show, where he describes release as *paramaśivabhāva.* Even for a few centuries after Śaṅkara, the works of those Advaitins who were strict followers of his school point as a rule to a Vaiṣṇava provenance, for instance, in their "benedictions" *(maṅgalācaraṇa).* The "tradition" of Śaṅkara's Śiva-nature appears to have been first established in the fourteenth century by Vidyāraṇya, the author of *Śaṅkaradigvijaya.* It was obviously nothing more than a product of fantasy, rooted in the name Śaṅkara, which of course is a synonym of Śiva or Rudra.

Therefore, when Gonda says on p. 201 that Śaṅkara's followers "give evidence of an inclination to Śaivism," it is not a correct generalization. There is a broad stream of Viṣṇuite Advaitism—not only insofar as the very earliest authors of Advaitavāda give evidence of the fact that their milieu was Vaiṣṇava, even if their philosophy itself did not give a mythological name to Brahman; there existed a Viṣṇuite Advaitism in early times, and perhaps already before Śaṅkara lived, also in the sense that there was a predominance of Viṣṇu-theism, while the nature of Viṣṇu was set forth in concepts derived from spirit-monism.

This is attested in the early period by the *Paramārthasāra* (attributed to Ādiśeṣa),[8] not taken into account by Gonda, and above all by the *Bhāgavatapurāṇa,* of which the Advaitic character[9] is not noticed by Gonda. I conjecture that the term *Bhāgavata* refers specially, though not exclusively, to Advaitic Vaiṣṇavism,[10] whereas the other ancient Vaiṣṇava group, the *Pāñcarātra,* was dualistic or pluralistic in its thinking, as we can see from the Vaiṣṇava Saṃhitās. The monistic-illusionistic tendencies of the Vaiṣṇavas (Bhāgavatas) can be explained as being due to their originally close relations with Mahāyāna Buddhism. Lamotte has pointed out the existence of these relations from Buddhist sources,[11] but they can be attested from the brahminical side also, namely in the *Viṣṇupurāṇa.*[12]

Gonda repeats on p. 83 the commonly accepted view that Śaṅkara established a monastic order and founded many cloisters. Years ago, I tried to verify this "tradition." I went through a large number of publications of South Indian inscriptions with a view to finding out references to cloisters *(maṭha)* of Advaitists. I found, so far as I can recollect, no mention of cloisters before the fourteenth century. In an ethnographic compilation,[13] I found a list of Directors of the main Advaitic cloister in Sringeri, which is supposed to have been established by Śaṅkara. The time-spans of individual Directors, from ordination to death, which are given there, are often improbably long for the earlier period. Of the ten Jagadgurus from Śaṅkara (according to this source, he was Director from 745 to 769) to Vidyāśaṅkara, the following periods from ordination to death are found: 90, 64, 89, 62, 83, and 105 years. One hundred five years are mentioned for Vidyāśaṅkara (1228–1333). After him appears the joint Directorship of Bhāratītīrtha (1328–1380) and Vidyāraṇya (1331–1386). After that, up to the year 1928, only once do we find a period exceeding 60 years (Narasiṃha Bhāratī 1817–1879) among the 22 Jagadgurus mentioned.

These dates, taken together with the absence of epigraphic evidence for Śaṅkara-maṭhas before the fourteenth century, I explain as follows: After Vijayanagara was devastated by Muslims and a general reconstruction was required, Vidyāraṇya, who was minister of the king of that empire, attempted a sort of deliberate Hindu cultural politics,[14] together with his brother Sāyaṇa. In order to render the authoritative literature of the Aryan religion more intelligible and easier to apply, the two brothers composed extensive commentaries on the Veda and on Dharma literature. With a sure instinct, Vidyāraṇya (who was called Mādhava before his ordination as a sannyāsin) also found other means, going beyond the merely literary, of making this religion secure. By means of legends, which he created, he made of Śaṅkara, whose philosophy he followed but who could never become popular with his elevated, exacting thoughts, a divine folk-hero who spread his teaching through his *digvijaya* ("universal conquest") all over India like a victorious conqueror, and whom therefore the Hindu, in his struggles with the powerful drive of Islam, could look up to. That this teaching was the crown of all "ways of seeing" *(darśana)* of the Āryas and Nāstikas—so that all other systems could at least represent partial truths, and hint at that peak of knowledge—this too was exhibited by him: in his "Summary of All Views" *(Sarvadarśanasaṃgraha).* Then he went on to establish an institution: the Śaṅkara Maṭha. He created fictions which could hardly be contradicted, the country having been totally devastated by Muslims. He announced that the Maṭha was established by Śaṅkara himself and had continuously existed since then. He appointed first the old Vidyāśaṅkara as the Director and announced that he had already occupied that position for many decades. This is how it could come about that in the list of Directors of the cloister the period of Vidyāśaṅkara is given as 105 years. After Vidyāśaṅkara's death the leadership was taken over by Vidyāraṇya's teacher Bhāratītīrtha, but soon he himself occupied that position jointly with him.

This is obviously a hypothetical construction based on a few documents, but it seems to me that the origin of the "tradition" prevalent today regarding Śaṅkara and his community can be roughly explained in the manner indicated. In the authoritative works of Śaṅkara, of course, there is not the slightest confirmation of this "tradition." If my description of the figure of Vidyāraṇya is correct, he might be considered in some sense a predecessor of Vivekananda. For he, too, has made of Śaṅkara something quite different from what he was earlier, and that again for purposes of defence, this time against Christianity.

The influence of Śaṅkara during the first centuries after his life was evidently not as strong as it may appear today. His influence is not identical with the Advaitic movement. This was already there, and apart from him there was also the influence of his rival Maṇḍana at work. The latter, moreover, was for centuries of philosophical discussion held in greater esteem than Śaṅkara as a representative of spirit-monism. It is only after Vācaspati Miśra (tenth century) harmonized the teachings of Śaṅkara and Maṇḍana and after Prakāśātman produced in his *Vivaraṇa* an imposing and fully articulated construction and further development of the system of the school of Śaṅkara that the stature of Śaṅkara the author of the *Bhāṣya* appears to have grown.

There is not the slightest indication in Śaṅkara's authentic works that he was "the great champion of Hindu unity," as Gonda describes him on p. 83, following the prevalent view. "Hindu unity" is something that lay completely outside Śaṅkara's field of vision. Such a tendency can be ascribed to the cultural politician Vidyāraṇya, but in his case, too, not without qualification, for he also fought really not for any unity, but for the dominance of his system, the Advaitavāda, above others. Śaṅkara energetically attacked the non-Advaitic religions and philosophical systems of "Hinduism" prevalent in his day; there is no trace of a "consciousness of the unity of Hinduism" to be noticed there.

While venturing such statements, however, it is important to distinguish between the authentic and the inauthentic works of Śaṅkara. If one does not do this, then the Śaṅkara mixed up with the inauthentic works becomes not, indeed, "a champion of Hindu unity" but a (rather impossible) collection of many of the opposite elements which Hinduism carries within itself. According to my researches, I regard as authentic, besides the *Brahmasūtrabhāṣya,* the following: the commentaries on the Upaniṣads, except those on the *Svetāśvatara* and *Nṛsiṃhapūrvatāpanīya* Upaniṣads, but inclusive of the commentary on *Māṇḍūkyakārikā,* also on the *Bhagavadgītā* and perhaps that on the *Adhyātmapaṭala* of the *Āpastambadharmasūtra,* and finally, *Upadeśasāhasrī.* The last is a collection (perhaps compiled by Śaṅkara's pupil Sureśvara) of all his independent writings. All other commentaries ascribed to him, as also the whole mass of tracts passing under the name of Śaṅkara (mostly Śaṅkarācārya), are not by Śaṅkara the author of the *Brahmasūtrabhāṣya.* The question how the mass of inauthentic writings could arise is relatively easy to answer. Once the Śaṅkara cloisters came into being in the fourteenth century (through the activity of Vidyāraṇya in the first place) and their Directors called themselves "Śaṅkarācāryas," it was naturally possible for any work composed by any of these ācāryas to circulate bona fide as a work of Śaṅkarācārya, the more so since a Śaṅkarācārya holds himself to be identical with the first Śaṅkara.

Notes

1. Editor's note: This is J. L. Mehta's translation of a section of a review article by Hacker: "Zur Geschichte und Beurteilung des Hinduismus. Kritik einiger verbreiteter Ansichten" ("On the History and Assessment of Hinduism. Critique of Some Common Views"). *Orientalistische Literaturzeitung* 59 (1964), cols. 231–45. The review article deals primarily with J. Gonda, *Die Religionen Indiens,* vol. 2: *Der jüngere Hinduismus* (Stuttgart, 1963).

2. Editor's note: In the work cited in n. 1. All further page references in Hacker's text are to this work.

3. On the origin of this chronology, see P. Deussen, *Das System des Vedānta* (Leipzig, 1883), p. 37, n. 23.

4. *Upadeśasāhasrī, Padyaprabandha* 18, 142 (= Dharmakīrti, *Pramāṇavārttika* 3, 354; also quoted by Sureśvara, *Bṛhadāraṇyakopaniṣadbhāṣyavārttika* 4,3,476).

5. See, for the time being, Kuppuswami Sastri's introduction to his edition of Maṇḍanamiśra's *Brahmasiddhi* (Madras 1937, Madras Government Oriental Manuscripts Series, vol. 4), pp. xlv–xlvii and lviii.

6. See P. Hacker, *Untersuchungen über Texte des frühen Advaitavāda* (Mainz: Akademie, 1950), pp. 14 and 24.

7. I have dealt with this in a (still unpublished) lecture to the Indological Section of the Congress of German Orientalists (Deutscher Orientalistentag) in Tübingen, 1949. [Editor's note: A revised English version of this lecture was published under the title "Relations of Early Advaitins to Vaiṣṇavism." *WZKSO* 9 (1965), pp. 147–54; also in: *Kl. Schr.,* pp. 205–12; and Chapter 3 in the present collection.]

8. Editions: Trivandrum Sanskrit Series, vol. 12 (1911); Acyutagranthamālā, vol. 9 (Kāśī, 1989 Vikrama Era); with English translation, introduction, and notes ed. by S. S. Suryanarayana Sastri (Bombay, 1941).

9. See P. Hacker, *Prahlāda* (Mainz: Akademie, 1959), pp. 110 and 122–28.

10. See also the reference to the Bhāgavata Saṃpradāya in: B.A. Saletore, *Ancient Karnataka,* vol. 1: *History of Tuḷuva* (Poona, 1936), pp. 449 ff.

11. E. Lamotte, *Histoire du bouddhisme indien* (Louvain, 1958), pp. 437 ff.

12. See P. Hacker, *Prahlāda,* pp. 89 f and 127; also *Orientalistische Literaturzeitung* 55 (1960), cols. 350 ff.

13. H. V. Nanjundayya and L. K. Ananthakrishna Iyer, *The Mysore Tribes and Castes,* vol. 2 (Mysore, 1928), pp. 457 f.

14. On Vidyāraṇya see, for instance, P. V. Kane, *History of Dharmaśāstra,* vol. 1 (Poona, 1930), pp. 374 ff.

15. See my contribution to the *Festschrift for W. Schubring* (Hamburg, 1951), p. 165, n. 4; and Kuppuswami Sastri (above, n. 5) pp. lix f.

16. I have presented some (not all) of the criteria which I apply in assessing the question of authenticity in *New Indian Antiquary* 9 (1947); [see Chapter 3 of the present collection]; ZDMG 100 (1950), pp. 248 ff. [Chapter 4 of the present collection]; and in my monograph *Vivarta* (Mainz: Akademie, 1953), pp. 24–29.

2

Relations of Early Advaitins to Vaiṣṇavism

After G. A. Jacob had observed that theistic terms in Śaṅkara's *Brahmasūtrabhāṣya* often appeared in passages where the logic of the system seemed to call for impersonalistic and monistic terms, and that Śaṅkara again and again ignored the distinction between *paraṃ brahma* and *īśvara* (cf. G. A. Jacob's edition of the *Vedāntasāra,* second ed., Bombay, 1911, Preface [dating back to 1893], pp. VII ff.), Rudolf Otto in his *Westöstliche Mystik* (second ed., Gotha, 1929, pp. 139 ff.; see *Mysticism East and West.* New York, 1970 [1932], pp. 121 ff.) presented a penetrating and elaborate study of the theistic basis or background perceptible in Śaṅkara's monistic thought. The fact brought out in relief by the two scholars indeed marks a feature which is of major relevance to an evaluation of the great thinker's personality and which distinguishes him from other philosophers of his school.

The observation of the theism included in and blended with Śaṅkara's monism raises three questions. The first is about the systematic context of the theism, and this has been treated by Rudolf Otto. Secondly, we have to ask about the historical context or background or the historical causes of the phenomenon. I think that this question can be answered with a fair amount of probability, but I will leave it for another study. The third question, the answer to which must be given before the second can be investigated, asks for an inquiry into the concrete type of that theistic background. This inquiry I will undertake in the present article.

Devotion, which is more than a philosophical doctrine about God, is in Hinduism usually directed to a definite mythological figure, mostly to Śiva or Viṣṇu or the Goddess. Therefore, if the theistic background of Śaṅkara's monism corresponded to a reality in his life, the question suggests itself as to whether it was of the Vaiṣṇava or Śaiva or of another type. Now it is true that Śaṅkara's main work, the *Brahmasūtrabhāṣya* (SBh), does not seem to reveal any preference for a particular deity in direct statements. The theistic background of his philosophy, though undeniable, is not immediately perceptible in its concrete outlines. Nevertheless it must be assumed that Śaṅkara's theism, as a constituent of his personal life, had a concrete shape conditioned by the family in which he was born, by his environment, or by devotional practice, though it was not directly reflected in his writings.

Now it is almost a common opinion, spread in India as well as in the West and frequently stated in books and articles, that the lower storey of the edifice of Śaṅkara's thought included a sanctuary of Śiva. But it appears to me that this opinion was circulated by as late a writer as Mādhava-Vidyāraṇya, the author of the *Śaṅkaradigvijaya,* who on the basis of the mere name Śaṅkara constructed the legend of the *bhāṣyakāra* having been an incorporation of the divine Śaṅkara or Śiva. For I cannot find the slightest trace of any partiality for, or even proximity to, Śaivism in Śaṅkara's main work—and, I may add, in all those writings which are indubitably or probably his productions. On the contrary, a few indications—not very conspicuous, it is true, and therefore, as far as I can see, not noticed by scholars so far, but nevertheless unambiguous—can be detected in the SBh to show that the Vaiṣṇava religion was, to say the least, more familiar to the author than Śaivism.

Firstly, the name *Śiva* is not used in the SBh. The deity denoted by this word is mentioned under the name of *Rudra* in a passage where myths are cited to substantiate certain statements (3, 3, 32). It is said there that Skanda was generated by Rudra. This is quite an impartial mention, not different from allusions to myths of other gods. No predilection for Śiva can be educed from it. On the contrary, the passage might even imply that the author was not a Śaiva. For as far as I know, Śaivas like to call their supreme deity by his honorific name Śiva, whereas a staunch Vaiṣṇava—who, as such, is *ekāntin*—avoids using *Śiva* as a proper name, preferring to designate the rival of his supreme god by the name *Rudra*. Moreover, the passage alluded to is the only impartial mention in the SBh of ideas connected with the figure of Śiva. As to the contemporary theology of Śaivism, it is well known that it is rejected without qualification in the polemical part of Śaṅkara's SBh (2, 2, 37–41).

Conspicuously different, however, is the case of Vaiṣṇavism. Exception made of the passage where the *Pāñcarātra* doctrine is criticized, Viṣṇu is mentioned under this name at least seven times and once each under the names of *Hari* and *Nārāyaṇa*. Let us now examine these passages. One of them (3, 3, 32) cites a myth, another (3, 2, 17) mentions *Nārāyaṇa* in connection with a *Mahābhārata* verse quoted. Neither of these two passages yields any material utilizable to answer our question. But in Sūtra 1, 2, 7 it is said that God can be made perceptible *(nicāyya)*, and in commenting on this passage Śaṅkara says: "It is taught that God, who is characterized by minuteness and other qualities, is perceptible, i.e., visible, in the lotus of the heart, just as Hari is in the *śālagrāma* stone. In this, it is a cognition of the Inner Sense which apprehends him. God, though omnipresent, graciously allows himself to be reverently meditated upon there" *(aṇīyastvādi-guṇopeta īśvaras tatra hṛdaya-puṇḍarīke nicāyyo draṣṭavya upadiśyate yathā śālagrāme Hariḥ. tatrāsya buddhi-vijñānaṃ grāhakam. sarvagato 'pīśvaras tatropāsyamānaḥ prasīdati)*. Here the *śālagrāma*, which is a Vaiṣṇava symbol, is referred to as comparable to the heart in which the supreme God is perceptible according to the *sūtra*. Hari is not compared with the *Lower Brahman*, which is constituted by a superimposition of illusory qualities on the Supreme, but with the transcendent *Highest Self*, that cannot become the object of meditation unless contemplated under a symbol. It is the Supreme Self that allows itself to be meditated upon in the heart as Viṣṇu is visualized in the *śālagrāma*. In the same sense Viṣṇu and his *śālagrāma* symbol are mentioned at two other places (1, 2, 14; 1, 3, 14). Furthermore, there are four passages (3, 3, 9; 4, 1, 3 twice; 4, 1, 5) where the superimposition of the spiritual vision of Viṣṇu on idols *(pratimā)* is cited as an instance of superimposition of religious ideas on things. In all these seven passages, Śaṅkara could as well have said in general that the vision of a deity is superimposed on a symbol or image, or, if he had hailed from a Śaiva environment or had really had a partiality for Śaivism, one would expect him to select the example of the *liṅga*, on which the vision of Śiva is superimposed. Instead, he cites examples from the cult of Viṣṇu seven times. This must point to a familiarity with the Vaiṣṇava religion, caused either by origin, environment, or other circumstances.

In Śaṅkara's *bhāṣyas* on the *Upaniṣads,* similar cases occur also, as, e.g., in Taitt. Up. Bh. 1, 6, 1; 1, 8, 1; Muṇḍ. Up. Bh. 2, 1, 4; Praśna-Up. Bh. 5, 2; Bṛh. Up. Bh. 1, 1, 1; 5, 1, 1; Chānd. Up. Bh. 6, 16, 3; 7, 1, 4; 8, 1, 1. A particularly interesting case in point is his commentary on Gauḍapāda's *Māṇḍūkyakārikā* 4, 1. Gauḍapāda here invokes a *Saṃbuddha,* who is *dvipadāṃ varaḥ.* There cannot be any reasonable doubt that the person meant is the Buddha, the Śākyamuni, since Gauḍapāda's monism owes much to idealistic Buddhism. But Śaṅkara in his commentary—which is certainly authentic, as can be shown by several criteria—attempts to explain away this reverence to the founder of the rival system. Though in another passage of the same commentary (on *kārikā* 4, 99) he frankly admits a proximity of Buddhistic idealism to Gauḍapāda's Advaitism, he stresses at the same place, commenting on Gauḍapāda's words *naitad buddhena bhāṣitam,* that his Advaitism differs from Buddhistic idealism in recognizing a Supreme Reality, which can be known only from the Upaniṣads *(jñāna-jñeya-jñātṛ-bheda-rahitaṃ paramārtha-tattvam advayam etan na buddhena bhāṣitam. yadyapi bāhyārtha-nirākaraṇaṃ jñānamātra-kalpanā cādvaya-vastu-sāmīpyam uktam, idaṃ tu paramārtha-tattvam advaitaṃ vedānteṣv eva vijñeyam).* So he may have thought it impossible that in *kārikā* 4, 1 Gauḍapāda should have paid reverence to the founder of a system in which, though it was akin to his, he found something to criticize in *kārikā* 4, 99. But if the *Saṃbuddha* of *kārikā* 4, 1 is not the Buddha, what person may be denoted by the word? There were many possibilities of interpretation once the most probable one was excluded. So Śaṅkara's option must be significant, because it inevitably must point in the direction of a preference and thus betray a partiality. Now he chose to interpret the *Saṃbuddha* as *Nārāyaṇa* the *Puruṣottama.* This means that he substituted for the Buddha of the original not an abstract Highest Being—which would, by the way, have been difficult on account of the additional words *dvipadāṃ varaḥ*—nor any human teacher, but the supreme deity of a concrete religion, and this religion is no other than that which we should expect after having examined the SBh, namely Vaiṣṇavism.

A certain proximity to, if not preference for, this religion may perhaps also be reflected in a few cases of names of imaginary persons used by Śaṅkara in exemplifications. The most frequent of them is, of course, *Devadatta,* and if a second person is required, his equally imaginary brother *Yajñadatta* is usually called upon. But there are a few cases of variations, and these again point to the sphere of Vaiṣṇavism, namely *Viṣṇumitra* (2, 2, 28; 3, 2, 7; 3, 4, 20) and *Kṛṣṇagupta* (4, 3, 5).

Now let us cast a glance into the Tarkakāṇḍa. It is true that Śaṅkara rejects the theology of the Vaiṣṇava system of *Pāñcarātra,* but it is worthy of note that his criticism is not so unqualified here as in the case of Śaiva theology. He controverts only the *vyūha* theory of the *Pāñcarātrins* but expressly approves of a considerable part of their system. He admits that in some respects, e.g., in the doctrine of God being the material as well as the efficient cause of the world, this system agrees with his Vedānta *(samānatvān na visaṃvādagocaraḥ),* and he states: "We do not controvert the doctrine that Nārāyaṇa, who is known to be higher than the Unevolved, who is the Supreme Self and the Self of All, has multiplied himself through himself into single forms . . . Nor do we raise any objection if it is intended to worship the Bhagavān with unceasing concentration of mind by approaching him (probably in his temple) or by other means" *(yat tāvad ucyate yo 'sau Nārāyaṇaḥ paro 'vyaktāt prasiddhaḥ paramātmā sarvātmā sa ātmanātmānam anekadhā vyūhyāvasthita iti, tan na nirākriyate . . . yad api tasya bhagavato 'bhigamanādi-lakṣaṇam ārādhanam ajasram ananyacittatayābhipreyate, tad api na pratiṣidhyate* 2, 2, 42). I think it cannot be overlooked that a marked sympathy for the Vaiṣṇava religion speaks from these words. This sympathy even goes beyond what might be expected from the point of view of strict Advaitism. For not only does Śaṅkara stress that the doctrine of God or the Brahman being the material as well as the efficient cause is common to both his system and that of Vaiṣṇavism, but he even identifies the Highest Self as taught by the Advaita system with a figure of mythology, namely with *Nārāyaṇa,* the *Bhagavān,* who is the highest deity of Vaiṣṇavism, and he expressly approves of Vaiṣṇava practices of worship and devotion. If he had had leanings towards Śaivism, or if he had, as the myth of our days would have it, maintained the equality or unity of all the religions or varieties of Hinduism, one would expect to find similar sympathetic statements at least in his treatment of the Śaiva system. But no trace of a similar sympathy for Śaiva doctrines or practices in discernible in the SBh.

We should take due notice of this fact, and we should utilize the result of our investigation when examining the problem of the authenticity of other works ascribed to Śaṅkara. We should cease either to repeat, on the authority of some of innumerable spurious works, the myth of Śaṅkara having had a particular predilection for Śaivism, or to make him the champion of an idea of unity which, to judge from all authentic documents, was quite foreign to his thought.

A special problem is Śaṅkara's conception of *māyā.* The history of this concept has still to be written before definite statements can be ventured as to the specific differences of its interpretations in Vaiṣṇavism and in the various schools of Śaivism. So much, however, can perhaps be said that Śaṅkara's notion of *māyā* tallies very well with the Vaiṣṇava conception of the term. Śaṅkara can, e.g., use the term to denote the miraculous power of *Parameśvara;* cp., e.g., *māyāmayaṃ rūpam* SBh 1, 1, 20.

In every philosophical work there is a place where convention requires the invocation of a deity, namely the *maṅgalācaraṇa* or *namaskāra* at the beginning and the end or at the beginning only or at the end only. Śaṅkara, however, deviates from this custom in most of his works. The reason for this seems to be stated in his *Vākyabhāṣya* on the *Kena Upaniṣad,* where he says: *na hi svārājye 'bhiṣikto brahmatvam gamitaḥ kaṃcana namitum icchati,* "For he who, having been led to be Brahman, is consecrated to sovereignty, does not wish to bow to anybody." Only a few of Śaṅkara's authentic works begin with *maṅgala* verses, namely the *Māṇḍūkyabhāṣya,* the *Taitt. Up. Bh.,* and the eighteenth metrical *prakaraṇa* of the *Upadeśasāhasrī,* and in all of them he invokes the neutral *Brahman* or the *Ātman.* The metrical invocation of *Nārāyaṇa* at the beginning of the *Gītābhāṣya* may not form an original part of the *bhāṣya,* since it is quotation. If it belonged to the *bhāṣya,* it may simply have been elicited by the Vaiṣṇava character of the Gītā and need not be any indication as to a religious preference of the author of the commentary. At the beginning of his *Kaṭha Up. Bh.* and of his *Bṛh. Up. Bh.* Śaṅkara voices his reverence only to the *saṃpradāyakartāraḥ,* i.e., to the teachers who propounded or expounded the doctrines of those Upaniṣads.

So Śaṅkara's own *maṅgalācaraṇas* yield nothing to answer the question as to his religious preferences. But the *maṅgala* verses of his disciples as well as of almost all authors of early Advaitism up to the end of the tenth century A.D. exhibit the same features as we found in the contents of Śaṅkara's SBh. There are no traces of association with Śaivism but several signs of proximity to Vaiṣṇavism. Sureśvara (in his *Naiṣkarmyasiddhi*), Toṭaka, the *Hastāmalakaślokāḥ,* Sarvajñātman and Ānandabodha all invoke Viṣṇu; Padmapāda adores the Brahman; Vimuktātman bows to his own self. It seems that the earliest masters of Śaṅkara's school, in the more restricted sense of this word, all belonged to Vaiṣṇava environments.

This may turn out the more significant if we consider, by contrast, the case of Maṇḍanamiśra. He seems to have been Śaṅkara's rival, probably his contemporary. However, the few and rather insignificant divergencies between his thought and that of Śaṅkara are scarcely sufficient to account for the rivalry. We may conjecture that there were differences of a more concrete nature, perhaps sociological. Now we find that towards the end of his *Brahmasiddhi* Maṇḍana calls the state of liberation *paramaśivabhāva*. It is true that Śaṅkara also uses the word *śiva*, but only as an adjective, e.g., in the verse portion of the Upadeśasāhasrī, and in this use the word does not seem to point to either Śaiva or Vaiṣṇava doctrines. But in the compound *paramaśivabhāva* the word *śiva* is probably not an adjective. For *paramaśiva* or *paraśiva* is a Śaiva term used in different systems to denote the Absolute (cp., to quote only one instance, *Pratyabhijñāhṛdaya* 3), transcending the manifestations of Śiva. Therefore, Maṇḍana's use of the word *paramaśivabhāva*, which may, *à la rigueur*, be explained as containing the adjective *śiva* but still inevitably suggests the typically Śaiva notion, most probably points to a religious preference. It suggests the idea of the state of deliverance being identity with the Absolute conceived as Transcendent Śiva. We may infer from this that Maṇḍana hailed from a Śaiva environment. If this is true, i.e., if Śaṅkara and Maṇḍana hailed from different religious environments, which naturally would more or less coincide with sociological differences, an additional explanation for the rivalry between the two great monists would suggest itself from this fact, and this would account for the fact that the few and rather insignificant divergencies between their respective doctrines were taken as an occasion for a stiff controversy. A few centuries later, when the concrete differences of the two schools were forgotten, Vācaspatimiśra could undertake the successful attempt of merging both systems, that of Śaṅkara and that of Maṇḍana, into one, and from that time onward Maṇḍana's doctrines survived as the so-called Vācaspati subschool in the one school of Advaitism.

The fact that radical Advaitism was cultivated in Vaiṣṇava circles is borne out also by the existence of texts that expressly profess Vaiṣṇavism and teach radical Advaitism at the same time. To this category belong certain passages of the *Bhāgavatapurāṇa* (which may date from a time not far distant from Śaṅkara's lifetime) and of the *Paramārthasāra* ascribed to Ādiśeṣa (which is at any rate earlier than the sixth century A.D., because one of its stanzas [83] is found quoted in the *Yuktidīpikā*[1] [p. 25]).

Note

1. I owe this information to the kindness of Prof. Oberhammer.

3

Śaṅkarācārya and Śaṅkarabhagavatpāda:

Preliminary Remarks Concerning the Authorship Problem

I. For many centuries the great Bhāṣyakāra of the Kevalādvaita school, a propagator of illusionism, has traditionally been styled Śaṅkarācārya. Some hundreds of writings are ascribed to the famous Ācarya. There can be no doubt that such a large number of works cannot have been written by a single man who, according to tradition, reached an age of only 32 years. Moreover, the variety of contents makes it highly improbable that all those works should have been composed by one and the same person. So it was inevitable that thc majority of historians should have taken the position that all those writings were provisionally to be regarded as spurious, with the only exception of Śaṅkara's main work, the *Brahmasūtrabhāṣya,* and that in the case of all the other commentaries and independent treatises the question of the authorship required investigation.

How was it possible that such a large number of writings could be wrongly attributed to the great teacher? Even if the possibility of a forgery is left out of account, it will not be difficult to give one possible answer to that question if it is taken into consideration that all the Jagadgurus of the Śṛṅgeri Maṭha, which is believed to have been founded by the famous Bhāṣyakāra, have borne the *title* of Śaṅkarācārya. So any literary work composed by one of these Ācāryas could rightly be called the production of a Śaṅkarācārya. There is one instance at the least of a text having been handed down by one tradition as a production of Śaṅkarācārya, whereas other traditions designated it as the work of a later Jagadguru of the Śṛṅgeri Maṭha. This is the case of the *Vākyasudhā,* otherwise called *Dṛgdṛśyaviveka,* which is ascribed by different traditions to Śaṅkara, to Bhāratītīrtha, and to Vidyāraṇya (T XII 7364). It is not surprising that the latter two Ācāryas should have come to be confounded as tradition speaks of a close collaboration between Vidyāraṇya and his teacher Bhāratītīrtha in composing another text, viz. the *Pañcadaśī,* but the ascription of the *Vākyasudhā* to Śaṅkarācārya will be best accounted for by the fact that both Vidyāraṇya and Bhāratītīrtha actually were Śaṅkarācāryas, as both were heads of the Śṛṅgeri monastery.

Bhāratītīrtha and Vidyāraṇya were influential teachers and famous authors, so it is natural that they should have preferred to be called by their own Sannyāsin names and that contemporary scribes should as a rule have used those names in the colophons of works composed by them. On the other hand, it may be assumed that authors who were themselves less renowned should have chosen to be called by the sacred title of Śaṅkarācārya rather than by their obscure Sannyāsin names and that they should have been styled thus by their contemporaries also. This may account for a good deal of the attributions of writings to Śaṅkarācārya.

Another occasion for works not composed by the great Śaṅkara to be erroneously assigned to him may have been the following. Anonymous texts used in the Śaṅkara Maṭhas for purposes of instruction may in the course of time have come to be attributed to the founder of the Maṭha. Texts circulating outside the Maṭhas may also, for reasons varying in the individual cases, have been believed to be produced by the most influential spiritual teacher India has known in the course of the past millennium. But it will hardly ever be possible to identify a case of this type.

Thirdly, the name of Śaṅkara is by no means a rare one, and there have certainly been several men who bore the name of Śaṅkara and were ācāryas too. Such men, or the transcribers of their writings, may have drawn a careful distinction between their literary productions and those of the great Bhāṣyakāra Śaṅkara. There is, e.g., a Śaṅkarācārya, the author of a *Tārārahasyavivṛttikā,* who is styled in the colophon *Gaurabhūmi-vāsi-mahāmahopādhyāya-śrī-śaṅkarācārya* (M I 512), a designation which is obviously intended to prevent confusion with the Bhāṣyakāra. But there may have been others who did not care to see their works distinguished from those of the great Śaṅkara, and if their doctrines were similar to his, it could easily happen that they ended by being identified with him in the memory of posterity.

Various other circumstances may have led to the identification of an author with the Bhāṣyakāra Śaṅkara. There is, for instance, the well-known story of Śaṅkara's dispute with the wife of Maṇḍanamiśra and of his entering the body of the dead king Amaru, which has been sufficient reason for several manuscripts to ascribe the *Amaruśataka* to Śaṅkarācārya (T VII 389 ff., H III 1759).

II. If we accept 'Śaṅkarācārya' to be the usual designation of the Bhāṣyakāra, we cannot but be puzzled over the fact that he is not called by that name, or by a combination of a name with a title, in ancient writings. As to his direct disciples, Padmapāda once calls him Śaṅkara,[1] whilst the prevalent designation in the text of the *Pañcapādikā* is Bhāṣyakāra and the title of Bhagavat is twice added to that word.[2] Sureśvara also calls him Śaṅkara[3] and uses the designations of Bhagavatpāda[4] and Bhagavatpūjyapāda.[5] It is true that the reference of the latter titles to Śaṅkara is not absolutely certain, as the name of Śaṅkara is not added to them and they are employed to designate the author of the *Upadeśasāhasrī,* a work belonging to the corpus of Śaṅkaran writings the authorship of which has not yet been settled,[6] but the context leaves very little doubt about these titles actually referring to Sureśvara's teacher. Toṭakācārya, another disciple of Śaṅkara, does not give his preceptor's name or title in his *Śrutisārasamuddharaṇa,* but his commentator Saccidānanda Yogīndra, in explaining stanza 178 of his work, mentions Bhagavatpāda as the name of Toṭakācārya's teacher (. . . *"tān gurūn" bhagavatpādākhyān "yāvadāyur namāmi"*). Vācaspatimiśra styles him "Bhagavān Bhāṣyakāra" in his *Bhāmatī* several times.[7] Jñānottama, an old commentator of Śureśvara's *Naiṣkarmyasiddhi,* never calls Sureśvara's teacher Śaṅkara but uses the designations Bhāṣyakāra,[8] Bhagavatpāda-Ācārya,[9] Bhagavatpūjyapāda-Ācārya,[10] and Ācārya.[11] The latter title and the addition of Ācārya to the second and third ones apparently are meant to allude to the fact that Śaṅkara was Sureśvara's Ācārya.

As far as Śaṅkara's contemporaries and immediate successors are concerned, we find:

1. The great teacher is sometimes called Śaṅkara without the addition of any title.
2. His usual title seems to have been Bhagavat. This word, when added to Bhāṣyakāra or combined with -pāda or -pūjyapāda, replaced the name.
3. The combination of the name of Śaṅkara with Ācarya does not seem to have been very usual. It was, of course, possible to form this combination, but the more solemn title of Bhagavat seems to have been preferred to Ācārya as a rule.[12]

In later Advaita literature Śaṅkara is also called Bhagavatpāda and Bhagavatpūjyapāda, the designation Śaṅkarācārya alternating with the old title. It will suffice for our purpose to quote a few instances. Ānandajñāna, who in his commentaries on the Bhāṣyas ascribed to Śaṅkara usually names him Bhāṣyakāra, composed the following stanza:

Bhagavatpādapādābjadvandvaṃ dvandvanibarhaṇam
Sureśvarādisadbhṛṅgair avalambitam ābhaje.[13]

Here the word Bhagavatpāda obviously refers to Śaṅkara, as the association with Sureśvara proves. Rāmatīrtha's commentary on the *Upadeśasāhasrī* begins with the words: *Iha bhagavatpādābhidho bhagavān bhāṣyakāraḥ . . . upadeśasāhasrīm . . . prakaṭīkurvan. . . .* The expression *vedāntasiddhānto bhagavatpādasammataḥ,* meaning "the Vedāntic doctrines as interpreted by Śaṅkara," is found in the introduction to a commentary on Madhusūdana's *Siddhāntabindu* (M VII 1497). To these quotations from texts two colophons may be added. In the colophon to a manuscript of the *Śrutisārasamuddharaṇa* of Toṭakācārya, the author is called Bhagavatpāda-śiṣya (M IV 1584). The *Bhāmatī* is called *śārīrakabhagavatpāda-bhāṣya-vibhāga* in the colophon to the fourth pāda of the third adhyāya (Nirṇayasāgar edition; C III 84; W I 608).

The habit of calling Śaṅkara Bhagavatpāda and Bhagavatpūjyapāda has not been discontinued in our day.[14] Those titles are, however, not confined to being applied to Śaṅkara; other Advaitins also are styled thus in colophons. For instance, Śaṅkara's teacher Govinda is Bhagavatpūjyapāda, Vimuktātman is Bhagavat, his teacher Avyayātman is Bhagavatpūjyapāda, Ānandajñāna and Govindānanda are Bhagavat, etc., whilst others bear different titles, as *yati* (Prakāśātman), *muni* (Citsukha), etc. But Śaṅkara is the Bhagavatpāda or Bhagavatpūjyapāda *par excellence,* as he is not seldom called thus in unambiguous contexts without his name being mentioned. This is a well-known fact, but nevertheless it does not seem superfluous to insist on it here, for, as we shall see, it is important to bear this fact in mind when the authorship problem is discussed.

III. We have found that Śaṅkara's contemporaries preferred to call him Bhagavat. Now it will perhaps prove useful to examine the manuscript colophons of writings ascribed to him. It may be assumed that in many cases an old tradition has been preserved in these colophons as they were transcribed mechanically from generation to generation.

I had to depend on the descriptions given in manuscript catalogues. I was able to go through a number of old catalogues and to examine one of recent date (T). The majority of the catalogues were, however, not utilizable, as they do not give full descriptions of the manuscripts, colophons are not reproduced in them, and all works attributed to Śaṅkara are indiscriminately described as productions of Śaṅkarācārya, whereas the question to which an answer was sought from the manuscript descriptions was just this: do the colophons attribute the several works to Śaṅkarācārya or to Śaṅkarabhagavat(pūjya)pāda?[15] Most of the materials have been drawn from T, C, and M. But as T also was utilizable only to a limited extent,[16] the material which could be extracted from the catalogues for the purposes of the present investigation is not so vast as might be expected from the number of catalogue items examined. Nevertheless, it will perhaps be sufficient for us to draw some conclusions.

Works ascribed to Śaṅkara (-Bhagavat or Ācārya)[17]

A. Works attributed to Śaṅkara-Bhagavat (bh) or Śaṅkara-Bhagavatpāda (p) or Śaṅkara-Bhagavatpūjyapāda (pp)

Advaitānubhūti. T XII 7148 (p).

Īśā-Upaniṣad-Bhāṣya. C I 174–5 (both bh). T III 1437–9 (3 times bh), H I 105a (p), Ān (bh), BI (bh). MG I 310 (bh).

Upadeśasāhasrī. T XII 7205 (pp), W I 614 (bh), Poona (bh; after the Gadyaprabandha: p), Ed. in "The Pandit" (bh; after the Gadyaprabandha: p).

Aitareya-Upaniṣad-Bhāṣya. C I 92 (bh), T III 1444–6 (three times bh), Ān (bh after all three adhyāyas), BI (final colophon: Śaṅkarācāryabhagavat, but after second adhyāya: bh), MG I 330 (p), 331 (bh).

Kaṭha-Upaniṣad-Bhāṣya. C I 178–9 (both bh), T III 1455 (bh), Ān (bh after all six vallīs), BI (bh); MG I 342 (p).

Kena-Upaniṣad-Pada-Bhāṣya. C I 176 (bh), T III 1456–8 (three times bh), T III 1460 (bh) Ān (after all four khaṇḍas: p); BI (bh).

Kena-Upaniṣad-Vākya-Bhāṣya. Ān (bh, final colophon only); MG I 387 (Śaṅkarācārya-Bhagavat); Poona (bh).

Chāndogya-Upaniṣad-Bhāṣya. C I 162 = Bik 215 (bn), T III 1476 (bh), T III 1478–82 (five times bh), Ān (in the colophons of the first and second Prapāṭhakas: p; in cols. of other chapters and in final col.: bh), BI (first prapāṭhaka: p; second–sixth Prapāṭhakas: bh); MG I 464 (bh).

Taittirīya-Upaniṣad-Bhāṣya. C I 147 (pp), T III 1487–9 (three times p with omission of the name), T III 1493 (pp), Ān (bh after all three adhyāyas), BI (bh after all three adhyāyas); MG I 505 (bh).

Praśna-Upaniṣad-Bhāṣya. C I 198 (bh), T III 1513–6 (four times bh), T III 1518 (bh), Ān (bh after all six praśnas), BI (bh); MG I 618 (p).

Bṛhadāraṇyaka-Upaniṣad-Bhāṣya. T III 1526–7 (both bh), Ān (bh after all six adhyāyas), BI (bh after all adhyāyas); MG I 644 (bh).

Brahmasūtra-Bhāṣya. T XII 7025 (p), T list, C III 140 (p), C III 145 (p), K (final col.: pp; the cols. of the other fifteen pādas give bh, p, and pp promiscuously), Nirṇ (pp; other pādas as mentioned under K), BI (pp; other pādas as K); Ān (final col.: pp; others as K).

Bhagavadgītā-Bhāṣya. T XV 8860 (pp), T list, Ān (bh after all adhyāyas); MG IV I 2048 (p).

Māṇḍūkya-Upaniṣad-Bhāṣya (with Gauḍapādīya-Bhāṣya or Āgamaśāstra-Vivaraṇa) C III 38 (bh), C III 59 (bh), C I 181 (bh), T III 1547–51 (five times bh), Ān (bh after all four prakaraṇas), BI (bh after all four prakaraṇas); MG I 704 (bh).

Muṇḍaka-Upaniṣad-Bhāṣya. C I 182 (bh), T III 1557–60 (four times bh), Ān (bh), BI (bh); MG I 719 (bh).

Vivekacūḍāmaṇi. T XII 7378–9 (both p), M II 347 (p), Poona (bh)

Śvetāśvatara-Upaniṣad-Bhāṣya. T III 1565 (p), BI (bh after adhyāyas I, III, IV, V, and VI).

Svātmapūjā. T XII 7400 (p).

Haritattvamuktāvali or Haritattvavyākhyā. M IV 1489 (p).

Harim-Īḍe-stotra. M III 1297 (bh).

Hastāmalakabhāṣya. C III 173 (bh), T XII 7411 (p).

B. Works mentioned more than once as composed by Śaṅkarācārya

(32 works which I have found mentioned not more than once each as Śaṅkarācārya's production, are not included in the list.)

Amaruśataka. H III 1759, T VII 389 ff.

Ātmānātmaviveka. M II 620, C III 48–9; MG 4559.

Kaupīnapañcaka. M VIII 127, T XII 7223.

Tripuṭī or Tripurī (-Upaniṣad). M I 14, W I 618.

Dakṣiṇāmūrtyaṣṭaka. T XII 7227, T list, (Dakṣiṇāmūrtistava) W I 615.

Daśaślokī. M IV 1535, T XII 7256, T list.

Nirañjanāṣṭaka. T XII 7281–3 (once "Śrīparamahaṃsaparivrājakācārya" only).

Nirvāṇaṣaṭka (also Cidānandaṣaṭka). T XII (7284–6).

Prabodhasudhākara. T XII, 7309 (in 7310 attributed to Dinakarācārya), C III 75 (Śaṅkarācārya designated as Govinda's disciple), M VIII 2845 (Śaṅkarācārya, Govinda's disciple).

Bālabodhasaṃgraha. T XII 7318–9.

Bālabodhinī. W I 618, T XII 7320–1, M I 175.

Vijñānanaukā. T XII 7377. (Vedāntavijñānanaukā) M II 715. (Vijñānanavaka) MIV 1720.

Vajrasūcī (-Upaniṣad). M I 36, C III 105.

Sahajāṣṭaka T XII 7390–1.

Svātmanirūpaṇa or Vedāntāryā or Svātmānandaprakāśikā. M III 1214. M V 1781, T XII 7392.

C. Works variously attributed: to Śaṅkarācārya (ā) and Śaṅkarabhagavat (bh, p, or pp)

Aparokṣānubhūti. M I 483 (ā), M III 1284 (ā), T XII 7151 (ā), Aparokṣānubhava) H III 1856 (pp, without preceding titles); MG IX 4540 (ā).

Ātmajñānopadeśavidhi. M I 176 (Śaṅkara, Govinda's disciple, no title following), W I 618 (ā), T XII 7161 ("a short vedāntic treatise of some unknown author in the manner of Śrī Śaṅkara's Upadeśasāhasrī").

Ātmabodha. T XII 7162 (p, without specification of teacher), T XII 7195 (ā), W I 617–8 (both ā), C III 39 (ā), C III 41 (ā, Govinda's disciple), Poona (bh); MG IX 4547 (ā), 4554 and 4556 (ā, Govinda's disciple).

Ātmavidyopadeśa (vidhi). M III 1310 (Śaṅkara, no title following), C III 45 (Śaṅkara, no title following).

Nṛsiṃhatāpanī-Upaniṣad-Bhāṣya. M I 24 (ā), T III 1509 (bh); MG I 581–5 (bh) 585–6 (Bhagavac-Chaṅkarācārya).

Mahāvākyavivaraṇa. T XII 7333 (Śrībhāṣyakāra), H III 1789 (ā), Haraprasād Shāstrī's Notices of Skt. Mss. (Calcutta, 1892) X 4133 (ā).

Vākyavṛtti. T XII 7347 and 7353 (both ā), W I 618 (ā), M I 178 (bh), H III 1793 (bh, without addition of name), (-vyākhyā) T XII 7354 (p).

Sanatsujātīya-Bhāṣya or -Vivaraṇa. T XII 7381 (ā), M IV 1494 (Śaṅkara-Bhagavatpūjyapāda-Śiṣya !), Poona (bh); MG IV 093 (bhagavatpāda, without name).

Conclusions

The list given above is far from being complete. But it would be impossible to compile a complete list of all colophons ascribing a treatise to Śaṅkara even if a comprehensive collection of catalogues could be made use of, because those catalogues that do not reproduce colophons omit distinguishing between Śaṅkarācārya on the one hand, Śaṅkara-Bhagavat, -Bhagavatpāda, or Bhagavatpūjyapāda on the other. It is, however, absolutely necessary to draw this distinction, as I hope to show in the following.

However scanty the materials presented here may be, they allow us to ascertain the following facts:

a. When variations of the title occur in the colophons to different sections (adhyāyas, pādas, etc.) of a work, only Bhagavat, Bhagavatpāda, and Bhagavatpūjyapāda alternate with one another, whereas Śaṅkarācārya does not seem to be interchangeable with the Bhagavat titles in the colophons of one and the same work. The only exceptions from this rule in the available material are the *Aitareya-Upaniṣad-Bhāṣya* and the *Kena-Upaniṣad-Vākya-Bhāṣya* (see list, section a), where the abnormal form Śaṅkara-Ācārya-Bhagavat occurs. But the irregularity of this form is easily explainable as the lapse of a modern scribe to whom the Ācārya form was more familiar than the Bhagavat form which he found in the manuscript he was copying; so he formed a contamination of both.

b. The forms containing the word Bhagavat are invariably accompanied by a specification of the teacher, who is always stated to be Govinda. On the other hand, when Śaṅkarācārya is stated to be the author of a text, a teacher is mentioned only in extremely rare cases. Such cases have been noted above under B, and C. Among the 32 works not included in the list one case of the compound Govinda-

Bhagavatpūjyapāda-śiṣya preceding the word Śaṅkarācārya was observed. This rareness of statements as to the teacher may fairly well be accounted for by the fact that the transcribers of the first copies were aware that Śaṅkarācārya was not the name but the title of the author whose work they were copying. It is quite natural that the teacher's name should not have been added to the title of a man who, besides his designation of Śaṅkarācārya (= Jagadguru), bore still a Sannyāsin name, for when he was the disciple of a teacher, he was not yet a Śaṅkara, and it was not as a Śaṅkara that he had received instruction. Again, it is probable that a scribe, who was the first to attribute to Śaṅkara a treatise which had circulated up to his time as anonymous, chose the simple colophon *Śaṅkarācārya-viracita* rather than one containing the teacher's name and further titles, and when such an ascription was effectuated at a late date, it could only be to Śaṅkarācārya, not to Śaṅkarabhagavat, as the Ācārya title seems to have become prevalent in the course of time.

The designations of Bhagavat, Bhagavatpāda, and Bhagavatpūjyapāda are almost invariably preceded by a series of titles, mostly Paramahaṃsa-parivrājakācārya, sometimes with the omission of -ācārya. These titles have been omitted in the list. But it is worth mentioning that even here a divergence between the Ācārya and the Bhagavat type is discernible: while the Bhagavat form is regularly preceded by titles of the description just mentioned, the Ācārya form is so only in the minority of the cases.

c. The Bhāṣyas of the three Prasthānas (early *Upaniṣads, Bhagavadgītā, Brahmasūtras*) as well as the *Gauḍapādīya-Bhāṣya* are always attributed to Śaṅkara-Bhagavat in the utilized material. Among the independent treatises the *Upadeśasāhasrī* and *Vivekacūḍāmaṇi* were found several times to be ascribed to Śaṅkara-Bhagavat. A few other works may perhaps also claim to have been composed by him.

As opposed to that group, a large number of writings, mostly independent ones, are assigned to Śaṅkarācārya, and some among them were in the available material found to be ascribed to the Ācārya several times. In some instances ascription varies between the Bhagavat and the Ācārya, but not in the case of the three-Prasthāna-Bhāṣyas.

It is only natural that some confusion should have occurred as Śaṅkarācārya has for centuries been regarded as always identical with Śaṅkara-Bhagavat, and it is even surprising that the confusions, as far as the colophons of the Prasthāna-Bhāṣyas are concerned, are so few in number.

At any rate, the observations set forth above—the formal divergencies between the two varieties of colophons and the association of each of them with a rather definite series of works—are so striking that they should not be neglected when the problem of authorship is discussed.

Since Śaṅkara's contemporaries styled him Bhagavat, Bhagavatpāda, and Bhagavatpūjyapāda, and the *Brahmasūtra-Bhāṣya,* which surely has been composed by him, is invariably ascribed to Śaṅkara-Bhagavat, -Bhagavatpāda, or -Bhagavatpūjyapāda in the colophons, we are entitled to regard provisionally as genuine those works that are described in their colophons as productions of the Bhagavat, whereas all the works that are usually attributed to Śaṅkara-Ācārya in the colophons are suspicious of being spurious.

So we find that, above all, the Bhāṣyas on the *Prasthānatrayī* can claim to be Śaṅkara's genuine productions.

IV. The authorship problem cannot of course be solved by the superficial method of examining colophons; the contents of the work require attention also. There may even be writings which, though described in all colophons as composed by the Bhagavat, are spurious all the same. The *Śvetāśvatara-Upaniṣad-Bhāṣya,* for instance, can hardly be regarded as genuine in its present shape. It may perhaps have been interpolated and remodeled by a later author, but this question will require special investigation.

On the other hand, it will not be difficult to prove the spuriousness of many of the works that pass as Śaṅkarācārya's productions or are alternately attributed to the Bhagavat and to the Ācārya if the phraseology and doctrines of the *Sūtrabhāṣya* are taken as a standard of comparison. Two of these writings shall now be singled out as specimens, and a few remarks as to the possibility of their being the Bhāṣyakāra's productions will be made.

A. The Sanatsujātīyabhāṣya

In the colophons examined above this text is ascribed once to the Bhagavat, once to a disciple of the Bhagavat, and once to the Ācārya. This does not speak much in favor of its having been composed by the Bhagavat.

The beginning of the text bears a striking resemblance to the first sentences of the long introduction to the *Śvetāśvatara-Bhāṣya.* This introduction is certainly spurious—its habit of frequently quoting long passages from the Purāṇa literature being opposed to the practice of all those works that may provisionally be regarded as the Bhāṣyakāra's productions—and it seems to have been prefixed to the genuine Bhāṣya. After the introductory clause (*idaṃ vivaraṇam alpagrantham . . . ārabhyate,* p. 248 of the BI edition), there is a fresh beginning on p. 274 (*brahmavādino vadantītyādi śvetāśvatarāṇāṃ mantropaniṣat. tasyā alpagranthā vṛttir ārabhyate)* that is quite similar in its form to the introductory phrases of Śaṅkara's commentaries on the *Bṛhadāraṇyaka, Kāṭhaka, Chāndogya, Muṇḍaka,* and *Māṇḍūkya Upaniṣads,* which also start by quoting the first words of the Upaniṣad. There is one expression at least, common to the *Sanatsujātīya* and *Śvetāśvatara Bhāṣyas,* which can hardly have been written by Śaṅkara-Bhagavat, viz.: *svāśrayayā svaviṣayayāvidyayā svānubhavagamyayā* (BI p. 248; Poona p. 437). The theories implied by this phrase have been developed by the Bhagavat's contemporaries and successors, not by him. Moreover, the *Sanatsujātīya* frequently specifies the sources of the quotations given in the text, which is very seldom done in Śaṅkara-Bhagavat's presumably genuine works. Further un-Śaṅkarean expressions might be added to the one quoted above—as for instance a passage on p. 455 (Poona), in the commentary on stanza 21: *na svataś cidānandādvitīyasya kāraṇatvam, kiṃtu māyāveśavaśāt*—but the question as to whether Śaṅkara-Bhagavat can have been the author of the text is definitively decided in the negative when we find a quotation from the *Brahmasūtrabhāṣya (avidyākṛtanāmarūpopādhyanurodhīśvaro bhavati,* from Sūtrabhāṣya II, 1, 14; Nirn. p. 382 1. 8; K p. 471 1.13) introduced by *uktaṃ hi* (Poona p. 447, commentary on stanza 8) and, subsequently, a quotation, probably from one of Sureśvara's Vārttikas, ushered in with the words *uktaṃ hi Sureśvarācāryaiḥ.* It is inconceivable that Śaṅkara should have cited his own disciple, styling him Ācārya.

B. The Sarva(darśana)siddhāntasaṃgraha (abbreviated: SSS)

This text is not mentioned in the list given above. In the edition[18] it is described as *Śaṅkarācārya-viracita* in the colophon to each of its twelve chapters. The edition is based on five manuscripts, and the editor mentions (preface, pp. XIII–XIV) that all of them ascribe the authorship to Śaṅkarācārya.

The editor in his preface seeks to prove that the text must have been composed by Śaṅkara the Bhāṣyakāra. Two German scholars have further propounded opinions as to the authorship of the text: H. Jacobi[19] emphatically denied the Bhāṣyakāra's authorship, whereas B. Liebich[20] argued for the probability or at least the possibility of the text's having been composed by the Bhāṣyakāra. I shall not examine the arguments advanced by the two scholars; neither of them takes the Vedānta chapter of the SSS into account, and in either case the reasoning does not seem to be very conclusive. But I think the question can be settled by a correct interpretation of two or three stanzas which are employed by Raṅgācārya to support the thesis of the "genuineness" of the work. The stanzas 20–22 of the first chapter read as follows:

> *Bhavaty uttaramīmāṃsā tv aṣṭādhyāyī dvidhā ca sā /*
> *Devatājñānakāṇḍābhyāṃ vyāsasūtraṃ dvayos samam // 20 //*
> *Pūrvādhyāyacatuṣkeṇa mantravācyātra devatā /*
> *Saṅkarṣaṇoditā tad dhi devatākāṇḍam ucyate // 21 //*
> *Bhāṣyaṃ caturbhir adhyāyair bhagavatpādanirmitam /*
> *Cakre vivaraṇaṃ tasya tad vedāntaṃ pracakṣate // 22 //*

Professor Raṅgācārya was certainly right in rejecting the reading *Śaṅkareṇoditā* and in preferring *Saṅkarṣaṇoditā*. But in interpreting the word *bhagavatpāda* he follows the commentary of Śeṣagovinda, a disciple of Madhusūdana Sarasvatī, who curiously explains the word as referring to Śaṅkara's teacher Govinda. It is true that Govinda is usually styled Bhagavat(pūjya)pāda also, but when we consider that a Brahmasūtrabhāṣya composed by Śaṅkara's teacher Govinda is entirely unknown,[21] whereas we should expect Śaṅkara in his own Bhāṣya to have alluded to the important fact that his teacher had also composed such a Bhāṣya, and when we take into account, on the other hand, that the title of Bhagavatpāda, wherever it occurs in Advaitic literature without a name following or preceding it, refers to Śaṅkara-Bhagavat (see above, pp. 3–4), then it comes out that Śeṣagovinda's explanation is utterly improbable and that it must be one of those *ad hoc* interpretations that are not seldom met with in commentaries. Śeṣagovinda was convinced that the author of the SSS and the great Bhāṣyakāra were identical; so he tried to explain away the obvious meaning of the word *bhagavatpāda*.

The fact that the SSS mentions a *Brahmasūtrabhāṣya* composed by the Bhagavatpāda suffices to make it appear very probable that the text has not been written by Śaṅkara-Bhagavatpāda. But further observations lead to the same conclusion. In the stanzas quoted above our Śaṅkarācārya speaks of an *Uttaramīmāṃsā* consisting of eight adhyāyas. This is very strange indeed, for we know only of Brahmasūtras divided into four adhyāyas, and these four adhyāyas have been commented upon by Śaṅkara-Bhagavatpāda. If this Śaṅkara-Bhagavatpāda were identical with the author of the SSS, who enunciated the theory of the eight adhyāyas, in his commentary on the second four adhyāyas (the Jñānakāṇḍa) he would very likely have referred to the fact that these constituted only the second part of the system, the first part being the Devatākāṇḍa. This Devatākāṇḍa (also called Saṅkarṣakāṇḍa or Saṅkarṣaṇakāṇḍa) is usually regarded as a text of the Karmamīmāṃsā (cf. Madhusūdana, *Prasthānabheda,* Ān. p. 6), composed by Jaimini, and Śaṅkara, who alludes to it in commenting on *Brahmasūtra* III.3.43, seems to reckon it as a distinct work, not as part of Vyāsa's sūtras. Moreover, there are in the SSS expressions and ideas that are foreign to Śaṅkara's authentic works. In XII.18 we find *vivarta,* and in XII.54 *saccidānanda,* two terms nowhere found in Śaṅkara's authentic works.[22] In XII.77–78 the *ekajīvavāda* is contrasted with the view that there are many individual souls. This points to a stage of development which had not yet been attained at the Bhāṣyakāra's time, and the juxtaposition of the three theories concerning the *jīva* as given in XII.77–79 is not in harmony with the phraseology and the ideas of Śaṅkara's main work. The *suṣupti* theory as enunciated in XII.81 also does not tally with the doctrine of the Sūtrabhāṣya.

On the other hand, the term *nāmarūpa* is to be expected in an exposition of the Vedāntavāda by the Bhagavatpāda; it is not, however, met with in the Vedānta chapter of the SSS.

The author of the SSS was a Vaiṣṇava, more specifically, a Kṛṣṇaite. The SSS proceeds from inferior systems to more valuable ones, and the Vedānta follows all the others, but still after the Vedānta the somewhat enigmatic Hiraṇyagarbhapakṣa is set forth, and at the conclusion of the whole work our Śaṅkarācārya declares that it is Kṛṣṇa who has taught to Uddhava "the path of those who have renounced all worldly attachments" *(avadhūta-mārga),* and that this path can be learned from the *Bhāgavata Purāṇa* (XII.99). Thus the Vaiṣṇava doctrine of deliverance, as proclaimed by Kṛṣṇa and transmitted in the *Bhāgavata Purāṇa,* is the highest wisdom. After these observations we shall not hesitate to interpret the Govinda who is identified with the Paramātman in XII.54 as Kṛṣṇa also; at any rate, this would be a much more plausible explanation than that propounded by Raṅgācārya, who thinks that Govinda here is the name of Śaṅkara's teacher (preface, pp. XII–XIII). The learned professor quotes two instances of a spiritual teacher being identified with the Supreme, but both of them are *maṅgala* stanzas, and it is of course quite another thing to identify one's teacher in a *maṅgalācaraṇa* than to do so in a context where nothing necessitates the teacher's name being mentioned.

As regards the author's Vaiṣṇava leanings, these might be interpreted as being not contradictory to the *Bhāṣyakāra's attitude.* For there can be no doubt that Śaṅkarabhagavat, who commented on the Brahmasūtras, stemmed from a Vaiṣṇava environment and treated Vaiṣṇava views with more toleration than those of the Śaivas.[23] But his philosophy includes no specifically Vaiṣṇava views, and, what distinguishes him most from the author of the SSS, he is very far from teaching the *avadhūta-mārga* and the doctrine of the *Bhāgavata Purāṇa* as being superior to pure Advaitism.

Abbreviations

The following abbreviations are used to indicate manuscript catalogues:

- Bik Rājendralāl Mitra, *A Catalogue of the Sanskrit Manuscripts in the Library of His Highness the Mahārāja of Bikāner* (Calcutta, 1880).
- C Hrishīkeśa Śāstrī and Śiva Chandra Gui, *A Descriptive Catalogue of Sanskrit Manuscripts in the Calcutta Sanskrit College;* vol. I, Vedic Mss. (Calcutta, 1895); vol. III, Philosophy Mss. (Calcutta, 1900).
- H E. Hultzsch, *Reports on Sanskrit Manuscripts in Southern India,* No. I–III (Madras, 1895–1905).
- M Rājendralāl Mitra, *Notices on Sanskrit Manuscripts,* vols. I–IX (Calcutta, 1870–1888).
- MG *A Descriptive Catalogue of the Sanskrit Manuscripts in the Government Oriental Manuscripts Library* (Madras).
- T P. P. S. Sastri, *A Descriptive Catalogue of the Sanskrit Manuscripts in the Tanjore Mahārāja Serfoji's Sarasvatī Mahāl Library,* Tanjore, vols. I–IX (Srirangam, 1928–1934).
- W Albrecht Weber, *Verzeichnis der Sanskrit-Handschriften der Königlichen Bibliothek Berlin,* vol. I (Berlin, 1853).

(Roman numerals refer to the volumes, Arabic figures indicate the items of the catalogues.)

For abbreviations concerning printed editions, see n. 16.

Notes

1. *Pañcapādikā,* Maṅgalācaraṇa, v. 3.

2. *Pañcapādikā,* Viz. S.S. edition, p. 29 line 9 and p. 39 line 4.

3. *Naiṣkarmyasiddhi* IV. 74 and 76.

4. Ibid. IV. 19.

5. Ibid. IV. 43.

6. By the investigations of Sengaku Mayeda (see his edition of the *Upadeśasāhasrī,* Tokyo, 1973, introd.), who made use of my method, the authenticity of this work is proved.

7. E.g., pp. 8 and 27 of the Nirṇayasāgar edition *(Brahmasūtra-Śāṅkarabhāṣyam* with the commentaries *Ratnaprabhā, Bhāmatī,* and *Nyāyanirṇaya,* ed. by Mahādeva Shāstrī Bākre, 2nd ed., Bombay, 1909).

8. E.g., in the commentary on *Naiṣk.* I.6 and IV.20.

9. Ibid. IV. 22.

10. Ibid. IV. 44.

11. Ibid. IV. 23 ff.

12. It would have been useful to examine Sureśvara's Vārttikas also, but they were not accessible to me. For the purpose of the present article, however, the utilized material seems to be sufficient as completeness is not aimed at here and it is only intended, in this section, to point to the fact that the solemn titles of Bhagavat, etc., were preferred by Śaṅkara's contemporaries. Sureśvara's *Pañcīkaraṇavārttika* has on purpose been left out of account here as the stanzas (1–2) mentioning Śaṅkara are apparently spurious (cf. P. Tuxen in: *Aus Indiens Kultur, Festgabe R. v. Garbe dargebracht,* Erlangen, 1927, p. 134).

13. V. 3 of the *maṅgalācaraṇa* introductory to the *Bṛhadāraṇyakopaniṣadbhāṣya.*

14. Cf., e.g., the Prastāvanā in the Nirṇayasāgar edition of the *Citsukhī,* 2nd ed., 1931), p. 1, line 20, and the introduction *(prāstāvikaṃ kiṃcit)* to the Ānandāśrama edition of Toṭakācārya's *Śrutisārasamuddharaṇa* (Anandāśrama S. S., vol. 103, 1936), p. 1, line 1.

15. The more important ones among the utilizable catalogues are specified above in the abbreviation list. One of the catalogues, though not giving colophons, distinguishes between Śaṅkarācārya and Śaṅkarabhagavat in the index (Kunja Vihari Kāvyatīrtha, *Catalogue of the Printed Books and Mss. in Sanskrit Belonging to the Oriental Library of the Asiatic Society of Bengal,* Calcutta, 1904). But while using the book one cannot get rid of the suspicion that the distinction is rather an arbitrary one, especially as the index adds *Govindabhagavatpūjyapāda-*

śiṣya to *Śaṅkarācārya,* not to *Śaṅkarabhagavat,* whereas, as we shall see, the overwhelming majority of the colophons as reproduced in other catalogues give that specification of the teacher just in the case of such writings as are attributed to Śaṅkarabhagavat. It seems rather incredible that all the Calcutta mss. should deviate from that rule. The fact that in other instances Śaṅkarabhagavat or Śaṅkarācārya has obviously been confounded with Śaṅkarānanda—commentaries called *dīpikā* here being attributed to Śaṅkarabhagavat or Śaṅkarācārya whereas they are elsewhere ascribed to Śaṅkarānanda and never to the Bhagavat or the Ācārya—adds to the impression of unreliability which the book produces. The book has therefore been left out of account.

16. Unfortunately, T, in such cases where the library possesses several mss. of one and the same work, as a rule gives the colophon of one of these mss. only, arranging the data of the rest in a list but omitting notes as to the colophons in the list. May we assume that the colophons of the mss. described in the list are identical with the one reproduced? It is probable, but we cannot be absolutely certain about it, for the compiler did not discriminate between Śaṅkarācārya and Śaṅkarabhagavat.

17. The following abbreviations are used to indicate printed editions:

Ān = Ānandāśrama Sanskrit Series
BI = Bibliotheca Indica
BSS = Bombay Sanskrit Series
K = Kāśī Sanskrit Series
Nirn. = Nirṇayasāgar Press (edition specified above, note 7)
Poona = Works of Shankaracharya, vol. IV: Minor Works (Poona, 1925)
Viz = Vizianagram Sanskrit Series

"T list" is added in some cases to indicate that the Tanjore catalogue contains a large list of further mss. which presumably have the same colophons as the one specified.

18. By M. Raṅgācārya (Madras, 1909).

19. In: *Deutsche Literaturzeitung,* 1921, column 724.

20. In: *Zeitschrift für Indologie und Iranistik,* 1923, pp. 124 ff.

21. A fragment of a *Brahmasūtrabhāṣya* by one Govinda is mentioned by Aufrecht in his *Catalogue of the Sanskrit Mss. in the University Library of Leipzig* (Leipzig, 1901), but it seems rather improbable that this fragment, which apparently is the production of a Kṛṣṇaite, should have been composed by Śaṅkara's teacher.

22. Cp. my work *Vivarta* (Wiesbaden, 1953); Paul Deussen, *Das System des Vedānta,* p. 228 [trans. C. Johnston, p. 212]; and my papers "Eigentümlichkeiten . . . " and "Śaṅkara der Yo˝in . . . " [i.e., Chapters 4 and 5 in this volume].

23. Cp. my paper "Relations of Early Advaitins to Vaiṣṇavism" [i.e., Chapter 2 in this volume].

4

Distinctive Features of the Doctrine and Terminology of Śaṅkara:

Avidyā, Nāmarūpa, Māyā, Īśvara

The purpose of this study is to lay some groundwork for answering the question: Which of the numerous writings[1] ascribed to Śaṅkara were really composed by him? In light of the significance of Vedānta for the intellectual history of India, this question[2] is of considerable importance.[3] Of course, before one can answer it, one must determine as completely and precisely as possible which views and which terms are peculiar to Śaṅkara as an individual thinker. This has not yet been achieved in an adequate manner; for until now Śaṅkara has been considered more as the exponent of a school than as an individual.[4] Although important findings about Śaṅkara's intellectual traits are presented in the well-known works of P. Deussen,[5] G. A. Jacob,[6] and R. Otto,[7] no one has hitherto pursued to a sufficient extent the question: What is unique to him in contrast to the views held by other masters of his school or those common to all Brahmanical philosophers of illusion? It therefore seems necessary to proceed in the present investigation on the basis of the only text for which Śaṅkara's authorship is undisputed.

Thus, in this study characteristic features will be culled from Śaṅkara's *magnum opus,* the *Brahmasūtrabhāṣya,*[8] and formulated so as to provide criteria for evaluating the authenticity of works for which Śaṅkara's authorship is in doubt. This task requires frequent comparisons with other Advaitins. Nevertheless, while statements about Śaṅkara will be supported by passages cited from the ŚBh, I shall generally refrain from using quotations to document statements about the teachings of others of his school. Since most of the claims will apply to a plurality of authors, such a procedure would require citing and interpreting such a large number of passages that the article would go far beyond its original goal and become a history of the Advaitavāda. The comparison with Śaṅkara's contemporaries and immediate followers seems to be most important; for in their case the differences from the teaching of the master are still slight, and our criteria of authenticity will be more certain the more precisely we ascertain those doctrinal and terminological differences which existed already in Śaṅkara's lifetime. For the few reports about Advaita prior to Śaṅkara (mainly comments of Haribhadra,[9] Kumārila,[10] and Jayanta,[11] authors of opposing schools), for Gauḍapāda,[12] Śaṅkara's contemporary Maṇḍanamiśra,[13] his direct pupils (Sureśvara,[14] Padmapāda,[15] and Toṭaka[16]), and Vimuktātman,[17] I base my remarks on my own investigations. Otherwise, I base my statements primarily on the presentation of Advaita in the first two volumes of *A History of Indian Philosophy* by S. Dasgupta (Cambridge, 1922–1932).

The four concept areas *avidyā, nāmarūpa, māyā,* and *īśvara* were chosen in recognition of the fact that it is especially with regard to these ideas that the peculiarities of Śaṅkara's thought and expression are evident.

The question of the historical and systematic context of Śaṅkara's thought can be dealt with only to a limited extent here. All that must, for the most part, be left to a presentation of the teachings of Śaṅkara which systematically evaluates all of his authentic writings, and to a history of the illusionistic-monistic philosophy of the Brahmins. The solution of the authenticity problems for which this study tries to pave the way would be a prerequisite for that.

I. Avidyā

A. The nature of avidyā

According to Ś.'s only definition, *avidyā* is the same as *adhyāsa: tam etam evaṃlakṣaṇam adhyāsaṃ paṇḍitā avidyeti manyante* (I,1,1, Introduction, K 51–52).[18] "Ignorance" is the "mutual superimposition" *(itaretarādhyāsa)* of subject *(viṣayin)* and object *(viṣaya),* the mutual transposing of self *(ātman)* and nonself *(anātman),* the unacceptable "combining of true and false" *(satyānṛte mithunīkṛtya,* I,1,1, Intro., K 34), which manifests itself, above all, in our habitual practice to view the nonself—body, senses, the inner sense—as the self (I,1,1, Intro. and I,3,2, K 308,8).

The fact that Ś. equates *avidyā* with the basic error of all worldly existence distinguishes him from all later Advaitins who considered *avidyā* a factor which causally conditions all error insofar as it is, so to speak, the stuff out of which every false idea is formed. Thus *mithyājñāna,* "false cognition," can also occur as a synonym for *avidyā* in Ś.'s text. In the consideration of the uses of *avidyā* in what follows (sec. I,4) we shall therefore also pay attention to the way in which *mithyājñāna* is used. It will turn out that this word occurs in the same contexts as *avidyā*. For Ś. *avidyā* is the same as *mithyājñāna;* for other Advaitins it is the cause of it.

B. Related factors

For Ś.'s successors and even several of his contemporaries and precursors, *avidyā* is something quite unique: as the material cause of all errors and the entire manifold world (which is a metaphysical error) nothing can really be coordinated with it. Ś., on the other hand, considers *avidyā* to fall under another, more general concept: *avidyā* is a *kleśa* (or *doṣa*—this word, however, does not appear in the SBh as a general concept which includes *avidyā*). It is the first, most important, and most dangerous member in a chain of other *kleśas* which are caused by it. This point of view is very close to that of the Yoga system. Yoga, too, considers ignorance as the first member in a series of psychic afflictions which encompasses, in order: *asmitā, rāga, dveṣa,* and *abhiniveśa* (*Yogasūtra* II,3). Here, the following sequences from the SBh are relevant:

ignorance, desire, and action (*avidyā-kāma-karma,* I,2,17, K 281,6):

ignorance, attachment, hate, fear, delusion (*avidyā, rāga, dveṣa, bhaya, moha,* I,3,2, K 308,8–10).

"Insofar as ignorance creates inequality, it is dependent on action, which is the result of traces of attachment and other afflictions (here Vācaspati specifies: hatred and delusion; *rāgādi-kleśa-vāsanākṣipta-karmāpekṣā tv avidyā vaiṣamyakarī syāt;* Vācaspati: *rāga-dveṣa-mohādayaḥ,* II,1,36, K 499,5). *Avidyā* thus belongs in a series together with action, affection, aversion, and delusion.

A series is merely alluded to in the following passages:

III,3,32, K 809,16: *avidyādi-kleśa*. (The synonymous expression *avidyādi-doṣa* is expanded much in the same sense as *Yogasūtra* II,3 by Ānandagiri in his discussion of *Chāndogya-Bhāṣya* III,14,2, which has been ascribed to Ś.: *ādi-padena asmitā-rāgadveṣābhiniveśādayo gṛhyante.*)

IV,2,7, K 935,14: *avidyādīn kleśān.*

III,2,5, K 711,6: *avidyādi-vyavadhānāt.*

C. The realm of avidyā *and the state of* avidyā

Avidyā is for Ś., in contrast to other Advaitins, more an affliction of the psyche (*kleśa*) than a cosmic power *(śakti)*. In this sense he speaks of a state of *avidyā* (*avidyāvasthā,* I,1,11, K 214,7f.; II,3,40, K 628,5; II,3,41, K 632,4 and 633,6). Those who find themselves in this state constitute "the realm of the ignorant" (*avidyāvad-viṣaya,* I,1,1, Intro., K 53–55 and 61,3). The totality of potential effects of the *avidyā*-state is "the realm of ignorance" (*avidyā-viṣaya,* I,1,11, K 214,7; I,2,12, K 275,8; I,2,20, K 286, 3–4; I,4,22, K 429, 1). All religious and worldly life takes place in this realm (*vyavahāra,* I,1,11; I,2,12; I,2,20; III,2,15, K 727,8). The expression "state of ignorance" can be used as a synonymous expression for "realm of ignorance" (I,1,11, K 214,7 and 214, 7–8).

D. The causality of avidyā

The following overview is intended to answer in detail the two questions: (1) What does *avidyā* cause? (2) How is the causal action of *avidyā* described?

The effects of *avidyā* listed in the left hand column have to *avidyā* *(av)* or *mithyājñāna (m)* the relationship given in the right-hand column:

The practice of identifying the body with the I or considering it as belonging to the I *(aham idam mamedam iti . . . lokavyavahāra)* . . .	is *m-nimitta* (I,1,1, Intro., K 34–40).
Transmigration . . .	has *av* as its *bīja* (I,1,1, K 84); is *av-kṛta* (II, 3, 50, K 643, 5);

	has *m* as its *kāraṇa* (II,1,14 K 466,12); has *m* as its *hetu* (II,1,4, K 179,2).
The entanglement of the Ātman in *saṃsāra (saṃsāritva)* . . .	is *av-kalpita* (I,1,4, K 161, 3–4); *av-kṛta* (I,2,11, K 272, 16).
Karman . . .	is *m-avaṣṭhambha* (IV,1,19, K 928,6).
The individualization of the soul *(jīvatva, jīva-bhāva, jaivaṃ rūpam, jīva-bheda, jīva-prājña-bheda, jīva-parameśvarayor bhedaḥ)* . . .	is *av-pratyupasthāpita* (I,3,19, K 338,4); *av-kalpita* (I,3,19, K 338, 17; I,4,6, K 400,9); *av-nimitta* (II,3,46, K 639, 9); *av-kṛta* (III,2,21, K 735,3); *m-kṛta* (I,3,19, K 336,10); *parameśvaraḥ . . . avidyayā . . . anekadhā vibhāvyate* (I,3,19, K, 338, 10); (relation of co-occurrence:) *yāvat . . . avidyāṃ nivartayan . . . ātmānaṃ na pratipadyate tāvaj jīvasya jīvatvam* (I,3,19, K 334, 6); *yāvat . . . avidyā na nivartate tāvat . . . jīvasya jīvatvam* (I,4,6, K 400,1).
The homogeneity of *jīva* and Īśvara is concealed *(sama-dharmatvaṃ tirohitam)* . . .	*av-ādi-vyavadhānāt* (II,2,5, K 711,6).
The individual soul *(śarīra, vijñānātman, jīva, ābhāsa = jīva)* . . .	is *av-kalpita* (I,1,17, K 221,11); *av-pratyupasthāpita* (II,3, 46, I 639,7); *av-kṛta* (II,3,50, K 643,5).
Embodiment (connection with the gross or subtle body: *kārya-karaṇopadhi, saśarīratva, buddhy-upādhi-sambandha, dehādy-upādhi-sambandha)* . . .	is *av-pratyupasthāpita* (I,2,20, K 285,16); *av-nimitta* (II,3,48,K641,7); *m-nimitta* (I,1,4,K 188,3); *m-puraḥsara* (II,3,30,K620,20); occurs *av-āveśa-vaśāt* (II,3,46 K 638,6).

Bondage *(bandha)* . . .	is *av-kṛta* (II,2,29, K 744, 3); *m-nimitta* (IV,2,8, K936,13).
The relationship of the object of suffering and the cause of suffering *(tapya-tāpaka-bhāva)* which exists between the soul and *saṃsāra* . . .	is *av-kṛta* (II,2,10,K516,3).
The nature of the soul as agent and experiencer *(kartṛtva, bhoktṛtva, upabhoga)* . . .	is *av-pratyupasthāpita* (II,3,40, K 628,3); *av-kṛta* (II,3,40, K 629, 13 and 15); *m-kalpita* (I,2,8, K 268, 10 and 11); *m-nimitta* (I,2,8, K268,5); *mithyājñānāt . . . pratipeda iva* (IV,1,13, K 921,18); (description of the relation as a co-occurrence in space or time:) *av-avasthāyām* (II,3,40, K 628,5; II,3,41, K632,4); *av-viṣaye* (I,2,12, K 275,8).
The *upādhis* . . .	are *av-pratyupasthāpita* (III,2,12, K 724,14; III,2, 15, K 727,8); *av-ātmaka* (II,1,14,K471,16).
Plurality or difference *(bheda, bheda-vyavahāra, nānātva, vibhāga [-vyavahāra], rūpa-bheda)* . . .	is *av-kalpita* (I,1,4, K 160, 2; II,1,27, K 491,9; II,1,31 K 494, 18); *av-kṛta* (II,2,26; K743,1); *m-kalpita* (I,4,10;K404,13); *paramātmani m-pratibaddha* (II,1,9, K 456,15); *m-vijṛmbhita* (II,1,14, K466, 7–8; II,1,22, K 484, 15–16); (indirect description of the relation as co-occurrence:) *m-asya anapoditatvāt . . . vibhāgaḥ* (II,1,9, K 456,10).
Suffering *(duḥkha, duḥkhopabhoga,* etc.) . . .	is *av-kṛta* (II,3,46,K638,7); *av-nimitta* (II,3,46,K639,8–9); *m-nimitta* (I,1,4, K187,8–9).

Mortality *(martyatva)* . . .	is *av-kāma-karma-kṛta* (I,2,17, K 281,6).
Name and form *(nāmarūpe)* . . .	(see section II,5).
The "components" *(kalāḥ)* (i.e., the sense faculties and basic constituents of the body) of one who knows Brahman . . .	are *av-nimitta* (IV,2,16 K 941,6).
The primal state of the world, "the Unmanifest" *(bīja-śaktir avyakta-śabda-nirdeśya)* . . .	is *av-ātmaka* (I,4,3, K392,3).
The material world *(prapañca, kārya-prapañca, dvaita)*[19] . . .	is *av-kṛta* (I,3,1, K 307,2; II,4,16, K 862,6); *av-pratyupasthāpita* (II,3,40, K 629,1); *av-adhyasta* (II,2,21, K 734,6–7).
That which has been created *(kārya)* . . .	is *av-adhyāropita* (II,1,9, K 455,15).
The matter from which elements and sense organs are formed *(mātrāḥ . . . bhūtendriya-lakṣaṇāḥ)* . . .	is *av-kṛta* (I,4,22,K428,14).
Error *(sarpādi-prapañca)*[20] . . .	is *av-adhyasta* (III,2,21, K 734,14).
Sattva (in this case, the inner sense) . . .	is *av-pratyupasthāpita* (I,2,12, K 275,5).
Awakening from deep sleep *(suṣuptād utthāna)* . . .	is *av-ātmaka-bīja-sadbhāva-kārita* (II,3,31, K 621,12).

If one wished to assign the causal operation of *avidyā* to one of the two categories of causal relation which the Vedānta distinguishes—material causation and efficient causation—then one might, because of the numerous occurrences of *avidyā-nimitta* and *mithyājñāna-nimitta,* be tempted to see here a relationship of efficient causation. Thus, a marked difference between Ś. and all other Advaitins, with the possible exception of Toṭaka, would be established: whereas they consider *avidyā* as *causa materialis,* it is *causa efficiens* for Ś. However, we are not justified in making such a sharp contrast; for the occasionally occurring expressions *avidyā-bīja* and *avidyātmaka* suggest, strictly speaking, a relationship of material causation. (The second expression, *avidyātmaka,* is employed with the *satkāryavāda* in mind: where the *upādhis* are formed from *avidyā* as their prime matter, they are "of the nature of *avidyā*" *(avidyātmaka),* since for the *satkāryavādin* the effect or product is identical with the material cause.) Nevertheless, in view of the frequency of *avidyā-nimitta* we cannot draw the conclusion that Ś. sees a *causa materialis* relationship here either. We must keep in mind that the causal connections between *avidyā* and its effects are, preponderately, indicated with unique expressions that are used only for these relations *(pratyupasthāpita,*[21] *adhyasta, adhyāropita, vijṛmbhita, kalpita),* or else with the very general and indefinite word *kṛta,* or with phrases which denote merely coexistence or succession. The preference for such expressions indicates that, as Ś. conceives it, one has to do here with a causal relationship of a very special kind. Nevertheless, this much can be affirmed with regard to the differentiation of the interpretation of Ś. from that of all other Advaitins—that in his case *avidyā* is never designated as material cause of the physical world. It is never referred to as *upādāna-kāraṇa* or *prakṛti,* whereas even Sureśvara, who is closer to Ś. than anyone else in his understanding of *avidyā,* uses the expression *upādāna* to refer to *avidyā.*

The frequent descriptions of causal chains, beginning with *avidyā* in SBh, also suggest that, as Ś. conceives it, the causality of *avidyā* is unique. This matter will be dealt with in the section on *nāmarūpa* (II,5). In that connection Ś.'s *avidyā* interpretation also will have to be further clarified.

E. Traditional attributes of avidyā *which are not found in Ś.*

I have attempted above to determine the positive features by which Ś.'s use of the term *avidyā* diverges from what is customary for others of his school. I shall now show what negatively distinguishes his interpretation from that of other (contemporary or later) Advaitins, that is, which conceptions are associated with the idea of *avidyā* by the latter but are unfamiliar to him.

It follows from what has been discussed up to this point that Ś. does not materialize *avidyā.* As a result the adjective *jaḍa,* which is constantly added to *avidyā* from Padmapāda onward (and is used by the Sāṃkhya school as a characterization of *prakṛti*), is missing in Ś. Moreover, the epithet *bhāva-rūpa,* which can be found in Advaita texts from Jñānottama onward, is missing. *Avidyā* is for Ś. not something "insentient" and "having the form of being," i.e., something positively existant. Even the theory, already current among Ś.'s contemporaries, that *avidyā* possesses a "power of dispersion" *(vikṣepa-śakti)* and a "power of concealment" *(āvaraṇa-śakti)* is foreign to the SBh.

Ś. does not raise *avidyā* to an eternal, metaphysical entity. Correspondingly, he does not use *anādi* ("beginningless"), constantly used by other authors to characterize *avidyā,* in connection with this word. To be sure, he once (I,1,1, Intro., K 63) calls *adhyāsa* "beginningless"; otherwise in the SBh as well as in the BS *saṃsāra* has this predicate. But *avidyā* he refers to only as "natural" (*naisargika,* III,2,15, K 727,8), which is a significantly less precise determination than the emphatic *anādi.*

Nowhere does Ś. explore the essence of *avidyā.* He makes only a few definite statements about it (I,1,1, Intro., see above, sec. I,1). Thus he never calls it *anirvacanīya.* This expression appears to have come into use during Ś.'s lifetime as a name for an essential characteristic of *avidyā*[22] and is subsequently employed by all Advaitins, with the exception of Ś.'s pupils Sureśvara and Toṭaka, as an epithet of *avidyā.* In the SBh the word occurs only as an adjective of *nāmarūpa* (see below, sec. II,4).

It is typical of Ś.'s aversion to purely theoretical matters that reflections on the bearer (*āśraya)* and object *(viṣaya)* of ignorance, as well as expressions which indicate *avidyā* as belonging to the Ātman, are lacking in the SBh. Ś.'s term *avidyāvat,* which indicates the *jīva* as "one who possesses *avidyā*" (e.g., I,4,1, K 390,7; I,4,3, K 392,13), could mislead one to ascribe to him the view that the individual soul is the bearer of *avidyā* (in other words, the thesis of Maṇḍanamiśra and Vācaspatimiśra), whereas one might gather from phrases such as *avidyātmikā . . . bījaśaktiḥ . . . parameśvarāśrayā* (I,4,3, K 392,3) that he considered Paramātman or Parameśvara as the *āśraya,* the substratum, of *avidyā.* But this discrepancy already indicates that Ś. was indifferent to the *āśraya* theories which are usually found in the treatises of other Advaitins and which must have already been in existence before him. *Avidyā-viṣaya* has in the passage of the SBh considered above (I,3) a completely different meaning than in the *avidyā* theory of other Advaitins: there it does not mean "object of ignorance" but "the sphere of the effects of *avidyā*"; and, while Ś. assigns *nāmarūpe* an *āśraya* (see below, sec. II,6), he does not do so for *avidyā.* Incidentally, even Sureśvara distinguishes himself from his master on this point, although his *avidyā* interpretation is otherwise very close to Ś.—even he speculates about "bearer and object of ignorance." Although briefly and implicitly, Ś. in one passage of the SBh (IV,1,3, K 907,19–908,2) makes it clear that for him theorizing about the *āśraya* of *avidyā* is unimportant and contrary to the spirit of the teaching:

Kasya punar ayam aprabodha iti cet. Yas tvaṃ pṛcchasi tasya sa iti vadāmaḥ. Nanv aham īśvara evoktaḥ srutyā. Yady evaṃ pratibuddho 'si nāsti kasyacid aprabodhaḥ.

Here all technical terms are avoided. Even *aprabodha* "unawakened state" replaces *avidyā*. The question, "To whom does this unawakened state belong?" would be formulated technically as, "What is the *āśraya* of *avidyā*?" The simple answer to this is: "It belongs to you who are asking." That is to say, there's no problem here at all! But the questioner does see a problem: "Has not revelation said that I am God?" In the case of absolute identity of God and the soul it would follow that God or Brahman is the *āśraya* of *avidyā*. But the second reply again leads away from the theory which the questioner had hinted at: "If you are awakened in this fashion, then there is no longer an unawakened state which belongs to anybody." In advance, attuned to the answers one is supposed to give, both answers are phrased so as to be terminologically unclear, although in such a way that one who is conversant with Advaita easily guesses their allusions. The answers are not philosophically exact; rather, they are pedagogically compelling. They intentionally ignore what the questions are hinting at. While avoiding everything abstract and general, they attempt to make it immediately comprehensible to the questioner that the important thing is "being awakened," that is, liberation, not the discovery of satisfactory solutions for the problems which emerge upon thinking through the concept of *avidyā*. For there is no more *avidyā* for one who is awakened, and so all problems associated with it have become irrelevant.[23]

F. *Paṇḍita-saṃmatiḥ*

My attempt to clarify the unique features of Ś.'s *avidyā* interpretation receives support from an unexpected quarter. In 1929 there was published in Bangalore a book with the title *Mūlāvidyā-nirāsaḥ, atha vā Śrī-Śaṅkara-hṛdayam,* composed by the modern Vedāntin Subrahmaṇya (Subba Rao).[24] In his endeavor to purify Ś.'s teaching from distortions, Subrahmanya rigorously contrasted a series of characteristics of Ś.'s teachings to received Advaita dogmas. In doing so he proceeds very much according to the traditional scholastic-dialectic method, in each case refuting the views which do not agree with Ś.'s standpoint. I give here some theses from his work:

Ata evāyam anātmānirvacanīyo mithyeti paṇḍitair nirgadyate (p. 134), "Therefore, the nonself is defined by scholars as 'undeterminable,' as 'false.' " Subrahmaṇya is closer to Ś.'s standpoint in referring *anirvacanīya* to the nonself, for Ś. refers it to *nāmarūpe,* and not to *avidyā*.

Mitho-viruddha-svabhāvayor ātmānātmanor yad anyonyatopādānam[25] *anyonya-dharmavattvenākalanaṃ ca tad etad ātmavido vyavaharanty avidyeti* (loc cit.). *Amum evādhyāsam avidyeti manyante tattvacintakāḥ.* (p. 135) "Self and nonself have mutually opposed essences. That one takes one to be the other and perceives the qualities of one in the other—that is what the knowers of the self call *avidyā*. . . . Precisely this superimposition is what philosophers understand by the word *avidyā*." Just as Ś., Subramaṇya identifies *avidyā* and *adhyāsa*.

Especially interesting is the summary which Subrahmaṇya gives of the traditional description of *avidyā*, which has been accepted for centuries but which deviates in almost every word from Ś.'s usage:

Atra muhyanti kecit: Nādhyāsa evāvidyā, kā nāma, cinmātrāśraya-viṣayā, anādy, anirvacanīyā, avidyā-māyādi-śabda-bhāginī kācic chaktir bhāva-rūpā, brahmātmaikatva-lakṣaṇa-vidyā-mātra-vidhvasyā. Adhyāsas tu tat-kāryam. . . . (p. 135)

Here we have an exemplary collection of almost all the characteristics of *avidyā* which are foreign to Ś. (and which for the most part have been discussed above): It is not *adhyāsa*, rather it is its cause; pure consciousness is its *āśraya* and at the same time its *viṣaya*;[26] it is beginningless and undeterminable; it can also be designated with the word *māyā* (this matter will be considered in section IV); it is a power (see section IV); it has the form of an existing thing. The only thing Ś. could say in agreement with this passage is that *avidyā* is to be destroyed merely through knowledge; he, too, speaks of the destruction or expulsion of ignorance (e.g., *vidhūya*, III,2,26, K 743,2).

II. Nāmarūpa

A. Nāmarūpa *as prime matter* (avyākṛte nāmarūpe)

The frequent occurrence of the word *nāmarūpa*[27] is a characteristic of Ś.'s language. He bases the concept primarily on two Upaniṣad passages: the *nāmarūpe vyākaravāṇi* of Chānd. Up. VI,3,2 (BS II,4,20) and, less often, the *nāmarūpayor nirvahitā* of Chānd. Up. VII,14,1 (BS I,3,41). His interpretation is that "name and form" were somehow already present at the time of the creation of the world. Creation was thus only a matter of separating them or bringing them forth. In any case, there are several places in the SBh where *nāmarūpe* are quite clearly understood as a kind of prime matter or primal state of the world. They are called in this reading "the undeveloped *nāmarūpe.*" At I,1,5 (K 202,2) the undeveloped *nāmarūpe* are the object which stands opposite the consciousness of Īśvara before the beginning of creation; at I,2,22 (K 290,16) they are identified with "the imperishable" *(akṣara),* and "the un-unfolded" *(avyākṛta)* and designated the seed potency *(bījaśakti*[28]), the substratum of which is the Lord (Īśvara). Also at II,1,14 (K 470,7) *nāmarūpe* are called "the seed" and, more specifically, "the seed of *saṃsāra* and the phenomenal world" *(saṃsāra-prapañca-bīja).* At I,4,2 (K 391,9) and, similarly, I,4,3 (I 391,11) the primal state *(prāg-avasthā)* of the world in which name and form are not yet unfolded *(avyākṛta)* or manifested *(abhivyakta)* is mentioned: the world had prior to the unfolding of name and form the potential, germ-like existence of the primal state (it was *bīja-śakty-avastha).* At II,1,17 (K 475,7) the state in which name and form are unfolded is contrasted with the original state in which they are not unfolded. At II,1,27 (K 491,11) unfolded and un-unfolded *nāmarūpe* are distinguished.

Quite often the *upādhis* of the soul, above all the body, are referred to as "made out of name and form" (*kṛta,* II,1,14, K 471,15; II,1,22, K 484,17; II,3,43, K 636,13; III,2,6, K 712,6); "developed" (*nirvṛtta,* II,3,46, K 638,8), or "formed" (*racita,* I,4,22, K 429,8) therefrom. Also in these contexts *nāmarūpe* are presented as a kind of prime matter. They are that which *avidyā* or *māyā* is for other Advaitins before and after Śaṅkara.

B. Nāmarūpa *as the phenomenal world* (vyākṛte nāmarūpe)

The theory of the un-unfolded *(avyākṛte) nāmarūpe* corresponds to the *satkāryavāda,* according to which nothing can come from nothing and everything already exists prior to its appearance in a potential, "causal" form. But this theory also corresponds to the view of the purely spiritual nature of Brahman as the creative principle: not directly from Brahman, but from the material *avyākṛte nāmarūpe* do the transformations *(vikāra)* of the world, i.e., the *vyākṛte nāmarūpe,* proceed. This theory is based on the Upaniṣad sentence, "Now, then, let me, having entered these three divinities with this living self, unfold name and form" (Chānd. Up. VI,3,2). But, here, a more natural reading of this passage is that the "three divinities"—heat, water, and food—are separated off from each other, and the result of this process is "name and form," i.e., the phenomenal world differentiated in individuals bearing different names and having different appearances. Grammatically, *nāmarūpe* should in this passage be regarded as an effected and not as an affected object.

Now, there are expressions in the SBh which can be construed in the sense that the world is developed, divided, or expanded into name and form. Among these are, to begin with, *nāmarūpavyākṛta* (I,1,5, K 199,9; I,4,15, K 416,13; II,1,17, K 475,15), *nāmarūpābhyāṃ vyākṛta* (I,1,2, K 100, I,3,41, K 382,9), and *nāmarūpābhyāṃ vyākriyamāṇa* (I,4,15, K 417,9). All four commentators—Padmapāda, Ānandagiri, Govindānanda, and Vācaspati—take the expression *nāmarūpābhyāṃ vyākṛta* (ad I,1,2, K 100) in the sense of "unfolded *into* name and form," and the first three explain *nāmarūpābhyāṃ* expressly as an *itthaṃbhāve* instrumental.[29] *Nāmarūpa* is also interpreted as the essence of the phenomenal world in the expressions "diversity of name and form" (*nāmarūpa-bheda* II,1,27, K 491, 15) and "expansion of name and form" (*nāmarūpa-prapañca,* II,1,21; repeatedly), perhaps also in the expression "the bringing about of name and form" (*nāmarūpa-nirvahaṇa* I,3,41, K 382,4; 382,13f.; *nāmarūpayor nirvahaṇam* 382,10). But *nāmarūpa-vikāra-bheda* (II,1,11, K 213,7) can probably only be understood as "the diversity of the products of transformation of *(avyākṛte) nāmarūpe.*" These transformations are then precisely the *vyākṛte nāmarūpe.* They stand in the same relation to *(avyākṛte) nāmarūpe* as foam, waves, etc., to the ocean, the latter being termed in the SBh "transformation products of the ocean" (*tad-vikāra,* II,1.13, K 463,13). There is, meanwhile, a group of passages that stand curiously between both interpretations. At SBh II,4,20, in the context of the explanation of the phrase *nāmarūpe vyākaravāṇi* of Chānd. Up. VI,3,2, the unfolding and unfolder of name and form are often mentioned *(nāmarūpayor vyākaraṇa, nāmarūpa-vyākaraṇa, nāmarūpa-vyākriyā* [this also at II,4,4, K 652, 16], *nāmarūpayor vyākartṛ).* Here, an interpretation of *nāmarūpa* in the sense of primal state is required: the prime matter or primal state *(nāmarūpa)* is unfolded *(vyā-kṛ)* into the world of appearance. Elsewhere, *nāmarūpa-vyākaraṇa* seems rather to mean "unfolding *into* name and form." Thus, at I,1,6 (K 205,9), where it is said that "at the beginning of the unfolding of *nāmarūpa*" water and heat (i.e., two of the three "divinities" mentioned at Chānd. Up. VI,2–3) "were employed," it indeed seems that water, heat (and food) are considered the prime matter, so that *nāmarūpa-vyākaraṇa* would have to refer to the unfolding *into* the manifest world. Also at II,1,17 (K 475,16) the context requires the assumption of this meaning: prior to the unfolding of name and form, the world was nothing, as it were.

In the case of such passages it is perhaps not even necessary to view the two interpretations as alternatives. Ś. was in fact a staunch adherent of the *satkāryavāda,* as were all early Vedāntins. For him material cause and product are identical, and the object to be *effected,* already latent in the subject, is at the same time also the object to be *affected.* With his term *nāmarūpa* Ś. brought about the consummate expression of this theory. Material cause and product, which are identical, are even designated by the same word. That which is formed out of *(avyākṛte) nāmarūpe* at the same time develops into *(vyākṛte) nāmarūpe.* It is a result of the *satkāryavāda,* taken here to its logical extreme, that the distinction between the two possibilities of interpretation is sometimes difficult.

Frequently in the SBh *nāmarūpe* unambiguously designates *vyākṛte nāmarūpe* as the constituents of the manifest phenomenal world, or portions thereof, and then the literal meaning of the expression (viz., "designation and visible form") is evident. Some examples of this usage follow:

1,2,14 (K 277, 6–9) and IV,3,14 (K 964, 15–18): Name and form are attributed to Brahman for the purpose of meditative worship, although Brahman is in reality without name and form.

I,1,22 (K 290,13): The embodied soul adopts its individualization according to name and form as real *(nāmarūpa-paricchedābhimānin).*

1,3,30 (K 363,9–10): Individuals *(viśeṣāḥ)* arise every time the world is created, carrying the same names and forms they had in previous creations.

I,4,2 (K 391,9): The world as it is is differentiated into unfolded names and forms *(vyākṛta-nāmarūpa-vibhinna).*

I,4,21 (K 426.2–3,6–7) and I,4,22 (K 427,7–8): The *jīva* is, according to Auḍulomi, the bearer of name and form, and it relinquishes them when it unites with Brahman. According to Kāśakṛtsna, however, name and form do not belong to the *jīva* but to the *upādhis.* They pertain only to the accidental conditions (body, *buddhi,* etc.) of the soul.

II,1,33 (K 496, 11–12): Everyday, empirical existence *(vyavahāra)* functions on the basis of name and form.

II,4,20 (K 673,4): Mountains, rivers, oceans, etc., are names and forms (plural).

Expressions in which the manifest world is referred to as *nāmarūpe* occur in the works of other Advaitins as well. But the use of this term in the sense of this prime matter or primal state of the world *(avyakta)* seems peculiar to Ś.

C. Related cosmic factors

According to one Upaniṣad passage (Bṛh. 1,6) this world consists of name, form, and work (*karman): trayaṃ vā idaṃ nāma rūpaṃ karma.* On that basis Ś. sometimes associates *karman* (or *kriyā*) with *nāmarūpe* (I,4,19, K 425,5 and I,4,22, K 427,14; implied at IV,3,14, K 964,15–16 by *nāmarūpādi*), and once he extends the series by adding "factors of action" and "retribution" (I,3,22, K 342,4, *nāmarūpa-kriyā-kāraka-phala-jāta*).[30]

D. Anirvacanīya *as modifier of* nāmarūpa

The word *anirvacanīya* is supplemented in the SBh by *tattvānyatvābhyām,* not, as for other authors, by *sadasadbhyām* or *sattvāsattvābhyām. Anirvacanīya,* "undeterminable," receives its content primarily through this addition, which states that as which something cannot be determined. It is therefore necessary at the outset to ask: What does *tattvānyatvābhyām* mean?, and especially: What does the *tattva* in the compound mean?

The question requires a detailed discussion, and so, to begin with, we will compile the relevant passages in the original. One of them contains instead of *anirvacanīya* a synonymous expression. Since, however, *tattvānyatvābhyām* is not missing, it is appropriate to consider this passage as well.

1. *Kiṃ punas tat karma yat prāg utpatter īśvara-jñānasya viṣayo bhavatīti. Tattvānyatvābhyām anirvacanīye nāmarūpe avyākṛte vyācikīrṣite iti; brūmaḥ* (I,1,5, K 201,11–202,2).

2. *Parameśvarādhīnā tv iyam asmābhiḥ prāg-avasthā jagato 'bhyupagamyate. . . . Avidyātmikā hi bīja-śaktir avyakta-śabda-nirdeśyā parameśvarāśrayā māyāmayī mahā-suptiḥ. . . . Tad etad avyaktaṃ kvacid ākāśa-śabda-nirdiṣṭam . . . kvacid akṣara-śabdoditam . . . kvacin māyeti sūcitam. . . . Avyaktā hi sā māyā tattvānyatva-nirūpaṇasyāśakyatvāt* (I,4,3, K 391, 16–392,10).

3. *Sarvajñasyeśvarasyātma-bhūta ivāvidyā-kalpite nāmarūpe tattvānyatvābhyām anirvacanīye saṃsāra-prapañca-bīja-bhūte sarvajñasyeśvarasya māyā-śaktiḥ prakṛtir iti ca śruti-smṛtyor abhilapyete* (II,1,14, K 471,6–8).

4. *Avidyā-kalpitena ca nāmarūpa-lakṣaṇena rūpa-bhedena vyākṛtā-vyākṛtātmakena tattvānyatvābhyām anirvacanīyena brahma pariṇāmādi-sarva-vyavahārāspadatvaṃ pratipadyate* (II,1,27, K 491,11–13).

In passage 2 *māyā* stands in place of *nāmarūpa,* though in the sense of the primal state *(avyakta)* which, as we have seen, is also called *(avyākrte) nāmarūpe.* We can thus include this passage for the sake of clarifying the sense of *tattvānyatvābhyām.* (In addition, we shall return to it under the discussion of the serial identifications, section IV.)

Two interpretations of *tattva* are possible. Either it means (a) "essence," "reality," or, what amounts to much the same thing, it is an abstract noun based on a *tat* which does not refer to a preceding or following noun. On this view, the *tattvena* analyzed out of the *dvandva* compound would be rendered literally as "as a that." Or it means (b) *tattva* is an abstract noun based on a demonstrative pronoun which does refer to some previously or subsequently mentioned noun. In translating it, then, the reference to the intended noun would have to be made explicit.

The word is taken in sense (b) by the commentator Ānandagiri in passages 1 and 3, and by Govindānanda in 3. For the other passages the commentators have nothing to say regarding *tattvānyatvābhyām.* Unfortunately, the earliest of the commentators, Vācaspati, explains none of the passages. With regard to 1, Ānandagiri explains that *nāmarūpe* are neither different nor not different from Brahman. They are therefore neither "that" (Brahman) nor "something else." With regard to 3 he says they are neither Īśvara nor something else (Govindānanda expounds these passages in the same way). This interpretation would be justifiable also in the case of 4, where the word *brahman* immediately follows *anirvacanīya.* But it is improbable for 2, since in that case the word *parameśvara* precedes *tattvānyatva* by a considerable distance.

Speaking decisively against this interpretation (b), however, is the fact that it is expressly stated in the continuation of text 3 (K 471,8–9) that God the Lord is *distinct* from name and form: *tābhyām anyaḥ sarvjña īśvaraḥ.* This emphasis on difference would be unintelligible if, by means of the *tattvānyatvābhyām* occurring just one line before, it were meant that name and form are neither different nor identical with Īśvara. Thus, we must set aside the explanation of the later commentators. In this matter we have another sign that Ś.'s interpretation of *nāmarūpe* was no longer familiar to them (cf. note 28). On the other hand, Vācaspati, who is the older interpreter, does not, as mentioned, expound Ś.'s expression *tattvānyatvābhyām anirvacanīya*. But he does in one place employ it himself independently of Ś.'s text where it is quite impossible to take the *tat-tva* as an abstract form derived from a demonstrative pronoun referring to a certain noun (*Bhāmatī* ad I,1,5, p. 103; 1.17 in the edition cited in note 29).

In passage 2, precisely where the reference of *tat-tva* to Parameśvara is least acceptable, it is said clearly that *māyā* does not admit of a determination as *tat* or *anyat,* because it exists as *avyakta,* not yet manifest, in the primal state. Perusing now the other passages, we find that 1 and 3 also deal with the primal state. And in 1 it is suggested by the immediately following *avyākṛte vyācikīrṣite* that *nāmarūpe* are "determinable neither as a that nor as something else," because they are not yet unfolded.

The only passage that does not treat of the primal state is 4. The idea suggested by this passage is that "the diversity of forms *(rūpabheda)* which is name and form" is "determinable neither as a that nor as something else," because it is (sometimes) "unfolded" and (sometimes) "not unfolded," in other words, because it exists not in a fixed state of being but only in a state of becoming *(pariṇāma).*

Ś., then, bases the concept *tattvānyatvābhyām anirvacanīya* on cosmological or, rather, predominantly, cosmogonic notions. He indicates with these words the instability of the primal state, which is not yet something but desires to be made into something *(vyācikīrṣita).* In a broad sense the expression describes the unsteadiness of that about which one can never say, "It is that" or "It is something else," for just as it wanted to unfold itself in the primal state, so now it always wants to transform itself and is never anything constant.

This is different from the interpretation of the other Advaitins who employ the word *anirvacanīya*. The difference becomes apparent as soon as *sadasadbhyām* replaces Ś.'s *tattvānyatvābhyām*. The thought that underlies *sadasadbhyām anirvacanīya,* exhaustively expounded by those philosophers, is that it is impossible to prove that—not *nāmarūpe*—but *avidyā* or *māyā* or its product (the world) is or is not.

Once in the SBh (above, passage 2) an expression synonymous with *anirvacanīya* occurs together with *māyā*. But *māyā* here stands, in a series of identifications, for *avyakta* or *(avyākṛte) nāmarūpe* (cf. below, sec. IV.2).

E. Nāmarūpa *and* avidyā

Nāmarūpe, as the quintessence of the world of appearance, encompass all that is not Brahman *(na ca brahmaṇo 'nyan nāmarūpābhyām arthāntaraṃ sambhavati,* I,3,41, K 382,8). But what is not Brahman-Ātman is illusory. *Nāmarūpe* are thus a *māyā,* an illusion (II,2,2, K 508,2), or, as Ś. most often expresses himself, it is *avidyā* that "makes" *nāmarūpe,* "brings them forth" or "toward" (the Ātman), "imagines" them, "superimposes" or "heaps" them upon the Ātman. *Avidyā* is "the essence" of *nāmarūpe.* The Sanskrit expressions are as follows:

1. *kṛta* (II,1.14, K 471,13; II,3,46, K 638,8; II,2,21, K 734,1; IV,3,14, K 964, 15, 18f.);
2. *pratyupasthāpita* (I,2,22, K 290,13; I,4,22, K 429,8; II,1,14, K 471, 15; II,1,22, K 484,17; II,2,2, K 508, 1f.; III,2,6, K 712,6);
3. *kalpita* (II,1,4, K 471,7; II,1,27, K 491,11,14f.; II,1,33, K 496, 11f.);
4. *adhyasta* (III,2,21, K 734,9f.);
5. *adhyāropita* (IV,3,14, K 964,5);
6. *ātmaka* (II,1,14, K 470,18).

Those are the same expressions which describe the functioning of *avidyā.* But one is struck by the fact that all specific causal notions like *kāraṇa, hetu,* or *nimitta* are missing. Besides the rather bland terms *-kṛta* and *-ātmaka,* there occur only words which are specially reserved for the designation of the functioning of *avidyā: pratyupasthāpita, kalpita, adhyasta, adhyāropita.* Thus, where the relationship of *avidyā* to the "world seed" *(jagad-bīja) nāmarūpa* is described,[31] it is emphasized by the choice of words, even more clearly than in other expressions for the functioning of *avidyā,* that the functioning of *avidyā* is of a quite special kind. Here, one would especially like to know what exactly *avidyā* is and who its bearer is, but Ś., of course, abstains from all theories on this matter.

In general, the peculiarity of the relationship between *avidyā* and *nāmarūpe* and its effects becomes evident from the numerous lengthy chains of words Ś. uses to describe the functioning of *avidyā* in combination with *nāmarūpe.* It is as if language is incapable of a precise formulation of this unusual relation, and only awkward, roundabout expressions can indicate what is intended. Most frequent of all is the concatenation *avidyā-nāmarūpa-upādhi: avidyā* posits *nāmarūpe,* and out of the latter an *upādhi* (usually the body) or *upādhis* are "made," "formed," "arise"; or else, the *nāmarūpe* are an *upādhi.* The *upādhi* is then, in turn, occasionally "cause" of another illusory appearance, or, the soul's failure to distinguish itself from the *upādhi* or *upādhis* is a delusion, and this error in turn causes the transmigration of the soul through *saṃsāra.* As some examples of such concatenations, which occur in multiple variations, I offer the following:

I,4,22 (K 429,8): The division *(bheda)* between individual soul and highest self is caused *(-nimitta)* by the *upādhis,* the body, etc. These are formed *(racita)* out of *nāmarūpe. Nāmarūpe* in turn are brought forth *(pratyupasthāpita)* by *avidyā.*

II,1,14 (K 471,13): Īśvara conforms to *nāmarūpe.* These are His *upādhi.* They are made *(-kṛta)* by *avidyā.*

II,1,22 (K 484,17): *Saṃsāra* is a delusion *(bhrānti).* It is caused *(-kṛta)* by the nondifferentiation *(aviveka)* of the *upādhis.* The *upādhis* are the physical complex. The latter is made *(-kṛta)* by *nāmarūpe.* These latter are brought forth *(pratyupasthāpita)* by *avidyā.*

II,3,46 (K 638,8): The state in which the *jīva* considers itself subject to pain is conditioned by a delusion *(bhrama-nimitta).* The latter consists in the nondistinction of the *upādhis (upādhy-aviveka).* Those—body, senses, etc.—in turn arise out of *nāmarūpe (-nirvṛtta). Nāmarūpe* are made *(-kṛta)* by *avidyā.*

III,2,6 (K 721,6): The latency *(tirobhāva)* of the knowledge and divine nature *(aiśvarya)* of the *jīva* is caused by a delusion *(bhrama-kṛta)* which consists in the soul not being able to distinguish itself *(aviveka)* from the *upādhis* of the body, etc., with which it is connected *(yoga).* The *upādhis* are made from *nāmarūpe (-kṛta).* The latter are brought forth *(pratyupasthāpita)* by *avidyā.*

Ś.'s sense of *avidyā*—one can't really say that he has a *concept* of *avidyā*—seems to me the most peculiar feature of his thought, and the terminology he uses to express this sense is one of the most unusual features of his language. Even his immediate disciples differ from their master in their *avidyā* phraseology. In particular, the *avidyā-nāmarūpe* chains occur, as far as I can tell, only in Ś.

If—contrary to the spirit of Ś.—we were to attempt to abstract something like a theory from the mentioned concatenations of causes, then we would have to say something like the following: *Avidyā* is a kind of potency which, in a completely unique process that cannot be compared with any other mechanism, "posits" the illusion of the material seed of the cosmos that stands opposite the Creator. Of course, one is not permitted to ask who it is who, at the time of the creation or prior thereto, possesses this illusion.

From an overwhelming majority of these passages[32] it is clear that *avidyā* and the world seed *(jagad-bīja)* are conceived by Ś. to be two different, though closely related, things. And that distinguishes Ś. again from the other teachers of his school, according to whose interpretation the prime matter of the cosmos falls together with the magical potency of illusion, *avidyā,* and with *māyā,* so that the term *nāmarūpa* becomes dispensable as a designation of the seed of the cosmos. The rendering of *avidyā* into a material thing, the prime matter of the cosmos, was already widespread prior to Ś. in Vedāntic and Vaiṣṇava circles.[33] He rejected it, to be sure, not with an explicit refutation but by means of his linguistic usage. That is to say, Ś. clearly always strove to follow the Upaniṣads closely in his method of thought and terminology. But one simply cannot extricate the theory of *avidyā* as prime matter from those texts. On the other hand, one can base the theory of *nāmarūpa* as the world seed on Upaniṣadic passages if, as shown above, one interprets them from the standpoint of the *satkāryavāda.* Moreover, in purāṇic thought *avidyā* is only another name for *prakṛti* and does not connote an illusion. Ś. thus could have feared that the word would have been misunderstood in a dualistic-realistic sense had he employed it in the sense of "prime matter."

Whether the peculiar usage of *nāmarūpa* in the sense of *avyakta* is Ś.'s innovation is something which we cannot determine at this time. That is indeed possible, for the usage disappears soon after Ś., as do several other unique features of his thought, and developments which were underway before Ś. resume. Only one or two generations remember Ś.'s *nāmarūpa* concept, as we can see from Vācaspati's *Bhāmatī* and Bhāskara's *Brahmasūtrabhāṣya,* which attacks Ś. Both of these may be dated around A.D. 850.[34]

F. Nāmarūpa *and* Īśvara

A monism less rigorous than Ś.'s in which consciousness or spirit is the ultimate principle is certainly possible. Such a monism could have the nonspiritual, material *(vyākṛte) nāmarūpe* arise directly out of the immaterial, spiritual principle of Brahman. It would not have to postulate a formless, original condition of the former—the *avyākṛte nāmarūpe.* Ś., however, takes the purely spiritual nature of Brahman seriously so that, almost against his will, *avyākṛte nāmarūpe* become a kind of *prakṛti*—he even calls them *prakṛti* in one place (II,1,14, K 471,8). But how does this idea relate to the ancient teaching of the BS, endorsed by Ś., that Brahman is the *prakṛti* of the world (I,4,23ff.) and—a thesis defended against the Sāṃkhya again and again—that no other nonspiritual principle of prime matter exists?

The purely spiritual Parameśvara or Brahman is the agent who unfolds *nāmarūpe* (I,3,41; II,4,20; II,4,4, K 652,16). But if *nāmarūpe* do not, as the *sūtras* seem to state, evolve out of Parameśvara but rather out of an original state of their own, then, of course, monism is threatened. And only the doctrine of illusion can restore it. We have already observed that *nāmarūpe* exist only in an illusory sense. They are only the effect of *avidyā*. The latter "imagines" *nāmarūpe* "as if they were the omniscient Īśvara Himself" *(sarvajñasyeśvarasyātma-bhūta ivāvidyā-kalpite nāmarūpe)*; they are His magical power *(māyā)*; they are His *upādhi*, to which He conforms (*anurodhin;* the preceding as per II,1,14, K 471; *upādhi* also at I,2,22, K 291,1), the "original state of name and form" is God's "divine power" (*daivī śakti*, I,4,9, K 403,13, here considered as something material!); God is the bearer, the substratum (*āśraya*, I,2,22, K 290,16) of name and form. These are the phrases with which Ś., sometimes more in the sense of a theory of illusion, other times more theistically, attempts to describe the relation of Īśvara to the *avyākṛte nāmarūpe* and to defend the unity of the origin of the cosmos.

The term *āśraya* calls for a comparison with Ś.'s use of *anirvacanīya*. Just as Ś. interprets cosmogonically the concept of the undeterminable, which other Advaitins explain in a logical and epistemological sense, here, too, he understands the concept of *āśraya* only in a cosmogonic sense. Whereas others conceive of Brahman as the *āśraya* of *avidyā* only epistemologically, Ś. speaks of Parameśvara-Brahman as the *āśraya* of *nāmarūpe* when it comes to the origin of the world (also I,4,3, K 392,4, where the original state is called *avyakta*). And where others depict pure Spirit in an ontological sense, as the *adhiṣṭhāna* of the world illusion, or in an epistemological sense, as the *adhiṣṭhāna* of any error, Ś. understands Brahman in a *cosmological* sense, as the *āspada* of the cosmic *vyavahāra* imagined by *avidyā* and fashioned out of name and form (II,1,27, K 491,13; cf. III,2,21, K 734,1: *brahmaṇi*). Ś. avoids epistemology and prefers, where he feels he has to theorize, an almost mythological cosmology. He perhaps believes that myths are an easier way to mystical *anubhava* than logical demonstrations. For he says in more than one place that cosmogonic myths are only a way to insight into the fundamental unity of Being, not ends in themselves or final truth (II,1,33, K 496,11; IV,3,14, K 959,9f.).

Sometimes the relation between Īśvara or Brahman and *nāmarūpe* is taken as one of illumination, in which case both terms again separate into two principles: "The manifestation of this entire complex of name-and-form, action, factors of action, and fruits of action is conditioned by the existence of the light of Brahman" *(sarvasyaivāsya nāmarūpa-kriyā-kāraka-phala-jātasya yābhivyaktiḥ sā brahma-jyotiḥ-sattānimittā,* I,3,22, K 342,4). Meanwhile, the light of Brahman is consciousness.

III. Māyā

A. Māyāvāda

The doctrine of the school of Ś. has been for centuries called *māyāvāda,* and so one would accordingly expect that in the SBh, the basic text of the school, *māyā* would often be talked about. That is, however, not at all the case. The word *māyā* occurs much less frequently than *nāmarūpa* and *avidyā*. The comparative frequency of these three words (counting only passages where the words are understood in the sense of the Advaitavāda), is respectively, about 2:7:10. Many times more frequent than any of these three, however, are such words as *ātman, paramātman, brahman, īśvara, parameśvara.* Furthermore, Ś. never calls his philosophy *māyāvāda,* although he forms quite a few compounds with *-vāda* and *-vādin*. Rather, he speaks only of *veda-, vedānta-, brahma-* and *ātma-vāda* or *-vādin,* for the principle of Brahman-Ātman is for him the only important thing. *Avidyā,* on the other hand, is only of secondary importance, and the word *māyā* has for him hardly any terminological weight; various notions are mixed together in his *māyā* concept. If one, therefore, wants to use some catchword to characterize what distinguishes Ś. from others, the word *māyāvāda* is hardly appropriate. He certainly develops no *theory* of *māyā*. But if the word indicates only allegiance to the school of illusionism, the theory that the phenomenal world is unreal, then it is, of course, applicable to him. Nevertheless, only with his disciples is the Advaita system a *māyāvāda* in the sense that it reflects on the nature of *māyā* and develops a theory of it. With them, indeed, *māyā* is sometimes much more the matter of concern than Brahman or liberation.

B. Māyā = *deception*

In this sense, the most general and least laden with philosophical and mythological connotations, the word *māyā* occurs once in the SBh in a series of expressions together with *alīka,* "untruth," and *vañcana,* "deception," "fraud" (II,3,6, K 586,3).

C. Special meaning: māyā = *magic*

In most passages where *māyā* and its derivatives occur in the SBh, the word either means "magic" or is based on that meaning. There is mention of the magician who, with sword and shield, climbs up a rope (I,1,17, K 221,12); the magician can multiply himself with magical power (I,3,19, K 338,11); he effortlessly reabsorbs that which he has created back into himself (I,1,21, K 483,15); he produces manifold creations (II,1,28, K 492,7); the magic succumbs to cancellation (*bādha,* II,2,29, K 555,11). This meaning of the word has in itself nothing to do with philosophy or religion, but it is frequently used in comparisons.

D. Māyā *as object of comparison*

The most characteristic thing about the use of *māyā* for Ś. is that in almost every case where the word is used to refer to something illusory the nonexistent apparition is *compared* to a *māyā,* i.e., a magical illusion. And mostly the comparison is carried out with a *yathā, iva,* or *-vat.* Less often, *māyā* appears as the second element of an *upamānottarapada-karmadhāraya.*

Examples:

1. with *yathā, iva,* or *-vat:*

I,1,17 (K 221,12). As the actual magician is distinct from his unreal double who climbs up the rope, so is Parameśvara distinct from the individual soul.

I,3,19 (K338,10): Parameśvara appears to be manifold through *avidyā* as the magician through his magic.

II,1,1 (K 437, 2–3): Īśvara is the cause of the persistence of the world as the magician is the cause of the persistence of his trick.

II,1,9 (K 455, 16–18): As the magician is not touched by his magic trick, the Paramātman is untouched by *saṃsāra.*

II,1,21 (K 483,15f.): As the magician can effortlessly and at will reabsorb in himself what he has conjured up, so could the individual soul absorb into itself that which it has created *(pūrvapakṣa).*

2. *karmadhārayas:*

samṣāra-māyā (II,1,9 K 455,18);

svapna-darśana-māyā (II,1,9, K 456,1);

nāmarūpa-māyā (II,2,2, K 508,1f.).

Not only is the illusory character of the phenomenon being compared to *māyā* brought to light, but also, sometimes especially, the fact that the creator of the phenomenon is untouched by his creation, or that his creating and annihilating are effortless, is brought out.

A further step beyond passages such as the ones cited above is taken when, leaving aside the comparison, something illusory is directly said to be a *māyā.* Thus, e.g., II,2,3 (K 707,5): *māyaiva sandhye sṛṣṭiḥ,* "The creation in a dream is an illusion." The adjectives *māyāmātra* and *māyāmaya* are mostly used with this meaning. *Māyāmātra* is (in *sūtra* III,2,3 itself, and several times in the *bhāṣya* thereto) used to refer to the dream state. It is also used to refer to the triad of states of the soul (waking, dreaming, deep sleep, II,1,9, K 456,3) as well as the entire manifest creation (*prapañca,* III,2,4, K 710,13). Ś. certainly does not associate with both adjectives the notion "consisting of *māyā*" in the sense of "consisting of the element of *māyā.*" That is clear, first, from the fact that they can occur simply as a contrast to *paramārtha* (III,1,1 K 705,5f.; III,2,4, K 709,1), and second, and above all, from the fact that Ś. does not, like other Advaitins, speak of *māyā* explicitly as a substance *(upādāna-kāraṇa)* out of which illusory things are made (the one place where *māyā* is identified with *avyakta* pertains to another context).[35] *Māyāmātra* and *mahāmāyā* are for him simply expressions handed down through his tradition to designate that which is "illusory"; for in fact one of them already occurs in this sense in the BS.

Summarizing our investigations up to now, we must conclude that *māyā* for Ś. is not the cause or the substance of what is illusory, but the illusory is compared with a *māyā,* or else it is said that the illusory *is* *māyā.*

E. Māyā *as the magical power of God*

Ś. does use *māyā* in another, quite different sense. Since the Ṛgveda there have been "positive" and "negative" meanings of *māyā.*[36] A "positive" *māyā* is the creative power of God as possessed especially by Viṣṇu—the *vaiṣṇavī māyā,* as it is called in the commentary on the *Bhagavadgītā* ascribed to Ś. It is surprising how often this usage of the word is to be found in the SBh. In approximately half of the places where the word occurs it is intended in this meaning or at least alludes to it. For the sake of bestowing grace upon his worshipper, Parameśvara can assume a "form consisting of *māyā*" (*māyāmayaṃ rūpam,* I,1,20, K 232,6; here, where we are dealing with the *māyā* of the highest God, one must see more in *māyā* than merely the concept "illusory" which we have just established), when the maintenance of the world by Īśvara is compared with the sustaining of a magical illusion by a magician (II,1,1), the meaning of *māyā* as "creative power" also comes to mind. Brahman or Īśvara possesses a "great miraculous power" (is *mahā-māya,* II,1,37, K 500,7 and II,2,4, K 509,5); only by means of his *māyā* is the Paramātman active, while he remains in himself without activity (*svarūpa-vyapāśrayam audāsīnyaṃ māyā-vyapāśrayaṃ ca pravartakatvam,* II,2,7, K 512,4).

F. *The dual meaning of* māyā *as a characteristic*

In the *Bhagavadgītā,* which certainly does not defend a doctrine of illusion, the *māyā* of the supreme God also has something deceptive about it. Whether there is a historical connection from this Viṣṇuitic concept of *māyā* to the illusionism of the Vedānta is a question which at this time we can only raise and not answer. But without a doubt Ś.'s concept of God, the notion of Īśvara or Brahman who possesses a great *māyā,* is influenced by the theology of Viṣṇuism. Yet it is equally certain, and generally recognized by researchers, that Ś.'s use of the word *māyā* has another source as well—the illusionism of the Mahāyāna. I have tried in the foregoing to separate as much as possible the illusionistic and theistic meanings. But Ś. himself could not have been very conscious of this difference. Certainly, for him, *māyā* was something illusory even in the sense of the creative power of God (*māyā-śakti,* II,1,14, K 471,8). In general, the creative aspect of Brahman is illusory (II,1,22, K 484,14–16). But the fact that two different historical starting points are discernible in Ś.'s use of the word *māyā* is in itself characteristic of him.[37] For his successors, the theistic component of the concept disappears. *Māyā* either becomes completely identical with *avidyā* or else it is distinguished from it only secondarily in speculative passages.

IV. The Relationship and Identification of Avidyā, Māyā, and Nāmarūpa

A. Relationship

In the preceding we were concerned with drawing, in each case, from a plurality of passages in which *avidyā, māyā,* and *nāmarūpa* occur, conclusions as precise as possible about the use of these expressions, while taking into account the inherent vagueness of the concepts. Thereby differences came to light, and we were called upon to apprehend these as clearly as possible. There were differences between the three concepts themselves as well as differences between Ś.'s interpretation of them and the interpretations of other adherents of his school. On the other hand, the three concepts are closely related.

Consider the sentence: "The one Parameśvara . . . appears in manifold manifestations through *avidyā,* as the magician through *māyā*" (I,3,19 K 338,10). One may not be justified in inferring an identity of *māyā* and *avidyā* from this sentence, since they are only compared, not equated. Nevertheless, the parallelism does indicate a certain similarity of the concepts. *Nāmarūpa* and *māyā* also resemble each other: the power of *māyā* with which God creates tends to congeal into a substance out of which He makes things, and this substance is the *avyākṛte nāmarūpe* (cf. above, III,5). Finally, *nāmarūpe* and *avidyā* are practically a single thing differentiated into two entities. Often a phenomenon that is described as directly fashioned by *avidyā* is at another time said to emerge out of the "*avidyā*-effected" *nāmarūpe,* and of course *nāmarūpe* are "essentially *avidyā*" (*avidyātmaka,* II,1,14, K 470,18). It is inherent in the nature of monistic-illusionistic thought that these three concepts, which are supposed to explain or at least allude to the transition from a purely spiritual Reality to an "untrue" material state, should tend to coincide.

B. Serial identifications

In a few places Ś. equates *nāmarūpa, māyā,* and *avidyā* expressly with each other and with other concepts. We should now consider these identifications in which theistic and illusionistic, Sāṃkhya and Vedānta, concepts come together.

1. *Akṣaram avyākṛtaṃ nāmarūpa-bījaśakti-rūpaṃ bhūta-sūkṣmam īśvarāśrayaṃ tasyaivopādhi-bhūtam . . .* (I,2,22, K 290,16–291,1). "The 'im-

perishable' is the un-unfolded, consisting of the seed potency which is name and form, the subtle form of the elements, whose substratum is Īśvara and which serves, in turn, as Īśvara's *upādhi*."

2. *Idam eva vyākṛta-nāmarūpa-vibhinnaṃ jagat prāg-avasthāyāṃ parityakta-vyākṛta-nāmarūpaṃ bījaśakty-avastham avyakta-śabda-yogyaṃ darśayati.... Parameśvarādhīnā tv iyam asmābhiḥ prāg-avasthā jagato 'bhyupagamyate, na svatantrā. Sā cāvaśyābhyupagantavyā, arthavatī hi sā. Na hi tayā vinā parameśvarasya sraṣṭṛtvaṃ sidhyati, śakti-rahitasya tasya pravṛtty-anupapatteḥ. Muktānāṃ ca punar anutpattiḥ. Kutaḥ. Vidyayā tasya bījaśakter dāhāt. Avidyātmikā hi bījaśaktir avyakta-śabda-nirdeśyā parameśvarāśrayā māyāmayī mahā-suptiḥ, yasyāṃ svarūpa-pratibodha-rahitāḥ śerate saṃsāriṇo jīvāḥ. Tad etad avyaktaṃ kvacid ākāśa-śabda-nirdiṣṭam.... Kvacid akṣara-śabdoditam.... Kvacin māyeti sūcitam.... Avyaktā hi sā māyā, tattvānyatva-nirūpaṇasyāśakyatvāt.... Avidyā hy avyaktam, avidyāvattvenaiva jīvasya sarvaḥ saṃvyavahāraḥ santato vartate* (I,4,2–3, K 391,9–392,14). "[The Upaniṣad passage Bṛh. Up. I,4,7] shows that 'this,' i.e., the world, which is fragmented in manifest names and forms, can, in its original state, when it exists in a state of seed potency in which name and form are not yet unfolded, be designated by the word 'the unmanifest.'... But we recognize that this original state of the world is dependent on the highest Lord and does not exist independently. And it is necessary to assume that there is such an [original state], for it serves a purpose. For without it a creative activity on the part of the highest Lord would not be possible, since He cannot act if He is without potency. Moreover, those who are liberated are not born again. Why? Because [for them] that seed potency is burned up by knowledge. For the seed potency is essentially ignorance, which can be referred to by the word 'the unmanifest'; which has the highest Lord as its substratum; and which is the great sleep consisting of *māyā* in which the souls lie, not yet awakened to their true nature, wandering in *saṃsāra*. The same 'unmanifest' is sometimes designated by the word 'ether' ... [citation of Bṛh. Up. III,8,11).... Sometimes it is expressed by the expression 'the imperishable' ... [Muṇḍ. Up. II,1,2].... Sometimes it is called *māyā* ... [Śvet. Up. IV,10].... *Māyā* is, namely, 'unmanifest,' since one can neither describe it by saying, 'It is this,' nor by saying, 'It is something else.' ... The unmanifest is ignorance. Only because the individual soul is ignorant does mundane existence continue."

3.... *saiva daivī śaktir avyākṛta-nāmarūpa nāmarūpayor prāg-avasthānenāpi mantreṇāmnāyate* (I,4,9, K 403, 12–14). "Precisely this divine power of creation, in which name and form are un-unfolded, is intended as the original state of name and form in this Vedic verse (Śvet. Up. IV,5)."

4. *Sarvajñasyeśvarasyātma-bhūta ivāvidyā-kalpite nāmarūpe tattvānyatvābhyām anirvacanīye saṃsāra-prapañca-bīja-bhūte sarvajñasyeśvarasya māyā-śaktiḥ prakṛtir iti ca śruti-smṛtyor abhilapyete* (II,1,14, K 471,6–8). "Name and form, which are imagined by ignorance to be the self of the omniscient Lord, which one can characterize neither by saying 'They are this,' nor, 'They are something else'; and which are the seed of *saṃsāra* and creation—they are spoken of in revelation and tradition as 'the *māyā*-power of the omniscient Lord' and as 'prime matter.' "

In all four texts *śakti* is conceived as something material. God cannot create if he does not have the corresponding power (text 2). But this power is not just a capacity. It is also a substance out of which God forms the world: the *śakti* of Īśvara is a *bīja-śakti*. And the prime matter is also the primary state of that which is to be created (text 2). Creative power, the material of creation, and the original state of the world thus coincide—a consequence of the substantialist way of thinking as well as the *satkāryavāda*.

Ś.'s preferred expression for the prime matter of creation is (*avyākṛte*) *nāmarūpe*. In these passages he also refers to it by the Upaniṣad concepts *avyakta* (texts 1 and 2), *avyākṛta* (1), *akṣara* (2), and *ākāśa* (2). Nevertheless, these concepts have no importance for Ś.'s philosophy other than in the series of identifications and in the passages concerned with the interpretation of these Upaniṣad passages.

Matters are different with the terms *māyā* and *avidyā*. These certainly have another meaning in other contexts. That they occur here as names of the prime matter of the universe seems to contradict our findings up to now. But one should note that the equation of *avidyā* and *māyā* with *nāmarūpa* and *avyakta* occurs only in series of identifications. When they stand alone they have their specific function, and in none of the many passages which we have considered in preceding sections are they interchangeable. But for Viṣṇuite theologians and for many adherents of purāṇic Sāṃkhya and the Vedānta long before Ś.'s time, *avidyā* was a name for prime matter, which could also be called *avyakta, māyā,* or *prakṛti*.[38] Ś. must have taken it into account that there would be some among his audience who were raised with such views and considered themselves Vedāntins.

We know further that for Ś. cosmogony was only of very minor importance (cf. above, I,3). For him it was not much a matter of concern exactly how the events of creation are presented or conceived nor, certainly, which terms are used. The account of creation in his system has only the propaedeutic function of drawing attention to the unity of being.

We will, therefore, be permitted to assume that Ś., in the series of identifications in text 2 above, tried to accommodate the interpretations of those for whom *avidyā* was a cosmogonic idea. He admits that one must postulate prime matter, whether one calls it *avidyā, māyā, prakṛti,* or *avyakta*. But the same text carries over into monism and illusionism: the prime matter or the original state of the universe exists only dependent on God and is illusory. It is *avidyā,* because all becoming, which exists only for ignorance, and through ignorance proceeds from it. For the liberated there is no becoming, no more rebirth, because for them ignorance is "burned up" by knowledge. Text 4 presents again the usual formula, according to which the original state of the world is not *avidyā,* but is "imagined" by it.

It may be that it was a pedagogical instinct—for the sake of leading the adherents of the *avyakta* cosmogony away from their more or less dualistic-realistic view toward his own monism and illusionism—that motivated Ś. occasionally to employ terms that were familiar to them, at the same time filling those terms with the content of his own theory. As far as the use of the expressions *māyā* and *prakṛti* goes, here it was also necessary to bring the doctrine of the Sāṃkhyistic and theistic Śvetāśvatara Upaniṣad in harmony with absolute monism.

We therefore conclude that for Ś. *avidyā* and *māyā* are one and the same thing, coinciding with *nāmarūpa,* only when they are explicitly referred to as the prime matter of the universe.

Schematized series of equivalent names of the prime matter of the universe also occur in Padmapāda[39] and Vimuktātman.[40] But in contrast to Ś. they equate *avidyā* and *māyā,* as other Advaitins do, in their general use of language, and *nāmarūpa* is hardly employed outside the series of identifications. In Vimuktātman the word is not even to be found in any of the series.

V. Īśvara

A. General and specific meaning

In its most general sense *īśvara* means "ruler"—a king *(rājan),* for example, is an *īśvara* (I,4, 23, K 431,8). In particular, however, gods, even those having limited domains, are occasionally called *īśvaras.* Īśvaras,

Hiraṇyagarbha foremost among them, continue, at the beginning of each new age, their previous activity by the kind permission of the highest Īśvara (I,3,30, K 361, 6–14; 363,9). They are entrusted with positions by Īśvara (III,3, 32, K 808,11). The sovereignty *(aiśvarya)* of the gods is dependent on the highest Īśvara (I,2,17, K 281,12). But only seldom does *īśvara* occur in the SBh with such a general meaning. The word almost always has the specific, pointed meaning: the *highest* Lord, Parameśvara. *Parameśvara* and *īśvara* are, in general, completely synonymous. In the following, therefore, I shall not distinguish between them.

It should also be made clear at the outset that *īśvara-parameśvara* is often synonymous with *paramātman* and *(paraṃ) brahma.* In the following I shall be concerned to show under what circumstances an identity is intended and under what circumstances differences in the use of *īśvara* and *brahman* appear.

B. *Īśvara per se*

The only positive characteristic that Ś. assigns to Brahman is its being spirit or consciousness (Deussen, *System des Vedānta,* pp. 145 ff. and 318f.). The *ānanda*-nature of Brahman traditionally taught in Vedānta is not challenged by Ś., but it is, remarkably, discussed only in places where a text Ś. is interpreting mentions it. Ś. describes Īśvara in precisely the same way: He is the only thing in the world that is consciousness (*na hi . . . īśvarād anyaś cetana-dhātur dvitīyaḥ . . . upalabhyate,* II,3,30, K 620,4; *vijñāna-dhātuḥ,* I,3,19, K 338,10); He is the sole subject of knowledge (*pratiṣidhyata eva . . . parameśvarād anyo draṣṭā śrotā vā,* I,1,17, K 221,9). But nowhere does Ś. say that Īśvara is *ānanda.*

Ś.'s reticence about the identification of Brahman or Īśvara with *ānanda,* held by all other Advaitins, is thus quite similar to his rejection of the materialization of *avidyā.* He does not attack the teaching of his fellow Advaitins if it happens not to correspond to his own, but he replaces it with other ideas and ignores it until exegetic considerations force him temporarily to confirm the prevalent view.

The other characteristics that apply both to Brahman and Īśvara are the most general conceivable: Īśvara is the sole *īśvara (ekeśvaratva,* III,2,35, K 748,15), just as there is no Ātman besides the Paramātman (III,2,26, K 749,8). He is omnipresent (*sarvagata,* e.g., I,2,7, K 266,9–12), like the Paramātman (e.g., K 266,3) or Brahman (e.g., K 266,13f.) or the Ātman (e.g., III,2,37, K 749, 10f.). Therefore He, too, is present in the body, though not just there (I,2,3, K 264,6). Because He, Īśvara, is the universal soul *(sarvātman),* one can say that He is man *(puruṣa)* or that He is *in* man (I,2,26, K 299,7). He is eternally perfect (*nitya-siddha,* e.g., I,1,20, K 230,1; *anādi-siddha,* IV,4,21, K 978,17)—a word which at the same time suggests the self-sufficiency of pure consciousness, *svataḥsiddhatva.*

Often the generality of the attributes amounts to the negation of all attributes. As the Ātman or Brahman is preferably characterized by negations, so too is Īśvara. Already such concepts as "eternal," "free," and "liberated" are, as far as we are concerned, essentially negations, and indeed the solemn epithet *nitya-śuddha-buddha-mukta* is ascribed to Īśvara (II,1,14, K 471,2) as well as Brahman (e.g., I,1,1, K 85,3). Then there is a whole series of negations: Īśvara has no body (II,2,40, K 571,1–3); He is not an agent (*kartṛ,* e.g., III,4,8, K 858,6), not an enjoyer (*nopabhoga-gandho 'pi . . . īśvarasya,* I,2,8, K 268, 12; cf. I,2,8, K 267,9); He has no defects *(doṣa)* and is without sin (*pāpman,* e.g., I,2,13, K 276,12); He does not identify the body as the self and thus also feels no suffering; He does not know the notion "I suffer" (*duḥkhābhimāna,* II,3,46, I 638,5–8); He is, like the Paramātman, forever constant (*kūṭastha-nitya* I,3,19, K 338,10; cf. 338,13f.); He is invisible (*na ca parameśvarasya rūpavattvaṃ yuktam,* I,1,20, K 230,4; *adṛśya,* I,2,21); He needs no support (*ādhāra,* K 230,6); His divinity (*aiśvarya,* K 230,12) knows no limits; He is not in *saṃsāra* (*asaṃsārin,* frequently); He is not known empirically *(lokataḥ)* but only from revelation (I,3,7, K 311,6f.). It is not necessary to document in detail the fact that all the above can also be said of Brahman.

C. *Īśvara and the individual soul*

Individual souls *(vijñānātman, jīva, śarīra)* and Īśvara are distinct—Ś. assures us of that time and again (I,1,17, K 221,11; I,1,21, K 233,1; I,2,8, K 267,8; I,2,20, K 285,9; III,2,5, K 711,5; III,3,34, K 813,10). The Paramātman also is "something other than the *jīva*" (I,3,19, K 338,16). On the other hand, other passages maintain precisely the opposite: Īśvara, Paramātman, or Brahman is identical with the individual soul (*īśvara:* I,1,5, K 203,2–6; I,4,6, K 398,10; I,4,22, K 426,16; III,2,6, K 712,9; *paramātman* or *para:* e.g., I,4,22, K 426,12; II,3,47, K 640, 14f.; *brahman,* e.g., I,1,31, K 256,18). The contradiction is explained and resolved through the doctrine of illusion. The difference is not absolutely real but *upādhi*-conditioned (I,2,20, K 285,16; *brahman,* I,1,31, K 257,1). The unity is concealed by the association of the soul with the body (*tirohita,*

III,2,6, K, 712,13) or by *avidyā* (*tirohita,* III,2,5, K 711,6) or by false knowledge (*mithyājñāna-kṛta,* I,3,19, K 336,10). Under the influence of *avidyā* Parameśvara multiplies Himself (*vibhāvyate,* I,3,19, K 338,11). The doctrine presented by BS II,3,43, that the soul is a portion of God, is modified by Ś. by adding "as it were" (K 636,2). The true essence of the Self is that of Parameśvara (III,4,8, K 859,4). The identity of the two is not such that the concepts "soul" and "God" are completely interchangeable. Rather, one must say that, although God does not have the same essence as the soul, the soul is in essence God (IV,1,3, K 907,9–12), or that it has the essential properties (*dharma)* of Parameśvara (I,3,19, K 333,8). God is more than the soul; He is the *true* soul, the Ātman (III,4,8, K 858,11).

One must divide the words which Ś. uses for the individual soul into two groups. One group—principally *jīva, vijñānātman,* and *śārīra*—expresses the illusory aspect of the soul, the *jaivaṃ rūpam,* which arises from association with the *upādhis* and is "established by ignorance" (*avidyā-pratyupasthāpita,* I,3,19, K 338,4). Only when using these expressions does Ś. say that the soul is *different* from God or that it is *essentially* God or Brahman (I,3,19, K 338,6 and 334,3f.). God is, *qua* the inner self of all beings, the *jīva* (II,3,47, with *īśvara, brahman,* and *para* used interchangeably in the discussion; I,4,22, K 426,12, *paramātman*). But in addition there are the two expressions *ātman* and *pratyagātman.* These also designate the individual soul, but in its real aspect. The *pratyagātman* is a state *(avasthā)* of Parameśvara (I,2,24, K 296,9f.); Parameśvara is to be regarded as the *ātman* (IV,1,3, K 906,10; here, *paramātman* and *brahman* are used interchangeably with *parameśvara* and *īśvara*). With the word *ātman* one indicates both the individual soul *(śārīra)* and Parameśvara (I,2,24, K 295,7). Indeed, the word refers primarily to Parameśvara (I,2,13, K 276,10).

It has not been my purpose in these remarks to describe once again the well-known soul monism of the Śāṅkara Vedānta. Rather, my intention was only to investigate those passages which make statements about the relationship of Īśvara to the soul, in order to discover if Ś.'s use of the word *īśvara* differs in this context from that of the words *brahman* and *paramātman.* But it turns out that, even restricting oneself to the passages where *īśvara* occurs, one can sketch a complete picture of soul monism—precisely the same picture that would result from a consideration of the passages where *brahman, para,* or *paramātman* occur. It is unnecessary to adduce for each individual case a parallel example for *brahman* or *paramātman* (although a few parallel passages were cited) in order to show that Ś. does not make any distinction in the use of the "personal" and the "impersonal" concept of God. Īśvara *per se* and Īśvara *qua* soul are the same as the highest Brahman.

D. Īśvara as Lord of the universe

The doctrine of the identity of God and the soul consists actually only in the denial of their separateness. The result is, once again, the theory of God's own nature. And this theory can only offer negative characterizations of God, with the one exception that God is the one spirit, i.e., principle of consciousness. All other positive statements about God are in fact diminutions of His true reality. Such statements are those concerning God as the Lord of the universe, as the Lord of souls, and as the object of meditation. We shall, proceeding now to consider these aspects of Īśvara, have to consider especially carefully certain differences from the concept of Brahman.

Īśvara is the creator or cause of the world (*sraṣṭṛ,* e.g., I,4,3, K 392,1; *kartṛ,* I,4,16, K 420,14; *jagad akalpayat,* I,3,30, K 364,5; *kāraṇam,* I,1,5, K 200,4, very frequently). He is the cause of the origin, continuation, and destruction of the world (II,1,14, K 471,2f.). He is the unmoved mover (II,2,2, K 507,14f.), the cause of all transformations (*vikāra;* I,2,23, K 292,6). His activity of creation presupposes omniscience, for the cause of the universe must be of a conscious nature (I,1,5). *Sarvajña* is a constant epithet of Īśvara. Naturally, he must also be omnipotent to carry out His huge task (*sarvaśakti,* often). His sovereignty *(aiśvarya)* has no limits (I,1,20, K 230,12). He creates alone (*advitīya,* I,4,14, K 414,5); the view that there is a special demiurge *(īśvara)* besides Parameśvara is explicitly rejected (III,3,6, K 775,10f.). Other "gods" *(īśvara),* such as Hiraṇyagarbha, Yama, and Agni, are dependent on Him for their sovereignty and assigned to their offices by Him (I,2,17, K 281,12; I,2,27, K 300,3; III,3,32, K 808,11; I,3,30, K 361). Not only the creation but every other transformation in the existing world is in the final analysis effected by God. He is in everything as its essence and creates every transformation according to His plan (II,3,13, K 599,4f.). His creating is without any motive. It is according to the language of the *sūtra* (II,1,33) a mere sport *(līlā).*

Out of what does God create the world? Two answers are given side by side:

1. God is not just the efficient but also the material cause of the world (*upādāna,* II,1,1, K 440,10f.; *prakṛti,* I,4,27, K 435,9; *bhūta-yoni,* I,2,21);

2. God has a creative power which is, in a material sense, conceived as the original state or prime matter out of which He forms the world (cf. above, sec. III, 5 and IV, 2).

The contradiction between the two views is again resolved through the doctrine of illusion or, as the case may be, the theory of different perspectives. Monism already announces itself with the idea that the original state is not independent, but depends on God (I,4,3)—that God is the "bearer" of the "seed potency" (I,2,22). Even more definitely monistic is the formulation, "*nāmarūpe* [in their original state] are, as it were, God himself" (II,1,14). *Nāmarūpe* are an *upādhi* of Īśvara to which He conforms (*anurodhī bhavati,* II,1,14, K 471,13; cf. I,2,22, K 290,16). *Upādhi* is for Ś. always something illusory (*avidyātmaka),* and so he explicitly concludes that *nāmarūpe* have only an illusory existence (see above, sec. II,E). In the language of the theory of different perspectives this means that the division of Īśvara into creator and material of creation is possible only from the standpoint of *vyavahāra.* The entire process of creation belongs to "the sphere of *nāmarūpa* or mundane existence, which is falsely projected by *avidyā*" (II,1,33). The sovereignty and omniscience of God have no absolutely real being (II,1,14, K 471,16–472,1; the concept of omniscience coincides for Ś. almost completely with that of being the creator, for creation is certainly only possible for one who is omniscient). What characterizes God as creator of the universe and Lord of the universe—his *sarvaśaktitva,* his *sarvajñatva,* his *īśvaratva*—is "dependent on restriction through illusory *upādhis.*" It is possible to conceive of God as ruler and creator *(īśvarādi-vyavahāra)* only in the context of mundane existence (*vyavahārāvasthā,* II,1,14, K 471–472).

The original state, the *śakti,* is an *upādhi* of Īśvara, and so we must consider that, regardless of whether *avidyā* "posits" the *upādhi* opposite God or identifies it falsely with God (just as it falsely identifies the *upādhi* *"buddhi"* with the *pratyagātman*), in both cases the creation is not absolutely real. And since the theory of creation as such is not the central issue, Ś. can, as the need arises, conform more to the doctrine of the BS, that God or Brahman is the *prakṛti,* or to the Purāṇic-Viṣṇuitic doctrine of *māyāśakti* as the prime matter which is dependent on God, for the purpose of the teaching about creation is always just to lead to monism.

Even in the theory of creation the concepts Īśvara and *(paraṃ)* Brahma or Paramātman are largely interchangeable, though not everywhere. One can say that this interchangeability extends throughout the whole theory of creation, with the single exception of the statement that the *īśvaratva* of Īśvara is illusory. To say that the *brahmatva* of Brahman is ultimately unreal is of course impermissible. But Brahman, too, is *sraṣṭṛ* (e.g., I,3,41, K 382,5), *kartṛ* (I,4,23, K 431,4), *jagat-kāraṇa* (very often), and, as such, intelligent (*īkṣitṛ,* I,1,5), omniscient, and omnipotent (*sarvajña, sarvaśakti,* e.g., I,1,2, K 101,2). And the Paramātman, too, is creator of the world (III,3,16, K 776,13ff.). At SBh II.1.1 *paramātman* and *paraṃ brahma* are found alongside *īśvara* as names of that which is both the efficient and material cause of the world. Only where the "division into ruler and ruled" (*īśitr-īśitavya-vibhāga,* III,2,38, K 750,1) is assigned to the *vyāvahāriky avasthā,* or where the *īśvaratva* of Īśvara is called illusory (II,1,14), is it said that this division does not really pertain to Brahman or Atman, or does so only from the empirical standpoint. Only in such places are Īśvara and Brahman or Paramātman presented as two distinct things.

The relation of Brahman and Īśvara is somewhat parallel to that between Paramātman and *jīva.* As the *jaivaṃ rūpam* of the *jīva* is nothing absolutely real, so the *īśvaratva* of Īśvara. But there is a marked difference: the term *īśvara* can be replaced for *brahman* everywhere, as our investigation up to now has confirmed again and again. *Jīva,* on the other hand, can never stand in place of *paramātman.* With the word *jīva,* just as with *śārīra* and *vijñānātman,* is always associated the idea of the soul in its illusory aspect. With *īśvara,* however, is seldom connected the notion that there is something illusory about it.

E. *Īśvara as the controller of individual fate*

There is a series of passages in the SBh where an influence of God on the action and behavior of the soul is spoken of, where Īśvara is conceived as the Lord of the inner world.

God is, in his aspect of "Lord" Who stands opposite souls, the controller of souls (*antaryāmin,* I,2,20, K 285,5), even of divine souls, such as that of the sun god (I,1,21, K 233,1). He is the immanent mover, the agent (*hetu-kartṛ,* II,3,41, K 633,12) in all activity. Even when the soul constructs its dream world, it is not inappropriate to speak of a creation of God, since God is the controller of the soul (*adhiṣṭhātṛ,* II,2,4, K 710,

8–10) in all its "states." Whatever the *jīva* undertakes, God causes *(kārayati)* it to do it, by taking into account the good or evil volition *(dharmādharmalakṣaṇaḥ prayatnaḥ)* of the soul (II,3,42, K 634,4). The soul, however, in the end has to attribute its fate to its own will. Therefore, the accusation that God is unjust or cruel cannot be made (II,1,34). Even the retribution of works is referred to God's impetus (He is *phala-hetu,* III,2,39; III,2,41). Here, therefore, one has to do with a dualistic relationship of the ruler to what he rules. Such a relationship, however, is only possible in the *vyāvahāriky avasthā* (III,2,38, K 750,1; II,1,14, K 471,16f.). Therefore, the *antaryāmin* aspect of Īśvara, or as the case may be, the division into *antaryāmin* and *śārīra,* is also illusory (I,2,20, K 285,16); for *śārīra* and Īśvara are, in essence, identical. But this identity is sometimes adduced to explain the action of God in the soul, which actually contradicts it insofar as it presupposes a difference! Even when the *jīva* "unfolds name and form" (i.e., plans something new, produces it, and gives it a name), it is ultimately God Who is active in this creation, for "the *jīva* is of course not absolutely distinct from Parameśvara" (II,4,10, K 673,5–9). Here, the text says: *tat-kṛtam* (= *jīva-kṛtam*) *api nāmarūpa-vyākaraṇaṃ parameśvara-kṛtaṃ bhavati,* not *parameśvara-kāritam,* so that one cannot any longer speak of the *adhiṣṭhātṛtva* of Īśvara. The passage indicates by its illogicality that Ś.'s Īśvara interpretation is not at all systematized or schematized, which distinguishes it from the Īśvara theory of later Advaitins.

The soul-guiding activity of God consists also, and above all, in His role in liberation. He is the basis of *saṃsāra* insofar as he permits it *(tad-anujñayā . . . saṃsārasya siddhiḥ),* and through His grace arises the knowledge which leads to liberation (*tad-anugraha-hetukenaiva ca vijñānena mokṣa-siddhiḥ,* II,3,41, K 633,8f.). To a few perfected beings *(saṃsiddha),* after they have exerted themselves and meditated on Parameśvara, the knowledge that God and the soul are identical is manifested *(āvirbhavati)* by God's grace *(prasāda).* "Therefore, bondage and liberation take place through the causality *(hetoḥ)* of God. From the ignorance of the being of God comes bondage, but from the knowledge of His being, liberation" (III,2,5, K 711,7–11). Here, the illusory aspect of Īśvara is completely forgotten. The knowledge of God, effected through God's grace, is the revelation of His identity with the soul. Personalistic piety and impersonalistic mysticism converge.

It is natural that in such passages the word *īśvara* is preferred. But synonyms can appear also. Thus, in the passage from II,3,41 cited above, *paramātman* occurs interchangeably with *īśvara.*

For the more personal-religious point of view that the BS seems to represent, communion with God is the goal of the pious seeker. Conforming himself to this point of view, Ś. speaks of those "who through worship of the *saguṇa* Brahman attain union with God" (*īśvara-sāyujyaṃ vrajanti,* IV,4,17, K 976,14; cf. IV,4,18, K 977,17). And these liberated beings remain dependent upon the will of God (IV,4,17, K 977,11). But it becomes apparent from parallel passages (IV,3,7–11 and especially IV,3,14, K 958,5ff.) that, according to Ś.'s point of view, those who have worshipped Īśvara through meditation arrive at the *saguṇa* Brahman. Thus, here, at least once, *īśvara* is a synonym of *saguṇaṃ brahma.*

In contrast to that are the countless passages where *īśvara* can only have the meaning of *paraṃ brahma,* and this usage is not unusual for Ś. even with respect to complete liberation. At IV,1,3 (K 906,13) it is said that with the *mahāvākya, ahaṃ brahmāsmi,* the Upaniṣad teaches one to comprehend Īśvara as the Ātman, and in the same place (K 908,1) Ś. calls the cognition *aham īśvaraḥ* (instead of the usual *ahaṃ brahmāsmi*) enlightenment, that is, liberation.

F. *Īśvara as object of meditation*

Meditation *(upāsanı, dhyāna)* is, according to the Advaita point of view, an action (I,1,4, K 167f.; IV,1,6, K 914,2), and as such it cannot yield liberation, since the latter is something that is not an effect. We have mentioned above that mediation refers to the lower Brahman, and that is understandable. Only as *saguṇa* can that which is in reality incomprehensible become a mental object. But Īśvara is identified as the object of meditation more frequently than the *saguṇa* Brahman. The Paramātman, Īśvara, qualified by attributes (*guṇa-viśeṣair viśiṣṭaḥ,* I,1,11, K 214,10f; cf. III,3,37), that is, so to speak, a *saguṇa* Īśvara, is the object of meditative worship *(upāsya).* Wherever the Ātman, hidden in all things, reveals itself with particular splendor, it is to be worshipped as *īśvara* (K 215,2, with reference to *Bhagavadgītā* X,41). Parameśvara, qualified by certain phenomenal qualities (*vikāra-dharmaiḥ . . . kaiścid viśiṣṭaḥ,* I,1,20, K 232,11), hence, a *saviśeṣaḥ* Parameśvaraḥ!, is meditated upon. Parameśvara is meditated upon by means of a symbol *(pratīka)* or by means of an *upādhi* or, according to Jaimini, directly (I,2,28, K 300,5). Īśvara is one; nevertheless, He is taught to have diverse attributes *(guṇa)* in various sections of the Veda for the purpose of meditative worship (III,3,58, K

848,2f.). Through *upāsana* God is revealed (*sākṣāt-kṛta,* III,3,59, K 849, 15–850,1).

However, *paraṃ brahma* is the object of meditation, too (I,2,1, K 262,3), and in order for one to be able to meditate on it, it is taught as having properties (*dharma,* K 262,5). It is furnished with attributes (*guṇa,* I,2,2, K 263,1–4; in K 263,4, *paramātman* is used as a synonym), and it is explicitly stated, "Because the attributes in question belong to the higher Brahman, it is inferred that the higher Brahman itself is taught as being the object of meditation" (K 263,20; cf. further I,3,13, K 322,1 *[paraṃ brahma]* and 323,13–15 *[paramātman]*). At I,2,7 it is discussed how Brahman, for the purpose of *upāsanā,* can be made to appear *(nicāyya)* infinitesimally small in the heart. In that passage the expressions *paramātman, brahman,* and *īśvara* are used interchangeably with the same meanings.

In those places where *upāsanā* is discussed, then, there is apparently a complete confusion of concepts. Brahman endowed with attributes, Īśvara, Īśvara endowed with attributes, Parameśvara, even the highest Brahman and the highest Ātman, are referred to as the object of meditation. Hence, all these concepts would seem to be, here, completely synonymous!

G. Īśvara, Paraṃ Brahma, Aparaṃ Brahma, and Paramātman

Recapitulating our results so far, we can say that the words *(paraṃ) brahma* or *paramātman* are almost always interchangeable with *īśvara;*[41] that *īśvara* can in most places be replaced by *(paraṃ) brahma* or *paramātaman;* and, finally, that when it comes to *upāsanā, aparaṃ brahma* as well as *(paraṃ) brahma* or *paramātman* can replace *īśvara.*

This use of language is characteristic of Ś. Comparisons with his disciples are, however, helpful only insofar as they establish that the word īśvara is used very seldom by them, whereas it occurs very frequently in the SBh. At the same time, the concept does not appear to have had much systematic development for them. But in later Vedānta *(Pañcadaśī, Vedāntasāra)* Īśvara is no longer confused with Brahman. He has been given a clearly defined place in the system, namely, He is Brahman associated with *māyā.*

How is this strange confusion on Ś.'s part to be explained? Undoubtedly, there are historical causes.[42] But the purpose of the present study forbids investigating them. Nevertheless, there are principles to be found in Ś.'s own thought system which help disentangle the confusion.

To begin with, it bears noting that there is a similarity between the way Ś. uses the words *avidyā, māyā,* and *nāmarūpa* and the terminological imprecision of his use of *īśvara* and *brahman.* In both cases one can arrive at a conclusion about the concepts Ś. associated with the words only after considering all the passages in which they occur. Definitions which distinguish the concepts are lacking. And only a *preferred* usage can be inferred from a majority of the passages in which they are employed (namely, for *avidyā–māyā–nāmarūpa,* a distinction of meanings; for *īśvara–(paraṃ) brahma–paramātman,* an identity of meaning). These preferred usages can occasionally be given up. Under the influence of certain opinions current in his day, *avidyā, māyā,* and *nāmarūpa,* which Ś. was inclined to distinguish, can in special circumstances fall together; on the other hand, in keeping with the basic illusionistic dogma of his system, Īśvara and *paraṃ* Brahma or Paramātman, which he intuitively (and possibly under the influence of non-illusionistic predecessors) was inclined not to distinguish, can occasionally be kept apart. In the latter case, Īśvara almost automatically becomes identical with *aparaṃ* Brahma.

According to this observation we must consider an aversion for definitions and a cavalier attitude toward conceptual systematization as a general distinguishing feature of the thought of Ś. Wherever one might find in a treatise the meticulous schematization so widespread in Indian thought, there one may appropriately doubt Ś.'s authorship.

Ś.'s lack of concern about terminology is evident in his theory of the Absolute in yet another way. Brahman receives *guṇas, dharmas,* or *viśeṣaṇas* really only by means of a *kalpanā* or *adhyāsa* or *adhyāropa,* that is, under the influence of *avidyā.* It becomes thereby *saguṇa, saviśeṣa,* hence conceivable as well as a potential object of meditation. The pure Brahman is of course *nirguṇa* or *nirviśeṣa(ṇa).* But again and again Ś. calls the characteristics of Brahman in itself—whether positive, such as spirit or consciousness, or negative, such as absence of sin, etc.—*guṇas, viśeṣaṇas,* or *dharmas* of Brahman or Īśvara! Now and then, though in fact quite infrequently, his disciple Sureśvara follows him in this practice, but after Vimuktātman, at the latest, it is strictly forbidden to speak of *guṇas* or *dharmas* of Brahman. One then says *svarūpa* instead of *guṇa* or *dharma* or *viśeṣaṇa.* Indeed, already for Ś.'s disciple Padmapāda it is apparently objectionable to speak of qualities of Brahman. Bliss, the experience of objects, and eternality may seem to be qualities of Brahman, he says, but they are in reality identical with him.[43]

Īśvara is for Ś. a concept that stands vaguely between *paraṃ* and *aparaṃ* Brahma. Mostly He is the former, infrequently the latter, and in some cases one is reluctant to decide (see above, p. 000). In the latter cases an intuitive theism has joined with an intellectual monism to form an illogical, but for that reason much more lively, combination. The extent to which Ś. goes with his identification of Īśvara with *paraṃ* Brahma is especially evident when he also distinguishes two forms *(rūpa)* of Parameśvara, a *saguṇa* and a *nirguṇa* (IV,4,19, K 978,8), just as he does of Brahman (I,1,11, K 213,7 and IV,3,14, K 964,12f.). And ultimately *paraṃ* and *aparaṃ brahma,* too, coincide (Ś. notes briefly at III,3,39, K 820,20; *guṇavatas tu brahmaṇa ekatvāt*). The lower Brahman is in fact not actually an entity unto itself. Only infrequently does it appear as such (e.g., IV,3,7ff.). It exists in general, so to speak, only for the purpose of worship (cf. II,1,14, K 472,17–19; III,2,14, K 726,13f.; III,2,15, K 727,3). One could almost say that it is only created by the meditating subject in the imagination. That which is worshipped in this meditation, however, is the one Brahman, the highest, which is only worshipped as something lesser because it is inconceivable without *guṇas.* Ś. can, therefore, for reasons internal to his system, use *īśvara, parameśvara, brahman, paraṃ brahma, aparaṃ brahma,* and *paramātman* at will in those passages where he speaks of worship. In their ultimate reality they are, according to his interpretation, one and the same.[44]

Notes

1. Aufrecht's *Catalogus Catalogorum* (together with supplements) already lists more than 300.

2. Cf. Winternitz, *Geschichte der indischen Literatur,* vol. 3 (Leipzig, 1922), pp. 433f.; O. Strauss, *Indische Philosophie* (München, 1924), pp. 242f.; H. v. Glasenapp, *Der Stufenweg zum Göttlichen* (Baden-Baden, 1948), pp. 9f., and *Die Philosophie der Inder* (Stuttgart, 1949), p. 187.

3. The only work known to me that systematically investigates the question of the authenticity of a work ascribed to Śaṅkara is the Breslau University dissertation of Käthe Marschner, inspired by O. Strauss, *Zur Verfasserfrage des dem Śaṅkarācārya zugeschriebenen Bṛhadāraṇyakopaniṣadbhāṣya* (Berlin-Charlottenburg, 1933). B. Faddegon's discussion of the authenticity of the *Gītābhāṣya* in his University of Leiden dissertation, *Çaṃkara's Gītābhāṣya, toegelicht en beoordeeld* (Amsterdam, 1906), pp. 63–71 and 95–98, is much too superficial. Scattered remarks in other studies which do no specifically investigate the authenticity question, of course, do not solve the problem.

4. That is true also for the book of Subrahmaṇya discussed below in section I,F. Although he contrasts Ś. to later Advaita, he, an orthodox Indian, is not concerned with historical and individual differences, but with the genuine Vedānta, and this he finds not only in Ś. but also Sureśvara and even Yājñavalkya.

5. G. Thibaut deserves credit for being the first to have demonstrated the difference of the teaching of Ś. from that of the *Brahmasūtras* through comparison of Ś. and Rāmānuja (*The Vedānta-Sūtras with the Commentary of Śaṅkarācārya*, part I, Sacred Books of the East, vol. 34 [Oxford, 1890], introduction). On the other hand, insofar as he relied for his interpretations on commentators and modern paṇḍits, he completely overlooked the difference between Ś. and his successors. Deussen, on the other hand, who was neither able nor willing to carry out the comparison with Rāmānuja, naturally did not notice that the teaching of the *sūtras* is different than Ś.'s. Nevertheless, he did exhibit an accurate feel for divergences in the later development of the doctrine from Ś.'s principal work. Cf. the preface to his translation of the *Sūtras des Vedānta* (Leipzig, 1883), p. XIII and *Das System des Vedānta* (Leipzig, 1887), p. 4. [*The System of the Vedānta*, Chicago, 1912, p. 4].

6. Cf. Sadānanda, *Vedāntasāra*, ed. G. A. Jacob, 2nd ed. (Bombay, 1911), pp. IV–IX.

7. *Westöstliche Mystik*, 2nd ed. (Gotha, 1929); trans.: *Mysticism East and West* (New York, 1932).

8. Abbreviated below as SBh; BS = *Brahmasūtra(s)*; Ś. = Śaṅkara.

9. *Śāstravārttāsamucaya*, Devcand Lalbhai Jaina-Pustakoddhāra 16 (Bombay, 1914).

10. *Ślokavārttika*, Chowkhambha Sanskrit Series (Benares, 1898–99); trans. by G. Jhā, Bibliotheca Indica (Calcutta, 1907).

11. *Nyāyamañjarī*, Vizianagram Sanskrit Series, vol. 8 (Benares, 1895).

12. *Māṇḍūkyakārikā*, Ānandāśrama Sanskrit Series, no. 10 (Poona, 1928).

13. *Brahmasiddhi*, ed. Kuppuswami Sastri, Madras Govt. Oriental Manuscript Series, no. 4 (Madras, 1937).

14. *Naiṣkarmyasiddhi*, ed. M. Hiriyanna, Bombay Sanskrit and Prakrit Series, no. 38 (Bombay, 1925).

15. *Pañcapādikā*, Vizianagram Sanskrit Series, vol. 2 (Benares, 1891); trans. by D. Venkataramiah, Gaekwad's Oriental Series, no. 107 (Baroda, 1947).

16. *Śrutisārasamuddharaṇa*, Ānandāśrama Sanskrit Series, no. 103 (Poona, 1936).

17. *Iṣṭasiddhi*, ed. M. Hiriyanna, Gaekwad's Oriental Series, no. 65 (Baroda, 1933). Editor's note: An obsolete reference by Hacker to the publication of his investigations has been omitted.

18. References are to SBh unless otherwise noted. After "K" follow page and line references according to the edition of the SBh in the Kāshī Sanskrit Series, no. 71 (Benares, 1931).

19. *Dvaita* is customarily translated by "duality." However, it does not usually mean "duality" in Śaṅkara's Vedānta, but "the state in which a second is present," hence, more or less, "second-ness." By this concept attention is directed not to two things, but only to the second of the two (the world). Thus, the word is often synonymous with *prapañca* (the world which, as the second thing, stands opposed to the Ātman).

20. Sensory illusion in which someone confuses a rope with a snake is a paradigm of an erroneous representation.

21. This word, which is especially characteristic of the language of the SBh, expresses the idea that *avidyā* brings something close (*upa*) (to the Ātman) and sets it over against (*prati*) it. In what follows, verbs such as "bring forth" or "toward," "place (in front of)," etc., will be used as approximate translations.

22. It is to be found in the preserved literature perhaps for the first time in Maṇḍanamiśra's *Brahmasiddhi*. The word is not to be found in Toṭaka, although that could have to do with the comparatively short length of his work. In addition, the style of Toṭaka's verses would allow only a paraphrase of the concept.

23. Concerning Ś.'s aversion to theories, cf. further my article "Vedānta-Studien" in *Die Welt des Orients*, vol. 1, especially pp. 248f. [see *Kl. Schr.*, pp. 59–68]. Concerning sequences of thought in the SBh which may be pedagogically determined, cf. below, section IV,2.

24. I am indebted to Swāmī Siddheswarānanda of the Ramakrishna Mission for this book. According to him, a lively controversy over the content of this book has taken place between its author, Kuppuswami Sastri, Hiriyanna, and other Indian scholars. Editor's note: Numerous works by Subba Rao appeared under his later monastic name Saccidānandendra Sarasvatī.

25. The edition has *anyonyatāpādānam*.

26. This is the view of Sureśvara in contrast to the doctrine of Maṇḍana and Vācaspati, according to whom the *jīva* is the *āśraya*, Brahman the *viṣaya*, of *avidyā*.

27. Usually in the dual form, *nāmarūpe*, in Ś. It occurs also, though less frequently, as the collective compound *nāmarūpam*.

28. The word *bīja* here is falsely related to Īśvara by the commentators Ānandagiri and Govindānanda. He is, according to them, the *bīja*. The theory of *nāmarūpe* as the cosmic seed was no longer known in Ānandagiri's time (14th century) nor, certainly, in the time of Govindānanda, who was much later. However, Vācaspati, the younger contemporary of Ś., still knew it; therefore, he clarifies *nāmarūpabīja* at II.1.14 (K 470f.) with the phrase *nāmarūpe eva bījam*.

Ānandagiri and Govindānanda naturally follow his explanation there, whereas in the case of I,2,22, where Vācaspati remains silent, they attempt an interpretation that works, not for Ś.'s system, but only the (later) one familiar to them. [Editor: See below, n. 44.]

29. Padmapāda, Pañcapādikā, p. 77,13; the latter three commentaries are to be found in the edition, *The Brahmasūtra-Shānkarabhāshyam with the commentaries Ratnaprabhā, Bhāmatī, and Nyāyanirṇaya* . . . , ed. M. S. Bakre (Bombay, 1909), p. 47. [Editor: On the *itthaṃbhāve* use of the instrumental, cf. Pāṇini II,3,21: *itthaṃbhūtalakṣaṇe*.]

30. I prefer, along with Thibaut, to interpret the series of words beginning with *nāmarūpa* and ending with *phala* as a *dvandva* (Deussen construes it differently).

31. Thus in the commentary on Chānd. Up. ascribed to Ś., VIII,14,1.

32. The series of identifications that appear to contradict the distinction of *avidyā, māyā,* and *nāmarūpa,* also typical of Ś., will be discussed later (sec. IV,B).

33. Cf. below, note 38.

34. For the dating of Bhāskara see Hiriyanna's introduction to his *Iṣṭasiddhi* edition (p. 65). For Bhāskara on *nāmarūpa* see his commentary on BS II,1,14. (Chowkhamba Sanskrit Series, p. 96). Editor's note: On the date of Vācaspati, see below, n. 44.

35. Cf. below, sec. IV,B.

36. Cf. L. Renou, "Les origines de la notion de māyā," *Journal de Psychologie normale et pathologique* 41 (1948), pp. 293ff.

37. Closely related to Ś.'s *māyā* interpretation, though not identical with it, is the interpretation of his *paramaguru* Gauḍapāda. In the *Māṇḍūkyakārikā māyā* also has the function of Ś.'s *avidyā*. It is a power that creates illusions. The word *avidyā* does not occur in Gauḍapāda's work.

38. A complete demonstration is not possible here. One can only refer to such passages as *Mahābhārata* XII,232,2 and 307,2; *Purāṇa Pañcalakṣaṇa* (ed. Kirfel), *Sarga,* II A 4,1–2 (p. 20) and II B 3,27 (p. 62); *Jayākhyasaṃhitā* (Gaekwad's Oriental Series, no. 54), IV,55c–56b; *Paramasaṃhitā* (Gaekwad's Oriental Series, no. 86), II,4. The refutation of the Vedānta theory of the creation of the world in Kumārila's *Ślokavārttika* (*Sambandhākṣepaparihāra,* 84f.) documents the interpretation of *avidyā* as prime matter among Vedāntins prior to Ś.

39. *Pañcapādikā,* p. 20, 11–13.

40. *Iṣṭasiddhi,* I,34 (p. 144).

41. To the cited passages should be added others of exclusively exegetical content. At I,1,20, in the context of an explanation of the phrase "the *puruṣa* in the sun and the eye," *parameśvara* and *paramātman* are used in the same sense;

at I,2,13–17: *brahman* and *parameśvara;* at I,2,24ff., in explaining the Vaiśvānara fire: *īśvara, parameśvara,* and *paramātman;* at I,3,10–12, in the discussion of what *akṣara* in Bṛh. Up. III,8,7f. means: *parameśvara, paraṃ brahma, brahman,* and *paramātman;* at I,3,14–18, in explaining the term *dahara* at Chānd. Up. VIII,1,1: *paramātman, parameśvara,* and *brahman; ākāśa* is at I,3,17 (K 330,16) a name of Parameśvara, at I,3,41 (K 382,6), of *paraṃ brahma;* at I,3,24f., in the explanation of *aṅguṣṭhamātra* (Kaṭh. Up. II,4,12), *paramātman* and *parameśvara* are used interchangeably; and at I,4,16 (K 419,7–9), in the explanation of Kauṣ. Up. IV,19, the term *paramātman* used previously (K 418,3f.) is replaced by *parameśvara.*

42. A comparison of the commentaries on the SBh by Ś. and Bhāskara could possibly reveal many older, traditional interpretations.

43. *Pañcapādikā,* p. 4,3f.

44. Editor's note: After the completion of this article, Hacker changed his views on the chronology of early Advaita Vedānta. He would no longer call Vācaspati a "younger contemporary of Ś." (See above, n. 28; also sec. II, E, conclusion; *Kl. Schr.,* p. 90), but assign him to the tenth century (see *Kl. Schr.,* pp. 110–19). For Śaṅkara himself, he replaced the traditional dates of 788–820 with the period prior to or around 700; see above, Chapter 1; also below, Chapter 6, n. 3. This did, however, not affect the results of his conceptual and philological analysis.

5

Śaṅkara the Yogin and Śaṅkara the Advaitin: Some Observations

1. The Problem of Argumentation in Śaṅkara Śaṅkara's method is mainly interpretative, simply because his work consists for the most part of commentaries in which he expounds authoritative texts which do not brook any contradiction. However, argumentative passages are also not rare. Purely argumentative, for example, is the second chapter of the prose part of US. The subject handled there is central to the system: the self. A teacher argues with a pupil longing for liberation from *saṃsāra*. Starting with the experience of suffering, he discourses first on nescience and superimposition *(adhyāropaṇā)*, then on the nature of the self. In the entire chapter no quotation from the Upaniṣads is given, in deliberate contrast with the first chapter, which employs the method of instruction according to the authority of the Veda. The doctrine of the self as self-sufficient *(svārtha)*, self-given *(svataḥsiddha)*, free *(svatantra)*, unalterably permanent *(kūṭastha, nitya)*, i.e., subsisting light of spirit, is developed solely on the basis of rational grounds in this didactic dialogue. It is the most systematic exposition of ātmology in the works of Śaṅkara.

Just for that reason one misses something. Surely, Śaṅkara is a monist—*ekatvavādin, aikātmyavādin.* Yet the doctrine that there is only one self, and that this alone is what truly is, emerges only in passing,[1] as if it followed obviously from what has been said. The sole argument for monism is: "That the light of the self . . . is without a second, follows from the fact that it is not absent in any of the various mental modifications" (*ātmajyotiṣaḥ . . . advaitabhāvaś ca sarva-pratyaya-bhedeṣu avyabhicārāt* 109). But the argument is weak. While elsewhere in the discussion all possible objections are examined, here the obvious objection, that sameness of essence does not mean identity of existence, remains unexamined.

The discussion of the self at KePBh 2,12,4 gives a similar impression. There in his debate with Mīmāṃsā and Vaiśeṣika, Śaṅkara rejects both an actualistic as well as a substantialistic view: the self is neither an agent nor can it be subsumed under the category of substance, it is neither *kartṛ,* nor *dravya.* Excepting for allusions to passages in the Upaniṣad, Śaṅkara has here also only the one argument for monism, that the self "sees" all mental modifications or functions of the inner sense: *sarva-pratyaya-darśitve copajananāpāya-varjita-dṛk-svarūpatā, nityatvaṃ, viśuddhasvarūpatvam, ātmatvaṃ nirviśeṣataikatvaṃ ca sarvabhūteṣu siddhaṃ syāt.*

A metaphysics of knowledge or gnoseological anthropology is to be found at BBh 4,3,2ff.[2] There it is explained how the self as the inner light pervades the faculty of knowledge, the body, and the objects of the external world. And even here the argument is not directed expressly in favor of monism. Correspondingly, illusionism is also limited. It has reference only to the connection between self and thing; the question of reality as a whole is not raised.

This result is surprising, for other Advaitins do argue in favor of monism, preferably negatively, by trying to show that becoming is an impossibility (Gauḍapāda) or that diversity *(bheda)* cannot be established (Maṇḍanamiśra, Vimuktātman and others). Why is monism so weakly developed on the basis of arguments in Śaṅkara despite his emphatic avowal of it? So much so that one can extract from his works a considerable body of doctrine regarding the self without having to make any mention of monism?

In his *Mysticism East and West* (German original: *Westöstliche Mystik*), Rudolf Otto has already brought to light similar unexpected matters in Śaṅkara's concept of Brahman.[3] We can generalize and say: When Śaṅkara philosophizes on the Absolute, his talk of an impersonal Brahman time and again slips over to that of a personal "Lord" or "Highest

Lord." The argumentation can, moreover, take the form of proper proofs of God,[4] though it is true that Śaṅkara operates with rational arguments only so long as he is concerned with the existence of God. At the conclusion of the demonstration at KeVBh 3,14,1 he speaks monistically: God is identical with the self of everyone *(sa cātmabhūtaḥ sarvasya),* and there is only one self *(ekasyātmanaḥ siddhiḥ).* But this is demonstrated not on rational grounds, but by means of quotations from the Veda.

The argument is then carried forward by means of an adaptation of criteria taken from Mīmāṃsā. The Upaniṣadic statements cannot be construed, as Mīmāṃsā postulates, merely as unauthoritative talk about something *(arthavāda).* They do not serve as complements, or as appendages, to something else (*ananyayogitva = ananyaśeṣatva* according to Ānandagiri). Therefore, they are authoritative or valid as means of knowledge, exactly like the portions of the Veda that prescribe ritual acts, which alone Mīmāṃsā admits as valid, and they generate a knowledge which cannot be acquired in any other way. "Such knowledge, once it has arisen, cannot be removed. Nor can it be contradicted. There is no negation to the effect that there is no God."[5] Śaṅkara formulates the argument in an extended sense, though in a very concise form, at BBh 1,4,7: "Whether a (Vedic) sentence is a means of knowledge or not does not depend upon whether it describes something actually existing or an action (a rite), but upon whether it produces determinate and fruitful knowledge."[6]

The criteria employed here derive for the most part from Mīmāṃsā, even though its basic principle of the sole validity of ritual injunctions is rejected; one criterion is derived from Nyāya. Commenting on MS 1,1,2, Śabarasvāmin says, "What is grasped as certain (or with definiteness, firmness), that cannot be false. An idea is false when, after it has arisen, it is overthrown by the insight: It is not so."[7] Śabara applies this consideration to the Vedic sentence, "He who desires heaven should sacrifice," and remarks, "What we learn from this sentence is not something which we can doubt, requiring us to ask whether heaven exists or not."[8] This basic principle of the absolute validity of knowledge gained from the word of the Veda, which Mīmāṃsā held to be applicable only in respect of injunctions, is extended by Śaṅkara and by Vedānta generally to the assertions of the Upaniṣads about the self. Since these produce in the meditating mystic knowledge which is definite, certain, and obtainable only in this way, and which is not contradicted nor sublated by another knowledge, therefore what the Upaniṣads assert is true, right, valid. Really speaking, the criterion is self-certitude itself; the Mīmāṃsā concepts serve the purpose of describing it and of affiliating it with a tradition. Even the last of Śaṅkara's criteria, namely that knowledge "has effects," i.e., is *phalavat,* accords only formally to a tradition, this time to that of the Nyāya system. In the very first words of his *Nyāyasūtrabhāṣya,* Vātsyāyana teaches: "While through a means of knowledge a thing becomes accessible, there arises a capacity for effective practical action and it is in this that a means of knowledge has its end."[9] Knowledge thus serves a purpose. This, according to Vātsyāyana, is an "exertion" *(samīhā),* and the capacity for this is the "relation to a result" *(phalenābhisaṃbandhaḥ).* That knowledge has a result or fruit is thus part of the meaning of right cognition and can therefore be employed as its criterion, as happens with Śaṅkara. But the fruit or result of Vedāntic knowledge is not, of course, any external or inner exertion, but rather an inner experience; it is "the removal of the evils which are the cause of *saṃsāra:* nescience, sorrow, delusion, fear etc."[10]

Śaṅkara can in this manner scientifically justify the fact that he does not argue rationally for monism but, apart from a small number of rudimentary arguments, merely refers to the texts (which generate experience) of the Upaniṣads. Nevertheless, it is striking that, in a thinker who normally does not in the least fight shy of providing rational grounds, the course of the argument here breaks off, just when it is faced with the central thesis of the system. We have here what is certainly a characteristic trait of Śaṅkara's personality: he wants to lead us to experience, not to argumentation;[11] but perhaps the concrete conditions on which this feature depends can be grasped more precisely.

Moreover, even the illusionism which constantly serves to complement the monism of spirit is weakly developed in Śaṅkara, not only in places where the proper theme is the self but also where "nescience" is expressly considered, as in the introduction to BSBh, USG 48–65, and GBh 13,2. The concept of the mutual superimposition of body and self only implies that the relation between these is ultimately unreal; it does not permit the problem of the reality or unreality of the objective as a whole to be attacked.

How is all this to be explained? Are there historical conditions which determine these peculiarities of Śaṅkara's thinking?

2. *Transition from Yoga to Advaita*

It seems to me, yes. I had already noted quite some time back that Śaṅkara's doctrine of nescience exhibits remarkable similarities, which at the same time distinguish him from other Advaitins, to the Yoga system.[12] Two years after I published this observation, a text came to light which poses a new problem for investigation in the history of philosophy: the *Yogasūtrabhāṣya-Vivaraṇa* of Śaṅkara-Bhagavatpāda.[13]

That the author of this text is designated as Bhagavat in the colophons may be taken as pointing to the author of the BSBh. All works really written by him are ascribed in the manuscripts to a Śaṅkara bearing the epithet of Bhagavat, Bhagavatpāda, or Bhagavatpūjyapāda, while, on the contrary, no work ascribed to a Śaṅkarācārya is by the author of the BSBh.[14] It is, of course, true that there are spuria also among the works ascribed to a Bhagavat, Bhagavatpāda, or Bhagavatpūjyapāda. Should the *Vivaraṇa* on the *Yogabhāṣya* be the work of the same Śaṅkara who has written the BSBh, and if we assume that he was at first a Yogin and later became an Advaitin, a number of peculiarities can be accounted for as being due to this change of affiliation, including the remarkable characteristics of his ātmology sketched above. Perhaps we may also be enabled then to say which of the Advaita works are earlier and which are later, according to the degree of their nearness to the way of speaking characteristic of Yoga. Because of limitations of space I can at present offer only a few observations.

Śaṅkara came without a doubt from a Viṣṇuite milieu.[15] Whereas Vedavyāsa's commentary begins, though admittedly not in all manuscripts, with an obeisance to Śiva, Śaṅkara begins and concludes his sub-commentary with an adoration to Viṣṇu. His strong theistic concern, which Rudolf Otto was the first to uncover in Śaṅkara's Advaita works, is manifested in Śaṅkara the Yogin by the fact that the longest *utsūtra* passage of his sub-commentary, fifteen pages of the published edition, deals with God, most of it with proofs of God.

What could have prompted the Yogin Śaṅkara to turn to Advaita? It is my conjecture that, in conjunction with his theism, it was the mysticism of the *Om* sound, which according to YS 1,27 is expressive of God and which Śaṅkara again mentions in the concluding *maṅgala* of YV. *Om* is dealt with in MāUp, and on this a new work had appeared, probably not much before Śaṅkara's time, which also taught a new kind of Yoga (*asparśa-yoga* MK 3,39; 4,2): Gauḍapāda's *Māṇḍūkyakārikā*. Let us assume tentatively that in order to learn this new doctrine of *Om* and this new Yoga, Śaṅkara went to school with an Advaita master, who instructed him in the MK and introduced him to the Advaita system, and that as a result he became a monist and was finally given the task of writing a commentary on Gauḍapāda's work by his teacher. This assumption enables us to order certain facts in quite a meaningful way.

At YBh 2,15 the [fourfold] division of the Yogaśāstra is compared with that of a system of therapeutics. Śaṅkara takes up this idea in the introduction to YV (p. 2), where he seeks to explain the purpose of the Yoga system. Thus Yoga is understood as a therapy. Śaṅkara again uses the same idea when in the introduction to the MāBh he wishes to state the purpose of the text to be explained, leaving out the fourfold division (which is appropriate only to the Yoga system); it is now the monistic teaching which leads the patient suffering from sorrow to the health of the self. In the introductions to other works of Śaṅkara, the idea of therapy *(cikitsita)* recurs once again in USP 19,1, while the notion of illness and health, with the omission of the concept of medical treatment, appears in USG 47. It may therefore be assumed that the three works in which the idea of therapeutic treatment is emphasized belong to the same period and are close to Yoga. For the latter is methodical practice, which can easily be compared to a therapy. Śaṅkara's Vedānta, on the contrary, does not mean to teach any method which through exercise may lead progressively to the goal of liberation. For this reason he later rejects Yoga (cf. below). In conformity with this, in USG (perhaps a late work) it is only the pupil who expects from his teacher some sort of therapeutic treatment; the teacher himself promises him nothing of the kind but only aims at leading him to knowledge.

The fact that Śaṅkara, otherwise so uneffusive, composed exuberant verses of obeisance at the beginning as well as the conclusion of his MāBh, seems to reflect here a real enthusiasm, stimulated by the illumination he believed he had received through his initiation into Advaita. Most of Śaṅkara's works contain no verses of obeisance.[16] If we now assume that in his early works—perhaps so long as his teacher was still alive or while he remained with his teacher—he appended verses of obeisance, but later gave up this practice (apart from the brief obeisance in prose to the *saṃpradāyakartāraḥ* at the beginning of the BBh and the KaBh), we find that the following are the earliest works of the Advaitin Śaṅkara: the MāBh, the TBh, and the first as well as the last three of the verse-*prakaraṇas* of US.[17] The assumption that just these works are the earliest will gain in probability if it can be shown that in MāBh there are striking reminiscences of Yoga, as yet unassimilated to Advaita, and that in the other *ex hypothesi* early writings there is a closeness to the diction of the MāBh. So far, it seems to me that this hypothesis is borne out at least in the case of three of the aforementioned writings: for the MāBh, the TBh, and the *prakaraṇa* USP 19. The diction of all other commentaries must, of course, be compared more thoroughly. For the present, I should like to mention only a couple of instances.

At MK 3,31 it is said: *manaso hy amanībhāve dvaitaṃ naivopalabhyate*. Śaṅkara explains in MāBh that this "de-manasization" of the *manas,* this annihilation of the function of the inner sense, occurs either in deep sleep or *vivekadarśanābhyāsa-vairāgyābhyām,* "through the practice of intuiting distinction and through the shedding of passions." This is formulated exactly according to YS 1,12. This sūtra teaches that the functions of the inner sense "are annihilated through practice and the shedding of passions," *abhyāsa-vairāgyābhyām tan-nirodhaḥ*. And Vyāsa completes the sense of *abhyāsa* by expanding it into *vivekadarśanābhyāsa,* thus using the same word which Śaṅkara adopts in MāBh. Now we must bear in mind that Śaṅkara otherwise adopts a very cautious, often deprecatory attitude toward the demand for the repetition of an idea ("I am Brahman") or the practice of meditation—cf., for example, USP 18,9–18 (objection) and 19ff. (refutation). In BSBh 4,1,2, he is bound by the sūtra; there he cannot do otherwise than recommend repetition, though even there he does it only with reservations. On the other hand, at BBh 1,4,7, where he speaks quite independently of the basic text, he not only rejects (against Mīmāṃsā) any commandment for the production of a series of ideas *(smṛti-saṃtati)* (Bhagavat p. 51, 26; Ān p. 128), but also expressly denies that Yoga with its exercises in *cittavṛtti-nirodha* (Bhagavat p. 52, 10; Ān p. 128f.) is a means to liberation, a *mokṣa-sādhana* (like BSBh 2,1,3). Thus the MāBh has on this point a closeness to Yoga which Śaṅkara rejects in other works. This finding (as well as the emergence of the idea of therapy, see above) can easily be explained through the hypothesis that the MāBh, as the earliest work of a Yogin converted to Advaita, still contains a residue of Yoga which had to be discarded in the process of further thinking through of the Advaita position.

Among the verse-*prakaraṇas* of US, the last one (19) stands particularly close to the thoughts and diction of the MK and the MāBh. That here (verse 1) the śāstra is conceived, as in YV and in MāBh, as therapeutic treatment *(cikitsita)* has already been mentioned. The disease here is *tṛṣṇā,* "thirst" or "desire," which, together with *avidyā,* "nescience," is called a *doṣa* in MāBh (1,9): *avidyā-tṛṣṇādi-doṣāḥ*. In verse 10 we encounter the image of *alāta (-cakra),* i.e., of the swinging torch, familiar to us from MK 4,47ff. and used in the same sense as in the MK. In verse 9 it was said that the subject, the object, and the process of knowing are an illusion simulated by the inner sense: "for, there is no evidence for an object distinct from knowing." Then we have in verse 10: "Or (one may also say): the fiction is equally duality-less; for it is not bound up with a thing. That is like a swinging torch."[18] Here the cleavage between subject and object is grasped as an illusion, produced by the inner sense, just as a torch swung around produces the illusion of fiery figures. This is exactly the view of the MāBh, whereas elsewhere (probably later) Śaṅkara employs the image of the torch in a different way; I shall come back to this in the next paragraph. As in MāBh everywhere, and in conformity with the language of the MK, at USP 19 the substantive *vikalpa,* along with the metre-determined *vikalpanā,* as also the causative of *kḷp* with and without prefixes, occurs very frequently to denote the unreality of the world. In other works of Śaṅkara the use of these words is decidedly rarer and is mostly limited to composite formations with *avidyā* and other words. Only in TBh, which also seems to be one of the early works because of its verse *maṅgala,* the term *vikalpa,* along with the verb forms, is still very frequently used to express illusionism. The ontological argument for monism, derived from the MK and disappearing in other, later writings of Śaṅkara, is once again developed at USP 19, 20–24: there cannot be any becoming; the self is without becoming (*aja,* a word which occurs 23 times in the MK). The argument is to be found in TBh also; it is summed up at TBh 2,8,4 (*Ān,* p. 90 bottom) in this sentence: *na hy anyasyānyabhāvāpattir upapadyate,* with which may be compared MK 3,21; 4,7 and 4,29; at each of these places in MK we find the half-verse, *prakṛter anyathābhāvo na kathaṃcid bhaviṣyati.*

3. Development within the Advaita Period Within his Advaita period Śaṅkara appears to have developed on certain points a more independent way of thinking, moving away from the standpoint of Gauḍapāda as adopted by him in MāBh. This is exemplified in the fact that the term *vikalpa* moves into the background, as also the ontological argument for monism, the place of which is taken by the arguments from the nature of knowledge and from the fact of experience.[19] A further consequence of this is a change in the conception of the subject-object relation, to which we may now turn. In anticipation it may be remarked that here also the TBh shows itself to be one of the probably early works, since it is, in various respects, still close to the way of thinking of the MāBh and of Gauḍapāda. The investigation is rendered a little complicated because the development of the conception of the subject-object relation must in part be discussed in its connection with the doctrine of *ānanda,* since some of the texts mention that relation only in conjunction with this doctrine.

According to the teaching of the MāBh, to which a brief reference was made a little while ago in our interpretation of USP 19,9–10, the one spiritual reality unfolds itself through vibration *(spandana)* of the inner sense (*manas* at MāUp 5; and *vijñāna,* MāBh 4,47; *citta,* 4,72) into the appearance (*ābhāsa* 4,47) of the subject and the object (*viṣayin* and *viṣaya* at MāUp 5 and MāBh 4,47 = *grāhaka* and *grāhya* 4,72f.).[20] This vibration is the world (*dvayaṃ*[21] *laukikam* 4,87; *lokaḥ* 4,88); it is a product of nescience (*avidyā* 4,47). In reality, the vibrating *citta* is unmoved and is the self itself (*cittaṃ paramārthata ātmaiva* 4,72). When, according to Śaṅkara, the exertion *(āyāsa)* of the vibration ceases, there emerges, according to the words of MāUp, the third quarter of the self, the "bliss-like" *(ānandamaya),* in deep sleep. Joy thus denotes negatively a cessation of the subject-object relation; positively it is the self itself. The "*citta* which has become Brahman" (*niṣpannaṃ brahma tat tadā* MK 3,46) is described at MK 3,47 as "highest pleasure, without becoming, with the un-becoming as the object of knowledge" *(sukham uttamam/ajam ajena jñeyena).* Śaṅkara's comment on this in MāBh is that this pleasure is "experienceable by the Yogin" *(yogipratyakṣam eva),* that it is "without becoming" because it is not directed to an object, and that it is "with" the "object of knowledge which is without becoming" inasmuch as it coincides with it *(avyatirikta).*

From this doctrine I shall first pick out the notion of the vibration of the inner sense, which is illustrated by the image of the rotating torch, and confront it with another, probably later idea of Śaṅkara; afterwards we shall consider the concept of *ānanda* in conjunction with the view of the subject-object relation in other works of Śaṅkara.

The image of the torch turns up again in the introduction to AiBh 2,1—a very important text on ātmology—but in quite a different sense than in the MK, in MāBh, and in USP 19. In AiBh 2,1 Śaṅkara distinguishes between the intermittent cognitive function of the senses and the subsisting seeing of the self, and says that it is an error to ascribe the intermittence to the self. The intermittent "external" seeing *(bāhyānityadṛṣṭiḥ)* is the object of the subsisting seeing of the self *(nityātmano dṛṣṭiḥ);* the latter is therefore generally identified with the former. "It is as if the seeing, having for its object things like a torch, characterized by the property of rotation, etc., were itself, as it were, rotating."[22] An expressive play of words: the torch rotates, is swung around; the visual perception likewise appears to rotate, because it follows the former and copies the image; but this is an illusion.[23] The rotation of the torch is here, as in the MK, in MāBh, and in USP 19,10 an object of comparison in so far as it produces an illusion. But in AiBh the illusion does not consist, as in other, earlier texts, in the subject-object bifurcation, but rather in not distinguishing the transsubjective self from the empirical *(vyāvahārika)* subject which in reality stands as an object over against the self. The disastrous illusion consists now not in a false division but in a false identification. Therefore that also which is compared with the rotation of the torch is no longer a psychic-mental vibration, like the comparison which was made at MK 4,47 between a *vijñānaṃ spanditam* and the *alātaṃ spanditam,* but a confusion resting upon a false identification suggested by the use of the root *bhram* instead of *spand.* Here the underlying conception of the subject-object relation is the same as is presented in the introduction to Śaṅkara's BSBh in greater detail and is referred to at a few other places in his later works; I shall revert to this presently.

Let us take up now the interpretation of the subject-object relation in conjunction with the *ānanda* doctrine. Of all the Upaniṣads the one which speaks most often of *ānanda* is the TUp. In the explications of this concept in TBh there is a noticeable difference which seems to mark the transition from Śaṅkara's earlier conception, which is influenced by the MK, to the later one.

At MāUp 5, where the bliss of deep sleep is dealt with, Śaṅkara explained the word *ānandamaya* as *ānandaprāyo nānanda eva:* the subject enjoying deep sleep is "bliss-full, not bliss itself." This interpretation signifies that in deep sleep there is nevertheless already an approximation to absolute bliss, which is then mentioned at MK 3,47 and designated as *sukha.* This interpretation of *ānandamaya* is similar to the one which in the pre-Advaitic Vedānta tradition held also for TUp 2,5, as attested by BS 1,1,13 *(vikāraśabdān neti cen na prācuryāt); ānanda-prāya* is, of course, about the same as *ānanda-pracura.* The only difference is that the "bliss-full *(ānandamaya = ānandapracura)* self" of TUp 2,5 was explained as the real self, whereas Śaṅkara characterizes the *ānandamaya ātmā* of MāUp 5 as a first stage, which in this Upaniṣad is followed by yet another, "fourth." In TBh, however, Śaṅkara deviates from the tradition:[24] the suffix *-maya* in *ānandamaya* denotes a product, a "transformation" (*vikāra,* the view rejected at BS 1,1,13!). In other words, the *ānandamaya ātmā* is not the self itself, but an effectuated self that has emerged or has been constructed out of the feeling of bliss.[25] The *ānandamaya* of TUp 2,8,5 is explained in the same sense by Śaṅkara. These interpretations distinguish the TBh from the MāBh and connect it with the BSBh on a point where Śaṅkara consciously deviates from the pre-Advaitic tradition.

On TUp 2,8,4, however, where in the text the expression "bliss of Brahman," *brahmaṇa ānandaḥ* occurs, where thus the question is not of something "bliss-like" but of bliss, Śaṅkara's exegesis moves entirely along the lines of his MāBh and deviates markedly from many places in his other, later commentaries, for here, the subject-object relation is under discussion. Bliss is explained in terms of the annihilation of the subject-object relation brought into being by nescience, of a liberation from this, of a coincidence of the subject and the object of bliss: *niraste tv avidyā-kṛte viṣaya-viṣayi-vibhāge vidyayā svābhāvikaḥ paripūrṇa eka ānando 'dvaito bhavati* (TBh 2,8,2 Ān p. 85); *sa eṣa paramānandaḥ svābhāviko 'dvaitatvād ānandānandinoś cāvibhāgo 'tra* (2,8,4 Ān p. 87). Negatively expressed: *abhinnaḥ svābhāvika ānandaḥ paramātmaiva na viṣaya-viṣayi-saṃbandha-janitaḥ* (2,8,5 Ān p. 88). And once again: *taṃ brahmaṇa ānandam . . . sarvaiṣaṇā-vinirmuktasyātma-bhūtaṃ viṣaya-viṣayi-saṃbandha-vinirmuktaṃ svābhāvikaṃ nityam avibhaktaṃ paramān-andaṃ brahmaṇo vidvān . . . na bibheti kutaścana* (2,9 Ān p. 96).[26]

In one work of Śaṅkara's which because of the verse of obeisance can be put down as possibly or probably early, namely in USP 17, there is an allusion to just this place in the Upaniṣad which was paraphrased and interpreted in the portion of the commentary just cited. USP 17,63 runs: *yasmād bhītāḥ pravartante vāṅ-manaḥ-pāvakādayaḥ / tad-ātmānanda-tattva-jño na bibheti kutaścana.* "Out of the fear of which move speech, mind, wind, and (all the forces in men and in the world)—he who knows the bliss of this self in its essence is afraid of nothing."

But the same verse-*prakaraṇa* of US contains (in verse 13) also the characterization of the self as *sac-cin-mātra,* thus with *ānanda* omitted. This is in agreement with the reservation which can ordinarily be observed in all genuine works of Śaṅkara, with the exception of MāBh and a few places in the TBh.[27] He mostly describes the self positively only as spirit (*cit* and other words). The second prose-*prakaraṇa* of US, which expounds the ātman doctrine in the greatest detail, deals with this alone.[28]

On the one hand, Śaṅkara is hesitant about characterizing the self as the primordial being *(sat);* on the other, such characterization is superfluous in his system. He has doubts because this would mean, according to his conception which is here influenced by the Vaiśeṣika system, the inclusion of the self, identical with Brahman, under a class: "Brahman, however, does not belong to any class, hence it cannot be named by words like 'being.' "[29] It is superfluous because he reduces all being to spirit: "that about which there is no absence of knowledge is being."[30] "All changes of the body, the organs, etc., exist only insofar as that which is the substrate of all exists: the essential self, the subsistent spirit."[31] "Brahman can be the substrate of anything only through causing manifestedness."[32] Although Śaṅkara's lukewarm interest in the concept of *sat* is thus based on systematic grounds, we may conjecture here also a connection with his Yoga origins, for Yoga determines the self solely as "spirit-power" (*citi-śakti* YS 4,34), whereas being, in this dualistic system, is relegated entirely to the side of primordial matter.

Śaṅkara's reservations with regard to the traditional characterization of the self (or Brahman) as primordial being have been sketched here in passing, because only with that in view can we fully comprehend his even more reserved attitude toward the equally traditional characterization of the self (and of Brahman) as *ānanda*. His aim is, above all, to prevent any misunderstanding of the doctrine of the absolute oneness of essence of the Absolute. In his explanation of the words *vijñānam ānandam brahma* at BUp 3,9,28,7, Śaṅkara says first that *ānanda* means that Brahman, described as *vijñāna,* is "not, like the knowledge of objects, permeated by sorrow," "but lucid, beneficent, incomparable, without exertion, eternally satisfied, always having the same essence."[33] In the thorough discussion which follows, he criticizes the view that this *ānanda* is felt or sensed. The liberated man is "like a handful of water poured into the ocean: he has then no separate existence so that he could experience Brahman which is *ānanda.* It is then senseless to say that the liberated man feels his self, which is of the nature of bliss."[34] And about Brahman also one cannot say that it feels its bliss: "Since Brahman experiences its bliss continuously, it is senseless to imagine that it experiences or does not experience. The experience of its own bliss by Brahman is continuous because it is its own essence."[35] The characterization of Brahman as *vijñāna* and *ānanda* is intended, Śaṅkara says in conclusion, as an explanation of essence *(svarūpānvākhyāna);* it should not be taken to mean that the bliss of the self is the object of a feeling *(saṃvedya).*

That *ānanda* is part of the nature of the self, is *svābhāvika* to it, was already declared by the TBh. But this text still speaks of an "inseparability of the subject and object of bliss" (*ānandānandinoś cāvibhāgaḥ,* see above). In the strict formulation of the doctrine of the oneness of the self's essence, identical with Brahman, as it is given in the BBh, there can be no question of such a coincidence. At BBh 4,4,6, in a discussion of the nature of liberation, Śaṅkara touches on the subject of *ānanda* again, independently of the Upaniṣad text interpreted here. He is critical of the view that liberation is the manifestation of a distinct new consciousness *(vijñāna)* and of a distinct new *ānanda.*[36] He argues thus: *vijñāna* and *ānanda* are essential properties *(dharma)* of the same substrate *(āśraya);* they can never, therefore, stand to each other in the relation of subject and object.[37] In view of the TBh we can add that it would be senseless and misleading to speak here of a cessation, a coincidence, or a nondistinction of subject and object of bliss.

This transformation of the *ānanda* doctrine reduces it to a minimalistic interpretation which disregards the content of the concept of *ānanda* or *sukha* when its appearance in a basic text requires its exegesis, as at BSBh 1,1,19 and ChBh 7,23–24,1, or which amounts to a merely negative explanation of the *ānanda* character of the Absolute, as at MuBh 1,2,7: *'ānanda-rūpam' sarvānarthaduḥkhāyāsaprahīnam.* It is a transformation which runs parallel to a transformation in the conception of the subject-object relation. So long as this relation is conceived as emerging from the one spiritual reality through vibration, and consequently is capable of dissolving again into that, we can, with this in mind, speak of a nondistinction of the subject and object of bliss. Śaṅkara knew that the doctrine of a consciousness seemingly dividing into subject and object, but in reality remaining pure, was of Buddhistic origin.[38] Nevertheless, he accepted it for a while (cf. MāBh 4,99). Later, however, he energetically distanced himself from Buddhism on this point. At BBh 4,3,7 he argues, in a very formalistic way, thus: that consciousness should appear as subject and object and thus be stained is impossible, for, what is, i.e., being (as such he takes pure consciousness), cannot have any connection with what is not, i.e., nonbeing. But when there is no connection with another (when the other is rather a property of being), the property intrinsic to a thing cannot be separated from it, for it belongs to its nature. For this reason, it is untenable to assume that through connection with another (reading *anya*), consciousness can be stained and can afterwards be purified.[39] This signifies the final rejection of the explanation of the subject-object relation as resulting from the vibration of pure consciousness.

A new interpretation of this relation is presented in greater detail in the introduction to BSBh and, in summary form, in GBh, 13, 26. Here the Mīmāṃsā doctrine, according to which 'the self' is what is meant by the word 'I,' is presupposed. Further, Śaṅkara goes to work here with the concepts of superimposition and nescience, which were probably in use even before Śaṅkara in a Vedānta which was not yet radically monistic. The effect of nescience is now no longer (as in MāBh and TBh) the subject-object relation as such, but the mutual superimposition of the subject on the object and of the object on the subject. By "object" is meant here specially the psychosomatic complex of body and inner sense. On the basis of Śaṅkara's other works, we can add (and Padmapāda will develop this point in his own manner) that the empirical *(vyāvahārika)* subject, the 'I,' is part of the objective realm; the self in its authentic character is beyond the subject as knower of things. But it is also present in the latter, as that which at all renders possible the "becoming manifest" of a thing. In the language of the AiBh text quoted above, it is the "subsistent contemplation of the self," *nityātmano dṛṣṭiḥ,* which is opposed to the "intermittent external contemplation," *bāhyānitya-dṛṣṭiḥ* (the 'I,' the psyche) as object. When the concept of the object is thus understood as inclusive of the 'I' and that of the subject in the sense of a "correlate of object" *(viṣayin),* evidently subject and object must be held to be, in the language of the BSBh introduction, absolutely distinct, "of contrary natures like light and darkness" *(tamaḥ-prakāśavad viruddha-svabhāvau).* True being then consists no longer (as in MāBh and TBh) in a unity of subject and object or in annulment of the opposition between the two, but it lies in the subject. Since the truth is realized through the insight into the unity of the self and the nullity of the objects, one can no longer with consistency speak of the self as being of the nature of bliss. To speak of *ānanda* is bound to awaken memory of the objective; even psychic states and functions, even a feeling of bliss, for example, are held to be objective. Śaṅkara therefore prefers not to speak of it. The insight immediately annuls itself as a psychical function; only the one spiritual reality is, as it has always been, beyond all time.

Other Vedāntins like Maṇḍanamiśra and Vimuktātman have sought to develop, it is true, the doctrine of the self as *ānanda* by means of monistic arguments in a less rigorous manner on this point than Śaṅkara, and that, too, in a direction in which Śaṅkara had still been moving in TBh:

> Worldly bliss attains its highest point when outer (objective) and inner (subjective) conditions are fully given. (The Upaniṣad) speaks of this as an example, in order to lead, through analogy, to the bliss of Brahman. For it is through this universally known bliss that the bliss which is attainable through the elimination of representations of objects can be grasped analogically. Even worldly pleasure is a

small part of just this bliss of Brahman. When consciousness is darkened by nescience and nescience mounts up, it (bliss) becomes in this world unsteady and worldly, for god Brahmā and others experience it as determined by their karma and, in accordance with their consciousness, by its association with objective conditions. But the more the power of nescience, desire, and karma declines, the more does bliss manifest itself in ever higher stages: that same bliss which is immediately known to those who are not struck down by desire, who know and are versed in the Vedas, is experienced by men, gandharvas, etc., multiplying itself hundredfold at each stage up to Brahmā Hiraṇyagarbha.[40]

Whether "Brahman-bliss" is here conceived as the bliss of the god Brahmā or as the bliss of the Absolute *(brahman)* remains, it must be admitted, uncertain. It is said, anyhow, that the degree of blessedness depends upon the degree of decrease in nescience and that the highest blessedness becomes "accessible through the elimination of objective representations," thus at least in deep meditation, pertaining to an apophatic Yoga, even if this bliss is not liberation itself.

4. Retrospect and Prospect Considering the resoluteness with which Śaṅkara professes the monism of spirit, it is all the more surprising that this central point of his system should be developed so weakly by means of arguments, as compared to the illusionism which is accessory to it and complements it. Śaṅkara can indeed provide some good reasons for his practice of referring mostly to the Upaniṣads when it comes to monism, but the problem remains (section 1).

If the YV is an early work of the same Śaṅkara who wrote the BSBh, and if in the course of his life he moved over from Yoga to Advaita, a solution easily suggests itself. The agreement of his avidyology with that of Yoga—all the more striking as on this point he diverges from other monists of spirit—as well as his habit of philosophizing about the self as also about God largely without regard to monism, is satisfactorily explained by the assumption that when thinking argumentatively, Śaṅkara largely moves along the lines, so familiar to him, of the Yoga system, which was not monistic. A couple of other facts also permit themselves to be coordinated meaningfully in this manner (section 2).

Assuming that Śaṅkara's Advaita period begins with the study of Gauḍapāda and the composition of the MāBh, we can see that he has gradually distanced himself somewhat from this starting point. Internal criteria agree with one that is external: those works which contain verses of obeisance prove to be probably earlier also when we analyze their contents. In any case, this can be established with some probability for four of these writings: for the pre-Vedāntic YV, the MāBh, the TBh, and for USP 19. USP 17 also appears to belong to the earlier period.

Works belonging to the later period are: USG, most of the *prakaraṇas* in USP, BBh, ChBh, KePBh, KeVBh, KaBh, MuBh, PBh, AiBh, ĪBh, GBh, and APV.

All these works (except for YV, which must be judged separately) have, quite apart from differences of development, an imposing number of common traits which mark them off from the works of other Advaitins, even those of the direct disciples of Śaṅkara. I refer for these criteria to my article, "Eigentümlichkeiten der Lehre und Terminologie Śaṅkaras" (in ZDMG 100, 1950), to my treatise "Vivarta" (Akademie Mainz, 1953), to my article, "Relations of Early Advaitins to Vaiṣṇavism" (in WZKSO 9, 1965) as well as to the works of Sengaku Mayeda, who has established the authenticity of the US, the GBh and the Ke-Bhāṣyas by applying my criteria.[41] For the MāBh, Tilman Vetter has collected together the marks of authenticity in his contribution to the present volume.[42] A couple of minor criteria are not yet mentioned perhaps in the works mentioned above; for example, the words *jaḍa* in the sense of *acetana,* and *sphuraṇa* or *sphūrti* in the sense of *abhivyakti,* as also *sva(yaṃ)-prakāśa (māna)* in the sense of *svayaṃjyotis* (cf. below, section 5) do not occur in the authentic works of Śaṅkara. It appears that the criteria used by us are a sieve, with mesh wide enough to sift out spuria, yet narrow enough to retain developments within the Advaita period of Śaṅkara. In any case, they have been repeatedly subjected to the only possible test by being applied to Advaita texts about which it is known that they have an author other than Śaṅkara, each time with the result that the criteria came into conflict with the text. So far as works ascribed to a Śaṅkara (Śaṅkarācārya or Śaṅkara-Bhagavat, -Bhagavatpāda or -Bhagavatpūjyapāda) are concerned, the result, so far as I can see, is that all independent works ascribed to him, with the exception of the twenty-two *prakaraṇas* collected in the US, as well as all commentaries not mentioned in the foregoing, are inauthentic.

From what has been presented so far, the hypothesis of a transition from Yoga to Advaita by Śaṅkara and of a development within his monistic period may appear perhaps fit for adoption. Nevertheless, it still remains to be shown how, precisely in his own Advaitic thinking, Śaṅkara has assimilated contents and modes of thought with which he was familiar in his Yoga period. When we do this, the finding at which we arrived in section 1 will be further clarified, and the hypothesis of this article, if correct, will gain in probability. At the same time we shall be able to grasp the originality of Śaṅkara with greater clarity.

5. Adaptation of the Doctrines of the Yoga System To begin with, let us briefly explain two terms: *samyagdarśana* and *pratyupasthāpita.*

Samyagdarśana is common in the Yoga system, e.g., YBh 2,15 p. 165; 168; 170. In Vedānta this term appears to be peculiar to Śaṅkara's vocabulary. He uses it often and has doubtless brought it along from his Yoga period.

Pratyupasthāpita describes the manner in which nescience produces its effect.[43] The word occurs only in conjunction with *avidyā* and is characteristic of Śaṅkara's terminology. Naturally, it could not be used so by Yoga, since this system is not monistic, nor illusionistic. But the beginnings of such usage can be seen to be present in YBh, in YV, and also in YD. *Pratyupasthāna* means in YD p. 98, 24 "the becoming present" *(maraṇam iti pūrva-kṛtasya karmaṇaḥ phala-bhoga-parisamāpteḥ sāmpratasya ca phala-bhogasya pratyupasthāne liṅgasya pūrva-śarīra-tyāgaḥ),* as well as BSBh 4,3,10 *(kārya-brahma-loka-pralaya-pratyupasthāne sati . . .).* Correspondingly, we have *pratyupasthita* in YBh 4,14 p. 340f. as "present" *(tatheti pratyupasthitam idaṃ sva-māhātmyena vastu).* Without the prefix *prati-,* but in causative form: *upasthāpita* at YBh 3,17 p. 266, at YV p. 267 paraphrased as *pratyupanīta,* thus with *prati-,* but another root. As a noun derived from the causative: *pratyupasthāpaka* at YV 1,6–7 p. 22. Inspired by the use of these words in the Yoga system, Śaṅkara as Vedāntin then described the effects caused by *avidyā* as "made present, made to appear, through *avidyā, avidyā-pratyupasthāpita.*

As is well-known, the psychology of Vedānta is very similar to Sāṃkhya, especially the variety of Sāṃkhya contained in Pātañjala-Yoga. In contrast to Sāṃkhya, Yoga leaves the inner sense undifferentiated, and Śaṅkara in particular almost wholly abstains from differentiating it. The Yoga system mostly calls it *citta,* but also *buddhi* and *manas;* Śaṅkara designates it as *antaḥkaraṇa, buddhi, manas,* or *citta,* mostly indiscriminately, or he distinguishes, sometimes merely verbally, between *manas* and *buddhi.* Neither in Yoga nor in Śaṅkara is *ahaṃkāra* a psychic faculty;

this word, just like *ahaṃpratyaya,* "the I concept," is used by Śaṅkara in YV 2,6–7 as a synonym for "I-am-ness," the *asmitā* of Yoga.[44]

The inner sense has functions which, in Yoga as in Śaṅkara, are called *vṛtti* or *pratyaya.* These terms seem to hark back to two distinct historical origins. *Vṛtti* is associated more with *citta, pratyaya* with *buddhi.* Five classes of *vṛtti* are enumerated in YS 1,6 *(pramāṇa-viparyaya-vikalpa-nidrā-smṛtayaḥ),* and many more *pratyaya* or *buddhidharma* in YBh 2,18 (a different version in YV): *grahaṇa, dhāraṇa, vijñāna* (only in YV), *ūha, apoha, tattvajñāna* (only in YBh), *kriyā, vacana, yathānyāyāvadhāraṇa* (the last three only in YV), *abhiniveśa.* The *vṛttis* are defined as "pure *pratyayas*" at YV 2,3 p. 126: *pratyayamātrā hi vṛttayaḥ.* Particularly characteristic of the Advaitin Śaṅkara, as compared to other Advaitins, seems the expression *bauddhaḥ pratyayaḥ* (representation of the inner sense). This is common also in YBh of Vyāsa (e.g., 2,20); in Śaṅkara it occurs as often in YV (e.g., 2,18) as in other places in his Advaita writings, where he speaks about the relation of the self to the psyche.

These functions, also called *buddhidharmāḥ* by Śaṅkara at YV 2,18 as well as at KeVBh 1,3, are superimposed *(adhyāropita)* on the self (YV 2,18: *puruṣa;* KeVBh 1,3: *sarvātman*), as if this were their agent. The reason for this, according to Vyāsa, is that the self *(puruṣa)* is "the enjoyer of the fruit" of these functions. Although the "enjoying" *(bhoga)* as such "is done by the *buddhi* and exists only in the *buddhi,*" it is "ascribed" *(vyapadiśyate)* to the *puruṣa,* just as victory and defeat, won or suffered by the soldiers, are ascribed to the king: "for he is the enjoyer of their fruit." The word "enjoyer" was meant to give expression to the inactivity and neutrality (*mādhyasthyam akartṛbhāvaś ca* SK 19) of *puruṣa.* There is in it something of both the real and the illusory. Already as a Yogin, Śaṅkara accentuated this illusionism, as against Vyāsa, by characterizing in sharper language than the latter the *bhoga* taking place in *buddhi* as a mental state qualified by nescience (*bhoga-rūpasyāvidyā-lakṣaṇasya pratyayasya. . . .* YV 2,18), and he reduced the sense of the word "enjoyer" to the act of pure sensing (*bhokteti grahaṇādi phalasyopalabdhā,* ibid.). After this reduction then, all that was required to get to the Vedānta standpoint was just to drop the terms "enjoyer" and "enjoying" (as an Advaitin Śaṅkara launched a vehement attack against Sāṃkhya because of its teaching that the self is a *bhoktṛ:* PBh 6,3 Ān p. 66ff.). That the self is of the nature of *cit(i), citiśakti, caitanya, dṛś(i), draṣṭṛ, sākṣin, upalabdhṛ,* and *upalabdhi* is a doctrine common to Sāṃkhya, Yoga, and Vedānta; the expression *nityopalabdhisvarūpa,* occurring frequently in the Advaita works of Śaṅkara, is already to be found in YV (e.g., p. 191; *nityopalabdhṛsvarūpa* p. 348).

That Śaṅkara's Vedānta should coincide so largely, indeed almost entirely, with Sāṃkhya-Yoga in respect of the doctrine of the inner sense and its relation to the self is by no means self-evident. One would have expected far-reaching points in common with the other school of Vedic interpretation, Mīmāṃsā; after all, an earlier commentator, Upavarṣa (perhaps identical with the Vṛttikāra), had even expounded the basic texts of both the schools, the *Mīmāṃsā-sūtras* and the *Brahma-sūtras.* But what Śaṅkara has in common with Mīmāṃsā is confined to just this one point of ātmology: to the doctrine that the self is that which we mean by the word "I" (and naturally he had to modify even this). For the time being it is not possible to decide to what extent Śaṅkara, with his points of agreement with the "ātmology" and psychology ("cittology") of Yoga, follows an already existing (pre-monistic) Vedānta tradition, since no work of this literature except the enigmatic BS is any longer extant. But since he differs from other Advaitins on those points in ātmology as well as in avidyology which connect him with Yoga, we may assume for the time being that his relations with this system were particularly close as a result of his earlier allegiance to it.

Let us return to the introduction to the YV already mentioned in section 2 above. There, the contents of Yoga are divided into four sections *(vyūha),* in analogy with the system of therapeutics *(cikitsā-śāstra)* and in accordance with YS 2,15ff:

1. "*Saṃsāra,* which is full of suffering, is to be avoided." (This corresponds with the doctrine of disease in therapeutics, *roga.*)
2. "Its cause is the connection between the subject and the object, which rests on nescience" (this is the "cause of disease," *roga-hetuḥ*).
3. "The means of avoidance is the unerring clarity of discriminating knowledge" (this is the "means of cure," *bhaiṣajya*).
4. "When this is attained, nescience is removed and with that the connection between subject and object ceases absolutely; this is avoidance, i.e., absoluteness" (in therapeutics: "health," *ārogya*).[45]

It may be remarked incidentally that this division has also a certain similarity with the four noble truths of the Buddha. However, the first and the third truths—suffering and its removal—are gathered together, and in accordance with the more positive view of Brahmanism, a section on the aim—absoluteness, corresponding to health—has been added.

It is, of course, not inapt to divide the Yoga doctrine in this manner. But it must be remarked, in the first place, that there are many things in the system of Pātañjala-Yoga which do not quite fit into this schema, e.g., the doctrine of magical perfection *(siddhi),* and second, that this system, as presented in the Sūtras, is not so divided. This division is an interpretation by Śaṅkara. And it is quite in conformity with the strongly practical, didactic, indeed therapeutic, interest of Śaṅkara, which we can observe everywhere in his Advaita writings.[46]

It is therefore worth noting that one text in which Śaṅkara the Advaitin presented what was essential in his doctrine, without reference to any texts requiring explanation and in a purely argumentative manner, reverts to the same schema of division which he had already set up as a Yogin. The idea of therapy had indeed now to move into the background (cf. above, section 2), but the disposition of the second prose-*prakaraṇa* of US corresponds exactly with the four-*vyūha* division. USG 45–47 deals with the suffering of *saṃsāra,* section 48 begins with the teaching on the cause of suffering: nescience. Without any sharp break this passes over gradually, from about section 58, into instruction in discriminating knowledge.[47] USG 109 depicts the attainment of the goal.

But the closeness to Yoga on many points can be seen not merely in the disposition but also in the details of the discussion, whether it be as criticism or as assimilation.

The suffering of saṃsāra rests on nescience: this is what Śaṅkara teaches in YV as well as in USG (48). What does nescience do? According to YS 2,5, it makes us regard what is ephemeral, impure, sorrowful, and not-self as enduring, as pure, as happiness, and as the self. That is an originally Buddhistic doctrine.[48] In Hinduism it is not merely adopted by Pātañjala-Yoga; with the exception of the impure which is regarded as pure, these erroneous assumptions are enumerated also by Prabhākara as "mistaken views which cause saṃsāra."[49] Śaṅkara the Advaitin would naturally accept this doctrine (cf. USG 15, for example, for the confusion between the self and the not-self). But it is expressed in a purely negative way (as early Buddhism preferred to do). On the contrary, where he explains nescience, Śaṅkara already indicates his positive aim by introducing his God-soul monism and his doctrine of the constant presence of the self: "You hold that which is the highest self and does not tarry in saṃsāra for its opposite, when you believe 'I am in saṃsāra'; about that which is not an agent, not an enjoyer and is (eternally) present, you believe that it is an agent, an enjoyer, and not (eternally) present. That is nescience" (USG 50). What is negative here is only the view that the self is not an agent and is not an enjoyer. In this, Śaṅkara continues what he had already taught as a Yogin. As we have seen, he had in fact turned away, already in YV, from the doctrine (accepted generally in Yoga) that the self is an "enjoyer." That the self is "present" *(vidyamāna)* is in effect nothing else than the doctrine of *nityopalabdhi* which Śaṅkara had already, as a Yogin, advocated and which he enters into in detail in the US sequence.

Nescience is superimposition (*adhyāropaṇā,* USG 51); superimposition *(adhyāsa)* is nescience (BSBh, introduction, K 52). The fact that Śaṅkara characterizes this definition in the introduction to BSBh as the view of the pandits, and in US lets the pupil present it as a knowledge which he has already acquired, suggests that he by no means regarded it as a doctrine peculiar to his Advaita. With Prabhākara, *adhyāsa* is simply a word for "error" (Bṛ on MS 1,1,5 p. 61). It is true that in Yoga the concept of superimposition is not used to explain the phenomenon of error in general; nevertheless, it is used to describe the error most important for the system, that of the superimposition of the functions of the inner sense on the self (e.g., YV 1,4 p. 14; YBh and YV 2,18 p. 181). Because this was the central and fundamental error also for the Advaitin Śaṅkara, he made the concept of superimposition the central point in his theory of nescience. Here he stopped half-way, with only a partial illusionism, as it is in essence present already in Sāṃkhya and Yoga: it is an error to ascribe to the body or to the inner sense what is proper to the self and vice versa. Advaita Vedānta, however, required a theory which could permit the world as such to be understood as an illusion; because the *adhyāsa* doctrine did not accomplish this, it lost its importance subsequent to Śaṅkara and was preserved only as a legacy of tradition.

Not only the incomplete illusionism of the *adhyāsa* doctrine, but to an even greater extent all the other pronouncements of Śaṅkara the Advaitin on nescience, agree so largely with Yoga that one is forced to notice the influence of this system here, even if we did not know that there is a *Yogabhāṣyavivaraṇa* by Śaṅkara-Bhagavat. Just as Vyāsa at YBh 1,8 equates error (*viparyaya = mithyājñāna,* YS 1,8) with *avidyā,* so also for the Advaitin Śaṅkara there is no difference between the concepts of *avidyā* or *ajñāna,* on the one hand, and *mithyājñāna,* on the other, whereas other Advaitins posit *avidyā (ajñāna)* as the cause of *mithyājñāna.* For the Advaitin Śaṅkara, just as in Yoga, *avidyā* is the cause of non-liberation, its consequences, and accompanying manifestations; for the other Advaitins it is the *causa materialis* of the world characterized by materiality and multiplicity. Just as in Yoga, so also in the thinking of the Advaitin Śaṅkara, *avidyā* is one of the many *kleśas* (or *doṣas*); for other Advaitins, it is something unique.[50] It remains to be added that it is not the Advaitin Śaṅkara who (in the introduction to BSBh K45) first refers to *adhyāsa,* in essential agreement with Prabhākara, as "having the form of memory" *(smṛtirūpa),*[51] but that already as a Yogin he had propounded the theory that error is "the representation, appearing in the form of clear knowledge, conjoined with the remembrance of another thing earlier perceived, of (a man) who has grasped (a thing) merely in general and not in its particularity."[52] It seems to me that the simplest explanation of these points of agreement is that in his argumentative thinking Śaṅkara as Advaitin continued to use, so far as this was at all possible, the concepts which were familiar to him from the school of Yoga.

According to the introduction to YV, nescience brings about, as we have seen, "a connection between subject and object: *draṣṭṛ-dṛśya-saṃyoga.* We have already discussed how Śaṅkara interpreted the subject-object relation under the influence of Gauḍapāda and how he later altered his view on this. Śaṅkara as Yogin looked upon the "connection" of the subject with the object as an effect (which has to be annulled) of nescience, and this view is closer to his later Advaita period than to the earlier, in which the influence of Gauḍapāda was even stronger. In the later period subject and object are, of course, absolutely separated and essentially different, and only nescience mutually superimposes them, throws them upon each other, thus producing something like a "connection." It cannot in fact be denied that this view is closer to Yoga than the theory (inspired by Buddhism through Gauḍapāda) of the bifurcation of the one spiritual reality into subject and object through the action of a vibration of the *manas* or *citta.* Nevertheless, Śaṅkara has here not simply reverted to the conception of Yoga. The concept of being connected, of *saṃyoga,* was no longer acceptable to him as an Advaitin. In the US this concept is brought into the discussion (USG 55) by the pupil; it is part of the role of the disciple also to give expression to views which are prevalent outside the Advaita system, so that they may then be accepted by the teacher (as in the case of *adhyāropaṇā*) or be criticized by him, as in the case of *saṃyoga.* The pupil opines that it is more appropriate to assume that the body and the self are connected with each other rather than superimposed upon each other. This fits in precisely with YS 2,17: *draṣṭṛ-dṛśyayoḥ saṃyogo heya-hetuḥ.* Of course, this connection is, also according to Yoga, conditioned by nescience (*tasya hetur avidyā,* YS 2,24; *tad-abhāvāt saṃyogābhāvaḥ* . . . 2,25), and in his comments on 2,18 Vyāsa also speaks of superimposition. But, having made superimposition the central point of his reflections on the nugatory and the perishable, he dropped the relatively cruder concept of "connection." It is no longer the case, as it still is in YV, that the connection is brought about through superimposition, for in the later view there is no "connection" at all of the subject with the object, but only a mutual "superimposition."

Some concepts, however, which are indissolubly associated with "connectedness" in the thinking of Yoga retain their meaning for Śaṅkara; they appear also in the sequence of the discussion in US. Being conjoined with another, being composite, signifies, according to an axiom of Sāṃkhya-Yoga, existing-for-another *(parārthatva),* not the existence of things joined together for each other, for they have become one, but generally existence for another, not-being-for-itself, not-being-independent. As an example of this both Vyāsa at YBh 4,24 and Śaṅkara (USG 55; KaBh 2,2,5) mention a house. However the "other," for which what has been joined together exists, is not, according to YBh 4,24, any other in general *(para-sāmānya-mātra),* but the self *(puruṣa).* Things exist "for" the *puruṣa,* for "the purpose of the *puruṣa,*" in two ways: either for "enjoying" or for "liberation." But this principle is widened into a general philosophical statement in the USG dialogue: the nonspiritual exists in general for the spiritual (56; 70f.). The unspiritual is here also what has been joined together *(saṃhata),* whereas the spiritual self is the absolutely simple. All things, through their existence for another, have in the end reference to the spiritual self.

There can hardly be any question of monism here; we may even go so far as to say that the notion of existence for the self actually excludes any kind of monism that allows true being only to the one self. With a slight, almost imperceptible adjustment, Śaṅkara has overcome the narrowness of Sāṃkhya-Yoga, in which the existence "for" the *puruṣa* was in the end only intended to demonstrate how the isolation of the *puruṣa* could be rendered possible, and laid down a significant principle which is nothing short of a challenge to go beyond spiritual monism in the direction of a philosophy of being which relies on analogy. This beginning, however, forthwith sank back into illusionism again; it had become possible only through the attempt to think Vedāntically along the lines of Sāṃkhya-Yoga.

In the context of the deliberations on the simplicity or being-for-itself of the spiritual self, in USG (71;73) as already in YV (4,19. 24), the Buddhistic view that a moment of consciousness *(saṃvid),* like a lamp, illumines both itself and other things, is rejected. It is not moments of consciousness that illumine themselves and an object; it is rather the self which "sees" the functions of the inner sense (*pratyayānupaśya,* YS 2,20) as objects (*dṛśya,* YS 4,19) and thus also the external objects which "become attached" to the inner sense or "mount" upon it (*buddhi-sattvopārūḍhāḥ sarve dharmāḥ,* YBh 2,17; *sva-buddhy-ārūḍham sarvam,* USG 73). The inner sense gets connected with the outer objects through the "canal" *(praṇālikā, praṇāḍikā)* of the senses; they "color" it *(uparāga)* in accordance with their form (*ākāra,* YBh and YV on YS 1,6–7, p. 19). The notion of the objectivity of the mental sphere, which has its origin in Sāṃkhya, is retained by Śaṅkara and by Vedānta generally; the concept of "coloring," however, is abandoned by Śaṅkara (Padmapāda will again accept it).

In the Buddhistic doctrine under attack, the metaphor of "illumination" was used. Within Sāṃkhya and Yoga this cannot be applied to the self, the *puruṣa.* "Illumination" or "light," *prakāśa,* is stated in YS 2,18 (beside *kriyā* and *sthiti*) as a characteristic of just the objective, so that "light" belongs to the *sattva-guṇa* ("activity" to the *rajo-guṇa,* "persistence" to the *tamo-guṇa*). Because the inner sense is distinguished by the dominance of *sattva,* it is of the nature of light.[53] Now in his discussion of YS 4,19 mentioned above, Śaṅkara refers to knowledge as being of the nature of light or as luminous (*jñānasya prakāśa-svarūpatvāt,* p. 350 bottom), again in agreement with the Prābhākara school of Mīmāṃsā (as in the explanation of error as having the "form of remembrance"). As an Advaitin he then worked out the notion of light into a full-fledged theory of illumination. Not only knowledge, but the self itself, is of the nature of light. It seems that it was his achievement to have built up this doctrine and that here he was not echoing any predecessor. True, he was inspired in this by (Prābhākara-) Mīmāṃsā, but the essential content of his doctrine was conceived by him in the interpretation of BUp 4,3,7 (to which we shall revert shortly). This is shown in the terminology: he always designates the nature of being a light-unto-itself of the self with the expression *svayaṃjyotis,* borrowed from BUp 4,3,9 (only in the verses of the US does *svayaṃprabha*[54] occur a couple of times: 10,3; 11,11); as against this, the Prābhākaras spoke of *svayaṃprakāśa (māna),*[55] a usage which is traceable among Advaitins since Padmapāda.

The doctrine of light had, in the first place, the advantage that it could describe the nature of the self as spirit more emphatically and vividly than was possible through the means of Yoga and Sāṃkhya. It is surely not a very convincing image of freedom to conceive of the self as "seeing," which it can do only in the light of the most subtle matter of which the inner sense is composed. In Śaṅkara's doctrine, made possible through the meeting of Yoga, Mīmāṃsā, and Vedānta, the inner sense (which one may also call psyche) and the self are to each other as *intellectus* and *lumen intellectuale.* Since the light of spirit was conceived merely as subsistent, this view did not go beyond the monism of spirit.

In the second place, the theory of light gave triumphant expression to the self-evident nature of the self *(svataḥsiddhatva),* and it was not any longer necessary to bother oneself, as in Sāṃkhya, about arguments. Because it is itself light, the self is better known than things which come to be given *(siddhi)* only in the process of knowledge, although, or rather just because, it can never become the object of knowledge. This doctrine, too, does not in itself necessitate monism.

In the course of the further discussion in USG it is shown how the self makes all functions of the psyche known, itself remaining invariably unaltered. This also in itself is the teaching of Yoga.[56] Śaṅkara, however, conjoins it with the concept of the "result of knowledge" *(pramāṇaphala),* as he had already, as Yogin, described it (perhaps again under the influence of Prābhākara-Mīmāṃsā) in connection with YBh 1,6–7, p. 22: *phalam . . . pauruṣeyaś citta-vṛtti-bodhaḥ* "the result . . . is the *puruṣa*'s taking notice of the functions of the inner sense." Only as Vedāntin has Śaṅkara combined into a unity the doctrines of the unchanging seeing and lighting of the self and of the result of knowledge; this constitutes the culminating point of the discussion of the US. Here again one can leave monism out of account.

As already suggested, in his interpretation of BUp 4,3,7 Śaṅkara has developed his doctrine of illumination as the central point of an anthropology. The self is the inner light *(antarjyotis),* which gives unity (*ekīkṛtya,* BBh, 4,3,7, Ān p. 535, Bhagavat p. 241, line 3) to the psychosomatic complex.[57] This light illuminates the inner sense—here for once differentiated into *buddhi* and *manas*—the senses and the whole body. It is for-itself *(svārtha);* the psychosomatic complex, of which all the other auxiliaries that enable its orientation are for-others *(parārtha),* can begin to function only through it *(vyavahārāya kalpate).* It is the *anugrāhaka* of the organs, that through the favor or grace of which alone they can function, for, all activity is accompanied by reference to I *(sābhimāna),* and the core of I is, as Śaṅkara takes for granted with Mīmāṃsā, the self (Ān p. 536, Bhagavat p. 241; the same doctrine summed up briefly at GBh 18,50, Bhagavat p. 280). Yoga concepts again are assimilated in this doctrine. Two of these have already been mentioned: *svārtha* and *parārtha.* Because of the fact that the inner sense "connects" *(saṃpṛkta, saṃyukta)* itself with the light of the self, it becomes an "organ for all," *sarvārtha-karaṇa,* as in YS 4,23, where it becomes *sarvārtha* through a mutual "coloring over" with the *puruṣa.* Thus—and only thus—the inner sense also becomes the "lamp," which, according to the Sāṃkhya-Yoga doctrine, it already is because of its sattva-nature. Moreover, the other organs are merely "doors" of the inner sense, *dvāra-mātrāṇi* (Ān p. 533, Bhagavat p. 240, line 16). We should recall here that at YV 1,6–7, p. 19, Śaṅkara had paraphrased the word *praṇālikā* (mentioned above) of the YBh with *dvāra.* The Yoga concept of mutual "coloring" does not fit in with the doctrine of light; it is substituted by that of "reflection" (*chāyā,* Ān p. 535, Bhagavat p. 241). The reflection emanates from the self, whereas its light in turn takes on the color of that which it illumines (Ān p. 537, Bhagavat p. 242).

The most striking similarity to Yoga is exhibited in the doctrine of illumination in Śaṅkara's interpretation of the word *samāna* at BUp 4,3,7: *sa samānaḥ sann ubhau lokāv anusaṃcarati.* An interpretation which is not forced will take the word as meaning "common" or "the same": The *puruṣa* wanders through both the worlds (that of waking and of dreaming) as "the same" or as "common to both." But Śaṅkara interprets the word in the sense of "similar," *sadṛśa,* in spite of the fact that he has first to search in the context for a word which might indicate that to which the *puruṣa* is similar. What he finds is: "similar to the heart," and this is taken to mean "similar to the inner sense." This forced interpretation was only possible because Śaṅkara called to mind YS 1,4, where there is mention of the "similarity" of the self with the functions of the inner sense: *vṛtti-sārūpyam,* and commenting on which in his YV, he had paraphrased *sarūpa* with *sadṛś.* In the context of the light theory, it is true, similarity acquires another sense than it had in Yoga.

The exposition given above may perhaps suffice to show that precisely where Śaṅkara thinks independently, he again and again inserts Yoga concepts in his speculation and argumentation in such a manner, it is true, that in the new context they become something different from what they were in the Yoga system. Since, however, they were unmonistic, they were helpful in permitting Śaṅkara to disregard or leave in suspense (without himself noticing it) the obligatory monism of his school when, with his eye on the matter in hand, he philosophized on the self. The original creation of the illumination theory thus came about in the fruitful encounter between the Upaniṣads, Yoga, and Mīmāṃsā, in which the self is acknowledged as the luminous principle of the inner unity of the person; the partial illusionism appended to this doctrine does not go organically with it.

Summary[58] Among the works ascribed to Śaṅkara-Bhagavat there is, beside those of Advaita contents, the *Yogabhāṣyavivaraṇa,* which is a subcommentary on Vedavyāsa's *Yogabhāṣya* and was published as late as 1952 (Madras Government Oriental Series, vol. 94). The identity of the author of this work with that of the *Brahmasūtrabhāṣya* can be established on the assumption that Śaṅkara was first an adherent of Pātañjala Yoga and then turned an Advaitin. This assumption can be substantiated by the observation, in the authentic Advaita works of Śaṅkara, of some features which, while bearing a striking resemblance to doctrines of the Yoga system, distinguish Śaṅkara's thought from that of other known Advaita authors. These features, especially peculiarities in the doctrines of Nescience and of the Self, are easily explainable as survivals of a Yogic way of thinking or as adaptations of Yoga ideas to the tenets of Advaita. A few Advaita works of Śaṅkara exhibit a closer proximity than the rest to the terminology and concepts of the Yoga system; this fact suggests that they are the earliest ones written after the author's transition from Yoga to Vedānta. It is conceivable that Śaṅkara was introduced into Advaita by a teacher who interpreted to him Gauḍapāda's *Māṇḍūkyakārikās,* and he did his work so well that the teacher entrusted him with writing a commentary on that poem. The *Māṇḍūkyabhāṣya* stands unique among Śaṅkara's writings by coming closest to Yoga, on the one hand, and exhibiting, on the other hand, some traits of monism which Śaṅkara seems to have dropped in his subsequent career. Closely related to the way of thinking of the *Māṇḍūkyabhāṣya* is Prakaraṇa 19 of the *Padyaprabandha* of the *Upadeśasāhasrī.* The *Taittirīyopaniṣadbhāṣya,* then, marks the transition from Śaṅkara's earlier period to his mature works. One of the main differences between the two periods concerns the interpretation of the subject-object relationship, which Śaṅkara had first explained as an illusory differentiation, consisting in a vibration of the mind, whereas he later described it as an illusory union, joining two absolutely distinct entities, namely the subject, which is real, and the object, which has but an illusory existence. The occurrence or non-occurrence of *maṅgala* verses also seems to deserve notice, for in some writings which include *maṅgalas,* initiatory or concluding, features are found that point to the early period, on the ground of the hypothesis delineated. It seems that Śaṅkara, who had introduced and concluded his *Yogabhāṣyavivaraṇa* with *maṅgala* verses, retained this practice in his Advaita period only as long as he remained in touch with his teacher.

The hypothesis presented here presupposes a solution of the problem of the authenticity of the works ascribed to Śaṅkara. The author of the present study has established a number of criteria, most of which are described in his earlier articles, and which seem to work as a sieve with a mesh wide enough to let pass spurious works and close enough to retain or admit even variations or developments among the authentic ones. The criteria have often been tested by being applied to Advaita works known to be composed by authors other than Śaṅkara, and each time the tested text proved to be at variance with the criteria. If they are applied to the writings attributed to Śaṅkara, it appears that all his independent works are collected in the 22 Prakaraṇas going under the name of *Upadeśasāhasrī,* all the rest being spurious. The authentic commentaries are those on the *Brahmasūtras,* on the *Bhagavadgītā,* on the *Adhyātmapaṭala* of the *Āpastamba-Dharmasūtra,* and on 10 Upaniṣads: *Bṛhadāraṇyaka, Chāndogya, Aitareya, Taittirīya, Kena* (both the *Padabhāṣya* and the *Vākyabhāṣya*), *Īśā, Kaṭha, Muṇḍaka, Praśna,* and *Māṇḍūkya,* the latter with Gauḍapāda's *Kārikās.*

It seems that three avenues of research have to be followed in conjunction and in mutual support: examination of the authenticity problem, reassessment of the doctrines peculiar to Śaṅkara, and investigation of the development of his thought.

Abbreviations

Ai	Aitareya
Ān	Ānandāśramasaṃskṛtagranthāvali
APV	Adhyātmapaṭalavivaraṇa
B	Bṛhadāraṇyaka
Bh	Bhāṣya
Bṛ	Bṛhatī of Prabhākara
BS	Brahmasūtra
Ch	Chāndogya
G	Bhagavadgītā
Ī	Īśā
K	Kashi Sanskrit Series

Ka	Kaṭha
Ke	Kena
KeP	Kena-Upaniṣad-Padabhāṣya
KeV	Kena-Upaniṣad-Vākyabhāṣya
Mā	Māṇḍūkya
MK	Māṇḍūkyakārikā of Gauḍapāda
MS	Mīmāṃsāsūtra
Mu	Muṇḍaka
P	Praśna
SK	Sāṃkhyakārikā
T	Taittirīya
Up	Upaniṣad (in the case of commentaries on Upaniṣads the sign Up is omitted, e.g., BBh)
US	Upadeśasāhasrī
USG	Upadeśasāhasrī-Gadyaprabandha
USP	Upadeśasāhasrī-Padyaprabandha
YBh	Yogasūtrabhāṣya of Vedavyāsa
YD	Yuktidīpikā
YS	Yogasūtra
YV	Yogasūtrabhāṣya-Vivaraṇa of Śaṅkara-Bhagavatpāda

Editions Used

All Upaniṣads with Śaṅkara's commentaries referred to in this article are found in the edition by Bhagavat: *Works of Shankaracharya,* vol. 2. Part 1 (Poona, 2nd ed., 1927) contains Ī, Ai, Ka, KeP, KeV, Ch, T, Mā with MK, Mu; part 2 (Poona, 2nd ed., 1928) contains B.

See also the Upaniṣads with Śaṅkara's commentaries in Ān: AiBh, 5th ed., 1931; BBh, 1st ed., 1891; ChBh, 1st ed., 1890; ĪBh, 5th ed., 1927; KaBh, 7th ed., 1935; KePBh and KeVBh, 5th ed., 1926; MāBh, 6th ed., 1936; MuBh, 6th ed., 1936; PBh, 5th ed., 1932; TBh, 5th ed., 1929.

APV in: *Minor Works;* see below, under US.

BS and BSBh: K 71, 1929–1931; also Madras University Sanskrit Series, no. 9 (*Prakaṭārthavivaraṇam,* vols. 1–2, 1935–1939); *The Brahmasūtra Śāṅkara Bhāṣya* with the commentaries *Bhāmatī,* etc. (Bombay: Nirṇayasāgar Press, 2nd ed., 1938).

US: with the commentary of Rāmatīrtha (Bombay: Nirṇayasāgar Press, 3rd ed., 1930); with English translation by Jagadananda (Mylapore,

Madras: Ramakrishna Math, 2nd ed., 1949); also in the edition by Bhagavat: *Works of Shankaracharya,* vol. 4: *Minor Works* (Poona, 1925). USG was translated into German by P. Hacker (Bonn: Röhrscheid, 1949).

GBh: *The Works of Shankaracharya,* vol. 1: *The Geetabhashya,* ed. by Bhagavat (Poona, 2nd ed., 1929).

MK: *The Āgamaśāstra of Gauḍapāda,* ed., trans. and annotated by Vidhushekhara Bhattacharyya (Calcutta: University, 1943).

YS and YBh with the *Ṭīkā* of Vācaspatimiśra: Ān 47, 3rd ed., 1932.

YS and YBh with YV: Madras Government Oriental Series, no. 94, 1952.

Bṛ: Madras University Sanskrit Series, no. 3, parts 1–2, 1934–1936.

SK with YD: Calcutta Sanskrit Series, vol. 23, 1938.

MS with the *Bhāṣya* of Śabarasvāmin: Ān 97; also in Bṛ. *Nyāyasūtra* with the *Bhāṣya* of Vātsyāyana: Ān 91.

Notes

1. USG 109; for earlier hints, see 50; 56; 64.

2. On this, see my article in *Die Welt des Orients* 3 (Wuppertal, 1948), pp. 242ff. [*Kl. Schr.*, pp. 61ff.].

3. Cf. also my articles in: *ZDMG* 100 (1950), pp. 276–286, and *Studia Missionalia* 13 (Rome, 1963), pp. 48–52 [see *Kl. Schr.*, pp. 99–109; 288–292; and Chapters 4, pp. 85–96 and 7, pp. 169–172 in this volume].

4. Cf. for BSBh Paul Deussen, *Das System des Vedānta* (Leipzig, 1883), pp. 133ff.; further, perhaps KeVBh 3,14,1, where the proof proceeds from the concept of karma.

5. *na cārthavādāḥ śakyante kalpayitum. ananyayogitve sati vijñānotpādakatvāt. na cotpannaṃ vijñānam bādhyate. apratiṣedhāc ca. na ceśvaro nāstīti niṣedho 'sti.* KeVBh 3,14,1 Ān p. 26.

6. *na vākyasya vastv-anvākhyānaṃ kriyānvākhyānaṃ vā prāmāṇyāprāmāṇyakāraṇaṃ, kiṃ tarhi niścita-phalavad-vijñānotpādakatvam.* Ān p. 130; Bhagavat, p. 52f.

7. *na ca niścitam avagamyamānam idaṃ mithyā syāt. yo hi janitvā pradhvaṃsate: naitad evam iti, sa mithyā-pratyayaḥ.* Ān p. 15; Bṛ p. 26.

8. *na ca 'svargakāmo yajeta' ity ato vacanāt saṃdigdham avagamyate: bhavati vā svargo na vā bhavatīti.* Ibid., preceding.

9. *pramāṇato 'rthapratipattau pravṛtti-sāmarthyād arthavat pramāṇam.*

10. *kiṃ vā na paśyasy avidyā-śoka-moha-bhayādi-saṃsāra-bīja-doṣa-nivṛttiṃ vijñāna-phalam.* BBh 1,4,7 Ān p. 130; Bhagavat p. 53.

11. Cf. for this my article mentioned above in: *Die Welt des Orients* 3 (1948). In addition, see also the important introduction to AiBh 2,1, where the apophatic method of leading toward experience is justified.

12. Cf. my article in: *ZDMG* 100 (1950), pp. 248f. [*Kl. Schr.*, pp. 71ff.].

13. Published in 1952 as Vol. 94 of the Madras Government Oriental Series, on the basis of a single manuscript.

14. Cf. my article, "Śaṅkarācārya and Śaṅkarabhagavatpāda" in *New Indian Antiquary*, vol. 9, nos. 5–6 (1947). The article, however, contains many mistakes, some of which completely alter the sense, because it was published without the author's corrections. [See Chapter 3 in this volume.]

15. Cf. my article in *WZKSO* 9 (1965), pp. 147ff. [*Kl. Schr.*, pp. 205ff.; Chapter 2 in this volume].

16. Cf. my article in: *WZKSO* 9 (1965), pp. 152f.

17. The US is by no means a unitary work; I consider it to be a collection of all the independent writings of Śaṅkara-Bhagavatpāda; these have come into existence at different times.

18. *draṣṭā ca dṛśyaṃ ca tathā ca darśanaṃ bhramas tu sarvas tava kalpito hi saḥ. dṛśeś ca bhinnam na hi dṛśyam īkṣyate* . . . (9); *vikalpanā vāpi tathādvayā bhaved avastuyogāt tad alātacakravat* . . . (10).

19. Cf. sections 1 and 5 of this article.

20. The pair of concepts *viṣaya/viṣayin* seems to go back historically to another origin than the pair *grāhya/grāhaka.* The latter is perhaps of Buddhistic origin. The first occurs in Yoga at YBh 4,23, where *viṣaya* (here characterizing specially the *citta*) paraphrases the term *dṛśya, viṣayin* (the *puruṣa*) the word *draṣṭṛ* of YS 4,23. The series *grahītṛ-grahaṇa-grāhya* is, on the contrary, used with reference to a Buddhistic philosopheme.

21. The terms *dvaya* = *dvaita* and *advaya* = *advaita* can be understood better on the basis of the (Buddhistically determined) ideas of Gauḍapāda than on that of the system of Śaṅkara or other Brahmanical ātman-monists. For, according to Gauḍapāda, the world arises as the "two-ness" *(dvaya, dvaita)* of subject and object through the vibration of the *citta,* and *paramārtha* is just the annulment of the polarity between the two, the coincidence of subject and object: this may then be meaningfully described as "not (any longer) two-ness" *(advaya, advaita).* Since, however, Śaṅkara explains the subject-object relation in quite a different way, as we shall see later, the word *dvaita* undergoes with him a change of meaning: it means, as evinced by numerous contexts in his works, simply "the world," synonymous with *prapañca* or *jagat.* The world is there conceived no longer as "twoness," but as the (not fully real) "second" alongside of the one spiritual reality, which is *advitīya* and in reality has no "second" beside it. Corre-

spondingly, *advaita* then means no longer "duality-less-ness, non-duality," but "that which has no second beside it." For characterizing Śaṅkara's position the term *aikātmyavāda*, "ātman-monism," is more appropriate than *advaitavāda*.

22. *yathā bhramaṇādi-dharmavad-alātādi-vastu-viṣaya-dṛṣṭir api bhramatīva tadvat.* Ān p. 65 below, Bhagavat p. 27, line 20.

23. "Rotating, being swung round" is denoted by the same word-root *bhram* as "to be under an illusion, to err."

24. As also later in BSBh, where he at first explains BS 1,1,12–19 according to tradition and, indeed, according to the assertions of Govindānanda and the author of the *Prakaṭārthavivaraṇa*, in agreement with the view of the Vṛttikāra, following which he then gives his own view, which he had already presented in TBh.

25. *kāryātman* TBh 2,5 Ān p. 67 bottom; *kārya-patita evānandamayo na para evātmā, ānanda iti vidyā-karmaṇoḥ phalam, tad-vikāra ānandamayaḥ.* Ān p. 68.

26. Characteristically, in the first quotation (from TBh 2,8,2) the word *advaita* occurs in connection with the concept of the coincidence of subject and object (here, bliss), i.e., in the sense of no-more-duality, as in MāBh; cf. above, note 21.

27. Cf. my remarks in: *ZDMG* 100, p. 276 bottom [*Kl. Schr.*, p. 99; Chapter 4, p. 86 in this volume].

28. Cf. further, *cin-mātra* USP 11, 4.7; 13, 2.

29. *na tu brahma jātimat, ato na sad-ādi-śabda-vācyam.* GBh 13,12.

30. *yad-viṣayā buddhir na vyabhicarati tat sat.* GBh 2,16.

31. *sarvā hi kārya-karaṇādi-vikriyā nitya-caitanyātma-svarūpe sarvāspada-bhūte saty eva bhavanti.* ĪBh 4, end.

32. *na hi brahmaṇo abhivyakti-nimittatva-vyatirekeṇa kasyacid ādhāratva-saṃbhavaḥ.* APV 6.

33. *na viṣayavijñānavad duḥkhānuviddhaṃ kiṃ tarhi prasannaṃ śivam atulam anāyāsaṃ nityatṛptam ekarasam.* BBh Bhagavat p. 222; Ān p. 495.

34. *jalāśaya ivodakāñjaliḥ kṣipto na pṛthaktvena vyavatiṣṭhate ānandātmaka-brahma-vijñānāya. tadā mukta ānandātmakam ātmānaṃ vedayate ity etad anarthakaṃ vākyam.* Bhagavat p. 224; Ān p. 499.

35. *brahmaṇaś ca nirantarātmānanda-vijñāne vijñānāvijñāna-kalpanānarthakyam. nirantaraṃ ced ātmānanda-viṣayaṃ brahmaṇo vijñānam, tad eva tasya svabhāva ity ātmānandaṃ vijānātīti kalpanānupapannā.* Ibid.

36. *mokṣe vijñānāntaram ānandāntaraṃ cābhivyajyate.* Bhagavat p. 287; Ān p. 634.

37. *na ca samānāśrayāṇāṃ ekasyātmabhūtāṇāṃ dharmāṇām itaretara-viṣaya-viṣayitvaṃ saṃbhavati.* Bhagavat p. 288; Ān p. 634.

38. References from Buddhist texts in Vidhushekhara Bhattacharyya, *The Āgamaśāstra...*, pp. 24f. and 172f.

39. *viṣaya-viṣayy-ābhāsatvaṃ ca yan malaṃ parikalpyate vijñānasya, tad apy anya-saṃsargābhāvād anupapannam. na hy avidyamānena vidyamānasya saṃsargaḥ syāt. asati cānya-saṃsarge yo dharmo dṛṣṭaḥ sa tat-svabhāvatvān na tena viyogam arhati... tasmād anitya-saṃsargeṇa malinatvaṃ tad-viśuddhiś ca vijñānasyetīyaṃ kalpanā andha-paraṃparaiva pramāṇa-śūnyety avagamyate.* Bhagavat pp. 247f., Ān 549.

40. *laukika ānando bāhyādhyātmika-sādhana-saṃpatti-nimitta utkṛṣṭaḥ, sa ya eṣa nirdiśyate brahmānandānugamārtham. anena hi prasiddhenānandena vyāvṛtta-viṣaya-buddhi-gamya ānando 'nugantuṃ śakyate. laukiko 'py ānando brahmānandasyaiva mātrāvidyayā tiraskriyamāṇe vijñāna utkṛṣyamāṇāyāṃ cāvidyāyāṃ brahmādibhiḥ karma-vaśād yathā-vijñānam viṣayādi-sādhana-saṃbandha-vaśāc ca vibhāvyamānaś ca loke 'navasthito laukikaḥ saṃpadyate. sa evāvidyā-kāma-karmāpakarṣeṇa manuṣya-gandharvādy-uttarottara-bhūmiṣv akāmahata-vidvac-chrotriya-pratyakṣo vibhāvyate śataguṇottarotkarṣeṇa yāvad dhiraṇyagarbhasya brahmaṇa ānanda iti.* TBh 2,8,1, Ān p. 84.

41. In: *JAOS* 85, no. 2, pp. 178–96; *WZKSO* 9 (1965), pp. 155–97; *IIJ* 10 (1967), pp. 33–55. For external criteria, cf. my article mentioned in note 14, above.

42. *WZKSO* 12/13, pp. 407–23.

43. Cf. *ZDMG* 100, pp. 250–54 [*Kl. Schr.*, pp. 73–77; Chapter 4, pp. 60–64 in this volume].

44. In USP 18 the word *ahaṃkartṛ* is frequent; it denotes the inner sense, in so far as it is the power which individualizes. The word is then taken up by Śaṅkara's pupil Padmapāda.

45. Śaṅkara's text: *duḥkha-pracuraḥ saṃsāro heyaḥ. tasyāvidyā-nimitto draṣṭṛ-dṛśya-saṃyogo hetuḥ. viveka-khyātir aviplavā hānopāyaḥ. viveka-khyātau ca satyām avidyā-nivṛttiḥ, tan-nivṛttāv ātyantiko draṣṭṛ-dṛśya-saṃyogoparamo hānam, tad eva kaivalyam.* (Editor's note: Cf. Vyāsa's presentation of this paradigm in YBh 2,15, as referred to by Hacker in section 2).

46. There is plenty of evidence for this interest. Cf. my remarks in: *Die Welt des Orients* 3 (1943), pp. 248f., and in ZDMG 100 (1950), pp. 255f. I have shown there that Śaṅkara was not interested in theoretical ideas, like the vehicle of nescience *(avidyāśraya)*. But Śaṅkara also says expressly: *avidyā kasya dṛśyate, iti praśno nirarthakaḥ* (GBh 13,2; ed. Bhagavat, p. 195 bottom).

47. The first prose chapter (USG 9–17; 23; 33–36) was already preparatory to this.

48. Cf. de la Vallée Poussin in: *Mélanges chin. et bouddh.* 5 (1936–37), p. 233.

49. *saṃsāra-hetavo viparīta-grahāḥ* Bṛ. on MS 1,1,5, p. 65f., Madras.

50. Cf. for these conclusions, my remarks in *ZDMG* 100, pp. 248–54 and 272–76 [*Kl. Schr.*, pp. 71–77; 95–99; Chapter 4, pp. 58–64 and 82–85 in this volume].

51. I take *-rūpa* in *smṛti-rūpa* in the sense which, as the second member of a bahuvrīhi, the word has for philosophers particularly: as it has the sense of "being such," it can almost be called an identifying suffix (having the same meaning as: *-bhūta, -ātmaka, -svarūpa, -śarīra*).

52. *agṛhīta-viśeṣasya sāmānya-mātra-buddhir upalabdha-pūrvānya-vastu-smṛty-upasaṃhitā . . . niścayākāreṇopajāyamānā viparyayaḥ*. YV 1,8, p. 33 bottom.

53. Cf. also YBh 1,2, p. 10: *prakhyā-svarūpaṃ hi citta-sattvam*, on which YV: *prakhyā prakhyānaṃ prakāśanam, sa hi sattva-guṇasya dharmaḥ;* further, SK 36 with YD. In the Yoga doctrine the self in turn becomes of the nature of light only in liberation, cf. YBh 3,55: *tadā puruṣaḥ svarūpa-mātra-jyotir amalaḥ kevalībhavati.* That is an even more mythical rather than philosophical (pertaining to the metaphysics of knowledge) view; cf. in epic Sāṃkhya: *jyotir-jvālā sumahatī jagāma tridivaṃ tadā.* Mahābhārata 12,200,20. Even in the Upaniṣad passage following which he develops his doctrine of the self-illumining self (BUp 4,3,9 Kāṇva; 4,3,10 Mādhy.) it is not said that the self is *always* "self-illumining," but that the "manikin in men" *(puruṣa)* is "self-illumining" in dream *(átrāyáṃ púruṣaḥ svayáṃjyotir bhávati).*

54. The word stems from the mythical sphere: cf. MuBh 3.1.7, where it is used to paraphrase *divya.* In the Pali canon *sayaṃpabha* is often an attribute of certain gods, cf. the reference in the Pali Dictionary of the PTS.

55. In Prabhākara himself this word does not seem to occur, but it is frequent in Śālikanātha; cf. Dharmakīrti, *Pramāṇavārttika* 2,327: *svayaṃ saiva prakāśate.*

56. YS 4,18: *sadā jñātaś citta-vṛttayas tat-prabhoḥ puruṣasyāpariṇāmitvāt;* YBh 4,33, p. 366: *kūṭastha-nityatā.*

57. *kārya-karaṇa-saṃghāta,* a word stemming from the Sāṃkhya-Yoga tradition: cf., e.g., YD 93,12 and YBh 2,3 (*-srotas* instead of *saṃghāta*). In Vedānta it is very frequently used by Śaṅkara in particular.

58. The "Summary" is in Hacker's original English (editor's note).

PART II

Nondualism and Its Implications: Understanding and Confrontation

6

The Theory of Degrees of Reality in Advaita Vedānta

I. The Hierarchy of Being European scholars generally understand by the term 'Vedānta' the school of Indian philosophy, consisting of several branches, which is dedicated to interpreting the teachings of the Upaniṣads.[1] Various theological systems of Hinduism present themselves as Vedānta; each claims to be *the* Vedānta. All schools of Vedānta but one[2] espouse, in accord with the Upaniṣads, a more or less radical monism. The most widespread of the schools, that of the famous master Śaṅkara,[3] is Advaita Vedānta or, more precisely, Kevalādvaita Vedānta, i.e., "Monism" or "Extreme Monism." Advaita Vedānta holds that only pure spirit or consciousness—called Ātman, Brahman, the Highest Ātman, the Highest Brahman, even the Highest Lord—truly exists. The plurality of individual souls is illusory; only the universal Self is real. The essence of the self is described as light of knowledge and subsistent bliss. It is one, simple, and without parts. It never changes: every form of becoming, be it birth, change, activity, or suffering, is foreign to it. The bliss, knowledge, and being that comprise its nature are one and the same.

The philosophical basis of this radical monism is an illusionism *(māyāvāda)* which is, in part, derived from the illusionism of later

Buddhism—the schools of relativism *(śūnyavāda)* or Madhyamaka and epistemological idealism *(vijñānavāda)* or Yogācāra. If only the One Consciousness is real, it is argued, then everything in our experience that is multiple, changing, and material—the entirety of phenomenal experience—is not truly real. Unreal, however, does not mean *nonexistent.* In order to understand the illusionism of Vedāntic monism it is important to realize that it is conceived with the goal of liberation in view; in Indian philosophy knowledge is never an end in itself, but always serves the purpose of liberation. The monist conceives of liberation as the condition in which the soul dwells in pure spirit or consciousness, *as* pure consciousness. In contrast to this One Consciousness, the world and everything in it is without value, and from there Advaita Vedānta took the further step of declaring that it is without any real *being.* But this lack of being is never of interest to the monist just as philosophical idea, but only in reference to the goal—liberation. Only for the wise or enlightened is the world unreal; for the unenlightened person who lives in the world, its reality remains unshaken. The concept of unreality is therefore relative, depending on the standpoint of the knower, and it functions, so to speak, as a comfort to the one who strives toward liberation: if it can be shown that the world has no real being, then it is sensible and feasible to strive for liberation according to the method Advaita Vedānta prescribes.

That which is not truly real, therefore, still has a certain aspect of being. Radical monistic thought was never satisfied with simply, paradoxically doing away with experience—with the many, the changing, and the material—as that which does not exist. Even in Gauḍapāda,[4] Śaṅkara, and Maṇḍanamiśra, the earliest Advaita philosophers whose works we possess, we find expressions which attribute to the world a certain degree of reality. Later philosophers, driven by polemics and apologetics, investigate the ontological status of the world in extended discussions and order it in a hierarchy of degrees of reality.[5] By means of this ordering the concept of unreality attains greater clarity. In this essay, therefore, we shall consider the various levels of being that are presented in Vedānta. We shall for the time being leave the Indian terms untranslated, explicating them in the course of our investigation.

First series: two levels

satya—asatya

Second series: five levels

sat—asat—sadasat—anirvacanīya—pañcamaprakāra

Third series: three levels
paramārthasat—vyāvahārikasat—prātibhāsikasat

1: First Series

In order to explain the first series we must leap ahead to consider what the first and second terms of the second series mean. The fourth term of the second series, however, presupposes in turn an understanding of the first series. We shall therefore begin with the term *sat.*

Sat means 'being' or 'existing.' In its ordinary, unphilosophical sense the word means the reality that is present to us in mundane experience; for that is what *is.* In its philosophical sense, for the strict monist, *sat* means only the self or Brahman. The characteristics of this reality, Brahman or the self, which exists *truly* and *in itself (an sich),* is that it is simple and one; it cannot change; it is spiritual, i.e., conscious, and it is not dependent on anything but exists through and for itself.

With this clarification we can proceed to consider the first series. *Satya* is that which corresponds to *sat,* the latter serving as a sort of standard. Thus in ordinary usage, *satya,* applied to statements, means 'true': a *true* statement corresponds to that which really exists. In an ontological sense, therefore, *satya* is that which corresponds to Brahman, being, insofar as it has similar characteristics. But since for the Advaitin there is only one *sat,* and nothing comes close to resembling it, the two concepts of *satya* and *sat* collapse into one. As far as linguistic usage goes, *satya* may perhaps be more emphatic: it refers to the *genuine, actual* reality of a thing. We shall therefore translate the word as 'truly existing.' As far as I can tell, the Advaita philosophers did not explicitly differentiate between *sat* and *satya.*

The negative expressions *asat* and *asatya* are more clearly distinguishable from each other than *sat* and *satya.* While *sat* and *satya* seem to coincide, *asat* and *asatya* are consciously kept apart. *Asat* is that which simply does not exist; *asatya,* on the other hand, means merely that something is without the features of true *sat,* which is not to say that it does not exist. *Asatya* is therefore that which does not *really* exist or which upon closer scrutiny *ought not* to exist, although somehow it does in an improper and ungenuine way. In ordinary usage *asatya* means 'untrue' or 'false.' Falsehood cannot, of course, claim any reality compared to the true or actual; yet at the same time it cannot be denied that, at least as an idea, it possesses a certain existence. This epistemological concept of falsehood the Advaitin transfers to ontology. We shall translate it as 'not truly existing.' We shall encounter it again in the second and third series and in that connection explicate further aspects of it. The common translation 'unreal' for *asatya* is misleading, at the very least.

2: Second Series

We have now dealt with *sat*. In regard to *asat* we should add that, strictly speaking, it is the absolutely nonexistent, that which never and nowhere was or will be. Examples are: a rabbit's horn, a man's horn, and a sky flower—things that do not and cannot exist. It would be superfluous to go into the highly sophisticated Indian theories of nonbeing here, since they were primarily developed in non-Vedāntic schools. Sometimes for the Vedānta philosopher, speaking loosely or in hyperbole, *asat* is equivalent to *asatya* or *anirvacanīya*.

Sad-asat means being-and-not-being, i.e., both the one as well as the other. This mode of reality was recognized outside of Vedānta by the Mīmāṃsā philosopher Kumārila and within Vedānta by the monistic but non-illusionistic Bhedābheda school. The latter defined the relation between the One Consciousness and the multiplicity of nonspiritual, material things as one of simultaneous identity and difference; accordingly, they explained the status of the empirical world as at the same time truly existing and not truly existing. We must explicate this idea briefly, even though it was rejected by the radical monists we are concerned with as illogical and impossible. In the first place, the contrast with *sadasat* will help to clarify the concept of *anirvacanīya* which we are about to discuss; and second, even though the Advaita philosophers do not recognize the concept of *sadasat,* they include it among the degrees of reality, so that with its inclusion the total number of degrees comes to five, and they are able to refer to one of the them as "the fifth kind." We shall have to say more about this below.

Anirvacanīya means indeterminable or unspecifiable: in the older texts (Śaṅkara, Maṇḍanamiśra) one adds *tattvānyatvābhyām,* in the more recent (since approximately the tenth century), *sadasadbhyām* or *sadasattvābhyām.* The first expression means "as a 'that' or an 'other,'" the second, "as being or nonbeing." We can ignore the difference in meaning these two phrases apparently originally had and say simply that *(tattvānyatvābhyām* or *sadasadbhyām) anirvacanīya* means: 'indeterminable either as real or unreal.' *Anirvacanīya* is thus the negation of *sadasat:* the former means *both* being *and* nonbeing, the latter *neither* being *nor* nonbeing. Concerning the history of these two peculiar concepts, which has yet to be investigated in any detail, we offer the following preliminary observations.

The concept of neither being nor nonbeing has apparently two sources in Brahmanical thought: one is cosmogonic speculation, the other the mystical theology of the All-in-One. The most important cosmogonic hymn of the Ṛg Veda (10,129) begins by describing the state prior to the origin of the world with the words: "There was at that time neither being nor nonbeing." Fifteen hundred years later Śaṅkara applies the expression *tattvānyatvābhyām anirvacanīya* to the primal state:[6] one cannot say that before its origin the world did *not* exist. The idea of creation *ex nihilo* was never conceived by the Indians. They believed, rather, that what was before the world had to be some kind of prime matter or primal condition. Precisely for that reason, however, one also cannot say that at that time there was *something;* for being has not yet arisen. But this cosmogonic notion of neither being nor nonbeing loses importance for philosophers after Śaṅkara. The philosophers of monistic mysticism, rather, found another use for the formula 'neither being nor nonbeing'—in the description of the Absolute. That which transcends all experience is preferably described in negative terms, and the most radical of all negations is the denial of both being and nonbeing.[7] It is clear that in this case being and nonbeing can only mean empirically determinate existence and its opposite; for in a strict metaphysical sense the Absolute is Being itself. Śaṅkara's disciple Sureśvara still speaks of the self or *ātman* as that which is above being and nonbeing.[8] The later Buddhist philosophers, too, characterize the Absolute with the formula 'neither-nor.'[9]

After the disciples of Śaṅkara, however, the use of the 'neither-nor' formula undergoes a radical change. Interpreting the teaching of the Upaniṣads in light of more recent philosophical developments, Advaita philosophers preferred to define the *ātman* as that which is self-evident and manifest per se and, especially from Maṇḍanamiśra on, as Being in general. One ceased to think of the *ātman* in terms of the mystical characterization of neither being nor nonbeing; somehow the self, which had always before been the incomprehensible par excellence, became the formally *indubitable.* To be sure, the older formulae continued to be used alongside the newer, particularly when it came to asserting that the self cannot really be *known* in the ordinary sense; and self-luminous consciousness had all along been recognized as one of the characteristics of the *ātman.* In a sense, the teaching did not change at all. The tradition-bound Indian philosopher, moreover, was not aware of any deviation from the past; he believed himself always only to be interpreting an old doctrine in a new way and never would have considered abolishing or even attacking it. Even modern research has hardly noticed the change that took place. Yet it is unmistakable that shortly after the reception of the theory of illusion, Vedānta became highly intellectualized and logicized; mysticism was thoroughly confined within the bounds of logic. The direction of concern shifted. The unknowability of the *ātman* was accounted for by making it the presupposition of all knowledge,[10] and this function of making cognition possible was characterized in terms of the concept of self-evidence as it had been developed in the epistemological controversies between Buddhist and Hindu philosophers (especially the Prābhākara school of Mīmāṃsā). In contrast to the self-evident self the world began to appear as a ghostly, illogical Unding that neither is nor is not. The world, and not just its primal state before becoming manifest, was described as "neither being nor nonbeing."

Meanwhile the concept of the indeterminable, that which is "neither-nor," found a new application outside cosmogony and mysticism, namely in the Advaita theory of error. All Indian philosophies intensely discuss the phenomenon of false cognition; the basic metaphysical and epistemological position of a school always becomes evident in its theory of error. Here we can only deal with radical Vedāntic monism. This school developed a theory of error centuries before it developed an account of valid cognition: the latter was achieved only in the seventeenth century,[11] the former was complete already in the tenth century.[12] This rather strange state of affairs was the result of the following circumstances. As I have already mentioned, all Indian philosophical reflection is directed toward the goal of liberation. The state of bondage, however, is generally believed to be caused by ignorance (not sin).[13] That is what one must eliminate in order to be free from rebirth; therefore, it is necessary to investigate what ignorance and error are. The philosopher of radical monism, or Advaitin, moreover considers all phenomenal experience to be illusory. Thus, for him error is primary, and that which is taken to be right cognition in everyday experience is, strictly speaking, just a special case of error. And so the whole world, the sum total of all objects of experience, is relegated to the level of an illusion.[14] In this manner one applies the results of one's investigation of sensory illusion to the world as a whole.

What is most important about the phenomenon of illusion is its ontological status, or degree of reality. One argued: the illusory object is *perceived,* therefore it is not unreal or nonexistent (not *asat*); for that which does not exist at all, e.g., the horn of a rabbit, is never perceived. On the other hand, it is sublated, i.e., removed from the realm of existence, by a subsequent correct cognition. Therefore it cannot be real or existent either (not *sat* or *satya*); for that which exists cannot be eliminated by knowledge. The ontological status of the illusory object, therefore, is to be described as "determinable as neither being nor nonbeing," and the main characteristic of the indeterminable is that it can be sublated; that which is indeterminable can be removed, suppressed, or eliminated by (true) cognition.

The world has the same degree of reality as the object of false perception. For it, too, is perceived—in everyday experience. Thus it cannot be *asat*. But it is also, in mystical experience, sublated. Therefore it cannot be *sat*.

Here it becomes clear that 'indeterminable' is a synonym of 'not truly existing.' The essence of that which does not truly exist lies in its indeterminability, and this in turn is equivalent to its eliminability through right cognition. Synonymous with 'not truly existing' and 'indeterminable' are all expressions which mean 'false' or 'untrue.'

The world is also to be characterized as "indeterminable" in relation to that which truly exists in itself, to *sat* or the self. For one can neither say that it is identical with *sat,* since the latter is spirit and one while the world is nonspiritual, insentient plurality, nor that it is different from it, for it is evident in experience that it has existence of some kind. Since in reality there is only one, indivisible Being, everything that exists, exists only insofar as it is endowed with the being of the One.

This purely negative manner of argumentation, which leads to the concept of the indeterminable whether one is investigating the ontological status of the world or its relationship to the One, distinguishes the radical monism of Advaita Vedānta from the above-mentioned Bhedābheda-Vedānta. The latter, in its formula 'both-and,' brings the Absolute and the world together; the former, through its 'neither-nor,' holds them strictly apart, while at the same time trying to conceive, through its doctrine of illusion, of some kind of (seemingly real) relationship between them. Both schools have in common that they grant only incomplete reality to the world: that is expressed both by the concept 'being-nonbeing' and the concept 'indeterminable.' Just as the older Advaitins, e.g., Sureśvara, had no qualms about applying the schema 'neither-nor' to the Absolute, so they also sometimes, like their Buddhist predecessors,[15] applied the notion of 'both-and' to the world.[16] But shortly after Śaṅkara it became fixed that only the world should be characterized in terms of 'neither-nor.' The world had become an illogical Unding. The self, on the other hand, became, so to speak, the patron saint of logicality.

A curious detail which I shall only briefly mention, and which also has an ancient Buddhist parallel, is the fifth degree of reality, called the *pañcamaprakāra* or "the fifth kind." The inventor of this bewildering concept is Vimuktātman. In investigating the state of transition from bondage to liberation, the condition known as "the elimination of ignorance," he finds that it is neither being, nor nonbeing, nor both, nor neither. Later Advaitins used the term 'the fifth kind' for this mode of existence.[17]

3: Third Series

The discussions of the series *satya—asatya* and *sat—asat—sadasat—anirvacanīya—pañcamaprakāra* are, until approximately the tenth century, in a certain respect incomplete. When the relation of the world to Brahman is reflected upon, then the former is *asatya,* the latter *satya.* But when the phenomenon of perceptual error within mundane experience is considered, then the world is *satya,* illusion on the other hand *asatya.* The world is thus *satya* or *asatya* depending on one's point of view; the concepts are relative, and that diminishes the clarity of the theory. Gradually, one came to see that it is necessary to distinguish two more degrees of reality within *asatya* and *anirvacanīya:* the "practically existent" *(vyāvahārika-sat),* which includes that which we experience through right cognition in everyday experience, and the "ficticiously existent" *(prātibhāsika-sat),* which is the status of illusion or error. The first is, in respect to that which truly exists *(sat),* so to speak illusion of the first degree; the second is illusion of the second degree.[18]

Both expressions, 'practically existent' and 'ficticiously existent,' had long been in use without, however, being clearly differentiated and ordered. One had attempted to prove that the indeterminable is quite capable of playing an active or passive role in knowledge and action, indeed, that this is precisely the nature of the indeterminable. On the other hand, it was later still permissible to characterize the world as mere appearance or false appearance, and it is still today quite common to compare the world to an illusion of the senses. But as a result of the sharper differentiation of the apparent from the real within the realm of the indeterminable, the world regained a measure of reality. It no longer stood quite on the same level as sensory illusion; for one recognized illusions of the first and second degree. Both are contrasted with the absolutely real, that which *is* in the highest sense *(paramārtha-sat),* viz., Brahman or the *ātman.* And so we get the three-membered series presented above (the third series). When it comes to translating the terms of this series into a Western language, it seems helpful to take into account the etymological content of the expressions and distinguish the *real* or truly existent *(paramārthasat)* from the *actual* or practically existent *(vyāvahārikasat):* that which truly is and that which exists practically are not the same thing for Advaita philosophers. For that which truly exists does not serve any function at all; it simply *is.* The essence of practical existence, on the other hand, which is first degree illusion, consists, as has been said, in its being involved in processes of knowing and acting. The third series, then, can be rendered by the three concepts: Reality—Actual Existence—False Appearance. The latter two levels are both "indeterminable," "false," and "not-truly-existent," but in different degrees. Of course, if one wanted, one could insert the terms *sadasat, asat,* and *pañcamaprakāra* into the series, so that six levels of reality would result.

II. Vimuktātman on the Ontological Status of the World

In order to document what I have set out above, as well as take it a step further, I shall translate and interpret a passage from the *Iṣṭasiddhi.*[19] This important work of Vimuktātman, a philosopher of probably the tenth century, is concerned especially with the clarification and defense of the concept of the indeterminable. Although this concept had been in use for centuries, Vimuktātman's work, which considers all the objections against it, appears to be the first comprehensive treatment of the topic. Vimuktātman belongs to the school of Śaṅkara. His views have had much influence and represent the predominant interpretation of Advaita Vedānta up to the present time.

At the conclusion of a discussion of Brahman, Vimuktātman asserts: "We ascertain, therefore, on the basis of revelation,[20] tradition,[21] logical argumentation, and direct experience, that Brahman alone and nothing else is real."

At this point he allows an opponent to speak (it is the practice in Indian philosophical treatises to introduce a new topic with a question or objection of an opponent):[22]

> ">If that is the case, then what is the mode of existence[23] of the world, which is a second thing (besides Brahman) and serves as the

object of perception and other means of knowledge?[24] If the world does not exist at all, then perception and the other means of knowledge do not have any object and hence are without validity; neither the ritual portion nor the knowledge portion (of the Veda)[25] would be valid, for their basis (i.e., the world, to which they refer) and their own existence[26] (insofar as the Veda itself belongs to the world) would be eliminated. Moreover, perception and the other means of knowledge (would not only be invalid, but) if the world, in which they are included, did not exist, they would not even exist! And revelation, tradition, and logical argumentation could not possibly exist. The consequence of all this is that Brahman as described above could not be demonstrated by these (means of knowledge).

"If, in order to avoid this predicament, one were to accept (the reality of) the world, then there are three possibilities: either the world is different from Brahman or identical with Brahman or both. For a real thing cannot exist (in relation to another) in any way other than these three. If, however, the world is not a real thing, then the stated consequence would follow; for it is certainly impossible that one could make use of anything that is not real, say, the horn of a man or a sky flower. But then if the world is a real thing, Brahman cannot be demonstrated to exist in any of the three relations.[27] It follows that, whether the world exists or not, the Upaniṣads cannot demonstrate Brahman. It is therefore inadmissible to say that man attains that which is (ultimately) desirable and avoids that which is undesirable through the vision (of Brahman).[28] Thus one must hold liberation to have a different nature, or else admit that there is no such thing as liberation.<

"To all this we reply: There is no defect at all in our position; for we believe that the world is made out of *māyā*.[29] And since *māyā,* together with its product (the world), is indeterminable either as something real or something unreal, the defects that would result from saying either that the world is real or that it is unreal do not affect our position. To be more explicit:[30] If the world has no reality, then monism need not be rejected. But if it is (also) not unreal, then the mentioned problems—in particular, that sense perception and the other means of knowledge become invalid—do not ensue. Thus, it does not follow that Brahman cannot be demonstrated. And, since *māyā* and its product cease to exist upon cognition of Brahman, it is not the case that liberation cannot be attained.

">But (says the opponent) I do not know any such thing as 'indeterminable *māyā*.'<

"I shall explain it to you (i.e., discuss it later).

">But if the world has no reality, then perception and the other means of knowledge would provide no valid cognition, and all the problems previously mentioned would result.[31]<

"When does it occur that perception and the other means of knowledge fail to provide valid knowledge because something real is not present?

">In the case of the (false) perception of a man's horn and the like.<

"No, (such things are not to be compared with the world; for they are altogether unreal, i.e., nonexistent, whereas) the world is *not unreal*. And if the world is to be considered similar to (a totally nonexistent object such as) a man's horn, insofar as it *lacks reality*, then it can be considered similar to that which is real, insofar as it *lacks unreality*.

">(If you will not accept that the world is on a par with a man's horn, then I offer another example:) That the means of knowledge do not provide valid knowledge when (their objects are) not real is evident in cases such as dreaming.<

"But then you do recognize something which is indeterminable; for you give up the example of the man's horn and cite instead a dream, which is without both reality and unreality.

">A dream, too, is real.<

"Well, then, lack of reality is not the basis of the invalidity of cognition; for even in the absence thereof (viz., unreality), invalid cognition occurs (namely, in the case of a dream, which you have just declared to be something *real*).

">A dream (let us say, then) is an illusory thing *(mithyāvastu)*.<

"But is *that* something real *(vastu)* or something unreal *(avastu)?* In either case, the problem just mentioned remains.

"One could perhaps argue as follows:[32] >The illusory thing is in fact two real entities which have been confused.[33] Or else, it is something real which appears as another real thing, so that a cognition having it as its object is false.[34]<

"Then one cannot say that sense perception and the other means of knowledge do not deliver valid knowledge in dreams; for their object is not like that in the dream state.[35] Now, one could say (using an idea accepted by the Advaitins): >Dream cognition is invalid, because its object is indeterminable; and the same will be true of waking cognition.<But that is not correct, because (waking cognition) is not (like dreaming cognition) sublated (by another, subsequent cognition which corrects it). Or, (we can ask:) why should not dreaming cognition be valid like waking cognition; for it has, just like waking cognition, something indeterminable as its object? If one responds,>Because it (dreaming cognition) is sublated,<then we would say: Invalidity, then, is due to the fact that (the cognition) is sublated and not to its object being something indeterminable.[36]

"Moreover, should one say that invalidity—which one wishes to maintain both for dreams and for waking cognitions—consists in the nonexistence of (the object) itself and its effects *after* (the cognition) is sublated, then I agree. But when it is alleged to be the nonexistence (of the object) *prior to* (sublation), then it is to be said in response that that is not the case even for dreaming. Should one say that sublation results from correct cognition of the true state of affairs in regard to the real thing, then I would agree to that too. But that the sublating cognition always exists, or that sublation occurs prior to the occurrence of this cognition—neither of these alternatives is true for dreaming. Therefore, just as in one's dream world, all worldly and Vedic involvement with actions, factors of action, modes of cognition, objects of cognition, and so forth, continues undisturbed, even though it is indeterminable, and a cognition that overthrows that experience arises from causes originating from within the dream itself[37]—so in regard to the waking state everything stands uncontradicted (i.e., all the experiences of the waking state retain their validity up until enlightenment).

">Since the illusory character of the world of waking experience is known prior to enlightenment,[38] practical activity in waking experience should not be possible. A dream, on the other hand, is not known to be illusory until one wakes up; so practical activity would be possible in it.<

"That is not a defect (in our theory). For it is well known that such phenomena as magical illusions, mirages, fata morgana, double vision, and loss of orientation do not cease prior to fully awakening (i.e., prior to direct apprehension of the true state of affairs), even though their illusory character is recognized (in the abstract).

">But even if the false appearance continues, practical activity in reference to and motivated by it is not possible (in such cases). Similarly, such (activity) would not occur in relation to this (world of appearance).<

"True. Even in this case (in regard to the world of waking experience) there is no such thing (as practical activity); there is only the appearance thereof, as in dreaming. And you, too, agree that the ficticious appearance of a magical illusion, etc., does not cease prior to awakening.[39]

"Therefore, as in dreaming, so in waking experience—there is no negation of the ficticious appearance of the world or of the practical activity therein prior to awakening. But practical activities, which are motivated by conviction in the real existence of the world, do not arise after insight into its false character is (fully) achieved. Actions and nonactions which are based on the knowledge of its illusory character, on the other hand, will occur. Moreover, those which are motivated merely by false appearances will also occur as before. For in common experience we observe that certain actions and abstentions, e.g., those in regard to sweet things that appear bitter, occur even though the falsehood (of the appearance) is recognized. Therefore, even though one recognizes the indeterminable nature of the world, practical activity is possible up until the attainment of enlightenment."[40]

Notes

1. In India 'Vedānta' is just a synonym of 'Upaniṣad.' The philosophy based upon the Upaniṣads is called *vedāntavāda* or *brahmavāda*.

2. This exception is the system of Madhva. Cf. H.v. Glasenapp, *Madhvas Philosophie des Vishnu-Glaubens,* Bonn, 1923. But even Madhva's teaching contains many remnants of the original Vedāntic monism.

3. He probably lived in the seventh century C.E. According to traditional belief, he lived around the turn of the eighth century, but that seems hardly

tenable. His teachings are concisely summarized in the *Upadeśasāhasrī* (trans. by Hacker, Bonn, 1949, *Religionsgeschichtliche Texte,* Heft 2).

4. His work, the *Māṇḍūkya-Kārikā,* is translated by P. Deussen in his *Sechzig Upanishads des Veda* (Leipzig, 1897). *The Āgamaśāstra of Gauḍapāda,* ed. by V. Bhattacharyya, Calcutta, 1943, is a new edition with an English translation.

5. In later Buddhism as well there are degrees of reality. Connections with Vedānta are obvious, and were this a historical investigation we would explicate them. But we shall not consider Buddhism in this study. The meanings and interconnections of concepts of reality in Vedānta diverge considerably from Buddhism and can be described independently of historical references to the latter.

6. See my article, "Distinctive Features of the Doctrine and Terminology of Śaṅkara" (Chapter 4 in this volume).

7. *Bhagavadgītā* 13,12; *Kaivalya Upaniṣad* 24; *Śvetāśvatara Upaniṣad* 4,18; perhaps also *Muṇḍaka Upaniṣad* 2,2,1.

8. Cf. my *Untersuchungen über Texte des frühen Advaitavāda, 1: Die Schüler Śaṅkaras* (Mainz, 1950), p. 39.

9. Candrakīrti, *Prasannapadā* (St. Petersburg, 1913), pp. 436,2 and 438,4. Cf. *Laṅkāvatārasūtra* (Kyoto, 1923), pp. 188f.

10. This doctrine is also found in the oldest Upaniṣads. See *Bṛhadāraṇyaka Upaniṣad* 3,7,18–23; 3,8,11.

11. By Dharmarāja Adhvarīndra in his *Vedāntaparibhāṣā,* ed. with English trans. by S. S. Suryanarayana Sastri, Adyar, 1942.

12. In Vimuktātman's *Iṣṭasiddhi.* See below.

13. Thus one sees God's essence to consist not in his holiness (this notion is almost unknown) but in his consciousness: the godhead is pure awareness or spirit.

14. When Indian philosophers discuss error, they consider almost exclusively sensory illusion. The commonest examples, trotted out over and over again, are: the rope which in half darkness appears as a snake and mother-of-pearl which is mistaken for silver. The snake and the silver are termed "illusory objects." In this way illusion is conceived to have an objective existence.

15. Cf. *Madhyamakāvatāra* 6,23 (cited on p. 176 of the *Āgamaśāstra of Gauḍapāda,* ed. V. Bhattacharyya), a subjective variant of the 'both-and' formula: all things have two appearances, according to whether one apprehends them from the state of enlightenment or the state of nonenlightenment.

16. Gauḍapāda, *Māṇḍūkyakārikā* 4, 68–70.

17. We may add here that the introduction of this term is traditionally attributed to Vimuktātman's successor Ānandabodha; see M. Hiriyanna's introduction to his edition of the *Iṣṭasiddhi,* pp. xxxvf.; P. Hacker, *Kl. Schr.,* p. 119, n. 2. Vimuktātman himself has the concept of a "fifth kind," but does not use the term *pañcamaprakāra* (editor's note).

18. It has not yet been determined who first divided the indeterminable into the practically existent and the ficticiously existent. This dichotomy does not occur in Vimuktātman (probably the tenth century); it occurs in Prakāśātman (*Pañcapādikāvivaraṇa,* p. 31, 1 ff.); later in the thirteenth century in Citsukha (*Tattvapradīpikā,* p. 83, 3 ff.) and still later in Dharmarāja (*Vedāntaparibhāṣā* II.27, p. 60, in the above-mentioned edition and translation).

19. Ed. M. Hiriyanna, Baroda, 1933. The translated passage is pp. 32ff. The translation attempts to achieve a compromise between accuracy and readability.

20. I.e., the Veda, which contains scripture of absolute authority that is considered to be not of human origin.

21. I.e., the ancient religious writings of secondary authority, e.g., the *Bhagavadgītā.*

22. The opponent will speak several times in the text that follows. His statements are set off by ><.

23. The word *gati,* literally 'path,' is frequently used by Vimuktātman in the sense of 'mode of existence,' 'degree of reality.' The word *prakāra* is more or less synonymous with it.

24. The other types of cognition or sources of knowledge are: inference, testimony (especially that provided by the Veda), comparison, implication, and nonapprehension.

25. The ritual portion consists essentially in the hymns and the Brāhmaṇas, the knowledge portion in the Upaniṣads.

26. *Āśrayāsiddhi* and *svarūpāsiddhi,* which are actually logical terms, are not, according to the commentary, used here in their technical senses.

27. I.e., as either different from or identical with, or both different from and identical with, the world. Vimuktātman has given the complete proof of this impossibility in the preceding section of his work.

28. The opponent formulates his argument so that in the end the existence of Brahman and even liberation are called into question. He does this for the following reason. The goal of all Indian philosophy is to prove the possibility of liberation and show the way to its realization. If any kind of systematic reasoning undermines the possibility of liberation, or if it can be shown that liberation is not what it is said to be by a particular system, then the entire system is overturned.

29. *Māyā* (which in its original meaning denotes 'magic') is in Advaita Vedānta the illusory prime matter of the world.

30. Noteworthy in the following is the purely negative argumentation.

31. As becomes evident in the next objection, the opponent does not comprehend that "being unreal" or "having no reality" (i.e., not *truly* existing, *avastutva*) is different from "being nonexistent" *(asat)*.

32. Two views are given which explain in different ways the extent to which something real is present in dreaming and the extent to which dreaming is illusory.

33. This is an allusion to the theory of error of the Prābhākara school of Mīmāṃsā.

34. This is an allusion to the theory of error of Nyāya and the Mīmāṃsā school of Kumārila.

35. Translator's note: The proposals just put forward by the opponent are based on interpreting illusion as a mistaking of one object for another. But obviously the illusory experience known as dreaming cannot be construed in that way.

36. Vimuktātman here stresses the fact that within the sphere of the indeterminable both valid and correct cognition are quite possible.

37. E.g., the roar of a tiger which one dreams, which awakens one from the dream.

38. Namely, through the instruction of Advaita philosophy.

39. We read *-anivṛttim;* see *Iṣṭasiddhi,* ed. Hiriyanna, p. 693 (Additions).

40. Vimuktātman here makes a sharp distinction between the abstract understanding of the world's lack of true being and the immediate experiencing of the One Spirit or Consciousness: The latter he holds to be possible, but one gets the impression from what he says that it is for him something quite foreign and remote. Editor's note: Hacker's notes 5, 34 and 37 have been replaced or omitted.

7

The Idea of the Person in the Thinking of Vedānta Philosophers

Among the philosophical schools of Hinduism, especially those have reflected on the nature of the person which had set themselves the task of interpreting the "Vedānta" texts, i.e., the Upaniṣads. Thus, these schools are called Vedānta systems in the West, or also, in short form, the Vedānta. Reflecting on the core or authentic being of man was for them no philosophical "theory," no purely intellectual hobby, and the instruction about it was not the business of "education" or "culture." Rather, such reflection was understood as a quest, and such instruction as a way toward the *true goal;* the quest as well as the guidance on the path had an unmistakable religious quality and intent. The abiding tendency of all Vedānta thinking is expressed in a statement transmitted in the *Āpastamba Dharmasūtra:*[1] "There is nothing higher than attaining the Self" *(ātmalābhān na paraṃ vidyate).*

The purpose of the present essay is not to give a comprehensive historical survey of Vedāntic thought relating to the person, the Self, the *ātman;* such a survey is, in any case, not yet possible given the present state of research. My knowledge of the philosophical Hindu doctrines that I present is based upon the study of the works of some representative thinkers of a relatively early period: Gauḍapāda (around 500 A.D.?),

Śaṅkara, Maṇḍanamiśra, Sureśvara, Padmapāda[2] (all of the seventh or eighth centuries), and Vimuktātman (around A.D. 900); all of these belong to the illusionistic and acosmic school of spiritual monism (Advaita), which is, insofar as complete and directly transmitted literary documents are concerned, the oldest Vedānta school (many texts representing other school traditions have been lost). In conclusion, I will present some preliminary comments on the concept of the person in *bhakti* theism and the schools of Vaiṣṇava Vedānta.

What I am concerned with here is indicated by the choice of the word *person.* Every European translation of an Indian term, after all, includes, to a greater or lesser degree, an equation with a term of our thought. Often, or more often than not, this happens unreflectedly; it is an (unavoidable) source of permanent misunderstandings on the part of such readers who do not read the texts in the original. By choosing the word person in this essay, not *equation* but an invitation to *comparison* is intended. By speaking of the *concept of the person* in Vedāntic thought, I consciously and, in part, explicitly *confront* this term with the concept of the person as it has been presented using Christian presuppositions by Max Scheler.

This is, it seems to me, a possible way not only to bring the Indian terms close to us, but also to clarify the question of the suitability of Vedānta terms for expressing Christian thought. Scheler's distinction of the mental from the spiritual person *(Geistperson)* can render substantial aid toward an understanding which is ready to appropriate as well as confront the Vedāntic concept of the *ātman.* However, for thought that operates with a binary division of soul and body and with the concept of the capacities of the soul *(Seelenvermögen),* access to the Vedānta (and Sāṃkhya) concept of the Ātman, the Puruṣa, the Self, or the person is made more difficult if not blocked from the outset (in Hinduism, the naturalistic Nyāya-Vaiśeṣika system corresponds to this way of thinking).

The Vedāntists of the school of spiritual monism (Advaita) determine the nature of the person by methods of opposition, differentiation, reduction and abstraction. All of this is meant as an interpretation of Upaniṣadic statements and traditional ideas of the school. The opposition to the objective, impersonal, "inert" leads only to the determination of the person as a subject, a soul, and an 'I.' The subject *(viṣayin)* stands in an absolute contrast to the sphere of the objective *(viṣaya),* the 'I' *(asmat-pratyaya)* to the 'you' *(yuṣmat-pratyaya)* and the 'it' *(idam-pratyaya),* that which is spiritual *(cit)* to the inert, insentient (*jaḍa*—this concept corresponds to a large extent to that of "stuff" or "matter," but does not mean exactly the same; in contrast to the Sāṃkhya, the abovementioned Advaita Vedānta thinkers avoid the term "matter"; *jaḍa* is that which is not "spiritual"). Only the method of reduction identifies the authentic core, i.e., the self.

Subsequent to the completion of this reduction, words that indicate "subject," "soul," 'I,' can also be retained. The interpretation strives to understand passages that come from the Upaniṣads more and more precisely and systematically according to concepts that come from the tradition of the Vedānta school.

The Vedānta teacher[3] leads his pupil to reflection on the nature of his person by asking him: "Who are you?" The pupil replies in accordance with Hindu categories by stating his caste and stage of life; he adds to this that he wants to be liberated from *saṃsāra,* the condition of being perpetually reborn. The teacher directs him to *distinguish* his true self from the body and to *reduce* his idea of the person to its authentic core. His body, his descent, his position in Hindu society: all of this is not he himself; and everything that happens in this empirical order, and what he himself does, has nothing to do with his true person. The pupil must learn to differentiate his Self from that which is mental or psychical as well.[4] When experiencing pain, for example, strictly speaking, it is not correct to say: "I feel pain." For, first of all, the pain is in a part of the body, and the body is not the person or the true 'I,' which is the self *(ātman)* only. Second, the mind or psyche, the inner sense, is the vehicle of the experience of pain, and this, too, does not belong to the authentic being of the self or the person. As pure subject, this (the self or the person) stands in opposition even to the psychical processes as subject: psychical or mental contents are the object of the person, The Vedāntist (as the Sāṃkhya philosopher) even understands everything that is psychical as subtle (imperceptible) *matter,* originating from and nourished by food, and the contents of the psyche and its functions have the form of modifications of this matter.[5]

The Vedāntic concept of the person thus draws a sharp line within the inner realm of what we may call the "soul." Even the 'I' and the "subject" are affected by it. Tentatively and, after the process of reduction has been completed, finally as well, these words also describe the core of the person. For, in the opinion of the Advaita Vedānta, the meaning of these terms includes, in addition to nonauthentic ingredients, also the authentic person; after reducing it to the personal core, the words remain applicable. The 'I' is a mixture of what is mental and nonauthentic, and the authentic core of the self, of the objective and the subjective.

Advaita Vedānta goes a part of the way with its sister school, the (Pūrva-) Mīmāṃsā, which defines the soul or the self as that which is meant by the word 'I.' But finally it moves away from the Mīmāṃsā and discards what is mental in the 'I.' It is only after this reduction that it can again use the word 'I' with reference to the self. In the realization of the Upaniṣadic sentence "I am Brahman," the identification with Brahman, whose being is true, *removes* the "I-ness" of the 'I.'[6] (For the present we shall leave the monistic implication of this sentence out of consideration; only the concept of the authentic core of the person is at stake here.) Only by the amalgamation of the self and the psyche or mind is it possible for the 'I,' which misapprehends itself, to act and suffer. Thus, the concept of the subject, too, is applicable to the self only after the reduction of its contents.[7] This reduction must remove that which is functional and incidental in the subject from the content of the term; what remains is pure nonobjectifiable consciousness. Thus, the self can, in Sanskrit, be indicated (though nonessentially) by *nomina agentis* such as 'the cognizer' as well as (certainly more essentially) by nouns indicating a process such as 'cognizing' and (even better) by words that indicate the result such as 'cognition' *(Erkenntnis)* as well as (most suitably) with pure nouns of verbal roots[8] that express the term 'to cognize' without differentiating between process and subject.

When I use the translation 'to cognize' it must be noted that the corresponding Indian word, say *jñāna,* has a considerably greater sphere of meaning than our 'to cognize' *(erkennen).* It indicates in point of fact almost *all* specifically *mental-spiritual (geistige)* acts. When Max Scheler describes the person as "the concrete 'consciousness of' " (in contrast to the consciousness as the phenomena in consciousness or the content of consciousness)—"all intentionally directed acts (also feeling something [e.g. values], wanting something [projects], judging about something [matters of fact], etc.)"[9]—he hits on that very reality which is intended by the concept of the ātman in Advaita Vedānta. One must not let oneself be distracted by the (certainly considerable) differences from the insight that the intended phenomenon is the same, and that a number of characteristics of the phenomenon are discussed in the same way by Scheler as by the Vedānta philosophers. An important difference naturally lies in the monistic tendency of the ātman concept; this will have to be discussed later. Furthermore, Scheler's concept of the person is very dynamic; the ātman concept in contrast appears to be so rigidly static that whoever views this characteristic alone is inclined to dismiss all comparableness. To speak of "acts" and "intentionality" appears at first to be completely out of the question. Finally, it should be stressed that Scheler's concept of the person is considerably richer and fuller than that of the ātman, so that it can become the central term of a system of *ethics.* This seems to be unthinkable in the case of the ātman.

However, a common feature can be seen in the fact that Scheler (in the same way as the Vedānta philosophers) sharply separates the person from anything that is psychical or mental in the 'I.' When he says: "The 'I' . . . is in every sense of the word still an object . . . the individual 'I' an object of inner perception,"[10] he expresses an insight that is propounded countless times by the Vedāntists; with it, he distances himself from philosophical views common in Europe which do not let the concept of the person emerge clearly, just as the Vedānta distances itself from the naturalistic concept of the soul of the Nyāya-Vaiśeṣika, which is subsumed under the category of substance.

Furthermore, sentences such as the following are significant in the present context: "The person is . . . the directly witnessed unit of experiencing—not only a thing conceived behind and apart from that which is experienced."[11] The person is the concrete, itself essential unity of being of essentially different acts, which by itself (thus not just *pros hēmās*) precedes . . . all differences in the nature of acts. The being of the person underlies all essentially different acts."[12] "Rather, there is in every fully concrete act the complete person, and the complete person 'varies' in and through each act; but its being never merges with any of its acts, and it is never 'altered' like an entity in the course of time."[13] All that sounds like a word-for-word exposition of the Vedāntic ātman concept if one (and this is certainly possible and admissible) leaves the dogmatic monism of this concept out of consideration for the time being and accepts that, in the final analysis, Vedānta would interpret the concept of 'variance' as used by Scheler illusionistically *(upādhi).*

When, for example, the Vedānta philosopher Padmapāda explains that the self is the "experiencing of an object" *(viṣayānubhava),* i.e., that it *is* the "experiencing of something," and is not merely made manifest through it, while in reality remaining behind or outside such (experiencing),[14] then it is difficult *not* to recognize, through all the differences in orientation which are so conspicuous in the context of this exposition, that the Indian refers to the same reality which Scheler means by "person." To the Vedānta as well, a (theoretical) idealism that mixes intellectualizations *(Vergedanklichungen)* that it posits as real into that which is given in cognition, is completely alien. Śaṅkara says: "Cognition arises out of (one of the) modes of evidence *(Bezeugungsarten);* however, (each of) these refers to an existing object."[15] The context in which this statement is made is not of interest to us here; the sentence has universal validity and is meant in that way. As modes of evidence, Śaṅkara's school as well as the Mīmāṃsā school of Kumārila classify six partly psychological-subjective, partly objective, ways by which cognition can be given an object: perception (external and internal), inference (including thought), communication, analogy, co-presence, absence. They attest to, certify, are authority that each given object actually exists and is such (as it is). Through them cognition always relates to something that has *being;* cognition corresponds to an *objective being.* With this sentence Advaita Vedānta distances itself (not yet in the writings of Gauḍapāda and Maṇḍanamiśra, but very strongly since Śaṅkara and his pupils) from all epistemological idealism[16] in a way very similar to Scheler. The historical opponent in this was the Buddhist "Consciousness-Only Doctrine" *(Vijñānavāda).* The illusionism and monism of Advaita Vedānta did not impede this turning toward objectivism; illusionism was objectified as well—we shall come back to the concept of objective illusion later—and in this form was intended to safeguard monism. But, as all idealistic constructions are alien to Advaita Vedānta (since Śaṅkara), the self in its view is not a hypostatized experience "in itself" or "per se," nor a "principle" of consciousness that lies behind the act (of experiencing),[17] nor an idea that would merely manifest itself in the awareness of truth. Instead, the self-evident, spiritual self *is* the "experiencing of the object," just as Scheler's "person" *is* "the inherently necessary and unique form of existence for the spirit"[18]—the "concrete, itself essential unity of being of essentially different acts."

Finally, the difference between Scheler's concept and the Advaitic concept of the person, as implied in the concept of act, can also be clarified to such an extent that it will become evident why what is meant by that term *could* not become explicit in the Advaita system, although the thinkers sometimes did face the essential nature of the "act." Scheler puts the actness of the act in the person itself; thus, it is an "existential unity of acts" for him. But these acts are something intrinsically different from psychic or mental "functions."[19] Advaita Vedānta also knows the concept of the "functions" *(vṛtti),* and it knows that they are *objects* of the self. But it could not let it become explicit that they are "objects of acts" because such a sentence would have endangered the traditional ontology (which we shall have to come back to) that supported monism. However, the "experiencing" *(anubhava)* of which Padmapāda speaks is certainly not a mental function or *vṛtti;*

otherwise it could not be *identified* with the self. Looking for a more comprehensive term, one cannot avoid saying, if one wants to use Scheler's terminology: it is an *act* of the person.

But that is only an *interpretation* of that which is meant *in essence* in, for instance, Padmapāda's lines of thinking. The concept of the act does not become verbally explicit. The Vedāntist is more interested in the *existential unity* of the acts than in the diverse *acts* as such. The idea of this existential unity is stated, for instance, in the following sentence from Sureśvara: "That which has an awareness of the division [that lies in the fact] that the grasper, the grasping, and that which is grasped (i.e., the subject, process, and object of mental cognition) [sometimes] are present and [sometimes] are not present, but which is different from the grasping, etc.: that is the Self."[20] Here the unity of being (of acts) in the "consciousness of . . ." is portrayed as permanent being to such a degree that it extends beyond the actuality of the acts. The self is seen, so to speak, as *one* permanent, continuous act in opposition to that which takes place or does not take place in the psyche or mind.

Even if the acts are seen as actualizations of the existence of the person, they are immediately transposed into the static mode which seems obligatory in Advaita. The Advaita Vedāntist views each of them insofar as it has been accomplished and therefore calls the "consciousness of . . ." the "*result* of a mode of evidence" *(pramāṇaphala);* i.e.: whenever perception, thought, etc. attest to the reality of something that exists, then the "result" of that lies in the fact *that* a consciousness of something real arises. (Linguistically these acts that are seen in terms of their having been accomplished are often indicated by nouns with the suffix *-ti: avagati, anubhūti, upalabdhi,*[21] among others.) In this connection the reference to an object in such acts is disregarded, though they occur only in relation to an object.

With regard to their dynamic and static implications, there is certainly a sharp contrast between Scheler's thought and that of the Vedānta. But the notion of the pervasiveness of the self in all acts of consciousness *(in allen geistigen Akten),* its total indwelling in every such act, its intrinsic nonobjectivity, its self-evidence, its spirituality, and, as a consequence of that, its self-sufficiency,[22] its existential unity, and its differentiation from the mental sphere: all these determinations leave no doubt that what they determine amounts to the *person* in Scheler's sense of the word. Above all, it is important to realize that they evidently cannot be understood as derivations from the notion of a *universal, monistic* Self. They are clearly an attempt to illuminate the nature of the *person.* The person, however, does not exist in a universal, monistic sense, but only as an individual person.

Of course, the adherence to monism caused the results of the research into the person to be immediately used for the development and expansion of the monistic ātman conception. This prevented such research from proceeding beyond the limits set by monism and from attaining a more complete grasp of the concept of person. For instance, the plurality of the acts of the person was indicated almost entirely with the one "cognizing," and the multitude of differentiations that was already performed in the language collapsed into synonymity. But in the expositions of the texts isolated thoughts can be found which, albeit with a certain illusionistic reticence, provide a somewhat fuller picture of the person, and which cannot be explained unless the real focus of spiritual attention for the Advaita thinker was the nature of the *person* and not a universal soul.

The notion of the "experiencing of an object," which was mentioned earlier, certainly belongs in this context. Moreover, the idea that adjacent things "are there for the purposes of the spiritual person, but that this can never be there for what is nonspiritual"[23] can hardly be transposed or interpreted in a monistic-illusionistic way. It could imply the *intentionality* of the acts of the person. "Meaning" and "purpose" are not differentiated in India (both are called *artha* or *prayojana*). But since this is so, the statement that things "exist for the purposes of the person," if viewed in a reverse direction, is the same as that the "person intends" or "means objects." The obligatory static interpretation of the concept of the person forced this inverted and thus hidden formulation of what presents itself as the "intention" of the acts of a person.

The image, furthermore, of the "self-luminous self" in whose "light" the body and the senses, which cannot exist for themselves, act and function,[24] does have a monistic thought behind it and as its goal, i.e., that the body and its actions in truth have no being at all, but that *only* the light of the self or the person (called here the *puruṣa*) has being. But in this form it cannot possibly have been contrived or thought out by a thinker for whom, in terms of his real intent, monism and illusionism would have been of primary importance; otherwise it would certainly have to look quite different. If it were really of primary concern that in truth *only* the light exists, why does it then take the trouble of *illuminating* and *enlightening*, and does not content itself with merely shining? What *interest* does that which has true being, the all-in-one, have in letting that which has no true being, which is illusion, function, controlled by its light? In point of fact, the thought that such an interest *exists* is inseparable from that image (of illumination). Against the will of the monistic thinker, as it were, the *intentionality* of the person which, of course, can only realize such intentionality through acts, is implied. Once again, the concept of the person as the conscious center of acts of an individual human being has affected the formulation of the thought; it has done so to such an extent that the transition to the obligatory monism of the Vedānta system becomes somewhat strenuous.

This implicit presence of the concepts of act and intention is not contradicted by the fact that the applicability of the term "agent" *(kartṛ)* to the person is rejected by the Vedānta system, for this term is obviously meant in a purely psychological sense. But it is also significant that these implications are not made explicit. It forms part of the nature of the person that it stands in *relationships* [i.e., modes of relating to . . .] that are peculiar to it and do not occur outside the being of the person: the relationship of "meaning" or "intention" with reference to an *object,* the relationship of "existing (or experiencing) together" with *other persons,* and the relationship of "self-transcendence" with reference to the "Person of persons," to the Supreme Self *(paramātman),* to God. The insight into the *uniqueness* and, as far as the person is concerned, *intrinsic necessity* of these relationships has in the West perhaps only most recently developed into clarity. There is always the danger of seeing the relationships considered here in all too close a proximity to other relationships—for example, of interpreting them in the manner of causality or of a relationship of possession—or of psychologizing them, thus blurring or obliterating their relational character and objectifying and reifying the person.

The most peculiar and fundamental difference between the Vedāntic concept of the ātman and the modern concept of the person lies in the fact that, according to the Vedānta, the nonobjective character, the spiritual nature, the self-evidence *(svataḥsiddhatva),* and the self-inherence *(svatantratva)* of the self can be secured only if it is categorically *denied* that the self is to be found in *any sort of relationship.* Nonindividuality is implicitly posited with this denial. Advaita Vedānta believes that this thesis is required by its extraordinarily static *ontology.* The consequence is that relations in which the person occurs either collapse into identities or are relegated to the realm of that which has no true being, the *vivarta,* that is, the objective illusion.

What prevented the Advaita thinkers from recognizing *explicitly* the inherence of acts and intentions in the nature of the person and from grasping the significance of the fact that it always occurs in relations was thus, seen conceptually, the presupposition of an excessively rigid ontology that was close to the philosophy of the Eleatics. Historically speaking, thinking about the self did not develop as an independent branch of research in India. In ancient times there were speculations on the core of the human being or the person *apart from* efforts to grasp conceptually the nature or ultimate ground of being, but both lines of thought merged into one very early. Since that time the being of all entities and the nature of the person have been identified, and the predicate "(truly) existent" *(sat)* or "(really) real" *(satya)* has been among the determinations of the person.

With that the foundation of a monism was laid that had its experiential origin in a mysticism that immersed itself into the self, saw no "second" reality apart from it, and experienced such awareness as the supreme truth *(das Wahre des Wahren)*. By adopting ideas from Buddhist philosophy, the tradition of this mysticism produced around 500 A.D. the extreme form of a systematic monism: that of the illusionistic or acosmic monistic (= Advaita) Vedānta. It is characterized as much by the depth of its statements on the self as by the radicality of its negation of the world.

The fundamental ontological statement of this system is: that which has being cannot come into existence, and that which comes into existence cannot have being, and the world is consequently an *illusion*.[25] That which has true being is only the self-evident *(svataḥsiddha)* self, which is the manifestness of what is manifest. This self is *one*. Vimuktātman proves this as follows: "If another spiritual entity *(ein anderes Geistiges)* were the object of the cognition of a spiritual entity, then it would be nonself; for it would be the object of the cognition (of another), as is a pot. But if it is not the object of a cognition of another, then it cannot be proven as existing vis-à-vis the other, for proof of existence comes about only in becoming the object of cognition. Thus there is no other spiritual entity (besides the one), be it known or unknown."[26] The demonstration is rigorous, but it overlooks the possibility of a manifestation through nonobjectifiable personal relationship. The concept of the One is once again defined with rigorous restrictions: What is one cannot have various "forms" *(rūpa)*. Therefore, in further analysis, the concept of the one excludes *coming into being* and *passing away*, and in general any kind of *differentiation*, including the possession of various *attributes*. The One is without attributes; all statements about it must be identical in content.[27]

Let us dwell on the concept of "differentiation" a little longer. It, too, is of an unreal rigidity. The corresponding Indian word, *bheda*, literally means "cleavage," "division." In Christian thought the doctrine of the trinity had already in antiquity provided an occasion to keep apart such terms as "distinction" *(distinctio),* "separation" *(separatio),* and "plurality" *(pluralitas).*[28] European scholasticism then put forth some distinctions of the *distinctio;* the scholasticism of the Indian monists, on the other hand, avoided such differentiations, although in Sanskrit they would have been easy to carry out, for they wanted to defend monism under any circumstances. That is, of course, relatively easy if the argumentation is designed, first of all, in a conceptual-deductive manner, second, in purely negative terms ("there is no *bheda*"), and, third, in such a way that one may shift between *distinctio, separatio* and *pluralitas* as needed, identifying these with the one *bheda.* In this way the Advaita philosophers in the course of the middle ages time and again put forth demonstrations against differentiation.

Then how does multiplicity—first of all as duality—come into being out of the One? In the beginning (in the extant literature, from Gauḍapāda [around 500 A.D.?] to Maṇḍanamiśra [around 700 A.D.]) the thinkers tried to answer this question by following the Buddhist "Consciousness-Only Doctrine" (Vijñānavāda). Thus Maṇḍanamiśra says:[29] "The subject-object relationship is only explainable if one assumes a unity (of subject and object), and specifically, in such a way that the subject itself, which is of a spiritual nature, develops in different directions into separate conditions or seemingly unfolds *(vipariṇāmād vivartanād vā).*" But soon an explanation for the "delusion" of multiplicity was found in the concept of the development of an *objective* illusion (which may seem very foreign to us); it was denoted by the word *vivarta,*[30] and its degree of reality was described by the expression "describable neither as being nor as nonbeing" *(sad-asadbhyām anirvacanīya).* All dynamics, all multiplicity, all coming-into-being, and all relatedness were shifted into the sphere of this illusion. The *vivarta* illusion has its neither-being-nor-nonbeing existence only somehow by virtue of the being of the One, the spiritual Self. "Somehow" is here a conscious, deliberate characterization. There is no real, rather only an illusory relationship between being and illusion; but "illusion" means just that—determinable neither as being nor as nonbeing, thus "somehow." This is true not only for this relationship. All relations are illusion, according to the Advaita. And illusion here is more illusory than it was ever conceived to be in Europe, for it is taught that the whole world is illusion, and that this illusion can be removed by true knowledge just as images in a dream, which are interpreted as objective illusions as well, are nullified by awakening.

This question, how a consciousness of objects is possible, is a complicated problem for this acosmic monism of the spirit. The spirit stands as a "consciousness of something" in opposition to an illusory something that is an objective illusory development of that very same spirit; and the "nescience" *(avidyā, ajñāna),* which individualizes and overlays that which is spirit, the material cause of all that is individual and illusory, is time and again partially "cancelled."[31] But in the context of the concept of the person, we are less interested in the theory of this partial and ephemeral "cancellation of nescience" than in a segment of the theory of the *complete* and *definitive* "cancellation of nescience" by the "awakening" *(prabodha, samyag-bodha)* from the cosmic māyā, when, as Gauḍapāda says, "the soul wakes up from the sleep of beginningless delusion."[32] The theory intends to prove the content of the experience of universal oneness as an ontological reality and as realizeable in practice. The most interesting question in our context is: How does this "awakening" come about?

The answer is very remarkable, not only because it implies that the process of cognizing, which leads to awakening, is itself still completely a part of the illusion. The most interesting point is how the *accomplishment* of the moment of transition from illusion to true being was conceived. Religious ceremonies, forms of worship, meditations and Yoga exercises have, in the view of the Advaita, no causative, rather only a predispositional significance. Awakening is a *cognitive realization;* but such realization cannot be brought about by *action,* rather only by an awareness of its object. Thus, argumentative reflections lead only to the verge of awakening. But how does awakening itself take place? Sureśvara, who has considered this point of the doctrine very thoroughly, tells us: By a *saying,* i.e., a saying of the Veda.[33] This refers specifically to the great "you are that" *(tat tvam asi)* of the Chāndogya Upaniṣad. It has the effect of a call that brings the Self to itself.

This doctrine, which is at once naive and sophisticated, shows in an eminent manner how profundity and absurdity interlock in Advaita thought. According to all ontological premises of the system, any transition from appearance to reality is impossible and unthinkable. 'Impossible' and 'unthinkable' are, elsewhere in this context, almost synonyms for 'not truly real.' Thus, all efforts to attain liberation would have to remain eternally within the cosmic dream. Furthermore, if the relationship between illusion and being itself is only illusion, it is inconceivable how, originating from being, a tendency toward self-cancellation could arise in illusion so that being alone would remain. Later—since Vimuktātman—it was explained that the transition has a degree of reality sui generis; subsequent to Ānandabodha it was called "the fifth type": neither being nor nonbeing, nor both at once, nor neither of the two—a deplorable game of terminology to cover up the weakest point in the system. Sureśvara's idea of the "call," on the other hand, may well betray a sense of the fact that that which has authentic being in the person can only be reached by means of the person; a call is, of course, directed in a very personal way to a person. But the Advaita philosopher cannot admit that the call that awakes the person originates from a person! He is not permitted to, according to the ontological premises of the system. The Veda belongs to the sphere of that which has no true being and is nonpersonal *(apauruṣeya);* but it is nevertheless supposed to awake the person by a personal call to its identity as the Self! Here a relationship of the Supreme Self to the self would be necessary. But it collapses into the absurdity of a causal process that crosses from the disappearing illusion into the ever-existing being of the Self. The Supreme Self, according to the ontology of the system, must be identical with the self; actually it is the self itself. Thus, a very personal act originating from something that is nonpersonal must be conceived. A naive as well as shrewd simile is supposed to make this understandable: the call causes an awakening in the way the vision of a tiger in a dream rouses a sleeping person from his sleep. But how did it come about that a sleeping person could have such a dream? We are not permitted to ask about this.

The doctrine that has just been described is not the only point in the Advaita edifice of ideas where we can see that the interpersonal relationship is required by the facts of the case and even somehow intended by the thinker himself, but that its comprehension is thwarted by conceptual constructions that isolate a mystical experience from its original context and turn it, in a forced and unreal manner, into an abstract ontology. I would also like to refer to the doctrine of the Self as beatitude, bliss, or happiness *(ānanda).* The very sober Śaṅkara did not appreciate this doctrine; he avoided it wherever he could. But, nevertheless, the tradition insisted that the Self was not only being *(sat)* and spirit *(cit),* but also bliss: *sac-cid-ānanda.* The doctrine of *ānanda* is, in turn, evidently an ontologization of a mystical experience detached from its frame of reference; it includes an insight into the nature of the person.

In the context of our examination, the following argument by Maṇḍanamiśra[34] is important:

> A reason for the inherent bliss of the Self is that it is the place *(āspada)* of supreme love *(preman)*. That it is the place of supreme love is, indeed, taught by the Veda: "This is more dear than a son." And that is general experience as well. Every being, even a worm, wishes: "I would not like not to be: I would like to be." But such a wish can only be explained if it is directed toward something that is dear to one. And love directs itself toward something that is full of happiness, not toward something unpleasant, nor toward something that is neither of the two, for one would hate in that case, or be indifferent.

Vimuktātman[35] develops the thought somewhat further:

> Everything else is dear for the sake of the Self, not for its own sake. Thus the Vedic revelation says: ". . . rather for the sake of the Self is everything dear" (i.e., desired or loved). But because everything is dear for the sake of the Self, then it is only the Self that is dear; for if the Self were not dear, then he would also not be dear who is there for its sake. But not for the sake of another is the Self dear to one, for it is not for the sake of another. . . . Also for man and wife (in the mutual surrender of love) the body is for the sake of another, but not the Self. But apart from happiness (bliss, beatitude) and that which is there for its sake, nothing else is generally assumed to be "dear." Therefore, only the Self and nothing else is happiness, as it is there for none and nothing else and as it is dear. That for whose sake everything is, but which is not for the sake of anything else, that is generally considered to be happiness. This general view is not possible for anything other than the Self, and thus only the Self is happiness.

After that Vimuktātman makes it clear that happiness is not (as some think) to be defined in a merely negative way as the cessation of unhappiness; rather it is the opposite: the cessation of unhappiness is an occasion which lets the happiness that is inherent in the Self become manifest. In conclusion then: "The Self is not for the sake of another. Rather, everything is for the sake of the Self. In the same way happiness is not for the sake of another. . . . thus happiness and Self have one and the same characteristic, and it follows from this that they are identical."[36] The happiness of experience is secondary *(amukhya)* happiness in contrast to the primary *(mukhya)* happiness which is the Self itself. These lines of thought remind us of Scheler's magnificent presentation of "bliss" (along with its negative counterpart, "despair"):

> In true bliss and despair, even already in cheerfulness *(serenitas animi)* and "peace of mind" everything that is merely a mode of the ego ("alles Ichzuständliche") appears as extinguished. These feelings seem to flow forth out of the fountainhead of the spiritual acts themselves, as it were, and to inundate everything that is given in these respective acts of the inner and outer worlds with its light and darkness. . . . A sequence of other experiences in a motivated chain of ideas may quite easily rob us of these feelings or cause them to appear at the end of the sequence of experiences. But once they are there, they detach themselves from the chain of motivations in a peculiar way and fulfil, from the core of the person, as it were, the totality of our existence and our "world." Then we can only "be" blissful or despairing, and not "feel," in a strict sense, bliss or despair, let alone "have" such feelings. But it forms a part of the nature of these feelings that they are either not experienced at all or they take possession of the totality of our being.[37]

From the essence of the matter—not only from the ontology of the Advaita—it is understandable that the bliss experienced in the mysticism of the Self was interpreted as *identical* with the Self. The conceptual unfolding of this experience forms an essential part of the Advaita doctrine of the Self; it shows, on the other hand, that that which is meant by the "Self" is the *person,* not primarily a universal spirit. The content of this experience was conceptualized with the help of statements of an ontology that are, in part, a dogmatization of the same experience, with the expectation of making it reproduceable. These statements ruled out mentioning bliss as an attribute of the Self along with two others (being, spirit); they required that *ānanda* with *sat* and *cit,* and each of these, and all three together, be identical *in nature* with the Self, for something that has true being cannot have, according to this doctrine, several attributes, not even any attributes at all; it must have an absolutely homogeneous "nature of its own" *(svarūpa).*

A series of further propositions supplements the statement about the mystical experience of the self as bliss and the ontological identification of being, spirit, and bliss. In part, they originate from the Upaniṣads; ultimately, they are, once again, in the service of monism:

1. Love is by nature self-love, and this is identical with the will to being.

2. (Thus it follows that): Love for other persons happens "for the sake of the Self"; ultimately, it is self-love.

3. Love is directed toward that which is blissful.

4. (It follows from 1 and 3 that): One loves one's own self because it is blissful.

5. Happiness or bliss is for its own sake and therefore identical with the Self, which is also for its own sake.

6. As "secondary happiness," the bliss of the Self is contained in all experiences of happiness.

The statements 4, 5, and 6 yield, in Vimuktātman's exposition, a kind of ontological proof of the Self from the fact of bliss and even of all experiences of happiness. This is in line with Maṇḍana's ontologically oriented proof, which refers to the concept of being to demonstrate the existence of brahman through sense perception.[38] In every perception we perceive that something *is,* i.e., *being* as such: this being *is* brahman itself. It is also in line with the proof of the existence of the Self developed by Śaṅkara *(Upadeśasāhasrī)* and others on the basis of the concept of "spirit." *That* someone becomes conscious of something (the consciousness-of) *is* self-evidently the Self. The three proofs taken together in conjunction with the ontological statements of the system yield the static being-spirit-bliss-monism of the Universal One. The remainder of reality is assigned to the sphere of illusion *(māyā),* of that which is not truly real *(asatya)* and determinable neither as being nor nonbeing *(sad-asadbhyām anirvacanīya),* of nescience *(avidyā),* and of illusory evolution *(vivarta).*

As a result, personal relationships, wherever they impose themselves on the investigation, are eliminated. To make the relationship of self to Supreme Self collapse into an absolute identity is the first and last goal of all cognitive efforts of this system. Thus, the awakening call had to be relegated to an impersonal and illusory realm. The question of "being with one another" of persons imposed itself where the act of love was examined in connection with bliss, but love was reduced to self-love and the relation collapsed. Personal relationships are described expressly in Vedānta texts as not being truly real. The "you" as philosophical expression of the person opposite to the "I" is identified expressly with the "it."

Love is a personal act: Vimuktātman's verbal efforts do not succeed in proving it to be static. But in the monism of the Vedānta this act is bent into a rigorous, grandiose, universal ontological egocentrism. That which is most personal in the person is perceived but immediately deformed. Nowhere does it become so clear as here why this system can have no real ethics; nowhere does it become so clear that prior to the revelation of God's divine love *(agapē)* even the most profound philosophy cannot lead to the realization of the authentic selfhood of the person. That "the human spirit," as Scheler says, "knows the divine spirit in a religious manner and only in this cognition possesses itself fully,"[39] that, in other words, only in the relationship to the Supreme Self does the self come to its authentic being *(Eigentlichkeit),* is stated in the monism of the Vedānta as well, but the relation has collapsed into identity.

However, perhaps one can say that in the statement of identity the relation was intended to a certain degree. Despite all the rigidity of the concepts of the monistic ontology, the focus of research was in fact directed toward the nature of the person; accordingly, the doctrine of the Self contains profound knowledge about the personal core of the human being. Likewise, this doctrine, while identifying the self and the Supreme Self, also includes essential statements about *God.* For example, it seems to do justice to the divine being when the Advaita Vedānta teaches that the distinction of substance and attribute and the assignment of several attributes does not befit the One, which is truly real. Augustine also taught something similar.[40] To be sure, statements such as this could be equally valid for an impersonal Absolute as for a personal God; yet Śaṅkara himself often speaks of the Absolute in such a way that it is unmistakable that he *means* the personal (or a quasi-personal) God. In his book *Westöstliche Mystik*[41] Rudolf Otto has correctly drawn attention to the "underlying foundation" of a "decided theism of a high form," which is ascertainable in the writings of Śaṅkara: "Here, too, the impersonal brahman rests, as it were, on a theistic foundation." In this connection Otto focussed more on the psychological realization of mysticism than on the philosophical system of the Vedānta. Seen from the standpoint of the latter, what Otto calls "the impersonal brahman on a theistic foundation" seems first of all to be a case of terminological confusion or at least negligence.[42] The theistic expressions "God" (*īśvara,* Lord), "Supreme Lord" *(parameśvara),* the designation "Supreme Self" *(paramātman),* which can be interpreted personally or impersonally, and *brahman* or *parabrahman,* which really can only be construed in an impersonal-monistic way, are in Śaṅkara's usage largely interchangeable. One cannot fail to see that in the concept of God, or rather in the concept of the Absolute, just as in the concept of the core of being in man, there is now and then a tension between personalistic intention and monistic presentation.

This tension cannot simply be explained and disposed of by saying that the monistic ontology was an insurmountable convention. This ontology, which had its origins in a conceptualization of mystical experience, was supposed to help reproduce that experience over and over again. If one considers this, then the tension appears as the problem how the thinker (who was always the teacher as well) could find the transition in thought between what he *realized* in his own intuition of the nature of the object and what the ontological reinterpretation of the monistic experience *promised* him as ultimate truth. Mysticism had not drowned in philosophy; rather philosophy had its only sense and purpose in constantly making mysticism possible again. The thinkers's own mystical experience, which determined (just as his own intellectual efforts) the varying degrees of his originality, may have contributed to the different forms of this tension and of the attempts to resolve it. As long as the ontologization was taken completely seriously, the tension could not be reconciled in a philosophical manner, for it is a transgression of domains and an inappropriate claim if the realization of *one* particular kind of mystical experience, namely, the absorption of the Self in itself, is detached from the frame of reference of this mysticism and formulated in statements that, with the claim of general validity, are presented as *the* truth.[43] Such statements are something different from those in which an insight into the nature of the person or the relationship to God in natural religion expresses itself.

With some schematization of the historical facts one can say that a solution of the said tension was sought in two ways, one sterile, one more fertile. The sterile one consisted in doing largely without any personal exploration of reality and without a mystical statement of one's own, and in applying all intellectual power to the conceptual penetration and defense of the established system. The more fertile way attempted once again the direct mystical statement; in the process, the transmitted ontological concepts were employed as means of expression. In this connection, the dynamism of the mystical *way* was again expressed in keeping with reality. Illusory problems, such as that of the transition to the mystical state, could not arise, for mysticism remained mysticism, each of a different kind, and did not present itself as ontology.

A noteworthy example of the latter kind, especially with regard to the understanding of the person, is the Prahlāda legend of the *Viṣṇupurāṇa*.[44] Its mysticism does not fit into any of the ontological systems of concepts that existed at the time of its composition. This comes out in the fact that the attempt to assign its statements to any specific monistic system is an immediate failure. "Prahlāda's monism is variable,"[45] for the statements are not meant as propositions about being; rather, each stands within a mystical situation.

In texts that are not philosophically independent, as in the above mentioned version of the Prahlāda legend, one cannot expect statements about the nature of the person, but it is possible (and interesting) to observe how the person *behaves* in this context. This mysticism is decidedly theistic: its monistic statements are a description of mystical events. Now it is very noteworthy (in this respect the text is unique) that here the relation between God and man, which is partly conceived in a more personalist mode, partly in a more substantialist one, is recognized as the presupposition of a relation between human persons, i.e., the relation of compassion. As I love Viṣṇu and Viṣṇu is in all beings, I must have compassion, even *bhakti,* for these beings: that is Prahlāda's theological ethic.

The question now arises whether this personalism of the *bhakti* mysticism also found expression in the concept of the person in theistic Vaiṣṇava Vedānta. I cannot answer this question satisfactorily; I have not enough insight into the very extensive literature of the theistic Vedānta. As far as I see now, the singular and, even in the Purāṇa literature, soon vanishing recognition of the personalist orientation and its connection with ethics was not adopted into a system. In contrast, the concept of the person of the theistic systematizers (in its demarcation against the mental sphere it is largely identical with that of Advaita Vedānta) has been enriched by some characteristics of personhood: the Self is individual and an "agent" *(kartṛ)*.[46] These are characteristics that were unavoidable in a system that taught divine love *(bhakti);* a purely static and nonindividual perception of the person does not permit the concept of divine love.

But it must also be said that this divine love sometimes appears in the literature in forms in which personhood itself is considerably impaired. The deity then becomes the occasion for the psychological generation of exquisite emotional enjoyments. A complete taxonomy was set up which classifies such feelings and describes those ideas about the deity through which the desired emotional enjoyments can be deliberately generated. For such delights the deity is at the service of the pious: "(The pious) make me amenable through *bhakti,*" says the god in the *Bhāgavatapurāṇa,*[47] and the theistic Vedāntist Vallabha (sixteenth century) incorporates the notion of making the deity serviceable for pleasure in his system.[48] Thus, in Hinduism, divine love did by no means consistently contribute to a deepening of the understanding of the person, especially because its connection with ethics was lost. The doctrine of the Self as bliss found here a new application, but one that once again diminishes the personal dimension.

Notes

1. 1,8,22,2.

2. Paul Deussen (*Das System des Vedānta,* Leipzig, 1883) interpreted Śaṅkara's *ātman* concept all too much from the point of view of Kantian philosophy. Without accepting Deussen's philosophical preconditions, I, too, have used a terminology in earlier works that could be interpreted in this direction: P. Hacker, *Untersuchungen über Texte des frühen Advaitavāda, 1: Die Schüler Śaṅkaras* (Mainz: Akademie, 1950); *Upadeshasāhasrī von Meister Shankara,* übersetzt von P. Hacker (Bonn, 1949). But I must refer to these works for further information. Cf. further: Surendranath Dasgupta, *History of Indian Philosophy,* vols. 1–5 (Cambridge, 1922–55); Olivier Lacombe, *L'Absolu selon le Védānta* (Paris, 1937).

3. The following is according to Śaṅkara, *Upadeśasāhasrī* (Gadya) 1, 9 ff.

4. Ibid., 1, 33 ff.

5. Cf., for instance, Sureśvara, *Naiṣkarmyasiddhi* 2, 15; 22; 91.

6. Sureśvara, *Naiṣkarmyasiddhi* 2, 28 f.

7. It is expressed in an Indian way by means of numerous nomina agentis derived from verbs that mean "to see," "to perceive," "to grasp," for example, *draṣṭṛ, upalabdhṛ, avagantṛ, pramātṛ, jñātṛ, grāhaka, grahitṛ;* as the subject of action: *kartṛ;* as the subject of experience: *bhoktṛ;* as "the correlate of what is objective": *viṣayin.*

8. *dṛś. cit.*

9. M. Scheler, *Der Formalismus in der Ethik und die materiale Wertethik* (Bern, 1954), p. 403.

10. Loc. cit., p. 397.

11. Ibid., p. 382.

12. Ibid., pp. 393 f.

13. Ibid., pp. 395 f.

14. Cf. my *Untersuchungen über Texte des frühen Advaitavāda,* pp. 132 f.

15. *jñānaṃ tu pramāṇa-janyam, pramāṇaṃ yathābhūta-vastu-viṣayam* (*Brahmasūtrabhāṣya* 1, 1,4). *Pramāṇa* is usually translated as "means of knowledge." Without wanting to reject this translation, I would like to come as near as possible to the original meaning of the word (i.e., "measure," "authority") through my translation ("modes of evidence") and explanation.

16. Cf. my essay "Vedānta-Studien: Bemerkungen zum Idealismus Śaṅkaras," in: *Die Welt des Orients* 3 (Wuppertal, 1948), pp. 240 ff.

17. In previous publications I have unfortunately sometimes used such expressions that blur outright a typical characteristic of Vedānta-thought, for example *Untersuchungen . . .*, p. 132 and *Upadeshasāhasrī*, pp. 50–52.

18. Scheler, loc. cit., p. 400 [see also pp. 393 f.; cf. above, n. 12].

19. Ibid., pp. 398 ff.

20. *grāhaka-grahaṇa-grāhya-bhāvābhāva-vibhāga-vit, grahaṇādeś ca yo bhinnaḥ sa ātmety avagamyatām* (*Bṛhadāraṇyakopaniṣadbhāṣyavārttika* 4, 3, 518).

21. Cf. Śaṅkara, *Upadeśasāhasrī* (Gadya) 2, 75–108.

22. *Upadeśasāhasrī* 1, 64 ff.: the term *svārtha.*

23. *Upadeśasāhasrī* 1,64–71.

24. *Bṛhadāraṇyaka Upaniṣad* 4, 3, 7 with Śaṅkara's commentary.

25. Cf., for instance, Gauḍapāda, *Māṇḍūkyakārikā* I, 17; III, 27; IV, 4–5; 29 (edition with translation and copious notes: *The Āgamaśāstra of Gauḍapāda.* Ed., trans. and annotated by Vidhushekara Bhattacharya, Calcutta, 1943).

26. *Iṣṭasiddhi* (Baroda, 1933), p. 240, lines 23 ff.

27. Cf. Vimuktātman, *Iṣṭasiddhi,* pp. 21–23.

28. Thus in Ambrosius, *De fide ad Gratianum* 4, 8, 91 (ML 16, 634).

29. *Brahmasiddhi* (Madras, 1937) p. 7, line 23.

30. Cf. P. Hacker, *Vivarta* (Mainz: Akademie, 1953).

31. Cf. P. Hacker, *Untersuchungen über Texte des frühen Advaitavāda,* pp. 144–48.

32. *Māṇḍūkyakārikā* (Āgamaśāstra) I, 16.

33. P. Hacker, *Untersuchungen über Texte des frühen Advaitavāda,* pp. 95–99.

34. *Brahmasiddhi,* p. 5, line 16.

35. *Iṣṭasiddhi,* p. 29, line 14.

36. *Iṣṭasiddhi,* p. 31, lines 7 ff.

37. Scheler, *Der Formalismus in der Ethik . . . ,* p. 355.

38. See my references in: *Beiträge zur indischen Philologie und Altertumskunde, W. Schubring . . . dargebracht* (Hamburg, 1951), pp. 164 ff.

39. Scheler, *Vom Ewigen im Menschen* (Bern, 1954), p. 191.

40. *De Trinitate* 7, 5, 10: Res ergo mutabiles neque simplices proprie dicuntur substantiae . . . manifestum est Deum abusive substantiam vocari. Ibid., 6, 7, 8; Non est ibi aliud beatum esse et aliud magnum esse aut sapientem aut verum aut bonum esse aut omnino ipsum esse.

41. Second ed. (Gotha, 1929), p. 139. Editor's note: For a slightly different translation, see *Mysticism East and West* (New York, 1970), p. 121.

42. Using philological methods I have examined these relationships in an article in *Zeitschrift der Deutschen Morgenländischen Gesellschaft* 100 (1950), pp. 276–86 [*Kl. Schr.,* pp. 99–109; see Chapter 4, pp. 85–96, in the present volume].

43. In other schools of Hinduism the experiences from other types of religious practice have been systematized likewise with the claim of universal validity; each school accused every other school of missing the ultimate truth and salvation. At the most, it could be granted to the representatives of other systems that their way was a remote preparation that might lead to salvation in a subsequent existence in the course of transmigration. If we wanted to imagine something in Christianity that would be similar to the Hindu systems or schools we would have to suppose that, for example, from the spiritual practices of Saint Francis or Saint Ignatius of Loyola, or from the mystical path and experiences of Saint John of the Cross, different ontological-conceptual systems had been devised and each one had then been presented with the claim of being *the* truth. Once we have made this assumption, the comparison with the heresies of Christianity immediately imposes itself. As little as a multiplicity of heresies, each of which claims to be *the true* form of its religion, represents an inner unity, just as little, or to an even lesser degree, can Hinduism claim to be an all-encompassing unity that contains within itself or admits the possibilities of the numerous antagonistic ways and systems. If this claim is made today, it is purely fictitious. Hinduism has no binding statement for all of its systems; thus, the various systems cannot be interpreted as formations of a pre-existing or underlying unity of "Hinduism." "Hinduism" is nothing but an expedient collective term for a group of cults and doctrines which, although mutually exclusive as totalities, nevertheless have a good deal in common as a result of exchange within the same geographical area.

44. Cf. P. Hacker, *Prahlāda, Werden und Wandlungen einer Idealgestalt, Beiträge zur Geschichte des Hinduismus* (Mainz: Adakemie, 1959), pp. 79–96.

45. Ibid., p. 92.

46. Cf., for instance, Olivier Lacombe, *L'Absolu selon le Védānta,* pp. 188 ff.

47. 9, 4, 66.

48. *Aṇubhāṣya* (Bombay, 1921), p. 26.

8

Śaṅkara's Conception of Man

The fundamental question of anthropology is posed by Śaṅkara himself in the first prose chapter of his *Upadeśasāhasrī*. The prose chapters of the *Upadeśasāhasrī* present a course of instruction in Advaita Vedānta. The teacher begins by reminding his pupil of passages from the Upaniṣads and the *Bhagavadgītā* which express the identity of the individual self with the Supreme Self. Then, "after the pupil has learned from Scripture and Tradition[1] the characteristics of the Supreme Self and has thus become desirous to cross the ocean of transmigratory existence," the teacher asks him, "Who are you, my dear?"

If we transpose this question from the situation of a teacher instructing his pupil into the language of a solitary philosopher, it turns out to be the inquiry about the nature of man, that is to say, the basic question or starting point of anthropology.

The pupil's answer naturally refers to what for an Advaitist is the lower level of reality. He mentions his caste and lineage, he speaks about his previous life and about how he eventually became an ascetic who has come to receive instruction from his spiritual guide. The teacher is not satisfied. He points out that all that the pupil has said concerns his body alone. The body, however, is bound to perish. Yet the pupil desires to escape from transmigratory existence. How can he reach this goal if he is nothing but what he has replied in answer to his teacher's question? "For, burned to ashes on this side of the river, you cannot cross to the other side."

This part of the teacher's instruction already includes an essential part of Śaṅkara's—and general Advaitic—anthropology. In answering the question, What is man?, the Advaitist thinks it inappropriate to refer to the body, to its faculties and potentialities, or to events in which it is involved.

Even the pupil who is receiving instruction from his teacher in the *Upadeśasāhasrī* has already realized this much. He draws a distinction between his ego and his body in saying, "I am different from the body . . . I have entered it, like a bird its nest, on account of merit and demerit accruing from acts I did [in previous existences in transmigration] . . . I have got tired of this going round and round in the wheel of transmigration, and have come to you, Sir, to put an end to this rotation."[2]

This implies, first, that the essential nature of man is that which is signified by the personal pronoun (I, thou, he), and second, that the body is not included in man's essence but is accidental to it. The being that is denoted by the personal pronoun remains essentially the same while continually assuming, and giving up again, countless bodies in the course of beginningless transmigration. This abiding substance of the human person is also denoted by the word 'self' *(ātman,* often more or less equivalent to what we call 'soul'). That the self is the entity signified by the personal pronoun, especially that of the first person singular *(I),* was a doctrine of the Mīmāṃsā schools, and all schools of the Vedānta agreed with them on this point. The pupil who is speaking in the *Upadeśasāhasrī* apparently received previous training, not only in a theistic system but also in Mīmāṃsā, so he takes it for granted that "the self is the object of the notion 'I' *(ātmā ahaṃ-pratyaya-viṣayaḥ).*"

Regarding the nature of the self, however, the Vedānta differed considerably from the Mīmāṃsā. It is well known that the central tenet of the Advaita Vedānta affirms the unity of the self or, to put it in other terms, the identity of the individual self and the Supreme Self who is God. It is precisely this monistic doctrine that the pupil in the *Upadeśasāhasrī* finds hard to accept. Since we are here concerned with Śaṅkara's anthropology, we can to a large extent leave his monism out of account. We are all the more justified in doing so because Śaṅkara himself often reasoned about the self without employing any specifically monistic concept.[3]

Vedānta schools generally described the nature of the self by the triad *sat, cit, ānanda.* These three words signify Being, Spirit, and Bliss. The self is not characterized or qualified by being, spirit, and bliss; rather, each of these terms stands for the whole of the self's essence or substance or nature. Śaṅkara, however, hesitated to describe the self as being and bliss without restriction. This is one of the peculiarities that distinguish him from other teachers of his school.[4] According to Śaṅkara, the self is essentially Spirit. His conception of the spiritual self comes very close to the notion of person as evolved by some modern Western philosophers, especially Max Scheler. There are also some striking resemblances to St. Thomas' idea of *lumen intellectuale.*[5]

Śaṅkara did not simply transmit the system of a school, adding a few arguments of his own; rather, his vision was focused mainly on vital problems of reality as such. In grappling with these problems he weighed the contributions of different schools of thought, utilizing whatever he found true or helpful and discarding what seemed to him to be futile. The Sāṃkhya as taught in the schools of Pātañjala Yoga, the Mīmāṃsā versions of Prabhākara and Kumārila, the radical monism and illusionism of Gauḍapāda, and the moderate monism and illusionism of some Vedānta schools of his time—the latter difficult for us to discern but to some extent inferable from some passages of Śaṅkara's works—all these schools or systems supplied him with conceptual tools. He utilized them all but committed himself to none of them exclusively. His only concern was the truth, whose supreme expression he saw in the Upaniṣads.

The systems of Nyāya, Vaiśeṣika, and Mīmāṃsā had evolved a concept, denoted by the word *ātman,* which more or less coincides with the notion of soul as current in Europe. In the Sāṃkhya school, however, of which the Pātañjala Yoga was a branch, there was no notion corresponding exactly to what we call 'soul.' What we, conventionally and traditionally, call *soul, anima, psyché,* belongs mainly to the domain of what the Sāṃkhya terms the Inner Sense (*antaḥkaraṇa,* comprising several faculties), but partly to the domain of the *puruṣa. Puruṣa* literally means "man." There was an ancient belief that within man there lived another being, a little man. This little man, simply called *puruṣa,* was held to account for the fact of consciousness and life in a human being. It was thus quite natural that *puruṣa* became a word to denote the spiritual essence of man, once thinkers had discovered the spirit to be man's distinctive quality. Therefore, we may very well translate *puruṣa* by "the self." A frequent synonym for *puruṣa* is *ātman* (the latter word has a different meaning here than in the Nyāya-Vaiśeṣika and Mīmāṃsā). But the self as conceived by the Sāṃkhya was rather a lame being. There is a well-known simile which compares the relation obtaining between the *puruṣa* and *prakṛti (materia prima)* to the relation existing between a lame man and a blind man who carries him. The first cannot walk, the second cannot see. Matter is blind, while the spirit can see but is unable to move. All psychic functions of man are processes occurring in the Inner Sense, which consists of subtle matter. They thus remain unconscious unless the *puruṣa* "sees" them. This is why the *puruṣa* is described as "the Seer" *(draṣṭṛ).*

This Sāṃkhya theory has one advantage over the traditional Western notion of soul. There is no split between the body and the soul, in so far as the soul is the Inner Sense. Both are conceived as a perfect unity. A number of Hindu legends and tales take it for granted that there are continuous passages between the psychic and the corporeal or material world. The Sāṃkhya thinkers recognized the truth implied in this popular belief and incorporated it into their system. But if there was no split between body and soul, there was the idea of another split which proved much more fatal than the differentiation of body and soul has ever been, granted that certain accusations of our day are to some extent justified. Man, according to the Sāṃkhya, is in reality no unity at all. It is only by delusion that we conceive the mind or the Inner Sense as possessing consciousness, or man as a unified being guided by a spiritual soul. Final emancipation consists precisely in understanding that this idea of unity is illusory and in isolating the lame spirit *(puruṣa)* from blind matter. Liberation from transmigration *(mukti, mokṣa)* is isolation *(kaivalya).*

The Vedānta theory of the self is greatly indebted to the Sāṃkhya. This holds also for Śaṅkara's version of the Vedānta. The principal texts in which he sets forth his doctrine of the self are the second prose chapter of his *Upadeśasāhasrī* and his commentary on *Bṛhadāraṇyaka Upaniṣad* 4, 3, 7. In both texts the monistic dogma is no essential part of the argumentation and is introduced, so to speak, only by way of an appendix. A few traits of the Sāṃkhya theory are retained, some are modified, while other ideas are added, partly in adaptation of doctrines of alien schools.

Śaṅkara retained the Sāṃkhya doctrine of the purely spiritual nature of the self. The functions or processes occurring in the psyche are the object of the self's "seeing." This seeing, however, is no action. Action involves change, but the self is immutable. If seen from a certain point of view, it seems that Śaṅkara's concept of the self differs from the Sāṃkhya only by his monism, which holds that there is but one self and that all plurality is an illusion, and by his rejection of the Sāṃkhya doctrine that the self "enjoys," i.e., experiences, objects. But this would be an inadequate perspective, similar to the judgment that St. Thomas' philosophy is nothing but an unsuccessful imitation of Aristotle. In reality, Aquinas carefully weighed and screened the contributions especially of the Arabs Avicenna and Averroes, and his genius is manifested precisely in the fact that through what seems to be only a slight readjustment, he succeeded in demonstrating a truth that his predecessors had perhaps intended but had actually obscured by undue radicalism or onesidedness. Śaṅkara's way of procedure bears a remote similarity to that of St. Thomas.

The Sāṃkhya taught that all things, including the psyche, exist "for the purpose" of the self. But this was understood in a rather narrow sense. In the unemancipated state, things are "for the purpose" of the self's "enjoyment," that is to say, the self, in "seeing" the things, produces experience. But such experience is only possible as long as man erroneously identifies his self with his psyche or Inner Sense. In a deeper sense, therefore, material things exist for the self's purpose in that they make possible its emancipation. Since the self is a "lame man," it cannot liberate itself. The "blind man" has to offer his help. Now the noblest thing made out of matter is the psyche or the Inner Sense. It is a process within the psyche which, when "seen" by the self, can result in the insight that spirit and matter, or more particularly the self and the psyche, are in reality absolutely distinct. This insight brings about the "isolation" of the self. It will not be embodied again. It ceases to transmigrate. Matter, and particularly the psyche, withdraws from it. The psyche merges into undifferentiated primary matter. Therefore, matter exists "for the purpose" of the self inasmuch as the subtle matter of the psyche is needed for bringing about the discernment that realizes the self's ultimate objective.

Śaṅkara gave a new orientation to this conception of "existing for the self's purpose." All that is nonspiritual is composed *(saṃhata)*, and what is composed does not have the objective of its existence within itself. It exists for another, it is *parārtha*. The spirit or the self, on the other hand, is absolutely simple in its essence; consequently, it exists "for its own purpose," it is *svārtha*. The Sāṃkhya doctrine of matter's "existing for the self's purpose" was intended to explain the possibility of the *puruṣa's* isolation; Śaṅkara's reinterpretation made of it a very important metaphysical proposition, stating that all things are oriented or disposed to being known by the spirit and that freedom is a distinctive characteristic of the spirit. Monism is disregarded here to such an extent that, taken strictly, Śaṅkara's doctrine of all things existing for the sake of the spirit would be at variance with his monistic dogma.

According to the Sāṃkhya, the self "sees" things or, more exactly, the representations of things in the psyche. Seeing presupposes light; one cannot see things in darkness. What entity supplies the light that enables the self to perceive objects? The Sāṃkhya taught that the Inner Sense consists of the most subtle material substance *(sattva)* which is itself luminous. Thus the *puruṣa* is in need of matter's light if it is to perform its only function, which is seeing. This is certainly not a very convincing expression of the superiority of the spirit over matter. Śaṅkara, as we have already seen, discovered freedom as an essential trait of the spirit. This entailed a fresh approach to the problem that can be metaphorically formulated in the question, What is the light that enables the spirit to perceive objects? In tackling this problem, he used a concept that the Prābhākara Mīmāṃsakas had adapted from Buddhist philosophy, but he expressed his solution in a term he took from an Upaniṣad text.

Buddhist philosophy taught that each consciousness-instant *(saṃvid),* like a lamp, illuminates itself and its object. From this doctrine the Prābhākaras had taken over the view that knowledge as such is luminous. But since they, unlike the Buddhists, acknowledged the existence of an abiding self as the substratum or agent of knowledge, they modified the theory. Knowledge, they explained, illuminates or manifests not only itself and its object but also the self which is the knower. Śaṅkara, however, found that it is neither the Inner Sense nor the act of cognition which is self-luminous, but the self itself. It need hardly be stressed that this doctrine expressed the spiritual nature of the self with incomparably greater precision than the theories of the Sāṃkhya, the Buddhists, and the Mīmāṃsakas had done. To express his doctrine of the self-luminosity of the self, Śaṅkara had recourse to a term he found in an Upaniṣad: *svayaṃjyotis* (Bṛh. 4, 3, 9). His choice of this term implicitly brings out his conviction that his doctrine was nothing but what was taught by the Veda.

Self-luminosity is a special aspect of the self's freedom. It implies that the self is known in a manner different from the way in which objects become known. The self is not an object. It is not necessary to prove, as the Sāṃkhya and the Nyāya had done, that the self exists. On the contrary, the self's luminosity is the presupposition for any object's being known. One may say in a paradox that the self is unknowable because it cannot become an object of knowledge, but it is at the same time better known than any object inasmuch as no object can be cognized save in the light of the self.

This light pervades the psyche, the senses, and the body, and thus binds into a unified whole the psycho-somatic complex of a human being. Since the self exists for its own sake, while all the material constituents of man, including the psyche, exist for the self's sake, it is the self that makes all bodily and psychic functions possible. In this doctrine Śaṅkara not only—once more—seems to forget his monistic dogma, but also—for once—gives a magnificent metaphysical explanation of the existential[6] unity of man. I deliberately use the term 'existential' unity, for Śaṅkara does not envisage man as a unity in essence or nature. Like the Sāṃkhya, he also affirms the split between the Self and the Inner Sense, and if he recognizes that man *exists* as a unity, his spirit-monism ultimately disparages existence as such.[7] Nevertheless, as long as he, facing reality, considers the existential unity of man, the restrictions and reservations which his monism and illusionism will ultimately bring in remain out of account, even to the extent of being in some measure contradicted.

We may formulate Śaṅkara's doctrine in the proposition: Man exists as a unity by virtue of the spiritual self pervading all his bodily and psychic constituents and functions. "As an emerald or any other gem, dropped for testing into milk or a similar liquid, imparts its lustre to them, so does this luminous self, being finer than even the heart or intellect, unify and impart its lustre to the body and organs, including the intellect, etc., although it is within the intellect; for these have varying degrees of fineness or grossness in a certain order, and the self is the innermost of them all."[8] The first constituent of man to catch the reflection of the light of the self is the intellect or intelligence *(buddhi).* Next comes the mind *(manas).* Both the intellect and the mind make up the Inner Sense which we may also call the psyche. The interpenetration of the self's light with the intellect is so intimate that even wise men *(vivekinaḥ)* as a rule identify both and are unable to distinguish them. Next to the Inner Sense, and through the mediation of the intellect, the light of the self pervades the senses, the organs, and the whole body. That this pervasion establishes an existential unity is expressly indicated by Śaṅkara's use of the verb 'to unify' *(ekī-kṛ)* in the passage quoted above.

Let us summarize Śaṅkara's theory. The spiritual self is essentially free *(svārtha).* It does not exist for the sake of things, but things exist for its sake. An aspect of its freedom is its self-luminosity *(svayaṃjyotiṣṭva)*. This involves self-evidence *(svataḥsiddhatva)*. Being luminous, the self not only "sees" objects but is itself the light in which objects become known. This implies that the self is never an object of cognition. It is the presupposition for things becoming objects of cognition. Neither can it, strictly speaking, be described as that which we call the subject of cognition. The subject of cognition is the self in its interpenetration with the Inner Sense or the psyche; this very interpenetration constitutes the Ego *(aham, ahaṃkartṛ)*. The self pervades not only the psyche but all constituents of a human being. It thus binds these constituents together into a whole. It is the principle of existential unity in a human being.

This doctrine seems to me to be Śaṅkara's most noteworthy contribution to anthropology. I omit, therefore, doctrines that seem to be of minor philosophic relevance. Among these is, for instance, Śaṅkara's cosmogonical explanation of how the Spirit—here understood in a monistic sense—becomes united to individual bodies.[9] Another anthropological doctrine, apparently inherited or adapted from Vedānta tradition, concerns the *prāṇa* or *mukhya prāṇa*.[10]

We must note, however, that in Śaṅkara's system monism and illusionism overshadow the theory of which a brief account has been given above. From the point of view of this monism and illusionism, it makes no sense at all to speak of anthropology or of a conception of man. In other words, this conception is simply an illusion. Man's supreme objective consists precisely in his realizing that the Self is only one, and that the interpenetration of the self with the psyche and the body, as well as the multiplicity of selves and human beings, is ultimately unreal. It is true that the road leading to this realization starts from the realm of illusion or unreality. This implies, for example, that as long as a man has not formally become a homeless ascetic *(sannyāsin)*, he has carefully to observe the code of Hindu *dharma*, that even the passage to the state of a *sannyāsin* is licit only for men who have been born as brahmins, and that the doctrine of the unity of the Self may never be used for minimizing the importance of the Hindu social order. Yet it would be a gross misunderstanding to infer from all this that Advaitists held that there was a continuous passage from the contingent to the Absolute or anything like *analogia entis*. Nevertheless, in Śaṅkara's time Advaitism was still in the making, and his monistic and illusionistic dogma could not paralyze his philosophical attention to reality. This is how it became possible for him to evolve the anthropological theory which I have attempted to delineate in the present article.

Notes

1. The terms 'scripture' and 'tradition' are only approximate renderings of the Indian *śruti* and *smṛti*. For the meaning of these terms the reader is referred to the handbooks on Hinduism. The quotation is from *Upadeśasāhasrī* I,9. I use the edition with English translation by Swami Jagadananda (second ed., Madras, 1949). In some cases I adopt the Swami's translation, but for some passages, as in the one quoted here, I give my own translation. An annotated German translation of the three prose chapters of the *Upadeśasāhasrī* was written by me and published by Ludwig Röhrscheid Verlag (Bonn, 1949).

2. *Upad.* I,12.

3. This is why I could discover a number of features common to Śaṅkara's concept of the Self and Max Scheler's notion of the Person. See my study "Die Idee der Person . . ." in *Studia Missionalia,* vol. 13, 1963, pp. 30–52 [i.e., Chapter 7 in this volume].

4. See my articles in *Zeitschrift der Deutschen Morgenländischen Gesellschaft,* vol. 100, 1950, pp. 246–86 and in *Festschrift für E. Frauwallner, Wiener Zeitschrift für die Kunde Süd- und Ostasiens,* vol. 12/13, 1968, pp. 119–48. [i.e., Chapters 4 and 5 in this volume].

5. For a comparison with Scheler, see my article mentioned in footnote 3; for a comparison with St. Thomas see my article "Essere e spirito nel Vedānta" in *Filosofia e Vita,* n.s. anno 10, no. 4, 1969, pp. 26–46 [i.e., Chapter 9 in this volume].

6. The context shows that I am not using this word in the modish sense (in which it refers to the existence, misinterpreted as a strange sort of essence, of the human individual only). All real things *are,* that is, they *exist* or have existence, and 'existential' means "of existence."

7. See my article "Essere e spirito" (mentioned in footnote 5), pp. 32 f. To the data considered there some striking passages from Śaṅkara's works can be added to show that existence ranks rather low in his system.

8. Śaṅkara's commentary on the *Bṛhadāraṇyaka Upaniṣad,* 4,3,7. I have used, with one slight alteration, the translation of Swami Mādhavānanda (*The Bṛhadāraṇyaka Up. with the comm. of Śaṅkarācārya,* 3rd ed., Mayavati, Almora, 1950, p. 612).

9. *Upadeśasāhasrī* I, 18–23.

10. Partly treated by Paul Deussen in his work, *Das System des Vedānta* (Leipzig, 1883), pp. 350–68 [trans. C. Johnston, Chicago, 1912, pp. 324–41]. Deussen took into account only Śaṅkara's *Brahmasūtrabhāṣya.* The works of Śaṅkara, however, contain further material.

9

Being and Spirit in Vedānta[1]

According to its Indian meaning, the word Vedānta refers to the Upaniṣads, those largely mystical texts at the "end of the Veda" which became the point of departure for one of the most important trends of Hindu philosophy and theology. In Europe, it is common to call these efforts of thought, which are exegetically committed to the Upaniṣads, Vedānta. In Indian terminology, one could call them *vedāntavāda,* which would be rendered more precisely as "Vedāntism" or "Upaniṣadism." In the following, I shall deal with the Upaniṣadic texts themselves as well as with philosophical ideas derived from these texts; for the sake of differentiation, I shall use the term 'Vedāntism' when I mean these philosophical ideas, but 'Vedānta' when I present the later doctrine in conjunction with that of the Upaniṣads.

The introduction of the famous Chapter VI of the *Chāndogya Upaniṣad* inquires about that teaching "whereby that which has not been heard of becomes heard of, that which has not been thought of becomes thought of, and that which is unknown becomes known"—that means, about the teaching which makes it possible to comprehend the totality of what there is under one single notion. With our European possibilities of thought, it is easy to guess what this notion is, but in India in the seventh or eight century B.C. it was not so easy; this notion is the concept of "being." It is, however, not taken in a strictly ontological sense, but rather in the sense of cosmology or philosophy of nature, primarily even in the sense of cosmogony. Being is here the "first being," the "original," "primal being" (*das Ur-Seiende*), an *ens primum* which is at the same time a kind of *materia prima*.

This approach already presupposes a prior history of thought. There had been attempts to derive being from nothing, or from nonbeing, but also the idea that prior to the beginning of all things, there had been "neither being nor nonbeing." The negative paradox "neither being nor nonbeing," which already appears in the early period in a Vedic hymn,[2] was later used in a very new sense in the ontology of the monistic and illusionistic Vedāntism; I shall return to this later. The text of *Chāndogya Upaniṣad VI* does not mention the "*neither* being *nor* nonbeing," but rejects explicitly the idea that being could have originated from nonbeing. It says: "To be sure, some people say . . . from nonbeing being was produced. But how could that be so? How from nonbeing could being be produced?"

The text describes the original being in the style of that genre of cosmogonic myths which appears frequently in late Vedic literature. In the beginning, being was by itself alone, "without a second." From its desire to multiply arose, first of all, three primary elements, i.e., fire, water, and "food." Through division and composition, the whole world, or (as we are told) "name and form," evolved out of these elements. In VI,3,3 the text states that for the sake of this evolution being itself "entered" into these elements "with its living self." Thus, the original being is included in all things as an incomprehensibly subtle essence to which every entity owes its being. This is what the text wants to demonstrate.

I could not avoid using the word 'essence.' But we should note that the conditions of what has been called "essentialism" with regard to the European history of philosophy are missing in India. That "essence" which constitutes the "being" of the *Chāndogya Upaniṣad* cannot be conceived independently of existence. *That* a thing is and *what* it is in its core—this is the same for the way of thinking which emanates from our text. The primal being has entered into the things as that whereby they have their existence, or even as their existence itself, and at the same time as their true essence. The essence of all things, i.e., the primal original being which has entered into them, is ultimately one. What distinguishes the things is only their "name"; it has its ontic foundation merely in language.

The cosmogonic account in the Upaniṣad is followed by a series of primitive experiments. There is no need to describe them. They all try to demonstrate that that which is in a thing, what the thing really is, is ultimately being itself. The twofold presentation contains the origin for two later systems of thought. In the cosmogonic presentation, we find the point of departure for a philosophy of emanation which was fully developed in the Sāṃkhya system; the demonstration of the *one* Being in all the manifold perceptible entities became the basis for that monism which was developed in Vedāntism. In Sāṃkhya, being is completely reified. As far as the word is concerned, the concept of 'being' is preserved in the guṇa *sattva*. This is the "quality of beingness" which is here a subtle, transparent stuff, one of the three constituents of primal matter and at the same time, in a psychological and ethical sense, reified goodness (the convertibility of "being," "good," and "true" which was a theme of medieval European thought, was not a matter of reflection in India; instead, it was simply expressed linguistically or semantically, that is, in the fact that the word for "being" also stands for "good" and "true"). In Sāṃkhya, primal matter has been substituted for the original being. Even in the Upaniṣad itself, the *ens primum* was at the same time conceived as a *materia prima*. But in Vedāntism, being continues to have a certain significance. For an inquiry about being and spirit in Indian thought, it thus makes sense to deal, above all, with the Vedānta, primarily with its monistic development.

In the logical and physical systems Nyāya and Vaiśeṣika (we may add this just to complete the picture), "beingness" *(sattā)* has been, in an exclusively logical perspective, built into the system as the most general generality (i.e., the highest universal). Apart from the Vedānta, only the philosophy of grammar as represented by the great Bhartṛhari, has produced noteworthy ideas about being. But the research on this system has just begun, and it would require a separate treatment. Thus we shall confine ourselves to the monistic Vedānta.

The ideas of *Chāndogya Upaniṣad VI* can, in European terms, be adequately interpreted as follows: the primal being, i.e., the original entity, "das Urseiende," as well as its essence or nature, or "*what* it is," *is* its being (or existence, "Sein"). An entity for which this is true can, however, only be one; according to Thomas Aquinas, God himself is his own *natura* or *essentia*, and his *essentia* is his *esse;* this is one of the reasons why there can only be one God.[3] Indeed, the text says explicitly that the primal being (i.e., original entity) was "one only, without a second." This original being is that whereby everything that has come into being is there, or even that *as* which it is there. Thus, we can say in a full sense of identity that it is the being of everything that has come into being. But since it is also its own self and essence, this implies that it is at the same time the essence and self of all things and persons, and that they are all identical in their depth. There was no suggestion of a recognition of the analogy of being; thus it was inevitable that the notion of a primal being, from which everything comes and which merges with its own products, would lead to a radical monism.

If the identity (applying later conceptual distinctions) is conceived only in a material sense, we have the Sāṃkhya scheme of thought, with its doctrine of the identity of the primal substance and its product; everything *is* in its essence and being its primal substrate, and all substrates are ultimately the primal matter. If, on the other hand, identity is conceived in a sense which includes being and spirit, then we arrive at the possibilities of monistic Vedāntism. The Upaniṣad does not explicitly distinguish the spirit from the being of things and leaves both directions of development open. It proposes identifications: the primal being is the self of the universe and at the same time the self of the individual person. To articulate this, the teacher in the Upaniṣad utters for his disciple, always at the end of a demonstration, nine times the famous words: "This subtleness (of the primal being, which is present in everything that has come into being as an imperceptibly fine essence) is the selfhood of the universe;[4] this (i.e., the primal being) is the truth; this is the self; you are that *(tat tvam asi).*"

The primal being is referred to as "truth" *(satya);* this has to be understood as that cosmic power which truth was in the ancient Indian world view.[5] Later the word was taken in the sense of "that which truly is, or exists"; this expresses the convertibility of "being" and "true" which we mentioned earlier: being is truth.

In the period of the Upaniṣads, various speculations were associated with the word 'self' *(ātman),* speculations in search of what is essential and truly real in man as well as in the universe. There was certainly no initial unanimity concerning the nature of this self. There was even the view that man had several selves; among these, however, a hierarchy was assumed. Our text identifies being, the basic principle and inherent fundamental force of the universe and man, with the self; this suggests, first of all, that what those speculations revolving around the word 'self' had tried to find had now been located in the primal being. But at the same time it implies a decision which was to have major consequences for the further development of the Vedānta. Not only being and essence, but also being and selfhood are completely identified. Vedāntism has never been able to break this identification, which was stipulated by the authoritative Upaniṣadic text.

In our text, the self is taken in a vitalistic sense. It is also called *jīva ātmā,* "living self," i.e., that whereby something that is alive has its identity as a living entity. The primal being itself has entered into that which has come into being *with* its living self, and that means also *as* living self. Later on, the vitalistic aspect disappeared. *Jīva,* literally "the living one," became a name for the individual self in contrast to the Highest or Universal Self. The Self, as that which truly is, or as being itself, is, according to the later view, beyond life and nonlife. In Hinduism, "life" does not have the character of absoluteness it has in Christianity; it is only taken in a biological sense.

In the period of the Upaniṣads, the view that the *self* is *spirit* gained increasing prominence. Vedāntism becomes almost a pure philosophy of the spirit; and thinking about being is usually dependent on the concept of spirituality. One of the most important starting points for this development lies in an idea which, with some variants, occurs several times in the *Bṛhadāraṇyaka Upaniṣad* (III,4,2; 7,23; 8,11). Here the self is described as "the unseen seer, the unheard hearer, the unthought thinker; apart from him, there is no knower" (III, 7,23).

Linguistically as well as in its way of thinking, this text is somewhat similar to the one from the *Chāndogya Upaniṣad* which we discussed earlier and where a search was made for that whereby the unknown becomes known. Both texts aim at something ultimate. The quest for that whereby the unknown becomes known is a search for being; the formula of the unknown knower refers to the spiritual or the spirit. In the same text (Bṛhadāraṇyaka Upaniṣad III,7,16–23) the self is defined as the "inner controller," which guides internally all the constituents of the human organism but is different from any one of these constituents. The inner controller in man, the unperceived perceiver, the unknown knower, is obviously the spiritual unity of the person, the center of all spiritual acts, which for this very reason is not accessible as an object to these acts. At the same time, the inner controller is also effective in all the constituents of the universe (*Bṛhadāraṇyaka Upaniṣad* III,7,3–15); this is in accordance with the way of thinking in many Upaniṣadic texts, in which cosmology and anthropology are integrated with one another. This way of thinking, too, tends toward monism as it will be fully developed in Vedāntism.

The two Upaniṣadic texts which we have discussed have gained greatest significance for Vedāntism. The concept of the self unites both. For the Vedāntist who tried to harmonize the readings of the Upaniṣads, the juxtaposition of such texts meant that the being which was mentioned in one text and the spirit discussed in other texts were one and the same. If we want to identify those Upaniṣadic thoughts on the theme "being and spirit" which were adopted and developed by Vedāntism, we may say in a brief summary and interpretation: eventually existence, essence, selfhood, and spirituality were completely integrated, and spirituality turned out to be the dominant element in this integration. Thus, we get a spiritual monism which excludes all such being that does not conform to this identification as nonessential and finally (probably under Buddhist influence) as illusory or as mere appearance.

However, judging by the extant sources, this result was reached only at least a thousand years after the composition of the early Upaniṣads. It is one of several possibilities to expand the many suggestions of the Upaniṣads into a system. It is that variant of Vedānta which became most influential in the history of Indian thought and to which I shall confine myself in my presentation.

Let us turn now to the oldest extant work of the radically monistic and illusionistic Vedāntism, i.e., the *Māṇḍūkyakārikā* of Gauḍapāda. The concept of spirit in this work, as well as its ideas about being, are strongly influenced by Buddhist philosophy. In a brief and schematic sense, we may say: the concept of spirit is influenced by Buddhist idealism (Yogācāra), and the ideas about being are influenced by Buddhist negativism (the Madhyamaka system). The arguments follow two lines. The one proceeds from the spirit, and the other questions being. Proceeding from the spirit: the opposition of subject and object is only an apparent, illusory vibration of the spirit, which is in reality unmoved. Regarding being: what *is* cannot *become* (come into being); what *becomes* (comes into being), cannot *be*. Truth is neither being nor nonbeing nor both nor neither (IV, 45).[6] It is referred to only negatively as "nonbecoming," or "that which does not come into being." The two lines of argumentation converge in the statement that "nonbecoming" is the spirit, called *vijñāna, citta* or *manas* (see IV, 45).[7] Here, being is not integrated with the spirit in such a manner that the integration would at least keep the "color" or connotation of being. Instead, being has been completely suppressed and superseded—so completely that we cannot even speak of a negation of being, nor of one of the two paradoxes of "both being and nonbeing" and "neither being nor nonbeing." Spirit alone remains.

This is a position which did not last in Vedāntism. On the one hand, Śaṅkara (ca. A.D. 680–720), who for some time worked with Gauḍapāda's concept, produced a purer concept of spirit—more clearly separated from the mental than it ever was in Europe. On the other hand, it does not conform to brahminical thought to refer to the ultimate and absolute using only negations. Gauḍapāda had used the hypernegation prepared in Buddhism: neither being nor nonbeing nor both nor neither. Śaṅkara agrees with Gauḍapāda (who is said to have been his teacher's teacher) insofar as for him, too, being is superseded by spirit; however, the absolute as spirit somehow retains the character, the "color" or connotation, of being.

One sentence from Gauḍapāda's radical argumentation would seem to deserve special prominence in our discussion. This is the sentence that the spirit can neither be called being nor nonbeing nor both together nor neither of the two.[8] This seems to imply the insight that being and spirit are not identical and, second, that the one cannot be derived from the other. This may be granted, even if we do not accept the monism, idealism, and illusionism of Gauḍapāda, that rigorous ascetic of the spirit. However, we are then still faced with the question concerning the relationship between being and spirit; this cannot be resolved by explaining away being.

Now let us turn to Śaṅkara. He rarely speaks about being, and only somewhat casually. For Gauḍapāda, the absolute was spirit in such an absolute sense that it was entirely beyond being and nonbeing; Śaṅkara, on the other hand, accepted the characterization of *brahman* as being and spirit (*sat* and *cit*), which apparently was already traditional by his time. But he showed little inclination to deal more explicitly with the element of being. On the one hand, this was so because he was afraid that labeling *brahman* as being might be misunderstood in conformity with a classifying philosophy of nature (such as the Vaiśeṣika), i.e., as affiliating the absolute with a class of things.[9] Like God in the doctrine of Thomas Aquinas,[10] Śaṅkara's *brahman* is *non in genere;* it does not belong to any class of things. Unfortunately, however, Śaṅkara included being, too, among the classes of things. In this he had to follow the Vaiśeṣika. Other achievements of thought to which he might have referred were not available to him. The Vaiśeṣika system regarded being as the most inclusive class of things, as *beingness,* which is the most general generality (or highest universal). Śaṅkara could not bring himself to rank the absolute with this class. If, on the other hand, 'being' is meant to designate the absolute (as *ens primum = esse tantum,* corresponding literally to the Indian *sanmātra* or *sattāmātra*), then this designation was in reality redundant according to Śaṅkara's way of thinking. In his doctrine, all things and everything that happens to them exist on the basis of the one absolute spirituality;[11] in a sense, this spirituality occupies, as a substitute, the place of absolute being.

Śaṅkara rejects the proposition that brahman is being *and* cognition.[12] In his view, the 'and' would jeopardize the absolutely unitary nature of the absolute. Although Śaṅkara, just as Thomas Aquinas, taught the absolute *simplicitas* of the absolute, the Hindu was radically different from the Christian insofar as he was incapable of thinking of the absolute being as *actus*.[13] This, in conjunction with an insufficient development of the idea of the analogy of being, implies that the Hindu philosopher who conceived the absolute in a more absolute sense than anybody else, could not provide this concept with much fullness; with Thomas, God contains in himself the "ideas."

Śaṅkara accepts the proposition (apparently advocated by others) that the being of brahman is its "intelligence" or cognition and that its cognition is its being; but he does not attach great importance to it.[14]

In two verses of the Kaṭha Upaniṣad (II,2,12f.), we are told that brahman can only be grasped in the statement "it is." Śaṅkara's explanation of this nucleus of an ontology, as found in his commentary on this passage, does *not* imply that the proposition "it is" refers to the authentic and pure *brahman*. Instead, the definition of brahman as *being* is only a preliminary one for him. It refers to *brahman* with attributes *(sopadhikaṃ brahma)*. Brahman is being insofar as it is the being or the basis of the entities which are there. But as noted earlier, this basis is considered to be primarily spirit. Furthermore, the idea of brahman as being is required for practical reasons; the negative characterizations, which have to demarcate brahman against anything that has come into being, should not be misunderstood as implying that brahman is *nothing*. The world, as the product of brahman, has qualifications which may be arranged in a series leading from the less subtle to the more subtle. The concept of being is located at the end and at the top of this series. In final liberation all concepts vanish, but the last and highest of them, the concept of being, is the closest possible approximation to what brahman really is, and to what cannot be attained by the senses, thought, and language. As such, brahman is beyond being and nonbeing, not an absolute Being *(Sein)* beyond all beings, but simply spirit.

The only positive characteristic of the absolute which Śaṅkara accepts without reservation is the spirit. His ideas about the spirit are the center of his system. We cannot say anything certain about the development of Vedāntism prior to Śaṅkara, because the pre-Śaṅkara literature of the school, with the exception of Gauḍapāda's work and the enigmatic *Brahmasūtras*, is lost. But it seems that in the philosophy of the spirit Śaṅkara achieved something new and original, the result of a cross-fertilization between an Upaniṣad interpretation no longer accessible to us, and the teachings of Gauḍapāda (who stands apart from this tradition) and other systems (Yoga, Mīmāṃsā).

Using the word 'spirit' with reference to Śaṅkara's system, I mean the Indian concept of *cit* or *caitanya*. The concept of *cit* has no precise equivalent in European languages. Seen from the standpoint of Vedāntism, Greek *nous,* Latin *intellectus* or *mens,* and similar concepts all denote more or less mental capacities in which the spirit *(cit)* is present but which are not spirit itself. They are more or less equivalent to what is called *citta* in Yoga, as well as Gauḍapāda and Śaṅkara. Yoga and Sāṃkhya had already distinguished between *cit* and *citi,* on the one hand, and *citta* or *buddhi,* on the other. *Cit* relates to *citta,* so we may interpret, just as being *(Sein)* relates to what there is *(Seiendes).* In the following, *cit* is rendered as "spirit," *citta* as "inner sense." But *citta* also corresponds to what we call "psyche" or "ego."

The spirituality of the *cit,* which constitutes the essence of the self according to Sāṃkhya and Yoga, was in these systems constantly characterized by the metaphor of "seeing" or "beholding" (we also find "enjoying," but we don't have to deal with this term here). If the self "sees," in which light does this happen? According to the Sāṃkhya, the most subtle constituent of primal matter, the *sattva* referred to earlier, is luminous. The "inner" sense *(citta, buddhi)* consists of *sattva.* The self sees or beholds in the light of the *sattva,* the inner sense. What it sees is, just as the light, in the inner sense. In the case of perception, this inner sense has, under the influence of the external senses, assumed the "form" *(ākāra)* of the objects, or has been "colored" by them *(uparāga).*[15] However, there was also another view which had infiltrated into brahminical philosophy (specifically the Mīmāṃsā system) from Buddhism; according to this view, knowledge itself, the process of cognition, is luminous.

Śaṅkara combined both of these philosophical ideas—that of the "seeing," "beholding" spiritual self *(cit, ātman)* and the receiving inner sense (which one might also call psyche, i.e., *citta, buddhi,* etc.), on the one hand, and the concept of self-luminosity, on the other. In this process both were modified. Now it was not the *act of cognition* that was luminous, neither as an individually occurring process nor through the individual "results" of cognition as they were "shining" in awareness. Instead, Śaṅkara defined *the self* itself as the self-luminous, subsistent light that was included and presupposed in every act or cognition, and not simply coinciding with it. Subsistent means: regardless of the intermittent processes of cognition, the self as such is light, by its very own essence and thus constantly; it is self-luminous. It beholds the processes of cognition, which occur in the inner sense (or in the psyche or the ego) in its own light; in this way, it turns them into conscious events.

By combining the metaphors of "beholding" and "shining" and by applying the idea of shining to the self instead of to cognition or inner sense, an interpretation of the self had become possible that led beyond the achievements of other systems. The doctrine of light had the advantage of describing the spiritual nature of the self more vigorously than had been possible with the conceptual tools of the other systems. The very nature of the spirit implies freedom. It is, however, not a very convincing portrayal of freedom if (as postulated by Yoga and Sāṃkhya) the spiritual self is supposed to "see" or "behold," but only in the light of the subtle matter which constitutes the inner sense (according to an old Sāṃkhya-Yoga doctrine, the self itself "shines" only in final liberation, in its release from matter.[16]

The spiritual nature of the self implies its self-manifestation *(svataḥsiddhatva).* To be known, the self does not require a subject-object relationship. This, too, was expressed in the doctrine of light. There was no need now, as had been the case in other systems, to work out inferences that were supposed to demonstrate the existence of the self. The self is the condition of the possibility of objects becoming known to a subject; thus the self itself is never an object. For this same reason, it is known more directly than the things which owe their manifestation *(siddhi)* as objects to its light.

The self cannot be included in any class or category. Against the Vaiśeṣika system, which is a philosophy of nature, Śaṅkara emphasized that the self is not one of the substances, and against the Mīmāṃsā system, that it is not an agent in the process of cognition.[17]

In conjunction with a passage from the *Bṛhadāraṇyaka Upaniṣad* (IV,3,7), Śaṅkara has used his doctrine of light as the center of a gnoseological anthropology. The self is the inner light *(antarjyotis)* that brings about the unity *(ekīkaroti)* of the psychosomatic complex. It illuminates the inner sense, the outward-oriented senses, and the entire body. It exists for its own sake *(svārtha).* Without it the psychosomatic complex cannot start functioning. All the other means of human orientation are for the sake of something else *(parārtha).* To express this without the light metaphor: all human behavior is accompanied by a reference to the ego, but according to Śaṅkara's presupposition (which he shares with the Mīmāṃsā), the self is the center of the ego. The inner sense becomes an "organ for everything" *(sarvārthakaraṇa)* only by virtue of the fact that it is "united" with the light of the self (as already taught by Yoga).

Without the reflection of the self, it could not become what it is supposed to be by itself, according to the Sāṃkhya and Yoga doctrine, something luminous, a "shining light." We may say that Śaṅkara understands the self as the spiritual unity of the person,[18] but with much more developed concepts than those employed by some Upaniṣadic texts. Here, Śaṅkara disregards his own monism to such an extent that some statements of his anthropological doctrine of light do not conform to monism at all.

Śaṅkara emphasizes that the self is constant, subsistent beholding and shining.[19] Even if no object is known and even in dreamless sleep, the self continues to be pure beholding and light itself. A similarity of this light with the *lumen intellectuale* which is taught by Thomas Aquinas is unmistakeable. According to Thomas, the *anima intellectiva* has a potential and an actual capacity, the *intellectus possibilis* and the *intellectus agens.* It is the function of the latter to abstract intelligible forms or general concepts *(species, formae)* from the sense images *(phantasmata).* These are received by the *intellectus possibilis,* and this produces actual cognition. The abstraction of the intelligible forms requires a spiritual light, the *lumen intellectuale.* The pure sense perception, though already spiritual, is not yet illuminated by the *lumen intellectuale.*

With Thomas, the spiritual light is thus restricted to intellectual cognition, to the formation of propositions. With Śaṅkara, on the other hand, it already illuminates the functions of the sense. Nonetheless, the doctrine of the *lumen intellectuale* comes quite close to the notion of the self as worked out by Śaṅkara. We may say: The relationship between the inner sense (which may also be called psyche or ego) and the self according to Śaṅkara corresponds more or less to that between Thomas' *anima intellectiva* and *lumen intellectuale* (*facit manifestationem;* see *Summa theologiae* 1,67,1c). Of course, Thomas did not separate the "light of the intellect" as sharply from the intellect as the philosophers of Sāṃkhya-Yoga and Vedāntism separated *cit* and *citta,* but a distinction is also possible according to the doctrine of Thomas.

The similarity with the Indian notion of the self manifests itself also in the historical fact that in Europe as well as in India there was a tendency to interpret the spiritual light in a monistic sense. In the West, approximately one hundred years prior to Thomas, the Arabic commentator of Aristotle, Averroes, had proposed the theory that the *intellectus agens* was one and the same in all men. In India, of course, that school of Vedāntism of which Śaṅkara was the leader was strictly monistic.

In his critical response to Averroism, Thomas, who followed the lead of Augustine, distinguished the spiritual light of the individual person from the absolute spirit without entirely separating it. He taught that the human intellect is capable of knowing and judging only because it "participates"[20] in God's spiritual light or because this light has been "impressed upon it directly by God."[21] The rational soul possesses the immaterial light not only potentially but actually.[22] Yet this is not the light of the absolute per se. Thomas also shows remarkable reserve in his two *Summae* with regard to the idea (which he does, however, not simply reject) that the *intellectus agens* is always knowing, regardless whether an object is being known or not.[23] This is so for the following reason. Aristotle's treatise "Of the Soul" says about the intellect *(nous),* which is "separate, without passion, unmixed, and essentially act," that it is "not sometimes knowing and sometimes not knowing."[24] The Arabs Avicenna and Averroes used this statement in support of their thesis that the *intellectus agens* is a substance separate from the soul. The Christian philosopher could not accept such a thesis.

With Śaṅkara and his school, monism is far more pronounced than with Averroes. Self and absolute self, *ātman* and *paramātman,* are in reality completely identical. The subsistence of "beholding" and "shining" in the self substantiates, according to Śaṅkara, the monism of his philosophy of the spirit. The fact that awareness occurs in all cognitions without exception, that it is in essence the same everywhere, proves for him that there is only *one* beholding and shining spirit, essentially and constantly beholding and shining, regardless of the intermittent processes of cognition in individual subjects. This is the only rational proof he presents for his spiritual monism. The obvious objection that essential unity does not have to be existential identity is not taken into account; this is a result of the ancient equation of self, essence, and existence. If the objection were taken seriously and if the absolute, subsistent light of the spirit would be related to the spiritual light, as it appears in individual cognitions, instead of being identified with it, then an analogy between the two would become evident. Of course, this is not an analogy of being, but an analogy of spirituality. However, the rigor of the Vedāntic concept of being recurs in its concept of spirit, although it seems rather relaxed as long as the human self as such is taken into consideration; accordingly, we can identify elements of a concept of person in the conception of the self.

The element of being, which Śaṅkara had neglected, becomes important in the work of his (perhaps somewhat younger) rival Maṇḍanamiśra. Maṇḍana's doctrine may be called radical ontologism. According to this doctrine, the absolute is, in a direct sense, being in general *(sattā)*. Being is the fact that something is there, and this is identically (and not just in a univocal sense) the same everywhere. Maṇḍana presents lengthy reflections on what being is *not;*[25] he rejects the views that it is being known, or the potential of being known. It could be possible that this was aimed at Śaṅkara. With Maṇḍana, being is certainly not lost in spirit. He also rejects the theory that being is the capacity of efficient action. With approval and adding his own commentary, Maṇḍana quotes the statement of an ancient Vedāntist (whose identity we do not know); according to it the general being is the "matrix of all distinctions," to which it relates just as matter relates to the things made from it. In it, all particularity has become extinct.[26] This is basically the same view as the one found in the Chāndogya text discussed earlier; it spoke of the primal being, and Maṇḍana developed its teachings into a radical ontological monism. Besides, Maṇḍana also knows the monism of the spirit. There are no reflections on the coexistence of spirit and being.

Thus Vedāntism presented two types of positive arguments, and in both ways a unity of essence was overinterpreted as identity of being. Either one would proceed, like Śaṅkara, from the essential unity of awareness in all cognitions, or like Maṇḍana, from the fact that all entities *are*. According to the one argument, the absolute was defined as spirit, according to the other, as being. Proceeding from the spirit (as was done by Śaṅkara in particular) could involve important reflections on the self. If there were reflections on the mutual relation between being and spirit, then this could only amount to merging being, more or less completely, in spirit.

Later on, Maṇḍana's argumentation from being was articulated even more sharply, for instance in Vidyāraṇya's *Pañcadaśī* in the fourteenth century. In a general fashion, Vidyāraṇya's considerations may be summarized as follows.[27] A thing *is,* and it has *attributes*. That it is, i.e., that it is qualified by being, means that the nature of being is present in it, too. The attributes, on the other hand, are different in each individual thing, and they do not belong to pure being. This has only *one* nature, and it is the same in all entities. That this nature seems to coincide with the attributes in a thing, or that the being of a thing appears as one of its attributes, is illusion, the result of *māyā*. Only that is truly real which is recurrent in all entities; and this is being alone.

To begin with, existence (or being-there) and essence (or being-so) have been put on the same level; both are supposed to be characteristics of a thing. But this is done just to separate them radically from one another—not, however, as existence and essence (being-there and being-so), but as two absolutely different kinds of being-so or essence. All being-so is objective appearance, because it veils and multiplies the unitary nature of being. Being alone *is,* and because its nature is absolutely unitary, all differentiated being-so must be mere appearance. This being, infinitely remote from an *actus essendi,* is mere self-identity, a rigid block.

But how can we explain that the particularities which constitute the difference of things adhere to the one being, or veil it? How is it possible that we can say: the things *are?* What is the kind of apparent being things have for themselves?

Obviously, Vedāntism could not answer such questions on the basis of a positive doctrine of being. Vidyāraṇya's line of thinking, which we just summarized, illustrates graphically what Vedāntists would do with being once it was treated positively in accordance with Maṇḍana's approach. Speaking of the being of *things* was possible only in a theory of appearance or illusion.

In monistic Vedāntism, the theory of illusion was cultivated with great dedication; it was supposed to demonstrate how the transition from appearance to being, i.e., release, is possible. Here, release means the knowledge of the sole reality of the one spiritual self, and that means also to *be* this self alone, to exist only as it. All entities apart from the one spiritual self are illusion. This illusion was described with images which, in part, had already been used by the Buddhist illusionism; the things of the world are like a mirage, like a rope that seems to be a snake, like mother of pearl that is considered to be silver. This implied a parallelism between sensory illusions, as they occur *in* the world, and that illusion which constitutes, according to the theory of the school, the entire world. One would explore the innerworldly illusion and then, by analogy with it, define the ontological character of the world. There was not much interest in the subjective conditions of illusion. Illusion was not explained as a subjective phenomenon but as objective appearance. In spite of its objectivity, such appearance can be nullified and supplanted by right knowledge. If I look closely and notice that not a snake, but a rope is lying in front of me, then the appearance of the snake is nullified and gone. Likewise, it is hoped that by recognizing the spiritual self as the one true reality, the world in its entirety will be annulled. In reality, nothing happens in this recognition, just as nothing happens in the cognitive annulment of the appearance of a snake. It is as it has always been. Only the void and veiling illusion has disappeared.

The following argument was presented to determine the ontological status of illusion: if something is perceived but may be annulled by subsequent cognition, then it cannot be defined as nonbeing or unreal, because it was perceived, and that which *is not* cannot be perceived. On the other hand, it cannot be defined as being or real, because it is annulled, and that which *is* cannot be nullified by mere cognition. Thus the object of an illusory cognition is "indefinable in terms of being and nonbeing" *(sadasadbhyām anirvacanīya)*. The words 'false' and 'untrue' *(mithyā, asatya)*, which are taken here in an ontological sense, have the same meaning.

Gradually the Vedāntists got used to distinguishing the case of innerworldly illusion more clearly from that kind of illusion as which they tried to identify the entire world.[28] The world is first-degree illusion, and sensory illusion is second-degree illusion. The distinction of two levels of illusion implied that the world was unintentionally credited with a higher degree of reality than that conceded by the older thinkers when they compared the world to sensory illusion. The intention of this comparison was an equalization in essence, i.e., in terms of their illusoriness. The theory of the three degrees of reality, on the other hand, established a distinction between the two levels of illusion specifically with reference to the intensity of their illusoriness. Both kinds of illusion are "indefinable in terms of being and nonbeing." But the illusion which is the world is "practically real" or "practically true" (*vyavahārasat* or *-satya*), whereas the second-degree illusion has only a "fictitious being" *(prātibhāsikasattva)*.

The absolute being *(pāramārthikasattva), brahman,* is the point of reference for both kinds of apparent being. Here, the characterization of the absolute as being comes again into play, although spirituality continues to be its primary determination. It is a characteristic trait of brahminical spiritual monism (brought into sharp focus in the defense against Mahāyāna Buddhism) that it does not tolerate negation without a positive, affirmative point of reference. This is the reason why brahminical monism instructs us to negate the world by means of knowledge; through such negation, it wants to bring about and intensify our readiness to see the positive absolute. This requires attention to its aspect of being. The absolute is that which is meant by the word 'is.' It is, according to Prakāśātman (approximately tenth century), the *astyartha;* Prakāśātman took a more affirmative approach to being than Śaṅkara did in the passage from his Kaṭha Upaniṣad commentary which we cited earlier. Being must be the focal point when those entities which exist in a practical sense only are negated. Being *is;* the entities only seem to be.

But how is it possible that being is present in all entities, i.e., in everything that appears to be? What is the relation between that which veils the presence of being in the entities, and being itself? The concept of a real relation was intolerable for the rigid spiritual monism. However, to prevent this monism from disintegrating into dualism or negativism, some kind of relation between being and appearance had to be recognized. In the period following Śaṅkara, the concept of apparent evolution *(vivarta)* was devised.[29] This is the absolute minimum of a relation. A relation of apparent evolution exists between something real and its illusory appearance, and this applies to illusions of both degrees. The relation between *brahman* and the world is the same as that which occurs, for instance, between a (practically) real rope and the illusory snake. It has the same ontological character as the illusory entity itself, i.e., it is "indefinable in terms of being and nonbeing." Apart from its ontological meaning, the concept of apparent evolution has also a cosmological and cosmogonic meaning. It is supposed to explain how the world arises from the absolute.[30]

It is of interest to compare this concept with the notion of *analogia entis.* These two doctrines have in common that they distinguish sharply between the absolute, subsistent being and the nonsubsistent contingent entities. They also share the idea that the contingent being is upheld by the absolute being alone. Thomas says: *res conservantur in esse a Deo* (*De potentia* q. 5a.1c; *Summa theologiae* I q. 1.104 a. 1c; *Summa contra gentiles* III 65.94). Vedāntism expresses a similar idea when it teaches that brahman is the locus or the substrate *(āspada, āśraya)* of the illusory world. Thomas distinguishes two types of analogy. In one case, two things are analogues by virtue of the relation they have to a third one; in the other, by virtue of the relation they have to one another in the sense that the one is the cause or origin of the other.[31] The relation between the absolute and the world is of the second type. The relationship of apparent evolution is conceived in a very similar sense; *brahman* is, indeed, the cause of the world. More precisely, Vedāntism postulates, as we have noted, that the absolute is the "locus" or the "substrate" of the evolution of the world. However, it cannot derive contingent being from the absolute through an act of creation. The existence of the world remains inexplicable. *Māyā,* the power of illusion, is its underlying material. Just like its product, the world, it is ontologically "false." *Brahman* is a cause only through *māyā.* Here, the equality of the doctrines of apparent evolution and *analogia entis* comes to an end. Aquinas' concept of being enabled him to conceive, in an adaptation of Platonic teachings, spiritual prototypes *(ideae, formae, species, rationes)* of all things in the absolute.[32] In this way, God was neither turned into a *causa materialis,* nor was there any need for an independent primal matter. The absolute remained fully absolute, pure *causa efficiens* and *causa materialis.*[33] The secret of the creation, never resolved by any attempt to circumscribe it philosophically, remained *God's* secret. Monistic Vedāntism, on the other hand, which tried to think the absolute in an absolute sense, had to pay a price; primal matter, which was considered to be independently real by other systems, became an inexplicable principle of illusion, i.e., *māyā* which ought not to be and which is annulled in final release. The secret degenerates into the uncanniness of the illusion; the absolute, on the other hand, is clarity per se, identical with what is spiritual in all men. That the absolute creates "through *māyā*" is only another expression for the apparent evolution, the *vivarta.* In this way, all things become ontologically "false." A statement found in Thomas, "simpliciter loquendo omnis res est vera, et nulla res est falsa,"[34] sounds like a deliberate rejection of this doctrine.

The minimalistic sense of relation implied in the doctrine of *vivarta* suggests a further comparison with Thomas. Although Thomas does not deny God's relation to the created world, he can only accept it as "notional," or as being "in thought." On the one hand, this has to do with the Aristotelian concept of relation, and on the other hand, with Thomas' view of the nature of God in contrast to that of the creatures. Aristotle's term for "relation" is *prós ti, ad aliquid,* "toward something." Thomas notes: "That of which it is said that it is toward something is somehow dependent on this."[35] But God is not dependent on anything. God is "beyond any order of the creation"[36] or "above" this order.[37] The creatures are causally oriented toward God, but not God toward the creatures.[38] Therefore, Thomas has often characterized God's relation to the created world as a "merely notional" one, as *rationis tantum* or *secundum rationem tantum.*[39] Partly depending on Avicenna, he lists various types of notional relations.[40] In one of these cases, there is a real relation in one direction, but only a notional one in the others. For instance, knowledge depends on its objects, i.e., it has a real relation to it, but the object has only a notional relation to knowledge. According to Thomas, the relation between God and the creatures is of a similar kind; the creatures are related to God in a real sense, but God's relation to the creatures is only a notional one.[41]

All this could also be said of a *vivarta* if we consider only the kind of relation and disregard the falsity of things implied in the concept of *vivarta.* The monistic Vedāntist, too, could say that all things are related to *brahman,* but not *brahman* to the things. But the Christian could hardly be satisfied with including God's relation to his creatures in the same category as the relation of the object of knowledge to knowledge itself. It seems that Thomas did notice that such an inclusion was insufficient. He presented a number of remarkable qualifications.[42] God's designation as creator and redeemer, which indicates a relation to the creatures, refers, though indirectly, to God's action, which is identical with his substance; God is really the "Lord." It is, however, significant that Thomas recognized the reality of relation in God only where he can (as in the present case) reduce the relation to the substance or where the relation subsists in God's own essence (as in the doctrine of trinity).

In the *Summa contra gentiles,* the inclusion in the scheme of "notional relations" appears modified; here the characterization of God's relation to the created world approximates those concepts which Thomas uses to explain in what sense positive predications concerning God are at all possible. To be sure, God's relations to the created world are not really contained in him, but on the other hand, they are not something outside of him.[43] This is in accordance with the thesis that nothing can be predicated of God and the created world in a univocal sense, but that, on the other hand, statements which attribute to God what is known from his creation are not merely equivocal.[44] We know God from the creation.[45] "All our knowledge about God is obtained from the creatures."[46]

"Our intellect, which starts from the senses in its cognition, does not transcend that mode which is found in the sensory things."[47] The case is similar when we apply the category of relation to God. "The relations are attributed to God solely in accordance with our mode of understanding, because other things are related to God." "Yet this understanding is not false."

> It does not detract from the divine simplicity if many relations are predicated of God, although (being in accordance with our mode of understanding) they do not signify his essence. Nothing prevents our intellect from understanding many things as being related in many ways to that which is simple in itself, so that it may consider this simple principle itself in the light of multiple relations. The simpler something is, so much greater is its potential, so many more things may derive from it, and so many more relations may thus be applied to it. Likewise, the point is the source for more figures than the line, and the line for more than the surface. Therefore, the very fact itself that so much is said with regard to God testifies to his supreme simplicity.[48]

"The simpler something is, the more relations accompany it."[49]

Perhaps Thomas could have developed his ideas concerning the applicability of the category of relation to God even more thoroughly if he had employed the concept of *analogy* not only in statements about God's nature and attributes, but had extended it explicitly to relations, because all predicaments—relation as well as substance, quality, and the seven others—can, strictly speaking, be applied to created things only. Nonetheless, positive predications about God are not *eo ipso* false. Moreover, they are not "merely notional." They express, within the possibilities of our reasoning power, truth in an analogous manner, and truth is *adaequatio intellectus ad rem.* The following statements made by Thomas with regard to names that denote God's nature could also be made when it comes to applying the category of relation to God: "Something can be named by us in accordance with the manner it can be understood by our intellect."[50] Anything that is said of God as well as the creatures is said in accordance with the fact that the creatures are oriented toward God as their principle and cause, in which all the perfections of the things exist in an eminent manner."[51] Our statements, those relating to substance as well as those dealing with relation, consider God's absolute simplicity in a variety of aspects. This is legitimate because God's simplicity is not homogeneity, uniformity, or voidness, but a fullness which transcends the possibilities of human understanding: *per unum simplex suum esse omnimodam perfectionem possidet.*[52]

The crucial difference between Thomas and monistic Vedāntism lies here, in the concept of the absolute, not in the formal concept of relation as such. Both our Christian philosopher and the Hindu philosophers of spiritual monism teach that the absolute is absolutely "simplex," and that it is being and spirit in identity. But the Christian philosopher understands this simple unity of being and spirit rather differently than the Hindu. For the Vedāntist, the absolute is the pure light of the spirit, without any content that might be determined by means of analogy, proceeding from the contingent world. For Thomas, God is spirit who knows his own nature "not only as it is in itself, but also in the manner in which the creatures, through some kind of similarity, can participate in it."[53] And this knowledge on the part of God is also the cause which brings the things into being.[54] Vedāntism conceives of the absolute in such a way that its relation to the world can only be a false appearance, a *vivarta.* According to Thomas, on the other hand, the relatedness of the created world to God allows him to conceive of a relation of God to the world which is not false, even if it is not a relation "toward something" *(ad aliquid).*

The concept of *vivarta* refers to being. It divides being into two kinds, which may be called subsistent and contingent being (disregarding the concept of falsity). However, no such distinction is made with regard to the spirit. The seeing light of the spirit in individual cognition is identical with the absolute spirit. Complex theories had to be worked out to explain how cognition of objects, as something different in different individuals, could be accounted for on the basis of spiritual monism and the doctrine of *vivarta.* Since Padmapāda, one of Śaṅkara's direct disciples, the metaphysical possibility of knowing objects was explained as follows: The same universal spirit was said to underlie the inner sense as well as the known thing in the "external" world, implying that the same spirit was delimited or determined *(avachinna)* internally by the inner sense, and externally by the thing, or that the inner sense as well as the thing were "apparent evolutions" *(vivarta)* of the one spirit.[55]

Speaking of degrees of being, the doctrine of illusory evolution attributes a character of being to what underlies all merely practical reality but conceives it primarily as spirit. The ontologism which we mentioned earlier and which (so it assumes) perceives the absolute in every entity, insofar as it is, seems to belong to a separate level of development. It can hardly have contributed to the formation of the doctrine of illusory evolution, because in contrast to ontologism, this doctrine ascribes *another* kind of being to the things than to the absolute. If, on the other hand, the spirit-based ontological *vivarta* were to be expanded into a twofold *vivarta* (i.e., a *vivarta* of absolute being and a *vivarta* of the absolute spirit, both always coexisting with each other), then the monistic premise would have been completely relinquished, and illusionism would be unnecessary. And this would lead us immediately to the problem of the relation between being and spirit. Reflecting on this problem appears once again as a task if we juxtapose the two highest accomplishments of Christian-European and Hindu metaphysics, i.e., Thomas Aquinas' concept of being and the Vedānta concept of spirit, specifically that of Śaṅkara.

Notes

1. An Italian version of this article was published in the journal *Filosofia e Vita,* vol. 10/4 (1969), pp. 26–46 [under the title "Essere e spirito nel Vedānta"; the original German version on which this translation is based was first pub-

lished in *Kl. Schr.*, pp. 293–319, under the title "Sein und Geist im Vedānta".] The topic of this article has been discussed earlier by Olivier Lacombe in one of the four chapters of his book *L'Absolu selon le Vedānta* (Paris, 1937). My reflections did not result from a critical response to Lacombe. Lacombe's presentation is based on texts by Śaṅkara and Rāmānuja. I restrict myself to the monistic Vedānta (leaving aside Rāmānuja), but within this tradition, I consider several authors. This by itself entails an assessment which differs in various respects from that given by Lacombe. Like Lacombe, I consider the comparison with Thomas Aquinas to be fruitful, but it seems to me that Lacombe equates too much, instead of merely comparing. In some cases (see, for instance, pp. 119f.), it seems that he does not interpret the texts with adequate precision.

2. *Ṛgveda X*, 129.

3. *Summa theologiae* I 9.11.3; *Summa contra gentiles* I, 42; *Compendium theologiae* 15.

4. Literally: "this subtleness—a having-this-as-its-self is all this."

5. Cf. Heinrich Lüders, *Varuṇa* (Göttingen, 1952–59), vol. 1, pp. 13 ff.; vol. 2, pp. 402ff.

6. This reference seems to be erroneous. The verse which comes closest to Hacker's statement would be IV, 83 [translator's note].

7. The term *vijñāna* appears in IV, 45; 47; 51f. For *citta*, see, for instance, IV, 20ff.; 46; for *manas*, III, 29ff. [translator's note].

8. See IV, 83f. [translator's note].

9. *Bhagavadgītābhāṣya* XIII, 12. Another reason why Śaṅkara was hesitant to characterize the absolute as *sat* is mentioned in my article "Notes on the Māṇḍūkyopaniṣad and Śaṅkara's Āgamaśāstravivaraṇa." *India Major. Congratulation Volume for J. Gonda* (Leiden, 1972), p. 125 [*Kl. Schr.*, p. 62]: Brahman is *sat* only insofar as it is the origin of the world.

10. *Summa theol.* I q.3.a.5; *Summa contra gent.* I. 25; *De potentia Dei* (i.e., *Quaestiones disputatae de potentia Dei*) q. 7a.3.

11. See *Bhāṣya* on *Īśā Upaniṣad* 4 (end); *Adhyātmapaṭalavivaraṇa* 6.

12. *Brahmasūtrabhāṣya* III,2,21.

13. Cf. Thomas, *De potentia Dei* q.7 (especially a. 1 corpus, prima ratio); q.1 a. 1 c: Deo autem convenit esse actum purum et primum, unde ipsi convenit maxime agere et suam similitudinem in alias diffundere.

14. *Brahmasūtrabhāṣya* III,2,21.

15. See *Yogabhāṣya* I, 6–7 with Śaṅkara's subcommentary.

16. See *Mahābhārata*, crit. ed. XII, 193, 19 (Bombay ed. XII, 200,20); *Yogabhāṣya* III,55.

17. *Padabhāṣya* on *Kena Upaniṣad* II,4.

18. Cf. P. Hacker, "Die Idee der Person im Denken von Vedānta-Philosophen." *Studia Missionalia* 13 (Rome, 1963), pp. 30–52 [in: *Kl. Schr.*, pp. 270–92; see the English trans., Chapter 7 in this volume.

19. On Śaṅkara's doctrine of the spirit, see especially the second prose chapter of his *Upadeśasāhasrī* (German trans. by P. Hacker, Bonn, 1949).

20. On *participatio,* cf. *Summa theol.* I. q. 12a. 11 and 3; q. 84 a. 5c.

21. See *De spiritualibus creaturis (Quaestiones disputatae)* a. 10 c: lumen intellectus agentis . . . est nobis immediate impressum a Deo.

22. Ibid., a. 10 ad 4: actu habet lumen immateriale.

23. Cf. *Summa theol.* I.q79 a. 4 ad 2; *Summa contra gent.* II,76 no. 1568 ff. (ed. Marietti).

24. *De anima* III, 5 (430 a, lines 17 and 22, ed Ross): houtos ho nous chōristos kai apathēs kai amigēs, tē ousiā on energeia . . . ouch hote men noei hote d'ou noei. Cf. the introduction to the edition by W. D. Ross (Oxford, 1961), pp. 41–48, and the commentary by Thomas Aquinas, III, *lectio* 10 (Marietti, no. 734 ff.); also Thomas, *Quaestiones disputatae: De anima* a. 5 obj. 1; *De spirit. creaturis* a. 10 obj. 3; *Summa contra gent.* II 76–78.

25. *Brahmasiddhi* III, 29 ff.

26. Ibid., I, 3.

27. *Pañcadaśī* II, 60 ff.

28. Cf. Klaus Cammann, *Das System des Advaita nach der Lehre Prakāśātmans* (Wiesbaden, 1965).

29. Cf. P. Hacker, *Vivarta* (Mainz: Akademie, 1953).

30. We may disregard here the epistemological (as well as metaphysical) aspect of *māyā,* which accounts for its designation as "nescience" *(avidyā, ajñāna).*

31. See *Summa theol.* I q. 12 a. 5; *Summa contra gent.* I,34; *De pot. Dei* q. 7 a. 7; *Compendium theol.* 27. In *De veritate* (q. 2 a. 11), Thomas distinguishes between *analogia proportionis* and *analogia proportionalitatis.* In the four later works which were just mentioned, he has abandoned this distinction; we may disregard it here. There is even less need to consider the *analogia attributionis* which Erich Przywara cites without giving a source; see his *Analogia Entis* (Einsiedeln, 2nd ed., 1962), p. 135.

32. *Summa theol.* I q. 15 a. 1–2; *De veritate* q. 3 a. 1–2.

33. *Summa theol.* I q. 44 a. 1–3; q. 45 a. 1.

34. *De veritate* q. 1 a. 10c.

35. *Summa contra gent.* II, 12 no. 913 (ed. Marietti).

36. *Summa theol.* I q. 13 a.7 c: extra totum ordinem creaturae.

37. *Quaestiones quodlibetales* I q. 2 a. 1 c: supra omnem ordinem naturae.

38. See the references in notes 33 and 34.

39. Ibid.; see also *De pot. Dei* q. 7 a. 11.

40. Cf. I *Sent* d. 26 q. 2 a. 1 (i.e., *Scriptum super sententiis magistri Petri Lombardi*); *De veritate* q. 1 a. 5 ad 16.

41. *Summa theol.* I q. 13 a. 7c; *De pot. Dei* q. 7a. 11c.

42. *De pot. Dei* q. 7 a. 11 ad 3.4; *Summa theol.* I q. 13 a. 7 ad 3.5.

43. *Summa contra gent.* II, 12–13.

44. Ibid., I, 32–33; *Summa theol.* I q. 13 a. 15; *De pot. Dei* q. 7a. 7c.

45. *Summa theol.* I q. 13 a. 1c.

46. *De pot. Dei* q. 7 a. 7c: omnis cognitio nostra de Deo ex creaturis sumitur.

47. *Summa contra gent.* I, 30 no. 277 (Marietti): intellectus autem noster, ex sensibus cognoscendi initium sumens, illum modum non transcendit qui in rebus sensibilibus invenitur. [Hacker's Latin quote concludes with the phrase: in quibus aliud est forma et habens formam; this is, however, not included in his German translation given in the main text.]

48. *Summa contra gent.* II, 13 no. 919: relinquitur quod (relationes Deo) attribuantur solum secundum intelligentiae modum, ex eo quod alia referuntur ad ipsum; no. 920: nec tamen intellectus est falsus; II, 14 no. 921: Patet enim ex his quod divinae simplicitati non derogat si multae relationes de ipso dicantur, quamvis eius essentiam non significent: quia sequuntur intelligendi modum. Nihil enim prohibet intellectum intellegere multa et multipliciter referri ad id quod est in se simplex, ut sic ipsum simplex sub multiplici relatione consideret. Et quanto aliquid est magis simplex tanto est majoris virtutis et plurium principium, ac per hoc multiplicius relatum intelligitur: sicut punctum plurium est principium quam linea, et linea quam superficies. Hoc igitur ipsum quod multa relative de Deo dicuntur, eius summae simplicitati attestatur.

49. *De pot. Dei* q. 7 a. 8 c.

50. *Summa theol.* I q. 13 a. 1 c.: secundum igitur quod aliquid a nobis intellectu cognosci potest, sic a nobis potest nominari.

51. *Summa theol.* I q. 13 a. 6 c: quidquid dicitur de Deo et creaturis, dicitur secundum quod est aliquis ordo creaturae ad Deum ut ad principium et causam, in qua praeexistunt excellenter omnes rerum perfectiones.

52. *Summa contra gent.* II, 31. no. 281.

53. *Summa theol.* I q. 15 a. 2 c: non solum secundum quod in se est, sed secundum quod est participabilis secundum aliquem modum similitudinis a creaturis.

54. *Summa theol.* I q. 14 a. 8 c.: Deus per intellectum suum causat res, cum suum esse sit suum intelligere.

55. Cf. Paul Hacker, *Untersuchungen über Texte des frühen Advaitavāda* (Mainz: Akademie, 1950), pp. 144 ff.; also the work cited in n. 28, pp. 132 ff.

10

Cit and Noûs, or the Concept of Spirit in Vedāntism and in Neoplatonism

Neoplatonism has more than once been compared with Indian philosophy, and especially with that multiform variety of Indian thought which is comprised under the designation of Vedānta or, as I prefer to call it when speaking of the later interpretations of the Upaniṣads, of Vedāntism. Historical dependence has been asserted especially in the case of Plotinus. But I wish to state right from the outset that I do not think that such dependence is proven in any way, though I would not deny the possibility that Plotinus may have had a vague knowledge of one or two Vedāntic doctrines, mediated to him through inexact translations or accounts.

Much more important than the fascinating resemblance of the two spirit-oriented philosophies is the fact that in spite of the common primacy of the spiritual, the conceptual formations and structures are so different that the distinctive terms of the Indian school of thought are almost normally misunderstood in the West. Let me illustrate this possibility of misunderstanding by what is perhaps the most striking example. There is no doubt that the German Paul Deussen was in his time the deepest specialist of Vedāntism in the West. In this scholar's book *The System of the Vedānta* (1883; English translation, 1912) we read in note 54 (p. 95; 90 trans.) that in a certain passage of Śaṅkara's *Brahmasūtrabhāṣya* there occurs "the monstrosity of an absolute perception," that is, the postulate of "a subject without an object." It seems incredible, but it is simply a fact, first, that precisely this "monstrosity" forms the very center of the system of monistic Vedāntism, of which Deussen undertook to give an account; second, that the most specialized specialist misunderstood the most central concept of the subject of his studies. It is this very "monstrosity" which I intend to elucidate in the following, in confrontation with Neoplatonism.

As I have already hinted, this confrontation is not meant to detect historical influences. It is simply an attempt to clarify concepts. Such clarification is a necessary prerequisite for a fruitful interpenetration of Indian and Western thinking in metaphysical speculation, nay, it is already a timid beginning of such interpenetration.

The comparison of Vedānta and Vedāntism with Neoplatonism is beset with difficulties. One of these consists in the enormous difference of the conceptual and argumentative stage of development in the two schools. I will try to explain what I mean by this statement. In the Upaniṣads, and I am thinking here especially of the later ones—*Kaṭha, Śvetāśvatara, Muṇḍaka, Maitrī,* and a few late passages in earlier Upaniṣads—we find concepts which, notwithstanding their profundity, are in a way indistinct, so that they are hard to define. In addition, argumentation is in quite a rudimentary state. On the other hand, later Vedāntism, beginning from the time of Śaṅkara, i.e., from the seventh century, combines concepts that are clear-cut and definable, though not very differentiated, with highly developed argumentation. In Neoplatonism, especially in Plotinus, it is extremely difficult, if not impossible, to define with precision the content even of the leading terms,[1] while, on the other hand, conceptual variety and argumentation are full-grown and refined. So we are confronted with an incongruity in either case, whether we compare with Neoplatonism the Upaniṣads, i.e., the Vedānta in the restricted sense of the word, or Vedāntism, i.e., the philosophy grown on the basis of the Upaniṣads.

Realization of these difficulties and incongruities is apt to deter one altogether from undertaking a comparison. Nevertheless, I will in the following present the result of a fresh approach. I am far from being a specialist in Neoplatonism. I wish to elucidate an *Indian* concept before an audience familiar with *Neoplatonism.* So I confine myself, on the Neoplatonic side, to that brief handbook which recommends itself also on account of the prominent role that it played for many centuries in the history of European thought, I mean to Proclus' *Stoicheíōsis theologikḗ.* Starting from, or on the basis of, or against the background of this book, with reference also to Plotinus, I will try to explain the difference of those two concepts which may be, and have been, translated by the same Western word, viz. by 'spirit,' the concepts of Sanskrit *cit* and Greek *noûs.* This will, of course, also necessitate digressions to other related concepts on both sides. In referring to Proclus, I gratefully used the admirable edition by E. R. Dodds with his English translation and commentary, without, however, sharing his opinion that such business belongs to the "Wissenschaft des Nichtwissenswerthen," i.e., to the science of that which is not worth knowing. For Plotinus I used the excellent edition, with German translation, published by F. Meiner.

In the title of this lecture I have quoted an Indian and a Greek term, *cit* and *noûs.* But this was more or less a makeshift. The meanings of the two words are connected by little more than the fact that both are usually translated by one and the same Western word. Still, I would justify the inclusion of the two words in the title, for, first, both the Indian and the Greek words do express something like what we mean when we speak of "Spirit" in philosophy; second, I wish to explain or at least to make a first attempt at explaining to students of Neoplatonism what is meant by *cit,* and to the Indologist by what means Neoplatonism in its most mature stage tried to give approximate expression to that reality which the Indian term faces. It seems in place to start from Neoplatonism, but since the meaning of the Indian term differs very much from that of the Greek one, it would be bewildering to start directly from the Greek term. Some metaphysical propositions of Proclus' book seem to provide promising starting-points.

I take proposition 15 as such a starting-point: "All that is capable of reverting upon itself is incorporeal" *(pân tò pròs heautò epistreptikòn asōmatón estin).* The notion, occurring in this proposition, of reverting upon oneself, was perhaps first conceived by the Stoics[2] and then taken over by the Neoplatonists. Now I could stop short here, remarking curtly that the Advaitic Vedāntist explicitly dismisses the notion of epistemological reflexivity as illogical, and that, therefore, further discussion is pointless, because "East is East and West is West and never the twain will meet."

The concept of reverting upon oneself has survived in Thomism down to our day. Proclus holds that this capability of reversion upon itself is an indication of an entity's being incorporeal, and the same argument recurs in St. Thomas' *Summa contra gentiles*[3] (II 49 Marietti no.

1254). The difference between Thomas and Proclus is that for Proclus there are three incorporeal entities, namely the One, Spirit, and Soul, each one subordinated to the preceding (proposition 20), while for Thomas the only incorporeal thing envisaged here is the *intellectus* or, more exactly, the soul of which the *intellectus* is a part.

Let me first explain why the idea of epistemological reflexivity is alien to Vedāntic thought (I am not speaking of Indian thought in general). At a very early time, probably in the first half of the last millennium before Christ, at the latest one or two centuries earlier than 500 B.C., one of those thinkers whose speculations were handed down in the Upaniṣads conceived a thought that, in my opinion, belongs to the greatest achievements of philosophy, both Eastern and Western. The clearest formulation of this thought is recorded at *Bṛhadāraṇyaka Upaniṣad* 3.4.2, but similar statements recur in four passages of the second, third, and fourth books of the same Upaniṣad (2,4,14; 3,7,23; 3,8,11; 4,5,15). This formulation reads (with a slight abbreviation): "You cannot see him who sees vision . . . , you cannot know him who knows knowledge" *(na dṛṣṭer draṣṭāraṃ paśyeḥ . . . , na vijñāter vijñātāraṃ vijānīyāḥ).* I think the formulation makes the idea conveyed appear self-evident. That principle which makes knowledge possible—knowledge of all kinds, sensorial perception as well as mental insight and discursive thinking—cannot naturally be grasped or comprehended by that of which it is the very basis of existence. Whatever names we may give to the principle that makes both mental and sensuous acts or events possible, whether we call it consciousness or spirit or thought or knowledge, it is absurd to assume that this principle should need an act of knowledge in order to attain that status which we call "to be known" or "to be manifest." It is absurd because that which makes a thing possible, or is the basis of it, cannot possibly itself be made possible by the thing which it makes possible. Such an absurdity, however, would happen in epistemological reflexivity.

Yet it is inconceivable that the greatest thinkers of the West should for centuries have acquiesced in a blatant absurdity. I am convinced that the Greeks who coined the term 'reverting upon oneself' actually faced a reality. But they did not view it from the same angle as the Indians, and accordingly they expressed it in a linguistic form totally different from the Vedāntist term. What Proclus means by 'reversion upon itself' is the self-manifestation, the self-revealing nature of the spiritual, which Proclus designates by the negative term 'incorporeal'—a term which is used by the Vedāntists also. In terms of post-upaniṣadic Vedāntism, spirit is not in need of a subject-object relationship in order to become manifest.

Precisely for this argument it is helpful for the thinker who intends to investigate the nature of Spirit to have, as the Indians had from very early times, a reflex awareness of the subject-object-relationship as an element of the structure of reality. For the negative proposition, "Spirit can never become an object," provides a vigorous support to the positive statement, "Spirit is self-revealing."

The denial of objectivity on the part of spirit naturally involves its proximity to the subject of knowledge. But according to the theory of Advaitic Vedāntism, the actual subject of knowledge is not spirit in its purity but spirit somehow intermingled with an objective element. I will revert to this point later.

The self-manifestation of spirit is expressed by an old term, which stemmed from mythic thinking and, through a long history, eventually developed into the symbol of one of the finest intellectual achievements of India. Like 'reverting upon oneself' its expression is a metaphor but, I think, a much more apposite one, namely 'self-luminous' (in Sanskrit *svayaṃ-jyotis* or, later, *svayaṃ-prakāśa*). 'Light,' 'shining,' is a self-explanatory and widely used metaphor to denote all acts and states of consciousness, cognition, and perception. Self-luminosity implies both the spirit's awareness of itself and its capability of making objects, both material and mental, appear in the range of consciousness. Here we are considering self-luminosity primarily from the ontological point of view (its epistemological relevance, in the Vedāntist context, will be studied later).

Taking up the comparison with Neoplatonism, we find that the metaphor of luminosity does not seem to be restricted there to states and events in the domain of consciousness or knowledge. The word *éllampsis,* e.g., has in Proclus' *Stoicheíōsis* always a purely ontological sense. However, there is a philosophical aspect that may be called epistemological ontology. If viewed from this aspect, a most surprising similarity between *cit* or *ātman* and *noûs* becomes perceptible. All the characteristics of self-luminosity are ascribed to *noûs* in a treatise of Plotinus (*Enn.* V,3,8,18–42), and besides luminosity "seeing" is also predicated of *noûs*—seeing, which is one of the characteristics of spirit in Vedāntism and of which I will treat later. We must, however, bear in mind, that the comparability of the passage presupposes our detaching it from its context, for the context is purely Neoplatonic; it speaks of the "intelligible World" and the relationship of Soul to Spirit, two themes entirely foreign to Vedāntic thought. Nevertheless, the similarity is surely significant, and the more so because the contexts in the two cultures are so different.

I will now translate an excerpt from the relevant passage in Plotinus, omitting ideas to which nothing corresponds in Vedāntism.

> It is Spirit which sees *(noûs dè horâ)*... "He who has received the light of the true things sees, as it were, the visible things in a higher degree... The life and the activity in Spirit are the *Primal Light which primarily shines for itself and is brilliancy to itself,* illuminating and simultaneously being illuminated, the true spirit-content, cognizing and being cognized, being seen by (or for) itself and not being in need of anything else for seeing, to itself self-sufficient for seeing—for that which it sees is itself—being known also from our side through even that, so that even from our side its knowledge comes to pass through itself. *(ho d' ekeîno tò phôs tôn alēthôn labòn hoîon blépei mâllon tà horatá... hē dè en tô nô zōē kaì enérgeia tò prôton phôs heautô lámpon prōtōs kaì pròs hautò lampēdōn, lámpon homoû kaì lampómenon, tò alēthôs noētón, kaì nooûn kaì nooúmenon, kaì heautô horōmenon kaì ou deómenon állou, hína ídē, hautô aútarkes pròs tò ideîn—kaì gàr hò horâ autó esti—ginōskómenon kaì par' hēmôn autô ekeínō, hōs kaì par' hēmôn tēn gnôsin autoû di' autoû gínesthai. Enn.* V,3,8,32–42).

Even here, where the similarity is so impressive, the differences between the Vedāntist and Neoplatonic views must not be overlooked. The light with which Spirit irradiates Soul has a content which is the "light of the true things," "that which is truly spirit-content" *(tò alēthôs noētón),* the Ideal Forms of the Intelligible World. The thought-pattern of spiritual reflexivity, too, so foreign to Vedāntism, is not absent from our passage. Moreover, the concept of *life* occurring here does not have any metaphysical function in the system of later Vedāntism. Nevertheless, the concept of self-revelation or self-luminosity is brought out with clarity and hymnic admiration. Parallels like these should be given due attention in ontologico-metaphysical as well as in epistemologico-metaphysical speculation.

The Neoplatonist's view that the intelligible light of *noûs* has a content, *noûs,* containing all Platonic Ideas, makes us understand why in his mind Spirit's reflection upon itself is not an absurdity, for Spirit carries, so to speak, its objects of knowledge within itself. By the same token, the Indian view of the contentless plenitude of Spirit *(cit, ātman)* can appear to be an absurdity or a "monstrosity" to the Westerner. The same context also accounts for the difference of meaning when both systems describe the Absolute or the Intelligible as "simple" (*haploûs, Stoich.*, prop. 47; *asaṃhata,* passim). In Neoplatonism this "simplicity" does not preclude spirit from being the sum of all Ideal Forms (*hólos mèn ho noûs tà pánta eídē, Enn.* V,9,8,4; *pâs noûs plḗrōma òn eidôn, Stoicheíōsis,* prop. 177).

The Indian *cit,* on the contrary, entirely un-Greek and un-Western, is simple in the strictest sense of this word; it is spirituality or intelligence abstracted from all contents or associates. Obviously the thinkers were aware that this abstraction, though of enormous philosophical relevance, was unknown in everyday life and even in other systems of philosophy. So they saw the need for a new term. In order to denote what they had discovered, they simply chose the root of a verb which means "to be conscious of," "to think," namely the verbal root *cit* (with or without the addition of an *-i*). The derivation from this root, *citta,* on the other hand, denotes "the mind" in philosophical and nonphilosophical parlance.

In proposition 47 of his *Stoicheíōsis,* Proclus speaks of entities that are "self-constituted" *(authypóstaton).* What is "self-constituted" is "simple" and "without parts" *(amerés);* on the other hand, he states that precisely "all that is capable of reversion upon itself" *(pròs heautò epistreptikón,* prop. 42) is "self-constituted." Now 'self-constituted' seems to be exactly the same as what is called in Sanskrit *svatassiddha* (substantive: *svatassiddhi*), i.e., an entity that constitutes itself by itself as existent and manifest, an entity that by itself establishes its existence and manifestation.

If I am right in explaining that the reality intended by the term 'reversion to itself' is the same as what the Indians mean by *svayaṃprakāśatā* or 'self-luminosity,' then my equation of the Greek concept "self-constituted" with the Indian *svatassiddha* is corroborated, the more so because, first, the two Greek terms are just as closely linked together as the corresponding Indian terms and, second, because both the Neoplatonist and the Vedāntist ascribe to the reality in question the further characteristics of being "without temporal origin" (*agénēton,* Proclus, prop. 45), "imperishable" (*áphtharton,* prop. 46), "being without parts" (*amerés,* prop. 47), and "perpetual" (*aídion,* prop. 48); corresponding Sanskrit terms, for which a number of synonyms could be substituted, would be *aja, akṣaya, akhaṇḍa* or *asaṃhata, nitya.* It would be pointless to cite occurrences, because examples abound from the time of the Upaniṣads, i.e., a time earlier than 500 B.C., down to the present time, since there are still adherents of Vedāntism.

Let us stop here for a while to survey the results we have so far arrived at in our comparison. We found two points in which the two systems seemed irreconcilable: first, the wider sense of the concept of "simple" in Neoplatonism as compared with Vedāntism. But you will see presently that on this point the divergent views can be harmonized to some extent if Vedāntist cosmology is taken into consideration. Second, we found the concept of *cit,* which at first sight seemed absolutely unique. However, we succeeded in discovering the concept of self-luminosity in Plotinus also, and this is a bridge which makes *cit* accessible, even though Neoplatonism did not undertake the rigid abstraction which severs *cit* from *citta.* On two other points both the Greek and the Indian system seemed to have in view the same reality, though viewing it from very different angles: "reversion upon oneself" corresponds to "self-luminosity"; "incorporeity" stands for "being spiritual." In addition, there were four terms which are simply identical: 'devoid of origin,' 'imperishable,' 'partless,' 'perpetual.'

I think these agreements suffice to show that what the Neoplatonist aimed at was much the same as what the Vedāntist intended to reach, namely, incorporeity. But while the Vedāntists understood this as a stage of pure spirit, Neoplatonism, which had not developed a conception of Spirit so pure as the Indian *cit,* felt it necessary ultimately to transcend Spirit in the direction of the One, which is beyond Spirit (as conceived in Neoplatonism) and beyond Being.

In order to understand both the similarities and the divergencies of the two systems, it may be useful at this point to form a clear idea of the different ways in which they conceived of the sphere of supreme realities. In both systems the supreme reality is described as a triad, but Vedāntism (in that form which we are considering here, which is also called Advaitism or spirit-monism) conceives of the triad as a substantial unity in which each of the three constituents, one of which is *cit* or spirit, is an aspect of the unity and in reality totally identical with it; in fact, the supreme reality itself, comprising all the three aspects, can sometimes be called "the One" *(eka).* Neoplatonism's triad, on the other hand, is subordinative, with *noûs* being subordinate to the One, and Soul to *noûs.*

The Indian triad, however, is similar to one of Proclus' triads (see W. Beierwaltes: *Proklos,* Frankfurt, 1965, pp. 93 ff.). Proclus has *ousía, zōḗ, noûs* (being, life, spirit; cp. Proclus, *Stoicheíōsis,* prop. 103), Vedāntism has 'being,' 'spirit,' and 'bliss' *(sat-cit-ānanda).* In this compound *cit* (spirit) occurs as the second member. In the Greek triad which I just quoted, there is not so much subordination as interpenetration. "Every element of this triad is all the three, but the three are in each element as themselves and at the same time after the manner of that in which they in-here" (Beierwaltes, op. cit., p. 95). The One as such is absent in this triad, which in its essence is an explication of the nature of the hypostasis *noûs* (Beierwaltes, op. cit., p. 97), which as such, of course, remains subordinate to the One.

One of the consequences of the subordinative structure of the hypostases in Neoplatonism is the different treatment of the problem of freedom of the Absolute in the Greek system as compared with the Indian. In Vedāntism freedom is represented as being inseparably linked up with the spiritual nature of the Absolute. The Absolute is shown to be free in two senses: in the sense of being independent of other entities *(svatantra)* and in the sense of not existing for another's sake *(svārtha)*. While the notion of independence needs no elaboration in Vedāntism,[4] which holds the Universal Spirit to be the Absolute, the concept of *svārtha* is thoroughly discussed (Śaṅkara's *Upadeśasāhasrī*, Gadyaprabandha, chapter 2). Neoplatonism ascribes freedom in every sense to the One alone. Plotinus, at the end of a long treatise "On free will and the One's will," states that the One alone is really free (*mónon toûto alētheía eleútheron, Enn.* VI,8,21,31). This seems to be consistent with the structure of the Neoplatonic system, which teaches two supreme realities in succession subordinate to the One, which is the Absolute.

Yet, I find it hard to reconcile with my Christian and Indian way of thinking to conceive of a Supreme that is free without being of the nature of spirit. And I find it questionable that there should be a subordinate hypostasis which is spiritual in an absolute sense, i.e., to the extent of being self-effulgent, but is lacking in absolute freedom. In an earlier study I tried to show even within the precincts of Hindu philosophy that it is an incomplete stage of insight if the inseparability of spirit and freedom has not been perceived.

A feature strikingly common to the Neoplatonic and the Advaitic idea of spirit is that both normally conceive of spirit as universal. This seems to be more or less inevitable, considering the similarity of the starting-points of the two systems and, especially, the still greater similarity of their respective goals. But I cannot enter here into this phenomenon; it would amount to something like metaphilosophy or theology. The individual existence of spirit is, of course, also envisaged in both systems. The thought-pattern by which Neoplatonism tries to solve the problem of the relationship between the universal and the individual spirit may perhaps, briefly and with some simplification, be described as existence of the superior in the inferior, of the universal in the individual. In India the various schools of Vedāntism have proposed different solutions. The system which I am considering, Advaitic Vedāntism, solves the problem in a way totally different from Neoplatonism.

We have reached here a point where the two systems radically diverge. The relationship between the universal spirit and the individual, the role of spirit in cosmogony or cosmology, and man's road to union with the Absolute are problems whose treatment bears very few similarities in the two systems; nay, the characteristic disparity of the two cultures becomes strikingly manifest here.

I cannot enlarge on the relationship between Spirit and Soul, first, because I have no insights to contribute to the knowledge of Neoplatonism, and second, because there is absolutely no analogy in Vedāntic thought to the relevant Greek doctrine. Simply in order not to leave the doctrine in question quite unmentioned and to provide a contrast to set off Indian doctrines which I am going to delineate, I will quote Proclus' proposition from the *Stoicheíōsis* (193), "Every soul takes its proximate origin from spirit" *(pâsa psychèprosechôs apò noû hyphéstēken),* and Plotinus' brief remark that soul is the spirit's outgoing activity (*enérgeia ex autoû, Enn.* VI,2,22,26; cf. V,1,3,5 *hoîon lógos hò en prophorâ*). In Vedāntism there is no differentiation between Spirit and Soul. Both words are indeed used in translations and English-written expositions, with spirit, however, occurring comparatively seldom. But the meaning of the words in such translations, of course, always depends on the Indian original they stand for. In speaking of Vedāntism (I leave out of account other Indian philosophical systems), 'soul' is often used as a translation of Sanskrit *ātman,* but this word is also, and mostly, rendered by 'the self.' I prefer this translation,[5] first, because it is strictly literal, since *ātman* also performs the function of the reflexive pronoun in Sanskrit; second, because the word is excellently suited to express the essential in man, that without which man is not man; third, because it is devoid of any preconceived content; fourth, because in metaphysics the expression 'The Supreme Self' easily offers itself as a term to denote the Personal Absolute by analogy.

The Self or *ātman* is, as I hinted before, a triune entity, in the monistic system mostly understood to be the Absolute. Its constituents or aspects or characteristics, each of which is the whole, are Existence, Spirit, and Bliss *(sac-cid-ānanda).* I venture to submit that the similarity between this triad and the Christian Trinity, on the one hand, and Proclus' "Being-Life-Spirit" triad, on the other hand, is no mere chance but is grounded in reality, the more so since this triad of Proclus does not so much imply subordination as interpenetration. The greatest divergence which separates the three triads is, I think, not the fact that they do not totally coincide at the conceptual level, but that the idea of three *Persons* with an identical substance is unknown to the Indian and rejected by the Hellenic philosophers.

The most prominent characteristic of the Self is doubtless Spirit. Śaṅkara, the most renowned teacher of the Advaita-Vedāntist school, treats of the Self almost exclusively as Spirit. The actionless activity, or rather the nature, of the Spirit is described by two metaphors: it 'sees' and it 'shines' or 'illuminates' (see Śaṅkara's *Upadeśasāhasrī,* Gadyaprabandha, chapter 2). What does it illuminate? First of all, it is important to note that, like the sun, it shines even when there is no object to be illuminated (this is what Deussen called a "monstrosity," as I noted before). Shining and Seeing is its nature and not an adventitious event. When there is an object of its illumination, this object is neither the outward world of things nor an "intelligible universe," a *kósmos noētós.* Vedāntist psychology, on this point similar to that of the Sāṃkhya system, posits a psychic entity which I prefer to call "Inner Sense" (others call it "Inner Organ"). It consists of subtle, imperceptible matter. Through the mediation of the senses, it receives impressions, in the literal sense of imprints, from what the Neoplatonists call "the Sensible World," *kósmos aisthētós;* besides this, the Inner Sense is also the agent, subject, or substratum of thinking, and in perception as well as in thinking it takes the form of fluctuations or modifications of the subtle matter that makes up its substance.[6] According to Advaitic Vedāntism, even these processes are raised to the level of consciousness only by the Spirit's "seeing" and "illuminating" them. There is no trace of a borderline, like the one which Neoplatonism draws, between the "sensible" and the "intelligible" world, and the Vedāntist's estimation of the sensible world and of pure thought is almost the reverse of the value-system of all Platonism. Pure thought is always suspect of being mere fancy.

But I said, "almost" the reverse because Vedāntism, far from being a pedestrian matter-of-fact philosophy, has developed such a pure and sublime concept of Spirit as no other philosophy, be it in India or in the West, has ever succeeded in discovering. I think it was an enormous achievement to abstract Spirit not only from its contents but also from those elements that seem inseparably linked up with it to form the Ego or the Subject of Knowledge. I may note here in passing that what Platonism intends to express by the conception of the "intelligible world," emerges in Vedāntism also, but at quite a different level. For the time being, I think it in place to try to explain how Advaitic Vedāntism, with its higher evaluation of direct perception (which it shares with all Indian systems of thought), could nonetheless attribute such an elevated rank to Spirit.

The argumentation which establishes this rank presupposes a highly developed awareness of the subject-object relationship. Its starting point is the axiom that the knowledge of a thing is dependent on the object, i.e., on the object being there, not on any activity of the knower. This statement is directed against idealists, but also against the view predominant among earlier Vedāntists who sought to attain to union with the Absolute or the Supreme by different kinds of activity,[7] namely by strict morality, asceticism, and meditation (which is mental activity). Śaṅkara appreciated all these activities without restraint, but he denied that they could bring about realization of the Absolute. He contended that this goal implied, or consisted in, *knowledge* of the Supreme; knowledge, however, can never be reached by any activity, mental or bodily. The thing sought to be known must become manifest; this is the only practicable method, or rather, there is no method, but knowledge must emerge of itself. Now the Absolute, in this context called Brahman, is certainly not an object like a thing or even an idea or a complex of ideas. Rather, it is the knower's own self.

Here the spirit-monism of the system comes up. A man's self, whose nature is pure spirit, is of course better known to him than any object, though this knowledge has not the form of a subject-object relationship. Consequently the Absolute is in reality that which is best known to everyone, because spirit-monism posits it to be identical with everyone's own self.

But why are people not actually aware of this? Here the illusionism of Advaitic Vedāntism is introduced. If Brahman is, as the system teaches, identical with each man's self without man's being conscious of it, this is the effect of Nescience *(avidyā),* the Vedāntist replies.

Nescience or ignorance is a notion that occurs in all systems of Hinduism, Buddhism, and Jainism. All these systems intend to show to man the road to everlasting release, understood as release from transmigration, with a positive content differently conceived of in the several systems, and the road to release consists in or includes right knowledge. To some extent, the notion is known to Hellenic philosophy also. Even Plotinus can occasionally mention ignorance (*agnoeîn, ágnoia; Enn.* V,1,1) as one of the causes of the soul's entering this world.[8] Advaitic Vedāntism, however, has in the course of many centuries bestowed a tremendous amount of ingenuity on constructing arguments and theories to demonstrate the nature and defend the existence of nescience; in my opinion, in all this huge literature on nescience and *māyā* (the Power of Illusion, more or less identical with nescience) there is, if not absolutely nothing, at any rate very little that is of philosophical relevance. I will not expatiate on this subject but mention only so much as seems to be indispensable for explaining the Vedāntist concept of spirit. The doctrine of nescience and *māyā,* as well as the monism of the system, seem to have been the price the Vedāntists had to pay for elaborating their doctrines of pure Spirit. I may note in passing that this price need not be paid, and the truth of the Vedāntist concept of Spirit, if differentiated into individual Spirit and Supreme Spirit or God, can very well be upheld if, instead of monism and illusionism, the thought-pattern of the analogy of being is made use of. But I cannot enlarge on this theme here. I may only note that this is, of course, another concept of analogy than that which occurs in Proclus and is referred to by Prof. Beierwaltes in his book on *Proklos* (pp. 73 ff.). I have now to treat of the doctrine, in so far as it is necessary to understand the Vedāntist concept of spirit, and of the theory of nescience or *māyā,* in so far as it is ancillary to that concept.

To begin with monism, it is largely based on tradition, but there were very different types of monism in the course of time. The system I am treating advocates radical spirit-monism. The only rational proof the great Śaṅkara has given for this theory includes a fallacy. Since in all acts of consciousness, no matter at what time, in what place, and in what person they occur, the quality or *essence* of consciousness is the same, Śaṅkara concludes that all acts of consciousness are also identical in *existence* (see his *Upadeśasāhasrī,* Gadyaprabandha, chapter 2). By the way, here we see the value of the medieval distinction between 'to be (there)' and 'to be thus,' or between existence and essence.

As regards nescience or *māyā* (we may skip here the differences established by some thinkers between the two words), it is, according to a later, but very common explanation (so that quotations are unnecessary) an inexplicable entity whose status of being can be described neither as existent nor as nonexistent. So far, I am ready to concede a certain philosophical relevance to the doctrine, for, from the metaphysical point of view, it is meaningful to distinguish degrees of reality. But later Vedāntism explained the whole world, all matter, manifoldness, time, space, and even all psychic events, as products of *māyā,* which was described as their material cause and as being, like their cause, neither existent nor nonexistent. *Māyā* has two powers, one veiling and one dispersing. It veils the nature of the Universal Spirit; it exercises dispersion in creating the illusion of a manifold world in space and time, material and psychic. This is how Vedāntism tries to solve the problem of individualization; it is simply an effect of *māyā*.

Most remarkable in our context is the fact that even the Supreme God (called *īśvara*, "the Lord"; India has developed different forms of quasi-monotheism, coexisting at a higher level with the traditional polytheism and in individual cases ousting it more or less) is associated with *māyā;* only in combination with this Power of Illusion is God the creator, preserver, and destroyer of the world. I mention this chiefly for one reason, for here we find a striking analogy to the "intelligible world" of Platonic ideas. *Māyā* is also called *Potency* (*śakti,* St. Thomas' active *potentia*),[9] and this makes creation possible. What is most astonishing, before creation all things exist as objects of the Highest God's contemplation, i.e., his ideas (see Śaṅkara, *Brahmasūtrabhāṣya* 1,1,5). Surely God is by nature Spirit, even in his association with *māyā,* an association that makes an equation with pre-Christian or Christian Neoplatonic ideas impossible, or at least requires adjustment. Nevertheless, there is a striking similarity in so far as the Vedāntist teaches that things preexist as God's ideas.

Another association with *māyā* (in this context preferably called nescience) occurs in the individual. The most refined product of nescience is the Inner Sense (designated by *buddhi* and other words). In English I sometimes translate it by 'mind,' and this is why 'mind' and 'spirit' in my translation-terminology are not interchangeable. The close association of Spirit *(cit)* and Inner Sense *(buddhi)* makes up what may be called the Ego *(ahaṃkartṛ)* in Śaṅkara's terminology, or the Subject of Knowledge. Release presupposes the extremely difficult mental severance of the spirit from its associate, i.e., the very Ego has to be, as it were, dissected. Only then, the system teaches, can pure Spirit shine forth.

I must now come to a conclusion. In spite of the enormous disparity of the two cultures, we found in the two systems an impressive number of terms that are partly almost literally translatable, partly interpretable as different ways of pointing to the same intended reality. Historical influences from either side are quite improbable. In two cases we found remarkable doctrines each of which is fully elaborated and cleansed from unnecessary associations in one of the two systems only. The first of these doctrines is the Platonic concept of Idea, which Neoplatonism has incorporated into *noûs,* thus preparing the way for classical Christian cosmology. If theistic metaphysics is to survive, if the doctrine of God is not to degenerate into an ideology ancillary to anthropology, it is indispensable that we should uphold this heritage of Platonism and Neoplatonism. In monistic Vedāntism, monism, with its corollary, illusionism, made it indeed hard to explain the origin of the perishable world from the Absolute; all the more notable is the fact that even in this system there emerges an adumbration of Platonic Ideas.

As regards the doctrine of Pure Spirit in Vedāntism, it is certainly one of the greatest achievements of philosophy. It is not logically necessary to associate it with monism and illusionism. Śaṅkara himself has shown this in demonstrating in a passage of his great commentary on the *Bṛhadāraṇyaka Upaniṣad* (4,3,7)[10] how Pure Spirit is the principle of unity that makes not only all mental and sensory acts possible, but whose light binds even vegetative processes, together with the consciousness-events, into the psycho-physical unity that is man. Śaṅkara seems here—whether deliberately or not, we cannot know—to have kept his monism and illusionism in suspense. It is deplorable that this fragment of great spirit-oriented anthropology was never elaborated. Nevertheless, it could help us, precisely with its irrefutable concept of pure spirit, to defy that materialism which nowadays has almost everywhere discarded the traditional notion of soul.

In these two, and probably even in more respects, the study of Vedāntism and Neoplatonism (and even more the comparison of the two systems as well as the comparison of classical Indian with classical Western systems of philosophy) seems to be of great relevance in our time, provided we recognize the value of great tradition in general and of metaphysics in particular.[11]

Notes

1. A. H. Armstrong, in his book *The Architecture of the Intelligible Universe in the Philosophy of Plotinus* (Cambridge, 1940, pp. 49 f.), lists no less than six "aspects" of *noûs*.

2. Cf. also Aristotle, *De Anima*, 430a 3.

3. Cf. also *Liber de causis*, prop. 15, with St. Thomas' comm. lect. 15.

4. Śaṅkara in his *Brahmasūtrabhāṣya* in most of the occurrences of *svatantra* denies that anything but the Spirit can be independent; a passage where *svatantra* is directly and positively connected with *ātman* (which is spirit), is to be found, e.g., in *Brahmasūtrabhāṣya* 2,3,36 at the end.

5. The concept of "real self" is not foreign to Neoplatonism; cf. W. Beierwaltes and H. U. v. Balthasar, *Grundfragen der Mystik* (Einsiedeln, 1974), p. 9, n. 2.

6. Here the *nooûn* and the *nooúmenon* are identical, in spite of Aristotle, *De Anima,* 430a 3, though the objects can be material, and the Inner Sense in any case consists of (subtle) matter.

7. See Śaṅkara, *Brahmasūtrabhāṣya* 1,1,4.

8. Proclus teaches that the philosopher's ascent to the One includes cleansing from ignorance, cf. Beierwaltes, *Proklos,* p. 285. What had been constructed in Advaitic Vedāntism, like a frightful fortification to defend the central mystery of spirit-monism, namely, the doctrine that the world is an illusion, neither being nor nonbeing, looms up occasionally and in quite a rudimentary form in Plotinus also: he can call matter, though in an *optativus potentialis* and in a certain respect only, "nonbeing," *mè ón* (*Enn.* 2,5,4,11).

9. *dýnamis* in an active sense occurs in Plotinus, *Enn.* 3,8,10,1.

10. Cf. my paper "A Note on Śaṅkara's Conception of Man," published in: *German Scholars on India, Contribution to Indian Studies,* ed. by the Cultural Department of the Embassy of the Fed. Republic of Germany New Delhi, vol. 1 (publ. by The Chowkhamba Sanskrit Series Office, Varanasi, 1973), pp. 99 ff., and my articles (in German and Italian) mentioned in the footnotes of this paper. [See Chapter 8 in this volume; especially notes 3–5.]

11. Editor's note: In the transliterations from the Greek, the *iota subscriptum* has been disregarded.

PART III

Neo-Hinduism and Modern Vedānta: Studies in Reinterpretation

11

Aspects of Neo-Hinduism as Contrasted with Surviving Traditional Hinduism

It has become customary to speak of a renaissance of Hinduism setting in toward the end of the nineteenth century. The term 'renaissance,' known from the cultural history of Europe, was used by a Hindu writer, D. S. Sarma, to designate the common traits of certain phenomena and movements in modern Hindu thought. Sarma's book *The Renaissance of Hinduism* came out in 1944. It seems to have been intended to supersede an earlier study written by a Christian missionary, namely J. N. Farquhar's *Modern Religious Movements in India,* which had appeared in 1915.

The dominating criterion used in Farquhar's treatment is "reform." This term was then taken over by Helmut von Glasenapp, who in 1928 wrote his German study *Religiöse Reformbewegungen im heutigen Indien.* Glasenapp's work seems to be largely dependent on Farquhar. Farquhar judged phenomena in the Indian life of the nineteenth and early twentieth centuries by the amount of reform they represented. His standards of evaluation were those of the European intellectual. It is understandable that the Hindu D. S. Sarma, writing on the same subject, replaced the term 'reform' with 'renaissance.' What mattered to him was not the fact that Hinduism, under the influence of foreigners, had undergone changes which might be described as reforms. Instead, he wanted to show that after a period of decay Hinduism had gradually recovered its vigor by its own resources.

It is an intriguing fact, however, that the phenomena which Sarma included under the term 'renaissance' largely coincide with those which Farquhar had labeled 'reform.' This shows graphically that both terms are somehow inadequate. In fact, both reflect a definite cultural partiality. The use of the term 'reform' betrays the European who wishes to bring betterment to India; 'renaissance,' on the other hand, indicates the atmosphere of Hindu nationalism. Nevertheless, if the terms are inadequate and therefore apt to mislead, they are not altogether incorrect. In the Indian cultural life of the nineteenth and early twentieth centuries there actually were events which, if evaluated from the angle of European culture, can be described as 'reforms.' But these very reforms were claimed by Hindus as their own achievement, which is quite correct inasmuch as Hindus effected the changes. Thus it is quite natural that Hindu nationalism saw these changes as a revival of Hinduism.

However, the inadequacy of the two terms makes it advisable to drop both. I do not know who invented the term Neo-Hinduism. I found it in an informative article by Robert Antoine who presented the Bengali writer Bankim Candra Caṭṭopādhyāya (Chatterjee) as "a pioneer of Neo-Hinduism."[1] The term 'Neo-Hinduism' seems appropriate to bring out the characteristic traits of what Farquhar liked to call reforms and what D. S. Sarma saw as a renaissance. Neo-Hinduism in fact claims to be Hinduism. But it is a novel Hinduism. Its substantial identity with earlier Hinduism is open to question. Even its comparability with the general features of the European Renaissance seems doubtful. I may note that as a synonym for 'Neo-Hindu' I occasionally use the word 'modernist.' This word also brings out the sense of the prefix 'Neo-.'

I started from the two terms 'reform' and 'renaissance' because these are perhaps more commonly known than the term 'Neo-Hinduism.' Moreover, the interesting coincidence of a reform oriented toward European patterns with a Hindu renaissance offers a preview of what Neo-Hinduism is.

Neo-Hindu literature begins around the 1870s. Prominent among the writers are Bankim Candra Caṭṭopādhyāya (1838–1894), Vivekananda (1862–1902), Aurobindo Ghose (1872–1950), Mohandās Karamcand Gandhi (1869–1947), and Radhakrishnan (1888–1975). Some others, beginning with Rām Mohan Rāy (1772–1833), may be described as forerunners. What distinguishes these from the writers of Neo-Hinduism proper is mainly the fact that Indian nationalism was not yet developed at their time.

Neo-Hinduism is not a unified system of ideas. In fact, it is chiefly because of one common trait that I classify religious thinkers as Neo-Hindus. Their intellectual formation is primarily or predominantly Western. It is European culture, and in several cases even the Christian religion, which has led them to embrace certain religious, ethical, social, and political values. But afterwards they connect these values with, and claim them as, part of the Hindu tradition.

The results of this process of assimilation are very similar to analogous events in the history of modern Indian languages. To a very large extent modern Indians think in concepts associated with English words. Even when they write in an Indian language, their mind is moving in the framework of these concepts. But loanwords from English, though abounding in the colloquial language, are taboo in writing. Especially when a writer is dealing with modern life, he is in need of Indian equivalents for English words. So Sanskrit terms are chosen to express the meanings of English words. The result is a language which outwardly looks purely Indian but which by its conceptual contents belongs to the type that an American linguist has described as "standard average European."

Similarly, typical Neo-Hindu concepts at first sight appear to be perfectly Indian, but closer analysis reveals that they include European contents. In this paper it is my aim to analyze some instances of this assimilation, to set them off against traditional Hinduism, and thus to delineate a few characteristics of Neo-Hinduism.

Traditional Hinduism is a religion, or rather a group of religions, today much more alive than Neo-Hinduism, which as a religion sometimes looks stillborn. But traditional Hinduism has one serious drawback. Unlike Neo-Hinduism, it has scarcely any publicity abroad. It does not produce any remarkable literature, least of all in English. My literary sources for surviving traditional Hinduism are mainly a number of tracts in Hindi which originally appeared in the monthly *Kalyāṇ* and were then published in book form by the Gītā Press in Gorakhpur.

What is the difference between Neo-Hinduism and contemporary traditional Hinduism?

As regards doctrines, there are some held by traditionalists but rejected more or less emphatically or re-interpreted by most or many Hindu modernists. But we should lose sight of the essentials if we were to try to find the decisive difference in the area of doctrine. This is all the more true inasmuch as traditional Hinduism is in no higher degree a unified and coherent doctrinal system than Neo-Hinduism. Even the dogma of the equality of all religions and the claim that Hinduism is tolerant by nature, characteristic though these opinions are for Neo-Hinduism, do not mark a difference from contemporary traditional Hinduism. Traditionalists often share these views, whereas Hindu modernists can occasionally stress the superiority of their religion more than the essential unity of all religions.

As regards openness for outside influences, Neo-Hinduism is certainly more willing than traditionalism to assimilate extraneous views. In fact, Neo-Hinduism essentially lives on such assimilation. But also traditionalism has not only actually undergone such influences; it sometimes even deliberately incorporates extraneous elements. Yet here is the point where the crucial disparity of the two ways of thinking, the Neo-Hinduistic and the traditionalistic, becomes discernible.

I used the term 'ways of thinking.' In fact, Neo-Hinduism and Hindu traditionalism are not two definite systems but rather two distinct mental attitudes. It may even happen that one and the same person combines elements of both ways of thinking. Traditional Hinduism assimilates and absorbs extraneous elements in a manner characteristically distinct from Neo-Hinduism. Unlike the latter, it maintains a living continuity with the past. Even in the past, Hindu groups often absorbed foreign elements. These certainly changed the appearance of the religion of the respective groups. But at the same time most of the old values retained their previous vitality.

In Neo-Hinduism, on the contrary, the continuity with the past is broken. The typical Neo-Hindu has at some period of his life lost his confidence in his native religion. Radhakrishnan, speaking of his college days, voices this feeling of frustration in the words: "I was strongly persuaded of the inefficiency of the Hindu religion to which I attributed the political downfall of India . . . I remember the cold sense of reality, the depressing feeling of defeat that crept over me, as a causal relation between the anaemic Hindu religion and our political failure forced itself on my mind during those years. What is wrong with Hindu religion?"[2]

Similar statements about Hindus losing faith in their religion occur in the works of Bankim Candra and Vivekananda. It is significant that it was not really in the religious field that these frustrated Hindus saw the inadequacy of Hinduism. Rather, it was primarily the political defeat that distressed and offended them. This implies that the ideal of nationalism, itself of European importation, had taken hold of their minds.

But this nationalism appears in a peculiarly Indian garb. Radhakrishnan attributed the political downfall not to political causes but to the intellectual incoherence and ethical rottenness of his national religion. Accordingly, he seeks the remedy for the evil not in political measures but in religious change. Hinduism, of course, must be preserved, since it is the national religion. But Radhakrishnan asks: "How can we make it somewhat more relevant to the intellectual climate and social environment of our time?"[3] Thus the national objective and the requirements of the present time are primary; religion is made subservient to them. Similarly, Bankim Candra strove to combat what he thought to be the effeminacy of his fellow countrymen, and thus to revivify their national pride and political efficiency. The means, however, by which he expected to accomplish this objective was again a modernization of the Hindu religion. Motivated by the same goals, Vivekananda presented his reinterpretation of the Vedānta, and even advocated the propagation of this Neo-Vedānta abroad, as a stimulus for reinvigorating the national feeling of the Hindus. From the recent past, the close intertwining of religion and politics in the thought of Gandhi is well known. These and other cases lead us to the conclusion that nationalism is the chief impulse of typical Neo-Hindu thinking.

After this general characterization, which inevitably was somewhat schematic, I will now analyze a few facts and ideas to further elucidate my subject.

Nearly all varieties of Hinduism practice the worship of idols. It is true that in the radical monism of Advaita Vedānta an image becomes what we may approximately call a symbol. Man superimposes on the image the idea that it is a god, because this idea is an aid to contemplative concentration. But the god represented by the idol is regarded as ultimately identical with the contemplator's own spiritual self. Thus idol-worship becomes a means of monistic self realization. It is clear that this reinterpretation is possible only on the basis of the common belief that the idol *is* the deity. In the realistic Mādhva sect, too, idols are reinterpreted as something like symbols. But this is not the common Hindu view. The *dharmaśāstras* teach or presuppose that the idol *is* the deity. This is most emphatically brought out by the ceremony of *prāṇapratiṣṭhā* which was developed in the course of the middle ages. This ceremony is intended to "establish life" in the image, that is to say, to make it identical with the god it represents. The theology of the Rāmānuja school also evidences the common view. This school teaches that the image is an *avatāra,* a descent or an embodiment of the deity. Being a descent of the god, the idol is of course identical with the god.

I have dwelt on this subject at some length because some Neo-Hindus deny that Hinduism includes the belief that idols are identical with the gods they represent and because this opinion has gained some publicity in the West. Mahātmā Gandhi stated: "Images are an aid to worship. No Hindu considers an image to be God. I do not consider idol-worship a sin."[4]

It has to be noted, however, that traditional Hinduism even today differs from views like those voiced by the Mahātmā. In one of the books of the Gītā Press I found a treatise on idol-worship. The treatise, probably in a deliberate if tacit opposition to Neo-Hindu views, is most emphatic in its insistence on the laws of the *dharmaśāstras.* The teaching of the treatise reflects a position exactly opposed to that of Gandhi. For the Mahātmā, idol-worship was not a sin because no Hindu identified an image with God. The traditionalist treatise, on the contrary, virtually declares that it is a sin *not* to consider the idol to be the god it represents.[5]

Why did Gandhi deem it necessary to state that he did not consider idol-worship a sin? The answer to this question is simple. Non-Hindu ideas, in this case Christian doctrine, had gained ascendancy over the Mahātmā's mind. So he reduced the function of the idol to a mere "aid to worship." He reinterpreted the Hindu practice in such a way that the Christian accusation no longer applied. This implies that he had assimilated from the outside the distinction between what was valuable or acceptable in this case and what not, but he claimed that this distinction stemmed from his native religion. This is a typical case of Neo-Hindu thinking.

The unflinching attitude of present-day traditional Hinduism in its defense of idol-worship is an outcome of its loyalty to the laws of *dharma.* I will revert to the concept of *dharma* presently. Let me first point out a few other facts.

As I indicated before, traditional Hinduism has not remained altogether closed to influences from the outside. A prominent example is the Bengali mystic Rāmakṛṣṇa (1836–86). It is true that Rāmakṛṣṇa's disciple Vivekananda has founded a religious association which he named after his master, namely the Rāmakṛṣṇa Mission, and that many members of this association, like its founder, have worked as vigorous propagators of the modernistic way of thinking. But this does not imply that Rāmakṛṣṇa himself was a Neo-Hindu. To all appearances, his connection with the tradition was quite unbroken. He was a staunch worshipper of the goddess Kālī, even a temple servant. Occasionally, however, he also practiced ways of spiritual realization *(sādhanā)* that are peculiar to other Hindu sects, notably Rāmaism, Kṛṣṇaism, and Advaitism. Moreover, he was not unsympathetic toward foreign religions. He conceived the idea of reconciling these religions with his own, or incorporating them into it, in a typically Hindu manner. He strove to realize by religious practice and meditative concentration the spiritual experiences of Islām and of Christianity. The attempts seemed successful inasmuch as he had visions of Muhammad and of Christ. So he took it for granted that the foreign religions were equal in value to his own religion. Still, Rāmakṛṣṇa's experiments involved not the slightest reinterpretation of traditional Hinduism, which, being a group of religions, has always been willing to absorb foreign elements. Neo-Hinduism, on the contrary, always implies reinterpretation.

Cases of assimilation of foreign elements are also found in the tracts of the Gītā Press which I mentioned before. These treatises deal with a vast number of subjects strictly on the basis of traditional texts. Yet the very style of their treatment betrays foreign, namely, Christian influence. It is clearly an imitation of the style of sermons or edifying essays with interspersed passages from the *śāstras* taking the place that quotations from the Bible have in Christian tracts or sermons. Moreover, there are in the Gītā Press tracts a number of leading concepts which in older Hindu literature were either absent or not so prominent as they are in the modern tracts, notably the notions of faith *(viśvās, śraddhā)* and prayer *(prārthanā)*. In the case of faith, the foreign influence is perceptible chiefly in the fact that traditionalistic tracts of our day speak of it much more often and with greater emphasis than texts of the past. This emphasis reveals a change of the relative position of faith in the spiritual system of religion. Faith is no longer, as it used to be in former times, one of the bare rudiments of religious practice, to be outgrown by gnosis *(jñāna)* and *bhakti;* it can now figure as one of the central impulsions of devotion. *Prārthanā,* which nowadays appears as an equivalent for "prayer," had hardly a religious meaning in Sanskrit, where it signified "entreaty," "solicitation," even in an erotic sense. Medieval theists, however, at least in Mahārāṣṭra, seem to have employed the word to express a specific religious attitude or an act of devotion. Thus Jñāneśvar, who in the thirteenth century composed a metrical commentary on the Bhagavadgītā in Marathi, used the verb *prārthanē* to denote not only petition but even the praise of adoration inspired by a feeling of awe.[6] In the nineteenth century, this meaning of the word seems to have coalesced with influences from Christianity. One of the Gītā Press tracts understands *prārthanā* as a means of establishing and maintaining contact with God. Ultimately, however, the prayer of petition as recommended by this tract takes on the form of the Hindu practice of *bhāvanā.*[7] The praying person seeks to realize the object of petition in a material sense by intense mental representation of it. The basis of this practice is the belief that man's soul is a part of the deity; hence, man's psychic effort can directly make use of God's unlimited power.[8] In this way prayer is completely Hinduized.

The willingness to assimilate foreign ideas goes even to the extent that a work of Christian origin can be remodeled in a Hinduized form. Among the Gītā Press tracts I discovered a booklet with the title "Faith in God" *(Bhagavān par viśvās).*[9] The very title seemed to me to point to foreign origin. I succeeded in identifying the source. It was Brother Lawrence's "Practice of the Presence of God."[10] A comparison with the original revealed that all references to Jesus Christ and to specifically Christian doctrines had been expunged. I will give one example. In the English version of the original there is the passage ". . . we ought, without anxiety, to expect the pardon of our sins from the Blood of Jesus Christ, laboring simply to love him with all our heart." The Hindu revision of this reads as follows: "When we love God with all our heart, our sins are automatically wiped out."[11] The characteristic difference consists not only in the omission in the Hindu version of Christ's expiatory suffering. In addition, the Christian's hope is changed into certainty, and forgiveness is turned into effacement, which is a mechanical process. In my translation I used the word 'automatically.' In the present context, this renders the sense of the Sanskrit or Hindi *svataḥ,* which literally means "of itself." The changes of the Hinduized text imply a depersonalization. The ideas of the original have been adjusted to the framework of Hindu *bhakti,* which is consistent with the law of *karman,* whereas the personalism of forgiveness of sin would amount to an abrogation of this law. Some ideas, however, seemed to the redactor to be compatible with Hinduism, even though they are hardly met with in Hindu scriptures. Thus he writes: "The spiritual practice of faith in God is the true kind of worship of God."[12] The importance which is here attached to faith clearly reveals Christian influence. This is all the more striking since the redactor has here exchanged a Christian idea which he could not assimilate for another Christian idea which he found acceptable, for instead of the sentence I have just quoted, the original states that "the way of faith was the spirit of the Church."

Thus assimilation of extraneous ideas occurs in present-day traditional Hinduism also. But a typical Neo-Hindu will not Hinduize Christian ideas in such a way. Taking his stand on the tenet of the equality of all religions, he will freely quote Christian writings but interpret them in a most latitudinarian sense. Examples of this kind abound in the works of Radhakrishnan.

Now let me turn to an analysis of the notion of *dharma*. This is perhaps the most instructive instance of a reinterpretation in Hindu modernism. I will treat it here in a very summary way.

Present-day traditional Hinduism defends the concept of *dharma* as it is found in the Hindu scriptures. This *dharma* comprises norms or patterns of conduct, most of which differ according to a man's caste and stage of life. Thus it necessarily presupposes the traditional social order of Hinduism. This is why it is described in Sanskrit as *varṇāśramadharma*. But just as in the past the norms that fall under *dharma* never formed a conceptually coherent whole or an immutable system, so even at present vindication of traditional *dharma* does not preclude the adoption of new values, which may even entail a readjustment of the system at some point or other. The system as a concrete whole remains unimpaired. A significant example is the ideal of service. In medieval Hinduism service *(sevā)* could only be rendered by a person of lower rank to one of higher station. Thus a Brahman, ranking higher than all other members of society, could serve a god or an idol but was forbidden to serve a human being. The *Manusmṛti* (4,6) condemns service done by a Brahman as being "a dog's behavior" *(śvavṛtti)*. In modern India, however, most probably under the influence of Christian ethics, service done to all beings has come to be regarded as a high ideal, obligatory on all classes. Thus, a modern text which expounds *dharma* quite in line with tradition, nonetheless includes *sevā* among forty principal virtues considered as constitutive of the *dharma* of *all* castes.[13] Yet the old rule of the *Manusmṛti* is not forgotten. Since, however, the text understands *sevā* in a positive sense, to express the virtue or duty of doing good to all beings, the old prohibition is now expressed by a different term: it is now "a slave's way of living" *(dāsavṛtti)* which a Brahman is forbidden to practice.[14] In this way, the old prohibition is essentially retained, but the fact of the adoption of a new value is reflected in the revaluation of an old term. Again, this adoption is not presented so as to appear to be the addition of a foreign idea to the system of values. The text connects the idea of *sevā* with the attitude of "being pleased with the well-being of all creatures,"[15] which has been an ethical value commonly recognized in India at least from the time when Buddhism was preponderant in the subcontinent, and which occurs in the Bhagavadgītā and in a considerable number of passages in the Great Epic. Yet the modern notion of *sevā,* as interpreted by the text under discussion, gives an active turn to what previously was essentially a mental disposition, and it is precisely this turn which reveals influence from outside. Nevertheless, the addition of the new value does not imply a transmutation of the traditional concept of *dharma.*

Most of the prominent Neo-Hindus, on the other hand, have reinterpreted *dharma* more or less radically according to Western models. Bankim Candra Caṭṭopādhāya was perhaps the first to offer such a reinterpretation. In order to evaluate his novel concept, we first have to note that the word *dharma* has other meanings besides the meaning "pattern of conduct" which I mentioned before. The word may also signify "an essential quality" of a thing. Moreover, many modern Indian languages use it as an equivalent of the European word 'religion.' Bankim achieved his reinterpretation by fusing all the three meanings I mentioned, namely (1) pattern of conduct, (2) essential quality, (3) religion.[16] Thus he arrived at the conclusion that religion is man's essential quality, denoted by the word 'humanity' *(manuṣyatva),* but it is at the same time a pattern of conduct, an ideal whose realization man is obliged to strive for.

All this looks very Western. In fact, Bankim remodeled Hinduism according to what he had learned from the positivists Auguste Comte and John Stuart Mill. Comte sought to replace the worship of God with the cult of humanity; Bankim, while retaining the belief in a Supreme Being, reduced religion to the practice of what corresponds to man's essential nature or his talents. Scarcely a trace of the old concept of *dharma* is left in this doctrine. Only the word *dharma* is retained. Like a container it has been emptied and then filled with a new content.

I do not know whether Bankim Candra's theological works, which are written in Bengali, have exercised a direct influence on other Hindu writers. The fact is, however, that a *dharma* concept very similar to his appears in the works of many Neo-Hindus who came after him. Possibly the works of Aurobindo Ghose, whose mother tongue was Bengali but who wrote in English, are the connecting link between Bankim Candra and later authors. In any event, Aurobindo, in his *Essays on the Gītā,* sets forth a concept of *dharma* very similar to that enunciated by Bankim Candra.[17] Individualism, included already in Bankim's concept, is intensified in Aurobindo's work. He emphasizes that each individual should freely develop the particular way of self-expression that flows from his "inner law of nature." Rabīndranāth Ṭhākur (Tagore), whose philosophical writings are documents of Neo-Hinduism, also betrays Bankim's influence in his notions of religion and *dharma*.[18]

Gandhi's concept of *dharma* is very personal; I may omit it here. In a work of his disciple Vinobā, however, we again meet with an interpretation of *dharma* which is closely related to that of Bankim Candra and Aurobindo, but unlike these authors, Vinobā stresses social obligations as part of man's *dharma*. Man's environment imposes on him the duty of service *(sevā)*, and this also constitutes his *dharma*.[19] As for Radhakrishnan's concept of *dharma*, it is little more than an echo of that of Aurobindo. Commenting on, or rather misinterpreting, the Sanskrit term *svadharma*, Radhakrishnan says: "Each one must try to understand his pyschological make-up and function in accordance with it."[20] Traditional Hindus, however, even today know very well that *svadharma* as such is not constituted by a man's psychic disposition or his personality but is determined by the caste in which he is born and the stage of life in which he finds himself, all this, including his psychic "make-up," being a consequence of his deeds in his previous existences. It is not surprising that precisely in the conception of *dharma* the divergence of modernistic from traditionalistic Hinduism is widest. For the practices of *dharma* are the very core of traditional Hinduism, and Neo-Hindus ordinarily have no active or living connection with these practices.

After this selection of a few ideas, which are not restricted to individual authors, I will now isolate some features of the thinking of prominent Neo-Hindu thinkers and writers, namely Vivekananda, Gandhi, Vinobā Bhāve, and Radhakrishnan.

Vivekananda's achievement in the history of Indian thought appears to have been a sort of revival of the spirit-monism which is known as the Advaita Vedānta. This philosophy had given a metaphysical orientation, an answer to man's ultimate questions, to many generations of Hindu intellectuals. At first sight one might be inclined to admit that Vivekananda succeeded in bringing about a genuine renewal. Among the pandits who today advocate the monistic Vedānta in accordance with tradition, there are not a few who are members of the Rāmakṛṣṇa order which was founded by Vivekananda. They bring out annotated translations of old texts, and occasionally, though rarely, even original studies are being produced quite on the lines of the traditional doctrines.

Unlike Bankim Candra and Aurobindo, who depreciated the monistic Vedānta, Vivekananda found that this philosophy alone, which he regarded as the most sublime accomplishment of the Indian mind, could provide a promising basis for a reinstatement of Hinduism. He saw in the Advaita Vedānta the bond that linked together the diverse varieties of Hinduism. In fact, he took it to be coterminous with Hinduism itself. But he did not simply restate the ancient doctrines. He modified them so as to make them appear relevant to the national and social problems of his time. The student of the history of Indian thought must ask himself whether this modification is a straight prolongation of the lines traced out by the ancient masters of the monistic Vedānta, or whether there is a break between the ideas of the old school and Vivekananda's presentation of the Vedānta.

The result of such scrutiny is that there actually is a break. The traditionalistic Advaitists hold that the world, in fact, all matter, all difference and diversity, all action, and all psychic phenomena are ultimately unreal. Phenomenal reality is a mere appearance, the inexplicable product of an inexplicable power of delusion which is called Nescience or Māyā. The sole reality is Brahman, which is pure Spirit, one only, impersonal and identical with man's true self. Realization of this absolute spiritual unity connotes insight into the nothingness of the Māyā and its products. This is final emancipation, in which transmigration comes to an end. The adept who wishes to attain the goal must totally renounce everything connected with the world. He has to abandon not only all possession of material goods and all secular action but also all religious ceremonies and even all attachment to human beings.

Vivekananda, however, while not rejecting renunciation and asceticism, discovered an ethical implication in Advaitism. He argued as follows. If a man realizes his identity with Brahman, which is the all-powerful Absolute, then he must feel that the compass of his potentialities is just as unlimited as Brahman itself. This will give him boundless self-confidence and irresistible power. He will thus become capable of working efficiently for the spiritual recovery of India, and this will bring about a national reconstruction.

In this way Vivekananda derived from the monistic dogma a practical consequence which every Advaitist of the old school must consider a fatal deviation from the road that alone leads to the goal. Vivekananda's practical application of Vedāntism reveals the Neo-Hindu whose primary concern is nationalism. His commitment to religion was surely genuine, but nationalism was part of this very commitment. Thus he was consistent in making the religious heritage subservient to the tackling of modern national problems. Since, however, nationalism had a firmer hold on his mind than the heritage, he did not notice that his adaptation altered the nature of the tradition to the extent of almost turning it into its opposite.[21]

Like other Bengali Neo-Hindus, Vivekananda was also influenced by positivism. Thus he not only repeated the Vedānta doctrine of the individual's identity with Brahman or God, but also taught that mankind as a whole is God. This implies that man's service for humanity is the true form of worship.

Another practical application for monism, equally irreconcilable with traditional Advaitism, was suggested to Vivekananda by the German philosopher and Indologist Paul Deussen, a posthumous disciple of Schopenhauer. Schopenhauer had taught that monism alone could provide a solid foundation for moral philosophy. Vivekananda learned from Deussen that this kind of monism, capable of serving as a basis for ethics, was taught in no other philosophy in such a pure form as it was in the Vedānta.[22] This view, however, involves two gross mistakes. First, Schopenhauer's monism was voluntaristic, while the Vedānta teaches spiritual monism. Second, ethics presupposes relationships, while the strict unity of radical spirit-monism effaces all relationships. Moreover, what is still more important in the framework of my study, there is not the slightest hint of an ethical implication of the monistic dogma in traditional Advaitism. On the contrary, the spiritual practice of Advaita Vedānta ultimately strives after a state which is beyond good and evil, that is to say (if a neologism be tolerated), a transethical state, which is actionless, not arbitrary behavior.

As regards Gandhi, it would be superficial to classify him as a mere politician. He was one of the most outstanding representatives of Neo-Hinduism. There were, however, some important remnants of traditionalism in his religious practice even more than in his thought. An example would be his habit of repeating the name of *Rām*. Gandhi even professed *Sanātana* Hinduism, and this term connotes an attitude analogous to what in other religions is called orthodoxy. He stated: "I believe in . . . all that goes by the name of Hindu scriptures, and therefore in *avatāras* and rebirth. I believe in *varṇāśramadharma*" (i.e., in traditional rules of conduct determined by one's caste and stage of life) . . . "I believe in the protection of the cow . . . I do not disbelieve in idol-worship."[23]

To fully understand this profession, which I have quoted in an abbreviated form, one must, however, take into consideration Gandhi's own interpretation of it. His belief in *avatāras* and rebirth, as well as his insistence on the protection of the cow, are certainly elements of traditional thinking. His respect for the Hindu scriptures, however, does not mean that he believed that these scriptures alone were divinely inspired, as traditionalists certainly do. Neither did he accept all their parts as divine revelation, nor did he claim exclusiveness for them. The Koran, the Avesta, and especially the New Testament with the Sermon on the Mount as its principal part, had for him equal dignity with the sacred texts of the Hindus. Furthermore, his profession of *varṇāśramadharma* did not imply what this word literally expresses. He was not willing to accept the rules laid down in the *dharmaśāstras* for the conduct of the Hindu castes and stages of life. He had his own interpretation, very modern, spiritualized, and ethicized, of the Hindu social order and the norms regulating its life. He asserted that this interpretation reflected the truly Vedic conception. But in this he was mistaken. As regards his view of idol-worship, I referred to it before. On the whole, we may say that in his religious views Gandhi was a modernist.

Of particular interest are Gandhi's ethical views. The predominant role which he ascribed to nonviolence *(ahiṃsā)* and service *(sevā)* is well known. As for service, I mentioned above, when speaking about *dharma,* that even traditional Hinduism has adopted *sevā* as one of the norms of conduct obligatory on all men. *Ahiṃsā,* on the other hand, is certainly an ancient Indian ideal. But one can gather from Gandhi's biography that he did not accept it directly from Hindu sources. Gandhi has confessed that the religious writings of Leo Tolstoy made a deep impression on him.[24] Now it is well known that Tolstoy saw the center of the gospel in the commandment not to resist evil. Since Gandhi was so willing to learn from Tolstoy's interpretation of the gospel, it is obvious that this doctrine must have influenced him. But he could at once identify it with a Hindu practice. We see here once more that an ideal becomes relevant to the Neo-Hindu as a consequence of impressions received from the outside; but he immediately connects the ideal with an element of the Hindu tradition. Still, Gandhi's notion of *ahiṃsā* had some aspects which are foreign to the Hindu tradition. First, he made *ahiṃsā* a norm for political action, which it had never been in the Hindu past. Second, he extended the meaning of *ahiṃsā* so as to include selflessness,[25] goodwill toward all life,[26] and even charity in the broadest sense, including love of one's enemy.[27] It is clearly the Christian ideal of love of one's neighbor which

Gandhi denoted by the old Hindu term. In traditional doctrine *ahiṃsā* had the purely negative meaning of abstention from killing or injuring living beings.

There is a movement, though apparently declining today, which strives to cultivate and propagate the ideas of Mahātmā Gandhi. One of the most important and interesting representatives of this Gandhist movement is Vinobā Bhāve (born 1895). What interests us in the framework of the present study is Vinobā's reinterpretation of the ideas and habits of the Hindu religion.

In his numerous speeches Vinobā seeks to inculcate in his listeners an attitude of altruism. He regards such an attitude as an essential prerequisite for the economic reforms he contemplates. He strives to arouse his listeners' interest by appealing to what ranks highest in their estimation and respect, namely their religious feelings. But this is surely more than a clever come-on. Vinobā seems honestly convinced that altruism, practiced in the economic field, is the most authentic form of religious practice. Cautiously but unmistakably, he sometimes hints that the practices of traditional Hinduism are susceptible to individualism and selfishness.[28] Their true fulfilment is their transposition into the field of social responsibility.

In the framework of his program, Vinobā has reinterpreted quite a number of Hindu religious ideas and practices.

He endeavors to stir people's respect and sympathy for the needy; so he identifies the poor with the Supreme Deity in speaking of *Daridra-Nārāyaṇa.*[29] *Nārāyaṇa* is a name of the Supreme God in Vaishṇavism; *daridra* means "poor, needy." In this identification of the needy with God, Vinobā utilizes the widespread Hindu belief that the human self is more or less identical or connatural with the deity.[30] Ancient Hindu texts, the Bhagavadgītā and others, also express the ideas that this identity or consubstantiality extends down to the lowest classes of society. But no thinker had ever drawn a practical, ethical conclusion from this view.

Vinobā demands that land owners should cede property to the landless. So he first teaches that all land primarily belongs to God.[31] When given to the poor, who are *Daridra-Nārāyaṇa,* the land becomes a sacrifice. Thus the idea of *bhūdān* arises. *Bhūdān* means "gift of land." By calling such gift a sacrifice *(yajña),* Vinobā stresses the religious meaning he wishes to associate with the donation. He said: "We must make sacrifices for the poor. I am asking for land. It is just a symbol of that spirit of sacrifice. In every heart there should be a desire to serve *Daridra-Nārāyaṇa.*"[32] Vinobā has invented still other kinds of sacrifice, all consisting in social service: *sampattidān* or gift of wealth, *shramdān* or labor gift, *premdān* or gift of love, *buddhidān* or gift of one's intelligence, and finally *jīvandān* or gift of one's life.

Other reinterpretations found in Vinobā's speeches concern notions like *Brahman* and practices like *bhakti* and idol-worship. *Brahman,* for Vinobā, means absolute equality. He wants to transpose it from the domain of metaphysics to social and economic life.[33] *Bhakti* and idol-worship are different though often combined forms of adoration in traditional Hinduism. *Bhakti* is primarily mental devotion, while idol-worship consists in exterior actions. For Vinobā, God is more or less identical with the totality of all human beings.[34] Accordingly, *bhakti* and idol-worship receive a new relevance for him. He does not attempt to abolish the old practices, but he adds a new meaning to the traditional one. He teaches that *bhakti* and idol-worship are also practiced in the mental attitude of altruism and in social service.[35]

I scarcely need point out in detail that all these ideas tally perfectly with the definition I gave of Neo-Hinduism. Ancient notions are seemingly retained, but Vinobā fills the words with a new content which obviously is not a product of the Indian mind. I may note in passing that the identification of society with God is the old positivist idea as adapted by Bankim Candra Caṭṭopādhyāya. The surprising discovery, however, of an economic relevance of the Hindu religion is certainly Vinobā's own contribution and at the same time a genuinely Hindu achievement.

I now turn to another and perhaps the most striking representative of Neo-Hinduism: Radhakrishnan. I feel that hardly any other writer combines the characteristic traits of the modernistic way of Hindu thinking in such an outstanding and comprehensive manner as he does. There can be no doubt that the most original Neo-Hindu thinker is Aurobindo; but Radhakrishnan seems to be the most typical. Influences of all earlier prominent Neo-Hindus can be traced in his work, notably Vivekananda, Aurobindo, Tagore, and Gandhi. Moreover, he applies the modernistic method to a number of problems that had not yet been taken up. I will single out only very few subjects.

Before doing so, I first must briefly analyze a way of thinking that is not restricted to Neo-Hinduism. In fact, it stems from hoary antiquity. In some publications of mine I have called it "inclusivism." It consists in claiming for, and thus including in, one's own religion what really belongs to an alien sect. The most outstanding example of such behavior is perhaps Tulsīdās. In Banaras, a city in which the cult of Śiva was predominant, he proclaimed devotion to Rāma. His ingenious safeguard against possible hostility from the alien sect was his teaching that worship of Śiva was all right, because Śiva himself was the foremost and noblest worshipper of Rāma. In this way Tulsīdās did not encroach on the religion of Śiva but claimed it in its entirety for his own. It seems that this method was employed especially by such religious groups as felt themselves inferior to their environment.

The same method has often been practiced by Neo-Hindus, notably Vivekananda and Radhakrishnan. They use it in a specifically modernistic concern, and this is why we must refer to it in a characterization of Neo-Hinduism, even though the method as such is an ancient heritage. I will presently consider an instance of inclusivism in Radhakrishnan's thought.

Like Vivekananda, Radhakrishnan professes Vedāntism. In the suggestive diction that makes his style so attractive and his thought at times so elusive, he says: "Every form of Hinduism is related to the common background of the Vedānta."[36] He continues: "The Vedānta is not *a* religion, but religion itself in its most universal and deepest significance."[37] It is almost impossible to define the precise meaning of such expressions as "related to the common background," and "the deepest significance" of religion. Nor is the notion of Vedānta very distinct in Radhakrishnan's work. In his book *An Idealist View of Life,*[38] which is perhaps the most noteworthy of his works, he speaks of "the consubstantiality of the spirit in man and God," which he holds to be "the conviction fundamental to all spiritual wisdom." This is certainly a Vedāntic idea but is not restricted to Indian thought. Nor does it express the degree of monism which Vivekananda professed. Generally speaking, Radhakrishnan's idealism is of a type that often seems more indebted to European than Indian sources. Nevertheless, both Vivekananda and Radhakrishnan hold that it is to the Vedānta that not only Hinduism but all religions ultimately, though unconsciously, tend. Thus the Vedānta is the unifying element in the multiplicity of the religious views and practices of Hinduism and of all religions. It is precisely the somewhat vague character of Radhakrishnan's Vedānta which makes it capable of such a role. But this unifying system or energy is an achievement of the Indian mind. We must remember that Radhakrishnan, like more or less all Hindus today, affirms that all religions are equal in their worth or essence or aim. If, however, the hidden goal or center or essence of all religions is the Vedānta, which primarily constitutes the spiritual unity of Hinduism, then all religions are in a way included in Hinduism. This is the most comprehensive application which the principle of inclusivism has ever found. Incidentally, it would perhaps be more accurate to speak of inclusivism in many cases where we are inclined to see Hindu tolerance.

Radhakrishnan's understanding of Vedānta is closely related to the notions of mysticism and spiritual experience. For him, the essence of religion is experience,[39] that is to say, the subjective side of man's relation to the Absolute. It appears fairly certain, however, that it was not from Hindu sages that Radhakrishnan received his primary information about or even initiation into spiritual experience. His books evidence, and a number of citations in them acknowledge, that the works of Western savants, for instance William James' book *The Varieties of Religious Experience,* provided him with categories for dealing with the subject. The idea, so characteristic of Radhakrishnan's thought, that mysticism is the very peak of religion, could have been drawn from James, who wrote that "personal religious experience has its root and center in mystical states of consciousness."[40] Radhakrishnan's books show that he has read the works of a great many Western mystics, both Christian and Moslem. And it was again Western scholars who taught him that mysticism in all religions was essentially homogeneous. But while Radhakrishnan assimilated from the West conceptual tools and, implicit in these, a humanistic or anthropocentric approach to religion, he must have become conscious of a definite superiority the moment he turned to Hindu systems of spirituality.

We may take Radhakrishnan's reaction to James' philosophy as a specimen of his way of viewing the problem of the Hindu religion as confronted with Western scholarship. On the one hand, he found in James an approach to religion which promised to allow him to keep abreast with achievements of modern scholarship. James thus seemed to provide an answer to the question which I quoted before and which had worried Radhakrishnan so much in his youth, namely the question: "How can we make our religion somewhat more relevant to the intellectual climate of our time?" On the other hand, Radhakrishnan must have felt that the Hindu approach was positively superior to the way in which Western scholars, James and others, treated religion. These scholars were speaking *about* religion, they were watching it *from without.* Only in somewhat timid words and by way of an appendix did James state his own beliefs. Hindu scriptures, however, as also those Hindu writers whom we call Indian philosophers, had always spoken *from within.* In other words, the Hindu sages and doctors had proclaimed or expounded or defended what they themselves were persuaded was true, whereas modern Western specialists in the science of religion investigated what others believed to be true. This Western attitude is foreign to many Hindus even today. When a Hindu comes to know that a Westerner is studying Hinduism or a system of Indian philosophy, he ordinarily presupposes that the Westerner professes what he is studying. Few Hindus command the intellectual elasticity which we can observe in Radhakrishnan and other leading Neo-Hindus.

Radhakrishnan did imbibe the results, if not the methods, of the Western scientific approach to religion. He accepted from the West the conceptual patterns which he has since used in interpreting the religious heritage of his native country. But at the same time he retained the typical Hindu attitude. In his work *An Idealist View of Life* he concluded his review of modern Western studies on religion by saying: "The different attempts to accommodate God to the needs of the modern mind are not quite successful in their ambition."[41] For Radhakrishnan, all these achievements of scholarship are outshone by the Indian, spiritualistic way of thinking. So he continues: "In the Eastern religions, the energy of the depth of the soul is something before which external existence pales into insignificance" (Ibid.). In a quotation I adduced earlier, Radhakrishnan said that in his youth he had thought that the Hindu religion was "anaemic." From the review, however, which he gives in *An Idealist View of Life* and in other works of his, it appears that after he had studied the theories of Western scholars. It was rather these theories that seemed to him effete. He conceived of a "philosophy of religion" which was very different from the elaborate but lifeless "science of religion" as enunciated by William James. "Philosophy of religion," Radhakrishnan states, "is religion come to an understanding of itself."[42] This is exactly the attitude which I described as "speaking from within."

Nevertheless, this attitude is only a formal element in Radhakrishnan's thought. He thinks he can combine this element with what he has learned from Western scholars. In his interpretations, the West stands for the scientific approach, while the East represents the religious impulse.[43] This implies that where he found true religion even in the West, he traced it ultimately to Eastern origin. This is one of the main ideas of his work *Eastern Religions and Western Thought*. The result of the combination of East and West is to be a religion which is "scientific, empirical and humanistic."[44]

These latter words reveal that in Radhakrishnan's thought the influence of the West eventually prevailed over what he calls "the East." William James' ideal of religion could be described in precisely the same words which Radhakrishnan uses, namely as a religion which is "scientific, empirical, and humanistic."

As regards experience, it is true that it has always held a prominent position in Hindu religious systems. Like William James, however, Radhakrishnan pits experience against dogma. Hindu sages, mystics, and doctors, on the contrary, have ordinarily been quite dogmatic in their outlook. So it would be hard to disprove that in Radhakrishnan's philosophy the primacy of experience was only secondarily connected with ideas of the Hindu tradition.

Thus the Western orientation is predominant in Radhakrishnan's project for a synthetic religion. This becomes most obvious in the way in which he portrays what he calls "the Hindu view of life." A European Indologist cannot help being amazed at finding this "Hindu view" so similar to ideas and outlooks in the history of Western thought. He cannot but smile when he reads, reprinted on the inside jacket of Radhakrishnan's work *The Hindu View of Life,* the opinion of a Quaker who wrote: "If what he describes in such masterly English . . . really be Hinduism, then there are many thousands of Friends who belong to that religion, though they call themselves Christians." It would perhaps be tedious to analyze here all the details in which Radhakrishnan presents Western or Christian ideas in a Hindu garb. I confine myself to a few examples.

Hindu philosophy or theology includes a notion which comes very close to what Christian doctrine calls revelation. It is true that most, though not all, Hindus do not understand revelation as emanating from the personal God. Among the schools that are specialized in the interpretation of the Vedic scriptures, the Mīmāṃsā teaches that these texts are authorless and have been existing from eternity, whereas the Vedānta holds that Brahman, the impersonal Absolute, is the source of the scriptures. In mythology, the god Brahman is not the author, but merely the proclaimer of the Vedas at the beginning of every aeon. Still, in all these varying teachings there is an analogy with the Christian concept insofar as revelation is held to be prior to man's experience. According to the traditional monistic Vedānta, the word of the revealed scriptures elicits man's experience, and this experience cannot be gained by any other means. Radhakrishnan, on the contrary, explains the original relationship between revelation and experience in an exactly inverse manner. For him, experience ranks first, and it is the criterion by which we can determine what an authoritative or revealed scripture is. He writes: "The records of the experiences of the great seers . . . are the Scriptures."[45] The

Vedas "are held to be authoritative on the ground that they express the experiences of the experts in the field of religion."[46] "Revelation and its reception are inseparably united."[47] On the latter point, Radhakrishnan agrees with Christian modernists, for instance Paul Tillich, whom he cites after the statement I have just quoted. Moreover, he does not hold, as traditionalists do, that the Vedas alone are authoritative, nor does he understand authoritativeness as precluding criticism.

Radhakrishnan's presentation of Hinduism in *The Hindu View of Life* follows a definition which is widespread in Western handbooks. This definition states that the elements common to the multitudinous varieties of Hinduism are:

1. acceptance of the authoritativeness of the Vedas,
2. the religious relevance of the social system of castes,
3. belief in the law of *karman* and rebirth or transmigration. As regards the Vedas, which represent revelation in Hinduism, I have briefly shown that Radhakrishnan's view differs from the traditional one in a typically Neo-Hindu fashion. The same holds true for his interpretation of the two other characteristics. I will not enter upon his interpretation of the caste system, which in many respects is surprising for an Indologist.

His views on *karman* and transmigration do not seem to be identical in all his works. In his Upton lectures of 1926, which were published under the title *The Hindu View of Life,* the *karman* doctrine appears in a rationalistic reinterpretation which combines the idea of a moral world order with elements of evolutionism and Christian ideas. I will quote a few excerpts. Radhakrishnan says: "The theory of Karma recognizes the rule of law not only in outward nature, but also in the world of mind and morals . . . We are every moment making our characters and shaping our destinies . . . (Karma) is the embodiment of the mind and will of God . . . There is room for repentance and consequent forgiveness in this scheme . . . The law of Karma encourages the sinner that it is never too late to mend."[48] It is needless to stress that most of these ideas are foreign to traditional Hinduism and were assimilated from the outside. Transmigration is not treated at all.

Three years later, however, in the Hibbert lectures for 1929, which were later published under the title *An Idealist View of Life,* Radhakrishnan presented an interpretation of the doctrine of transmigration also.

Principles of an evolutionistic philosophy provided him with the necessary guidelines for this interpretation. "The human self," he says, "is an emergent aspect of the world process and not a substance different in kind from the process itself."[49] Within this inclusion in the world process, "the connection with the past at the human stage is denoted by the word 'Karma' in the Hindu systems."[50] Man is determined by the past and at the same time free for "creative advance into the future."[51] "The law of Karma says that each individual will get the return according to the energy he puts forth."[52] On the basis of such views, Radhakrishnan comes to the conclusion that "the hypothesis" of rebirth "is a reasonable one."[53] In particular, his thesis that the self is "a continuous process"[54] helps him to find that "hypothesis" reasonable. The process has a meaning or a goal. It is a "gradual improvement," a "growth into personality."[55] It cannot be completed in one lifetime.

In evaluating this theory it would be unfair simply to censure the method of explaining concepts of a foreign culture or religion with the aid of ideas that are familiar to the Western reader. But the scholar who practices such conceptual adaptation must be alert to the danger of misrepresentation. Radhakrishnan does not seem to have avoided this danger. He alleges that the Hindu theory of the world process connotes a continuous evolution toward a definite goal. But this is exactly the opposite of what *saṃsāra,* the Sanskrit word denoting the world process, implies. The *saṃsāra* process is unending, blind, and meaningless. It is true that one of the Hindu systems of thought, namely the Sāṃkhya, includes an element of teleology in teaching that Primary Matter unconsciously tends to bring about the Spirit's release from transmigration.[56] But the operation of Primary Matter is not the same as the process of *saṃsāra,* and Radhakrishnan's vindication of *saṃsāra* as "a movement with a meaning" and "a growth into personality"[57] is nearly the opposite of the ideas of the Sāṃkhya philosophers. As a matter of fact, he does not attempt to connect his idea of purposeful *saṃsāra* with the Sāṃkhya philosophy. But there is no system in Indian philosophy at all that teaches that *saṃsāra* has a purpose. The teleological element in Radhakrishnan's interpretation of *saṃsāra* has doubtless been suggested to him by Christian thinking.

What Radhakrishnan presents in *An Idealist View of Life* and in all his other books is his personal view. This view is extremely interesting inasmuch as it shows how an unusually widely read Hindu, sensitive to spiritual values, reacts to the present-day critical situation. If it can claim a general significance, then only as a document of one form of what I have called Neo-Hinduism.

Let me now present some theses which recapitulate, and to some extent supplement, what I said about the characteristic traits of Neo-Hinduism:

1. Typical Neo-Hindus have received their ideas of religious, ethical, social, and political values not from their native religion but from the outside, from Western philosophies or from Christianity.

2. These values are, however, identified with elements of the native heritage; in other words, native elements are reinterpreted so as to express ideals that were assimilated from foreign sources.

3. This modernization, though amounting to a Westernization, is an outcome of nationalism, which is the chief impulse of Neo-Hindu thinking.

4. Although nationalism is ultimately an importation from the West, it has a somewhat different meaning here than in the West. National pride in India is not primarily grounded in reminiscences of the political history or in political ideals but in the consciousness of the cultural, in particular religious, achievements of the native country.

5. This cultural nationalism includes the idea that India has a message to proclaim to the world.

6. Neo-Hinduism asserts that Hinduism is a spiritual unity.

7. Neo-Hinduism claims to be tolerant.

8. Neo-Hindus hold that all religions are equal in essence or value.

9. This doctrine is established essentially with the aid of the ancient practice of inclusivism.[58] If this is taken into account, the doctrine of the equality of all religions turns out to be an assertion of the superiority of Hinduism.

10. In some of these points, surviving traditional Hinduism can agree with Neo-Hinduism. Since, however, traditionalism professes the old *dharma* and thus has a living contact with the Hindu heritage, its behavior is widely different from that of

Hindu modernism. For instance, like the Neo-Hindus many or most traditionalists are also nationalists. But regarding the relative priority of religion and nation the two ways of thinking diverge. Schematically, one may say that Neo-Hindus, notwithstanding their Western orientation, profess Hinduism because they feel themselves committed to their nation and consequently to their national religion, while traditionalists profess nationalism on the ground of their loyalty to the Hindu tradition and consequently to the motherland of this tradition.

11. There are persons who may be described as representing a pure form of Neo-Hinduism, for example Aurobindo and Radhakrishnan, but there are many who retain beliefs and practices of traditional Hinduism notwithstanding their leanings toward modernism.
12. Although traditional Hinduism lacks publicity, it seems to have an incomparably greater vitality than Neo-Hinduism.
13. Both varieties of Hinduism, as well as all religions, are at present challenged by the onslaught of Marxism.[59]

Notes

1. In: *Indica, The Indian Historical Research Institute Silver Jubilee Commemoration Volume* (Bombay, 1953).

2. See *Contemporary Indian Philosophy* (London, 1936), p. 258; 2nd ed., (London, 1952), pp. 475 f.

3. Ibid.

4. See *Young India,* 6.10.1921. Reprinted in: M. K. Gandhi, *Hindu Dharma* (Ahmedabad, 1950), p. 8.

5. Hanumānprasād Poddār, *Lok-paralok kā sudhār,* Bhāg 3 (Gorakhpur: Gītā Press, saṃvat 2008), pp. 45 f. Editor's note: On Poddār and the notion of "surviving traditional Hinduism", see Introduction, n.71.

6. Jñāneśvarī 11.328: *ānika eka sāviyāci bhayabhīru / sarvasvē dharūni tujhī moharu / tuja prārthitāti karu / joḍoniyā.* This paraphrases Gītā 11.21b: *kecid bhītāḥ prāñjalayo gṛṇanti.*

7. See my book, *Prahlāda* (Wiesbaden, 1959), Index s.v. *bhāvanā.*

8. Cf. *Satsang-sudhār* (Gorakhpur: Gītā Press, saṃvat 2009), pp. 5–16.

9. Gorakhpur, 2nd ed., saṃvat 2008.

10. An English version of this booklet was published in London (H. R. Allenson), 1906.

11. *saṃpūrṇ hṛdayō ke dvārā Bhagavān se prem karne par hamāre pāpō kā svataḥ mārjan ho jātā hai.* Op. cit., p. 14.

12. *Bhagavadviśvās kī sādhanā hī Bhagavān kī saccī ārādhanā hai.* Op. cit., p. 6.

13. Cf. *Tattvacintāmaṇi,* Bhāg 1 (Gorakhpur: Gītā Press, 8th ed., saṃvat 2007), p. 286.

14. Op. cit., p. 288.

15. p. 286: *sab bhūtō ke hit mé rat honā.* Cf. Bh. Gītā 5.25, 12.4 and many parallels listed in *The Pratīka Index of the Mahābhārata,* vol. 6 (1972), pp. 4067 f.

16. For particulars see my article in: *Zeitschrift für Missionswissenschaft und Religionswissenschaft,* vol. 42 (1958) pp. 3–8, where relevant passages from Bankim's works are also referred to [i.e., "Der Dharmabegriff des Neuhinduismus"; see Chapter 12 in this volume].

17. Aurobindo's *Essays on the Gītā* first appeared in 1921–28. I have used the edition published in New York, 1950. Relevant passages are found there on pp. 458–61, 463, 465, 467.

18. R. Tagore, *The Religion of Man* (London, 4th ed., 1953), pp. 17, 143–45, 154, 181.

19. Vinobā Bhāve, *Gītāpravacanē* (Wardha, 3rd ed., 1954), sections 3,6,14, 78, 79, 104,105.

20. Radhakrishnan, *The Bhagavadgītā* (London, 3rd impr., 1953), p. 147.

21. Cf. my article in: *Evangelische Missionszeitschrift,* 1971, pp. 1–15 [i.e., "Der religiöse Nationalismus Vivekanandas"; see Chapter 14 in this volume].

22. See my article in: *Saeculum,* vol. 12 (1961), pp. 385 ff. [i.e., "Schopenhauer und die Ethik des Hinduismus"; see Chapter 13 in this volume].

23. See *Young India,* 6.10.1921; reprinted in: M. K. Gandhi, *Hindu Dharma* (Ahmedabad 1950), p. 7.

24. M. K. Gandhi, *An Autobiography . . .*, trans. by M. Desai (Ahmedabad, 2nd ed., 1940), pp. 172 and 198.

25. See *Young India,* 4.11.1926. Gandhi, *Hindu Dharma,* p. 199.

26. See *Young India,* 9.3.1922. Gandhi, *Hindu Dharma,* p. 186.

27. See *Speeches and Writings of Mahatma Gandhi* (Madras: G. A. Natesan, 4th ed.), p. 346. Also in: *Selections from Gandhi,* ed. by N. K. Bose (Ahmedabad, 1948, p. 151, no. 404.

28. See, for instance, Suresh Ramabhai, *Vinoba and his Mission* (Sevagram, Wardha, 1954), p. 123. I refer to this book because it is perhaps more easily accessible than Vinobā's speeches. It is however these speeches, as reported in newspapers and published in Hindi booklets, from which I have drawn my information about Vinobā's views.

29. Op. cit., pp. 52, 59, 123.

30. Op. cit., p. 169: "We rely on the indwelling Godhead . . ."

31. Op. cit., p. 164.

32. Op. cit., p. 59. See also p. 123: " . . . he said . . . real dharma lay in serving God as Daridra-Nārāyaṇa."

33. Op. cit., p. 31.

34. See, e.g., *Vinobā ke vicār,* Bhāg 2 (Naī Dillī, 3rd ed., 1952), p. 198.

35. According to a passage (p. 188) in the book referred to in the preceding note, service rendered to the people, especially to villagers, is idol-worship performed in a spirit of *bhakti,* because the collectivity of the people is God.

36. Radhakrishnan, *The Hindu View of Life* (London, 9th impr., 1954), p. 22.

37. Op. cit., p. 23.

38. 4th impr., London, 1951. The quotation is from p. 103.

39. *Contemporary Indian Philosophy* (London, 2nd ed., 1952), p. 492.

40. W. James, *The Varieties of Religious Experience* (new ed., London, 1952), p. 370.

41. p. 82.

42. *An Idealist View of Life,* p. 84.

43. Radhakrishnan, *East and West* (London, 1955), p. 120.

44. Op. cit., p. 129.

45. Radhakrishnan, *The Brahma Sūtra* (London, 1960), p. 113.

46. *The Hindu View of Life,* p. 17.

47. *The Brahma Sūtra,* p. 112.

48. *The Hindu View of Life,* pp. 72, 73 f, 76.

49. *An Idealist View of Life,* p. 266.

50. Op. cit., p. 275.

51. Op. cit., pp. 274, 276, 301.

52. p. 276.

53. p. 287.

54. p. 295.

55. pp. 297, 301.

56. *puruṣa-vimokṣa-nimittaṃ tathā pravṛttiḥ pradhānasya.* Sāṃkhyakārikā 57.

57. *An Idealist View of Life,* p. 301.

58. For the attitude of *inclusivism* (so characteristic of Indian religions from the early times down to our day, but not perceived by researchers, and therefore constantly confused with "tolerance") see also my paper "Zur Geschichte und Beurteilung des Hinduismus" [*Kl. Schr.,* pp. 476–83; especially 480 ff.].

59. This statement was made in 1970 (editor's note).

12

The Concept of Dharma in Neo-Hinduism

Since the beginning of the nineteenth century, Hindu thinkers acquainted with modern Western ideas and the teachings of Christianity have developed views which were intended to preserve and adapt the Indian tradition and make it effective in a wholly new climate of thought. These endeavors, familiar today to many Europeans, especially through the writings of Radhakrishnan, are conveniently referred to by the term "Neo-Hinduism." A historical presentation of Neo-Hinduism (together with the survival of traditional currents) was undertaken by the Anglican missionary J. N. Farquhar;[1] D. S. Sarma[2] presented the same subject from the Hindu point of view, including events in the intellectual history of Hinduism which had occurred after Farquhar. In both works, however, few sources are used thoroughly except those written in English. The importance of the literature in Indian languages for the study of modern Indian movements of thought, and the need for detailed investigation, is impressively shown in the rich essay by R. Antoine, S.J., "A Pioneer of Neo-Hinduism,"[3] which gives valuable information on the religious ideas of the Bengali poet and thinker Bankim Chandra Chatterjee[4] (1838–94) and investigates his relationship with the European positivists.

For a better understanding of the origin and spread of Neo-Hindu ideas, more detailed investigations would be desirable. Such investigations would, first, show which works of Western thought provided the Neo-Hindus with the tools with which they handled their traditional material. Father Antoine's study is an important beginning in this direction.

Second, they should show how traditional Hindu concepts were reinterpreted through modern philosophical ideas; this is the aim of the present essay.

Third, the Indian development of the new ideas, taking place alongside the continued influx of fresh influences from the West, and the reinterpretation of traditional ideas, should be investigated—a task which can probably only be carried out extensively in India, since much of the relevant literature might be unobtainable in Europe. It seems that as a result of this Indian development many ideas have today become almost canonical; this is true of the subject of the following study.

Fourth, we must take note of a motif which has prevailed for a long time among Neo-Hindu thinkers: the desire to prove that Hinduism is a religion equal or even superior to Christianity. Here, as well as in the attempts to modernize ancient Hindu ideas, positivism—and also in the last few decades modernistic and liberal Christian theology—have been of great help; the clarification of this process is another task for research.

Reinterpretations can be best studied by means of modern expositions of traditional texts. One ancient text in particular has retained its value for Neo-Hinduism, and is perhaps more popular today than at any time in its long history: the *Bhagavadgītā*. Several leading modern thinkers have written commentaries on it, and there is a vast wealth of books and essays by lesser writers who try to show the essence of Hinduism by means of the *Gītā*.

The concept *dharma* plays a significant role in the teaching of the Gītā, and modern interpreters have generally treated this concept as one of the most important ideas in the poem. Before dealing with the modern adaptations of the concept, we must ask what *dharma* means in traditional Hinduism.

First, *dharma* is *religious law* or order. This includes not only ritual and moral matters, but also the whole legal system as well as a mass of custom. Thus *dharma* means, among other things, the whole outward side of religion, and so the word is used in modern Indian languages to translate the term 'religion.'

Second, *dharma* is also *law being fulfilled;* every act done according to the law is *dharma.*

Third, *dharma* is *law fulfilled,* i.e., what is called "good karma." In Hindu belief, an act congeals, as it were, into a stuff which clings to the soul, determining its fate after death; if an act is done according to *dharma,* then its residue, on which transmigration depends, is also called *dharma.*

We must also note that while some laws are for all men, others only affect particular *varṇas*[5] and stages of life. Thus to study the Veda is the *dharma* of the Brahmins only. Veda study and chastity are the *dharma* of the first stage of life (the student), pious living is that of the second stage (the householder), etc. In referring to the specific *dharma* which is binding on an individual by reason of his membership of a specific *varṇa* and stage of life (not by reason of his uniqueness), the term 'individual *dharma,' svadharma,* is used. It is this meaning of the word *dharma* that appears in the *Bhagavadgītā*—the *dharma* of a particular *varṇa.*

In order to understand the Neo-Hindu reinterpretation of the concept, which we shall discuss presently, we must finally note a fourth ancient meaning of the word which is entirely separate from the three specifically religious meanings described above.[6] *Dharma* in this fourth sense means *essential property,* and is quite neutral; it does not necessarily mean "good property."

The first author to give a consciously Hindu, and at the same time consciously modern, interpretation of the *Bhagavadgītā* was Bankim Chandra Chatterjee, mentioned above. His commentary, unfinished but nonetheless important, began to be published in 1886. Another work, *Principles of Religion* (*Dharmatattva,* 1888), contains important elements of *Gītā* interpretation and a presentation of the new concept of *dharma.*[7] Bankim seems to have been the first to develop this concept, for if the concept had already been known, it would be hard to see why Bankim established it at such length, and with reference to Positivist thought; he could have referred to Indian authors. We should also expect that in that case Vivekananda (1863–1902), another Bengali who, like Bankim, was one of the fathers of Neo-Hinduism and worked a little later, would have known the concept; but Vivekananda's view of *dharma* is quite traditional.[8] Later, however, the basis of Bankim's concept of *dharma,* with some variations in different authors, became almost canonical.

Our starting point is the discussion of the nature of *dharma* given by Bankim in his *Principles of Religion* in the form of a dialogue between teacher and pupil.[9] The question is asked, What is the *dharma* of man? (by which is meant, What is the religion of man?—*dharma* in the usual modern Indian sense is expressly equated with the English word 'religion'). But in the course of the discussion Bankim shifts the meaning of the word. He makes the teacher say: "We need not call this eternal entity *(padārtha)* religion; if we call it *dharma,* there will be no confusion." But it is precisely here that Bankim introduces confusion. For he now makes the teacher ask, What is the *dharma* of the whole of mankind, of Christians as well as Buddhists, Hindus, and Muslims? That is, he shifts the meaning of the word *dharma* from "religion" to "essential property." The bewildered pupil is still thinking of *dharma* in the sense of "religion," and of course cannot say what is the *dharma,* in this sense, of the whole of mankind. The teacher then asks a leading question: "What is the *dharma* of a magnet?" Here, the pupil sees that "essential property" is meant; so he answers: "to attract iron." Similarly, he is able to say that the *dharma* (essential property) of fire is to burn. When the teacher asks again about the *dharma* of man, the only possible answer is a very general abstraction: the *dharma* or essential common property of man is of course humanity, *manuṣyatva.* By this juggling with the different meanings of the word *dharma,* Bankim arrives, apparently without leaving Indian soil, at a conclusion that he had of course first learned from John Stuart Mill and Auguste Comte: the religion of man is humanity, *l'humanité, manuṣyatva.* However, Bankim differs from his positivist teachers in matters of content, as will be seen from his interpretation of the Gītā.

There are not many verses dealing with *dharma* in the Gītā, but they are important in the context of the poem. In order to raise Arjuna from his despondency, Krishna instructs him first about the immortality of the soul and the mortality of the body, and next about his (Arjuna's) *dharma.* Thus, in the opening situation of the Gītā, the beginning of the battle and Arjuna's despondency, the concept of *dharma* is one of the points on which Arjuna is to base his decision. Krishna says to Arjuna (II, 31ff.): "You must consider your *dharma* (i.e., the way of life of your *varṇa* and your duty resulting from it) and not tremble. For a member of the warrior *varṇa* there is no higher good than a fight according to *dharma* (i.e., a lawful one, a *justum bellum,* so to speak). "Happy, Arjuna, are warriors who find the opportunity for such a fight; it is an open door to heaven. If you will not carry out this *dharma*-required fight, you will lose your own *dharma* (cf. below) and glory, and acquire sin (i.e., bad *karman,* the substance of evil deeds)."

Thus *dharma* is here *law to be fulfilled,* duty. It is called *sva-dharma,* that is, the *dharma* that belongs to a particular man (Arjuna) as a member of a particular *varṇa* (i.e., the *kṣatriya*). If this *dharma* has been fulfilled in the form of a righteous act, it congeals into a power which determines his fate in his next existence, so that Arjuna will be reborn in heaven. If it is not fulfilled, then the substance of evil deeds—sin—will be accumulated, leading to bad rebirth. In verse 33 the expression "to lose one's own *dharma*" occurs. It is usually translated: "You will abandon, or neglect, your own duty (the duty of the warrior *varna*)." But since we are here speaking of the *consequence* of an omission, that is, of an evil deed, it seems to me better to understand *dharma* in the third of the meanings listed above: a metaphysically congealed act.[10] The sense is then: "You will lose the merit you already possess, the substance of the acts you have done."

This, it seems to me, is how the passage should be interpreted from the point of view of traditional Hinduism. Let us take another verse (III 35): "It is better to fulfil your own *dharma* badly than another's well. It is better to die in your own *dharma,* for it is dangerous to perform another's *dharma.*" This verse shows how important the boundaries of the *varṇas* and stages of life were to the Hindu. Against many modern interpretations, it should be pointed out that the verse shows clearly that there is no question of talents or inclinations. For if a man can perform his own dharma—the action required for his own stage of life and *varṇa*—badly, and another's well, that means that he lacks the talent and inclination for the one but has them for the other.[11] But that has nothing to do with *dharma. Dharma* is an entirely supra-individual order; it concerns the individual primarily as a duty which he must fulfil. To perform another's *dharma* is a breach of the *varṇa* system, which is one of the worst evils for traditional Hindus.

We turn now to Bankim's interpretation. He sums up the content of Krishna's teaching thus: "everyone must follow his *svadharma.*"[12] And he continues:

> What does *sva-dharma* consist of? For the ancient pandits such as Śaṅkara, this term was easily explained. (They would have said:) Arjuna is a Kshatriya, so Arjuna's *svadharma* is the *dharma* of the warrior, to fight. But (Bankim goes on to ask,) does this explanation tell us everything? For the Hindus, who follow the order of varṇa and stage of life, *dharma* can indeed be determined by varna; we have understood that. But then what is *svadharma* for the

> non-Hindus? . . . Most people are outside the *varṇa* system; have they no *svadharma?* Has the Lord ordained no *dharma* for them? He has created millions and millions of people; has he ordained a *dharma* only for the Indians, and made all the others *dharma*-less? Is the *dharma* proclaimed by Bhagavān for the Hindus only? Are not the non-Hindus also his children? No, the religion of Bhagavān *(bhāgavata dharma)* is not so narrow-minded.

From the standpoint of traditional Hinduism, however, a different answer must be given from the one given here by Bankim. Even when *bhakti* piety oversteps caste barriers, this never leads to any abandonment of either the caste system or the belief that the *dharma* is given only to the Indians, not to the Mlecchas. Even today we may read in tracts by traditionally thinking Hindus that the highest achievement of a pious non-Hindu is to be reborn in a high Hindu caste in his next existence. As an individual he can never become a Hindu and so enter the system of *dharma.* The Bhagavadgītā itself adheres in principle to this view.

It is obvious that Bankim once again mixes two meanings of the word *dharma:* the modern meaning "religion" and the old meaning of the duty determined by *varṇa* and stage of life. When he says "The religion of Bhagavān is not so narrow-minded," the word for "religion" in the original is of course *dharma.* Certainly the religion of Krishna includes bhakti piety which transcends all boundaries. But that same religion also includes the doctrine of the boundaries of *dharma,* determined by *varṇa* and stage of life, and this *dharma* cannot be extended. But just as in another passage by identifying *dharma* as essential property, Bankim arrived at the concept of humanity as identical with religion, so in this passage by compounding *dharma* as religion with *dharma* as duty determined by *varṇa,* he arrives at the idea of the universality of Hinduism.

This second confusion also leads to a third. Bankim continues: "Whoever thinks that the Lord of the world is so *dharma*-less is like the Christians," and in a footnote he adds: "The Christians believe that whoever does not worship Jesus Christ will be thrown into hell forever by the Lord of the world." Here, two very distinct concepts of exclusiveness are blended together. The exclusiveness of Hinduism is based on birth and geographical location, but Bankim refuses to recognize this attitude as essential to his religion. On the contrary, he attributes to Christianity an attitude which allows a people or a culture to be condemned to *dharma*-lessness (and that means also religionlessness) and does not see, or ignores, that the exclusiveness of Christianity is of quite a different kind, being based on the spirit and on faith. This enables him to rank his ideal Hinduism as superior to Christianity.

Bankim now returns in his Gītā commentary to the idea that we have already learned from his *Principles of Religion.* He says: "That which constitutes humanity *(jāhā laïyā manuṣyatva)* is the *dharma* of mankind." Thus the natural properties possessed by man as man are also his religion. But we have here not merely an identification of the meanings "religion" and "essential property." The first meaning in the above list is also brought in: legal order to be fulfilled. For Bankim does not treat humanity merely as something already realized. It is much rather an ideal which we must make real, an order to be fulfilled, a task, a duty. Indeed, nothing is left of the ancient concept but the formal shell (order to be fulfilled). The ancient content is replaced by modern, individualistic ideas: the *dharma* of man is the proper exercise *(vihita anuśīlana)* of his psychic and physical dispositions *(vṛtti)* or powers *(śakti).* Bankim thus arrives at an interpretation which is exactly the opposite of what we stated to be the implication of Gītā III, 35, interpreted above: that *dharma* has nothing to do with individual talents or inclinations.

Bankim next uses his concept of *dharma* to reduce the *varṇa* system to a universal human basis. The principle of hereditary occupations, which to the traditional Hindu seems essential and which is in fact the basis of the system's perpetuation, he regards as inessential. What he retains is a typology of human activities built on a broad classification of talents. Accordingly, in his view the choice of *svadharma* is free, but once *svadharma* has been chosen it is a duty.[13]

Bankim calls his new concept of *dharma* an "interpretation of the word of God (i.e., of the Bhagavadgītā) in view of the social changes which have occurred in course of time and in accordance with the science of society."[14] But in fact all that remains of the ancient concept is the formal element of duty, and this, too, Bankim could have taken from Europe—from Kant, whom he valued very highly, or from John Stuart Mill.

Bankim's thought, presented in the form of a new interpretation of the most universally respected religious text in Hinduism, seductively combined ancient and completely modern material into an apparent unity. This must be the reason for its success. The equation of religion with humanity, which he borrowed from Positivism and passed off as Hindu by playing with the various meanings of the word *dharma,* is continued in the anti-supernatural, radically humanist tendency which is characteristic of much Neo-Hindu thought; moreover, the separation of the concept of *dharma* from the system of *varṇa* and stage of life, and the accompanying psychological interpretation of the concept, has become customary with many writers. The *dharmas* are often differentiated, as in Bankim, as types of talent, and the term is also often given a radically individualistic interpretation.

Before turning to later interpretations of *dharma,* we must return once more to the *Bhagavadgītā*. Verse III 35, discussed above, has a parallel in XVIII 47: "One's own *dharma (svadharma),* even if devoid of qualities *(viguṇa)* is better than another's *dharma* well done. When one performs the work required by one's own nature *(svabhāva),* one incurs[15] no sin." Bankim's commentary ends before this verse. But anyone who has adopted his interpretation will find it confirmed here. For here we have a direct statement that the work of one's *svadharma* is "required by one's own nature," and work "born of one's own nature" is mentioned several times in the preceding verses, so what is easier for modern man than to infer that here *svadharma* is traced back to the character of the person in question? One of the latest commentaries explains accordingly:[16] "Each individual has his inborn nature, *svabhāva,* and to make it effective in his life is his duty, *svadharma.*" Further: "Each one must try to understand his psychophysical make-up and function in accordance with it." Another author similarly sees *svadharma* as "the *dharma* of an individual," and simply equates it with *svabhāva,* essential nature.[17]

But, as we have already seen in our discussion of BhG. III 35, in the Gītā the different *svadharmas* are not determined by an individual's talents. We must now examine what is meant by *svabhāva* in the eighteenth chapter of the poem. For the relation between *svabhāva* and *svadharma,* which is expounded there, has been repeatedly re-evaluated by modern interpreters.

The eighteenth chapter of the Gītā presents a series of typologies. Knowledge, act, and agent; intelligence *(buddhi),* firmness *(dhṛti),* and happiness *(sukha)* are each divided into three types, and each type is determined by the predominance of one of the three *guṇas*[18] of the Sāṃkhya philosophy (XVIII 18–39). The specific activities of the four *varṇas* are also distinguished, we are told, by "the *guṇas* proceeding from their nature" (*svabhāva-prabhavair guṇaih* XVIII 41). The reference to the three guṇas of Sāṃkhya is here omitted, no doubt primarily because there are four *varṇas* but only three *guṇas,* so that the distribution would have been difficult. But it is clear that the specific properties enumerated in verse 42 as "the work, springing from their nature, of brahmins" (calm, self-control, asceticism, purity, patience, uprightness, wisdom, discrimination, faith), are regarded as resulting from the highest *guṇa (sattva),* and that the qualities described as "the work, resulting from their nature, of warriors" (valor, power, firmness, skill, not fleeing in battle, generosity, lordship—verse 43), are at least partly derived from the second *guṇa (rajas).* Finally, the third and fourth *varṇas* are allotted not traits of character but specific activities: the vaiśya practices agriculture, cattle-raising, and commerce, and the śūdra is a servant (verse 44).

The context should leave us in no doubt that the nature or *svabhāva* referred to here is the specific property of a person's *varṇa,* and this nature is of course regarded, in accordance with Sāṃkhya doctrine, as subtle matter consisting of a modification of the original matter or *prakṛti.* The fact that traits of character are given as the "work" of the two upper *varṇas* is one of those attempts to interpret varṇa differences ethically, which are to be found elsewhere in the great epic in which the Gītā is inserted. What is certainly not meant is that a calm, controlled, upright, wise man should be counted as a brahmin by virtue of these characteristics alone, without reference to his origin. A Hindu who believes in transmigration must rather regard a person's possession of particular characteristics as the result of the moral merit of the acts he has performed in a previous existence. If somebody is born as a brahmin, this is because he has earned such excellent *karman* that he possesses the high qualities belonging to that *varṇa,* and can therefore put them into practice; if he does not put them into practice, that is a sin which he voluntarily incurs in his present existence. In this sense, the teaching in Gītā XVIII 40–48 is both individualistic and typological, but principally typological. By the acts which a person has performed as an individual, he gains his *varṇa* in a later birth, and these acts also enable him to realize the character of that *varṇa*—if he wants to. This seems to me to be the correct interpretation of the Gītā passage. An individual's own inborn work, the work determined by his nature, appears unambiguously from the context of the passage to be the work that belongs to him on the basis of his *varṇa,* and a person's own nature or *svabhāva* is nothing else than the character of his *varṇa.*

But it is also clear that the characterological typology of the two upper *varṇas* includes a spiritual element which extends beyond the caste system. When modern interpreters make use of this fact, they use the Bhagavadgītā, which teaches the caste system, as a weapon against that system, which has become a great stumbling block for modernized Indians. In this connection we will discuss some ideas from Aurobindo

Ghose's *Essays on the Gita.*[19] Aurobindo, one of the most prolific thinkers in modern India, draws on Bankim in his interpretation of *dharma,* and has had a strong influence on present-day thinkers, especially Radhakrishnan.

He writes:

> What the Gita is concerned with is not the validity of the Aryan social order now abolished or in a state of deliquescence—if that were all, its principle of the Swabhava and Swadharma would have no permanent truth or value[20]—but the relation of a man's outward life to his inward being, the evolution of his action from his soul and the inner law of nature.
>
> And we see in fact that the Gita itself indicates very clearly its intention when it describes the work of the Brahmin and the Kshatriya not in terms of external function . . . but entirely in terms of internal character.

Thus the tendency already present in the Gītā to internalize, to transfer from the physical to the mental sphere, gives Aurobindo the opportunity to modernize the concept of *dharma.* And in Aurobindo, as often in modern Europe, radical internalization quickly leads to radical individualism. The Gītā urges each person to do the work belonging to his status, even if it is "devoid of qualities" (*viguṇa* III 35; XVIII 47) or "faulty" (*sadoṣa* XVIII 48); but Aurobindo tries to find support in the Gītā for a view of life which would escape from social ties and finds the fulfillment of the purpose of existence in the individual alone: "Life, state, society, family, all surrounding powers seem to be in a league to lay their yoke on our spirit, compel us into their molds, impose on us their mechanical interest and rough immediate convenience." He deduces from the Gītā the doctrine that "the functions of a man ought to be determined by his natural turn, gift, and capacities," that the individual should "develop freely" and in so doing will be best able to serve society. He carries his justification of individualism into the realm of religion itself:

> . . . each of us has a principle and will of our own becoming; each soul is a force of self-consciousness that formulates an idea of the Divine in it and guides by that its action and evolution, its progressive self-finding, its constant varying self-expression, its apparently uncertain but secretly inevitable growth to fullness. That is our Swabhava, our own real nature; that is our truth of being which is

> finding now only a constant partial expression in our various becoming in the world. The law of action determined by this Swabhava is our right law of self-shaping, function, working, our Swadharma.

Here, just as in Bankim, an individual's talents are regarded as being at the same time a duty, and in presenting these very modern ideas the Sanskrit terms *svabhāva* and *svadharma* are used.

Aurobindo, like Bankim, retains the four varṇas as representing four main types of endowment, but "these are not fundamental divisions, but stages of self-development in our manhood"; an individual man can realize in himself the characteristics of all four successively in the course of his upward development. "The inner Swadharma is not bound to any outward social or other form of action, occupation or function."

The poet Rabindranath Tagore also had—at least for a time—a view of *dharma* that clearly betrays the influence of Bankim in its evolutionism and radical humanism; in Tagore, as in Bankim, the concept of God is an idea of perfected humanity. In 1930 he gave a series of lectures in Oxford on *The Religion of Man*,[21] by which he clearly means not only a religion which man has, but also a religion of which man is the object. Roughly following ancient monistic *(advaita)* ideas, Tagore distinguishes between the individual and "Man the Eternal, the Eternal Man" or "Man the great," by which he means the supra-individual idea of human personality, the "transcendental" "pervading personality" of "Supreme Man." "The idea of the humanity of our God, or the divinity of Man the Eternal," explains Tagore, is the subject of his Oxford lectures. Even more expressly than Bankim he equates *dharma* in the sense of religion with *dharma* in the sense of essential property, and maintains with Bankim: "Humanity is the *dharma* of human beings." "Religion consists in the endeavor of men to cultivate and express those qualities which are inherent in the nature of Man the Eternal, and to have faith in him," to reconcile the impulses of man's brute nature, which are concerned with immediate needs, with those tendencies which are "the life current of universal humanity."

Mahātmā Gāndhī's view of *dharma* is completely different and very much his own. He shows no trace of the influence of Bankim or Aurobindo. Although he attacks the evils of caste, he upholds the basis of the system, the principle of hereditary occupations. In the concept of *svadharma,* especially on the basis of Gītā III 35, he recognizes his idea of *svadeśī,* i.e., he sees in this verse the religious justification for his claim that man owes his service above all to those who are nearest to him by birth and situation. In politics, this means the service of one's own land; in economics, it means using the products of one's own land. Commenting on this verse, he writes:

> Pure service of one's neighbors cannot be disservice to those who are remotely situated; rather the contrary. A man who allows himself to be lured by the distant scene and runs to the ends of the earth for service is not only foiled in his ambition but fails also in his duty toward his neighbors. That seems to me to be the sense of this verse. Interpreted in terms of one's physical environment this gives us the law of *swadeshi. Swadeshi* is *swadharma* applied to one's immediate environment.[22]

Gandhi's disciples have also attempted to establish a new concept of *dharma.* We will now discuss the interpretation by Gandhi's disciple Vinobā Bhāve (1895–1982), who in recent years has become known outside India through his advocacy of "land gift" *(bhūdān).* He has published a series of *Talks on the Gītā,* given to his fellow-prisoners in 1932 when he was imprisoned for his part in the independence movement.[23] In his view the doctrine of *svadharma* is the main purpose of the Gītā; in this he agrees not only with Bankim but also with the medieval commentator Rāmānuja.

In Vinobā's view of *dharma,* ideas inspired by his master Gandhi are not well integrated with an individualism traceable to Bankim and Aurobindo's influence. He begins as a radical individualist; in his first talk he states plainly: "The two hundred people here in front of me have two hundred different *dharmas.*" Individual dharmas are also variable: "My *dharma* is not the same today as it was ten years ago, and in ten years' time it will no longer be the same as today." Vinobā, like Bankim, makes *dharma* dependent on *vṛtti* (though not, as Bankim does, on several *vṛttis*); the word can be translated as "psychological disposition" or "character." "As the disposition changes through thought and experience, the old *dharma* is lost and a new one is acquired." His idea that the aim of compliance with *svadharma* is the unfolding *(vikāsa)* of the personality also shows the influence of the psychological individualism of Bankim and Aurobindo. *Dharma* is understood as the essential property not of each individual but of mankind as such, when he explains the fundamental verse III 35 by means of comparisons which all speak of man simply as a member of mankind. For instance, he says that man cannot, because he loves the sun, leave the earth and live on the sun, because that would not be his *dharma*. With this idea Vinobā contradicts himself, since he has on the contrary gone beyond Bankim's allocation of dharmas to types to an allocation of dharmas to individuals.

In his last talk (No. 18) he seems to be trying to resolve the contradiction. However, since he introduces new terms without making clear their relation to the previous ones, the attempt is not entirely successful. He distinguishes between changeable and unchangeable *svadharma*, but instead of deriving the changeability from subjective experience, as in the first talk, he now uses the traditional Hindu legal terminology, in which *svadharma* is determined by *varṇa* and stage of life *(āśrama)*. Since a man passes through several *āśramas* (student, householder, hermit, wandering ascetic), his *dharma*, which is determined by the current *āśrama*, changes; but the dharma of the *varṇa* is unchanging. Vinobā does not explain what a modernized *āśrama-dharma* might be like. Speaking of *varṇa-dharma*, he says that if we regard it as a form of social organization, it admits of exceptions; so that according to Vinobā *varṇa-dharma* also is not entirely unchanging.

Vinobā, as a disciple of Gandhi, accepts the social basis of the caste system: the principle of hereditary occupations. But he does not repeat the teachings of Hindu law on the dharmas of particular castes; instead, he relates the *svadharma* of each individual only to the social milieu in which he finds himself at a given time. In the eighteenth chapter of the Gītā, as we have seen, *svadharma* is derived from *svabhāva*. Vinobā explains this idea by means of the doctrine that a man's *svadharma* is a duty given by nature *(nisargataḥ prāpta)*. In using the expression "given by nature," he is apparently thinking also of the individual character disposition; in his eighteenth talk he repeats once more that when a man is considering whether a particular action is his *svadharma*, he should also ask himself whether it suits his *vṛtti*. But in his thought, the idea that *svadharma* is conditioned by the individual's psychology does not play anything like the role in Vinobā's thought that it plays in Aurobindo's. Rather, he constantly stresses that true *svadharma comes to* man. One need not seek it, one should not seek it; it gives itself spontaneously, it is determined by the environment in which one is born. And its content is service *(sevā)* to those nearest to one. Accordingly, Vinobā distinguishes three constituents of *dharma:* duty to one's country *(svadeśī dharma)*, which includes among other things the economic duty to buy only the products of one's country; duty to one's own caste or people *(svajātīya dharma);*[24] and the duty resulting from the time to which one belongs *(svakālīna dharma).*

All this belongs to Gandhian or "Gandhianizing" thought. Vinobā also follows his master in connecting the idea of *svadharma* with the injunction to act without desire for fruit; for Gandhi held that the central doctrine of the Gītā was the command to act without desire and without concern for results. True *svadharma,* which one accepts as arising from one's circumstances, is according to Vinobā always free from desire *(niṣkāma);* so that it is also *sāttvika,* i.e., corresponds to the highest of the three psychological qualities of the Sāṃkhya philosophy.

The efforts of Neo-Hinduism to develop a new concept of *dharma* are an attempt, using principles borrowed from European positivism and modernism, to find a new norm for ethical and social relationships, such as traditional Hinduism had in its countless rules of *dharma*—a *new* norm, expressing both the essence of the national religion as it is interpreted today, and the requirements of a new age, to which people believe they must do justice. The history of these attempts shows how quickly the thought of a modern thinker can take on almost the significance of dogma. The Gandhians are trying to establish a new concept of *dharma* on a basis of sociology and social ethics, but the habit (apparently started by Bankim Chandra Chatterjee) of giving a psychological and finally individual basis to *dharma,* has such a strong hold on the minds of Indian thinkers that Vinobā does not succeed in freeing himself from it, or in subordinating its subjectivism to his own purpose, which is obviously directed toward an objective order. The radically individual, psychological view of *dharma* stands in Vinobā's work side by side with the social interpretation.

Notes

1. J. N. Farquhar: *Modern Religious Movements in India* (New York, 1915). Less detailed: H. v. Glasenapp: *Religiöse Reformbewegungen im heutigen Indien* (Leipzig, 1928).

2. D. S. Sarma: *Studies in the Renaissance of Hinduism* (Benares, 1944).

3. In: *Indica, The Indian Historical Research Institute Silver Jubilee Commemoration Volume* (Bombay, 1953).

4. This is the part-anglicized form of the name. In Bengali, in the usual transcription: Bankim Candra Caṭṭopādhyāya.

5. The original uses the word *Kaste* ("caste") throughout. However, as the reference both in Hacker's article and the writings which he describes is to the theoretical four-term system, and not to the observable system of hundreds of castes, I have nearly always translated it as *varṇa* (translator's note).

6. To illustrate the semantic distance for his German readers, Hacker adds at the end of this sentence: "and has no more to do with them than, for instance, when we use the word 'Vermögen' in the sense of 'ability,' we remember that the same word also means 'wealth.' " For additional observations on the semantic and conceptual developments of *dharma* in traditional and modern Hinduism, which expand and sometimes modify Hacker's statements, see W. Halbfass, *India and Europe,* Chapters 17 and 18 (translator's and editor's notes).

7. Bankim's collected works in the original Bengali have been published in nine volumes by the Baṅgīya Sāhitya Pariṣat, Calcutta, 1938–41.

8. Cf. Vivekananda: *Complete Works,* vol. 5, Mayavati, 6th ed., 1954, pp. 349ff., esp. p. 358. (In the 7th ed., vol. 5, pp. 446–57, esp. 456).

9. P. 11 of *Dharmatattva* in the above edition of Bankim's works. Cf. also pp. 143ff.

10. This is also the view of the medieval commentator *Rāmānuja.*

11. In the original "has the talent and inclination for the one but not for the other" ("für das eine Begabung und Neigung hat, für das andere dagegen nicht"). I have taken the liberty of reversing the words "has" and "lacks" to make the apparently intended sense clearer (translator's note).

12. *Śrīmadbhagavadgītā,* pp. 25ff. in the above edition.

13. To obviate misunderstanding, the original uses the English word *duty* here.

14. *Śrīmadbhagavadgītā,* p. 28, bottom.

15. Because sin is regarded as a kind of substance, one speaks not of "doing sin" but of "incurring, obtaining sin"; cf. the translation of Gītā II, 33; p. 260 above).

16. S. Radhakrishnan: *The Bhagavadgītā* (London, 1948), pp. 364; 147 (on Gītā XVIII 41 and III 35).

17. P. N. Rao: *The Bhagavadgītā and the Changing World* (Ahmedabad, 1953), p. 113.

18. The *guṇas* are qualities of the original cosmic matter *(prakṛti),* but are regarded as substances. Cf. E. Frauwallner: *Geschichte der indischen Philosophie,* vol. 1 (Salzburg, 1953), pp. 306ff. (Hacker translates *guṇa* throughout as *Grundqualität,* "underlying quality"; translator's note).

19. Sri Aurobindo: *Essays on the Gita,* first published in Aurobindo's periodical *Arya,* August 1916–July 1920; first published in book form 1921–28. The

edition used was published in New York in 1950; the passages referred to are on pp. 458–61, 463, 465, 467. (Also in the edition published by Sri Aurobindo International Center of Education, Pondicherry, 1959, pp. 698–99, 701, 702, 705, 709, 712, numbered by printer's error as 598–99, 601, etc.; translator's note).

20. The equation of truth with value is characteristic of Neo-Hinduism.

21. R. Tagore: *The Religion of Man* (London, 4th ed., 1943; the passages referred to are on pp. 17, 143–45, 154, and 181 (but not in that order. In the Unwin paperback edition of 1961 they are: 11, 95, 89; translator).

22. Mahadev Desai: *The Gītā according to Gandhi* (Ahmedabad, 1946), pp. 188f. (1948 ed., pp. 185f. I have quoted the paragraph in full; Hacker omits a few words.) Cf. M. K. Gandhi: *From Yeravda Mandir,* Ahmedabad (3rd ed., 1945), p. 63.

23. Marathi original: Vinobā Bhāve: *Gītāpravacenẽ* (Wardha, 3rd ed., 1954); Hindi translation: Vinobā Bhāve: *Gītāpravacan* (New Delhi, 5th ed., 1952). The ideas discussed here appear mainly in sections 3, 6, 14, 78, 79, 104, 105 (on Gītā I, II, IV, XIV, XVIII). (English translation: Vinoba Bhave: *Talks on the Gītā.* New York, Macmillan, 1960; translator).

24. Sanskrit and the New Indo-Aryan languages have no word for the concept of people or nation. Instead they use the word *jāti,* which means also "family," "species," "lineage," or "caste."

13

Schopenhauer and Hindu Ethics

Arthur Schopenhauer, as is well known, taught that the ethical significance of action depends on a "penetration of the *principium individuationis*"; the good man "recognizes directly and without reasoning that the in-itself of his own manifestation is also that of others, the will to live, which constitutes the inner nature of everything and lives in all."[1] He found this same recognition expressed in the famous *tat tvam asi* ("that art thou") of the *Chāndogya Upaniṣad:*[2]

> Individuation is mere appearance . . . the multiplicity and diversity of individuals are mere appearance; that is, they exist only in my idea. . . . My real inner being exists in every living being, as directly as it reveals itself to me alone through my own self-awareness. It is this recognition, expressed in Sanskrit with the standard formula *tat tvam asi,* meaning "That art thou," that emerges as compassion, which is the basis of all genuine, that is unselfish, virtue, and of which every good action is the actual expression.[3]

For corroboration, Schopenhauer refers to the *Bhagavadgītā,* Chapter 13, verses 27 and 28. In translation, these read: "He who sees that the highest

Lord dwells alike in all beings, not perishing when they perish, is the one who sees. For, seeing the Lord dwelling alike in all, he does not harm the self by the self, so he goes to the highest goal."[4] To support his foundation of ethics, which we will call the *tat tvam asi* ethic, Schopenhauer thus refers to two passages in Sanskrit literature: part of an Upaniṣad and two verses of the *Bhagavadgītā*. A historian or Indologist who is aware of this cannot avoid the question whether, or how far, Schopenhauer is right in claiming these two texts for his system. To answer this question, we must first investigate the meaning of the words quoted in their original context. This depends on philological considerations; these, however, can be conveyed through a translation, and we shall do so here. Next, we must ask how the passages have been interpreted in the history of Hinduism. These initial investigations (sections 1–2 below) will show that before the beginning of European influence, *tat tvam asi* was certainly not, and the *Bhagavadgītā* passage probably not, used in an ethical sense, at any rate not in the sense understood by Schopenhauer.

However, the *Bhagavadgītā* does contain the germs of a truly metaphysical or theological foundation for ethics, similar to Schopenhauer's but characteristically distinct from it (see section 2 below). They were developed further in the *Viṣṇu Purāṇa* (see section 3), and taken up by a nineteenth-century Hindu thinker (see section 4).

This development was apparently not continued in the modernized Hinduism of the twentieth century. Instead, we find the *tat tvam asi* ethic. The question when and how this ethic was adopted can be answered precisely and with certainty, using specific sources (see sections 5–6). In the twentieth century, leading representatives of Hindu thought have championed this ethic, in one case in a polemical exchange with a Western scholar (see section 6). Its adoption is not an isolated occurrence. When considered systematically, and viewed together with structurally similar phenomena, it appears as a process which exhibits a characteristic of Neo-Hindu thought (see section 7).

A similar question to the one which will be examined historically and philologically in sections 2 and 3, and systematically in section 7, was put many years ago by the secretary of the Schopenhauer Society to Otto Strauss, then Professor of Indology at Kiel. It was worded as follows: "Did Schopenhauer correctly understand the Indian philosophical and religious ideas that were available to him—mainly the Upanishads and Buddhism?" Strauss answered the question in a lecture which presented some fundamentals of Hindu and Buddhist ethics, without reference to Schopenhauer, and then concluded with a quotation from

Schopenhauer's *The World as Will and Idea.*[5] This quotation tells us that for Schopenhauer, as for Hinduism, "the moral virtues are really not the ultimate end, but only a step toward it." Schopenhauer found the essence of the Christian doctrine of original sin in "the assertion of the will to live: the denial of the will to live, in consequence of the appearance of a better knowledge, is, on the other hand, salvation. Between these two . . . lies the sphere of morality; it accompanies man as a light upon his path from the assertion to the denial of the will.[6]

Strauss thus contents himself with establishing one point of resemblance: that for Hinduism (and also Buddhism), as for Schopenhauer, ethics are "not the ultimate end." But he fails to bring out the difference which appears already in the word "light." From the standpoint of the radical monism of the spirit, which has, after all, been the strongest form of the higher Hinduism for centuries, morality cannot be called a "light" on the way to saving knowledge. It does, indeed, serve as a remote preparation, but it can also become an obstacle. The only "light," from this standpoint, is cognitive realization. Besides, Strauss does not touch on the important questions of whether the metaphysical doctrine, which is expressed from a Hindu point of view in the texts cited by Schopenhauer, can be used as a foundation of ethics in Schopenhauer's sense at all, and whether the Hindus themselves have understood these texts in an ethical sense or drawn ethical consequences from them.

1. "That art thou" What is the meaning of the sentence 'That art thou,' which occurs nine times in sections 8–16 of Chapter 6 of the *Chāndogya Upaniṣad?* Uddālaka Āruṇi is teaching his son Śvetaketu about Being *(sat).* This is a subtle, imperceptible substance, the highest deity, the essence of the universe, truth, and the Self. When a living being dies, it goes into Being, and whatever comes to be, comes out of Being. Even plants are seen as living beings in India, so that Uddālaka can say that it is this subtle Being or Self, hidden in a seed, that enables the seed to grow into a tree. It is the "life" *(jīva)* or "living Self" *(jīva ātman)* in a growing tree. But it is also "truth" *(satya).* In later Vedānta philosophy, this has been understood as meaning that Being, or the Self, is that which truly is, or the only reality. Deussen, who did not recognize the difference between the developed Vedānta and the ideas of the Upaniṣads, translated *satya* as "the real" *(das Reale)* in the dialogue of Uddālaka and Śvetaketu in the *Chāndogya Upaniṣad.* But Uddālaka's thought had not yet reached the degree of abstraction that is contained in this term. In ancient Indian belief, truth is a powerful *substance*. It is contained in every true utterance. Its power is shown, for instance, in the ordeal in which someone proves the truth of his words by grasping a red-hot ax without being burned;[7] he is protected by truth, and truth, as Uddālaka teaches, is identical with the "highest deity." This highest deity is the soul of the universe; it is Being, and it is the living Self in living beings.

Uddālaka uses nine arguments to show his son the nature of Being, and each of these nine passages ends with the words: "This subtle thing is that which is the essence (or soul) of the whole world; it is truth, it is the Self; that art thou, Śvetaketu!"[7] Thus Uddālaka does not just teach his monism of being in a general form; again and again he leads his son to apply the teaching to himself, to include himself consciously in the substance of the universal One, to identify himself with it: 'That art thou!'

If we leave aside the expressions 'the highest deity,' 'Being,' 'the subtle [imperceptible] thing,' and 'the Self,' there are two descriptions of the universal One which claim our attention: 'truth' and 'life.'

The first of these two eludes classification in any terms we are familiar with. Truth is a substance with an independent existence, but is manifest in a true utterance through the truthfulness of the speaker. Its irresistible power can be put to use in wishes ("as this is true, so let that be true!"), in curses, and in ordeals. In this notion, ethics and magic are inseparably combined. The reason why truth is identified with Being seems to be that the ancient Indians knew nothing more powerful than truth, and that the all-encompassing, all-pervading, all-effecting, universal Being must naturally include this power also. This is at the same time the starting-point of the progressive abstraction by which the universal One came to be called True Being. The term "truth" for the universal One survived in this form in the later Vedānta philosophy.

This was not the case with the designation of the universal One as 'life' or the 'living Self.' While the word *jīva,* or *jīva ātmā,* was retained, the vitalism which characterizes Uddālaka's philosophy was very soon abandoned. Already in the time of the earliest Upaniṣads, it was accepted that True Being, Brahman, or the Self was essentially spiritual. It is "self-illuminating," objectless, subsistent cognition, or consciousness. The metaphysic of Vedānta became a radical monism of the spirit, a monism of consciousness. All vital and volitional features were strictly excluded from the universal One, and eventually banished to the realm of the unreal.

In the philosophy and practice of Vedānta, *tat tvam asi* has become one of the "great sentences" in which the true content of the whole Veda is concentrated. The treatises of the great Vedānta teachers tell us frequently and in detail what this sentence means, why it is authoritative, what it does, and how it performs its function.[8] 'That' refers to the sole reality, the purely spiritual Brahman; 'thou' is the individual soul. The sentence acts as a call or an exclamation. When it is rightly heard, it brings about an awakening from the sleep of unknowing, an awakening into the state in which one is Brahman only. According to the medieval interpreters, Śvetaketu was rather a slow learner. His father had to call to him nine times "That art thou" before he would wake up.

Tat tvam asi was thus drawn completely into the service of a radical monism of consciousness and a purely intellectual program of salvation. As far as we know, there was no trace of its being used ethically, as Schopenhauer used it. Such a use would be logically impossible. Schopenhauer, who knew no Sanskrit and read Indian texts in translations that were quite faulty in places, did not clearly recognize or fully estimate the fundamental difference between his monism of the will and the Vedāntic monism of cognition or consciousness. If his thesis, that the essence of the world is will, were correct, the ethical use of *tat tvam asi* would indeed be a logically tenable consequence: "that," which is the other, namely the metaphysical will, is also "thou." For ethics are concerned with volition, and if my volition is identical with that of another, it is perhaps understandable that, by intuitively equating my own self with that of the other, I should act in his interest exactly as in my own. My love of my neighbor would, however, be really love of self, so it would be questionable whether we could continue to talk of ethics.

Vedāntic monism, however, has explicitly banished all volition and all action to the realm of the unreal. Sympathetic identification with another, which according to Schopenhauer is the essential attitude of a good person, would be seen by Vedāntins of all schools as straying from the path of salvation. The universal One is to be reached not by ethical identification, but by intellectual abstraction. There is no route from the monism of consciousness to ethics. As Albert Schweitzer rightly said, it is supra-ethical.[9] The view that my cognition is a manifestation of a universal cognitive substance which is the only reality, and that all volition and action are an unreal objective appearance, cannot be the basis of any volitional behavior toward another. Whether Uddālaka Āruṇi's vitalistic monism could have taken an ethical direction if the development into a radical monism of the spirit had not taken place is an idle question. What is certain is that it could not have taken such a direction in ancient or in medieval India.

This was clearly recognized by the historian of philosophy and Indologist Paul Deussen, who was one of the best scholars of Śankara and Vedānta. He was a true follower of Schopenhauer's philosophy, which he regarded as the highest pinnacle of human knowledge. He evidently became an Indologist for the sake of Schopenhauer's philosophy, and like his master he was interested in ethics as much as in metaphysics. He was concerned to represent Schopenhauer's philosophy as a bridge between the metaphysics of Vedānta and Christian ethics as he understood them. We can assume that he would have been delighted to find Indian thinkers making the same ethical use of *tat tvam asi* as his master. But he had to recognize that they did not, and that it was impossible in Vedānta.

We are, Deussen wrote, "apt to judge the value of a philosophical system by the ethical consequences which it has produced or which can be drawn from it," following the biblical text 'Ye shall know them by their fruits' (Matthew 7, 16).

> But it is possible for a tree to be good and yet produce no fruit, or no good fruit—perhaps because its blossom has been touched too soon by the frosty wind of the knowledge of truth. This is what may have actually happened in India. Seldom has eternal philosophical truth been so precisely and aptly expressed as in the doctrine of the saving knowledge of the ātman. Yet this same knowledge is like that frosty wind which arrests development and freezes life. Whoever knows himself to be the ātman is removed for ever from all desire and therefore from the possibility of immoral action, but he is equally devoid of any impulse to any activity whatsoever.[10]

Moreover, Deussen holds that the doctrine that the self or universal ātman "is of a purely spiritual nature, pure consciousness *(caitanya)*" is "the basic error of the Vedānta system, which among other things deprives it of any true morality, however close the purest form of such a morality may be to its principles."[11]

This opinion shows that Deussen's interest in ethics and his commitment to Schopenhauer's teaching were much stronger than his approval of Vedānta. He judged Vedānta by a standard provided by Schopenhauer, not the other way round. Yet he tried to give even the

Vedāntic monism of consciousness a place in his system, as in the following:

> If, according to Schopenhauer's great teaching, it is the will and not the intellect that is the core of a human being, then Christianity has the superior merit that its central and essential demand is for a rebirth of the will. But if a human being is not mere will but also intellect, then that Christian rebirth of the will must appear from the other point of view as a rebirth of consciousness, as the Upaniṣads teach. "Thou shouldst love thy neighbor as thyself," says the Bible. But why am I expected to do this, since I have feelings in myself and not in someone else? "Because," the Veda adds in explanation, "in truth your neighbor is your own self, and what separates you from him is mere illusion."[12]

But this attempted harmonization is forced. By combining Schopenhauer's philosophy with Vedānta, the monism suddenly becomes a dualism; a human being is no longer only will, but also intellect. And in attempting to make use of Vedāntic monism, Deussen lets in two inaccuracies. The Vedāntin's goal is consciousness of being-nothing-but-consciousness, and this cannot rightly be generalized as 'rebirth of consciousness.' Besides, this consciousness or cognition is not of an identity of one's own self with that of another person, but of an identity of one's own self with an impersonal universal One. Deussen never noted the difference between Uddālaka's vitalistic monism and the monism of cognition or consciousness which prevailed in the Upaniṣads and which reigned alone in later Vedānta. He made an honest effort to justify Schopenhauer's reference to *tat tvam asi* as a foundation for ethics, but his attempt cannot be considered successful.

2. "Do not harm the self by the self" What is the meaning of the other passage, *Bhagavadgītā,* 13, 27–28, which Schopenhauer cites to support his monistic foundation of ethics? In particular, what is the meaning of the phrase in verse 28: 'does not harm the self by the self?' If we begin by asking Deussen, we find that he maintained Schopenhauer's view that the verse provides a monistic basis for ethics. These two verses were the one passage in Hindu literature which Deussen thought could be used to support his and Schopenhauer's ethics; he was therefore in the habit of quoting them.[13] He took the "highest Lord" mentioned in these verses as the universal self—in the sense of Schopenhauer's 'will,' naturally—which is identical with the individual self of every being. He who has recognized the identity not only of the individual self of every being with the "highest Lord," but also of his own self with his neighbor's, "does not harm" his neighbor because, as he has recognized, he would then be harming "his own self" in his neighbor "by his own self." According to Schopenhauer and Deussen, this is the sense of the verse in the *Bhagavadgītā.*[14] Is this interpretation correct?

Let us first see how the context can help us to understand the verses. There is no mention of ethics in the surrounding verses. But that matters little for our problems, for in any case, *Bhagavadgītā* 13, 27–28 appears to be a little self-contained unit which does not entirely fit its surroundings.[15] This part of the text could have been put together from a number of small pieces, as clearly often happens in the later Upaniṣads, which are close to the *Gītā* in many ways. It is impossible to see the *Gītā* as the work of a single author; nevertheless its various parts belong to a single circle of thought. It contains many repetitions, and later parts could have been composed on the model of older parts of the same poem.

The phrase 'he does not harm the self by the self' in *Bhagavadgītā* 13, 28[16] calls for explanation. What does 'the self by the self' mean? Collocations of the accusative *(ātmānam)* or nominative *(ātmā)* of the word for 'self' with the instrumental *(ātmanā)* 'by the self' or locative *(ātmani)* 'in the self,' or both, are common in the *Bhagavadgītā.*[17] When connected with verbs meaning 'to see' or 'to have pleasure,' they are an emphatic expression of mystical introspection: "Many see the self by the self in the self through meditation" (13, 24). When used in a merely concrete sense, they can be rendered simply by 'oneself, himself'; this sense can occur with other verbs also, as "He should lift himself up by himself" (6, 5).[18]

But what does 'harm' mean here? The Sanskrit verb *hiṃs (hinasti)* can either mean simply 'harm' or 'annihilate, destroy, kill.' There is a parallel in *Gītā* 16, 21, where "destruction of the self" is mentioned using a verb of similar meaning.[19] There, destruction of the self consists of yielding to sexual desire, anger, or greed, and so going to hell. These words give an idea of what we can understand by the "destruction" or "loss" of the self, which, according to the teaching of all the Upaniṣads, cannot be literally destroyed or lost.

Within the *Bhagavadgītā,* I would next cite as parallels 6, 20; 6, 30. In 6, 20cd the true yoga (6, 23) is described: "Where, seeing the self by the self, he finds contentment in the self."[20] In 6, 30 Kṛṣṇa, the universal God in human form, says: "For him who sees me in everything and everything in me, I am not destroyed (or lost), and he is not destroyed (or lost) for me."[21] Both verses refer to mystic insight. In the first, the yogin is immersed in himself without thinking of a God, while in the second, his vision is very similar to our *Gītā* verse 13, 28. The only difference is that he not only sees God in everything, as in 13, 27–28, but also sees everything in God. The result, in the case of mere vision of the self (6, 20) is described as 'contentment,' and in the case of the vision of God (6, 30) as a state in which God and the soul are not destroyed or lost for one another. Other passages, outside the *Gītā,* speak of happiness or freedom from pain as a result of seeing the Self or God.[22] Could not the expression 'he does not harm himself' (or 'his self') describe an experience such as contentment, happiness, freedom from sorrow, or that in which God and the self are not lost or destroyed in relation to one another? The last, particularly, comes very close to 'not harming.' 'He does not harm his self' would then mean 'he does not cause himself sorrow' by losing or destroying God, as *Gītā* 6, 30 puts it.

There is another parallel in the *Īśā Upaniṣad,* verses 1; 3; 6; 7:[23]

1. Everything here which moves in the world is to be clothed with the Lord. When you have given it up, you may enjoy it;[24] do not covet anyone's goods.
3. Demonic those worlds are called, covered in blind darkness; to them, after death, go all who kill the Self (or 'their self').
6. But he who sees all beings in the Self (or 'in himself') and the Self (or 'himself') in all beings, he does not shrink from them.[25]
7. When all beings have become the self of the knower, what bewilderment, what sorrow is there for him who sees the unity?

These four verses are very similar to *Bhagavadgītā* 13, 27–28. There is this much difference, that the Upaniṣad starts by telling us to see all things in God ("everything is to be clothed with the Lord") and then speaks of seeing the Self. We may suppose, of course, that the Self is identified with the Lord, but the change of expression is not without significance, especially in comparison with *Gītā* 13, 27–28, which speak of seeing the Lord in all things, not all things in the Lord, nor all things in the Self. Common to both passages, however, are the expression 'Lord,'[26] the theo-monistic vision, and the possibility of "destroying the self." The *Gītā* also presents in many places the view expressed in the first two verses of the *Īśā Upaniṣad*—especially the second, omitted here—which combines outward activity with inward renunciation. This view is just as unusual in Hinduism as the idea that it is possible to destroy the self. This corroborates the conjecture that the *Īśā Upaniṣad* comes from the same circles as the *Gītā*.

In any case, the connection between the expressions 'harm the self' in the *Gītā* and 'killers of the self' in the Upaniṣad is undeniable. *Īśā Upaniṣad* 3 says that "killing the self" leads to "demonic worlds." *Gītā* 13, 28 does not say this, but according to *Gītā* 16, 21, "destruction of the self" is a "gate of hell," which is metaphysically the same as what is said in *Īśā Upaniṣad* 3. According to *Gītā* 16, 21, 'destruction of the self' means greed; and *Īśā Upaniṣad* 1 tells us not to covet others' goods. The positive counterpart of this is inward renunciation, which is an indispensable precondition for contemplation, a common Indian idea. On the other hand, both *Gītā* 13, 28 and *Īśā Upaniṣad* 3, 6–7 show that failure to see the unity is in turn identical with harming or killing the self.

By putting together the results of our comparison of *Gītā* 13, 28 with *Gītā* 6, 20; 6, 30; 16, 21 and *Īśā Upaniṣad* 1; 3; 6; 7, we can define the content and associations of the concept of harming/destroying/killing the self with some certainty: one harms or destroys the self when one yields to greed, for this renders impossible the insight which sees the Lord or Self in all beings and all beings in the Lord or Self. That means that contemplative bliss is not reached, and God and the Self are "lost" or "dead" to each other; consequently rebirth continues after death, beginning with some very painful form of existence. We may infer that, according to the view underlying these passages, the true nature of the self is realized when the unity is seen. An attitude in which the true nature of the self is misapprehended is said to harm, destroy, or kill the self. Rebirth continues so long as this state of authentic existence is not reached.

The moral injunction to avoid greed, which is implied in *Gītā* 16, 21 and expressed in *Īśā Upaniṣad* 1, is not based on the idea that one recognizes one's own self in another and therefore treats him as one's own self; it is based on the idea that greed makes contemplation impossible, while renunciation is a necessary precondition for true vision. Here, as usual in Hinduism and Buddhism, morality has value only as a preliminary to mystical knowledge, and it is only because of this interconnection between ethical behavior and knowledge that the omission of one or the other could be thought of as "destruction of the self."

A discussion of the Schopenhauer-Deussen interpretation of *Bhagavadgītā* 13, 28 would not be complete without asking whether there is any metaphysical or theological basis for ethics in the *Gītā* at all. So we must look at the verses which speak of goodwill toward all beings. In some passages it is suggested that such goodwill leads to God or to salvation, for instance, that the well-wisher is dear to God.[27] We also find the idea that the vision of God or the Self (God "alike in all beings") leads to goodwill, especially in 6, 31; 32, where it is said that the yogin who sees and worships God in all beings, "regards [everything] in all [beings], be it pleasure or pain, as if it were his own."[28]

This sentence does indeed contain a basis—a theological basis—for the ethical imperative. But it is quite different from the one that was outlined by Schopenhauer and taken up by Deussen. It is not that I have goodwill for my fellow-being because he is essentially identical with me; it is rather that because the same God dwells in me and in him, I behave toward him not *as being* my own self but *as if he were* my own self.[29] That is a kind of monism, but it is neither Śaṅkara's absolute monism of consciousness or cognition (with its corollory of illusionism) nor Schopenhauer's monism of will. The doctrine is suggested rather than fully stated in the *Bhagavadgītā;* it is developed later in the *Viṣṇu Purāṇa,* to which I shall return. It is essential to this doctrine, as distinct from Schopenhauer's, that it sees *three* participants in ethical behavior: the subject, his neighbor, and God. The ethical imperative arises from the belief that God is in the subject and in his neighbor, while the *tat tvam asi* ethic sees only *two* participants: the subject and his neighbor, who are identical with one another in their metaphysical essence.

Could not this idea also be contained in the phrase 'He harms not the self by the self?' For three persons could be spoken of in connection with this phrase also: God, whom the yogin sees in all things, a self (accusative), and other self (instrumental). But then both selves would equally be the Lord whom the mystic sees. The verse would then mean: "Since he sees the Lord dwelling in all things alike, he harms not the self [of the Lord, which is in his neighbor] by the self [of the Lord, which is in himself]." As a parallel to this idea we could cite *Bhagavadgītā* 17, 6, which says that by excessive asceticism one tortures God who is in the body,[30] and again 16, 18, where Kṛṣṇa says that egoism, force, pride, desire, and anger are hatred, i.e., hostile behavior toward himself, the universal God, "in one's own and in others' bodies."[31] But this would be a forced interpretation, first because, as our investigation has shown, the words 'the self by the self' represent a mystical-emphatic form of the reflexive pronoun and do not refer to two selves, and second because it depends on the identification of the 'Lord' and 'the self,' which obliges us to supply a great deal that is not stated. Besides, it would be quite unlikely, because it would force us to ignore the content of the idea of "destroying the self" which we have ascertained from the *Īśā Upaniṣad* together with three verses of the *Gītā*. It remains quite impossible to interpret the verse as containing the *tat tvam asi* ethic. It would be absurd to assume that this ethic, which is never clearly expressed, was implied in words that must be understood in a quite different way, as our examination of parallel texts has readily shown.[32] On the other hand, verses such as 16, 18 combine easily with 6, 31–32 to present an ethic which bases the ethical imperative on the idea that the same God dwells in one's neighbor and in oneself. The basic idea of the *tat tvam asi* ethic, that one's neighbor's self is identical with one's own self, is quite different.

Some verses in chapter 12 of the *Laws of Manu* come very close to some of the *Gītā* passages we have dealt with.

> 12, 91: He who sees the self [or himself] in all beings, and all beings in the self, sacrifices to the self and reaches sovereignty.
>
> 12, 118: He should see all things, being and nonbeing, in the self, with concentration. For when he sees all in the self, he does not turn his mind to wrong.
>
> 12, 125: He who thus sees the self by the self in all beings, reaches equality with all things, and goes to Brahman, the highest state.[33]

All three verses speak of seeing the self, but the self referred to is understood as the universal self, or God. The first verse shows that seeing identity leads to mystical and contemplative heights. The second seems to come close to the *tat tvam asi* ethic, in the same way as *Gītā* 13, 28, but according to the above findings we may, and perhaps must, agree with the Indian commentator Kullūka, who explains: "Since he sees all things in the self, he does not turn his mind to wrong, because he has no passions of desire or loathing." In other words, it is not because he identifies his will with another's (as the *tat tvam asi* ethic teaches) that he does not think of doing wrong (against another, or in general), but because the vision of the self is necessarily associated with ascetic suppression of the passions. That is the same idea as we found in the *Bhagavadgītā* and *Īśā Upaniṣad*. In the third verse from Manu, we can see that the vision of the self and mystical identification are concerned with union with the absolute, not with the foundation of ethics.

We must now consider the interpretations placed on *Gītā* 13, 28 in medieval India. I have examined nineteen commentaries,[34] of which fifteen explain this verse. The oldest extant commentary was composed by the spiritual monist Śaṅkara (that very thinker whose system Deussen viewed as the peak of Indian philosophy) in the seventh or eighth century C.E. He knows nothing of an ethical interpretation of the verse. Basing his exposition on his own system, he explains that the individual self, imprisoned in metaphysical ignorance, does not know its identity with the true, universal self and mistakes what is nonself for the self. The nonself is the body together with the psychical apparatus. So long as the self is ignorant, this complex incurs repeated death and rebirth. According to Śaṅkara, what the *Gītā* means by the words 'He destroys the self by the self' is that the ignorant person continually condemns to death what he takes to be the self, namely the psycho-physical complex. Here, the "self" which is destroyed is only erroneously taken to be the self, and is really the psycho-physical complex. The real self of the ignorant person, on the other hand, is also continually destroyed by his ignorance, since it is concealed by it.

This interpretation, which is shared by the commentators belonging to Śaṅkara's school,[35] is thoroughly forced. However, if we set aside that part of it which results from the Advaita system, we are left with the view that the fallen state into which one is thrown by "destruction of the self" results from failure to realize the knowledge of unity. To destroy or harm the self, therefore, is to fail to recognize the true relation between the individual and the highest self. To that extent, Śaṅkara's school agrees with an important part of the results of our comparison with parallel texts. Continuation of rebirth is, of course, essentially the same as what the *Īśā Upaniṣad* means by 'blind darkness,' and what the *Gītā* means when it speaks of God and the soul being lost to each other.

The same ideas recur in the commentaries of other schools. The unreleased state, that is, rebirth, and ignorance of the true relation of God and the soul, are injury or destruction of the self. Monistic Śaivas,[36] followers of the Vaiṣṇava "qualified monism" *(viśiṣṭādvaita)*[37] and of "pure monism" *(śuddhādvaita)*,[38] authors both early[39] and late,[40] are all agreed on this. They cannot have taken their interpretation from Śaṅkara's twisted exegesis; they certainly drew on commentaries older than Śaṅkara. It must be assumed, then, that the exegetical tradition retained a great deal from the centuries before Śaṅkara, especially as the view agreed on by the commentaries is confirmed by parallel passages. Many commentators, moreover, cite *Īśā Upaniṣad* 3, which contains the word 'slayer of the self';[41] many also cite a verse from the *Mahābhārata,* which in its context condemns those who dissemble themselves: "He who shows himself as other than he is—what evil has he not done? He is a thief who steals himself."[42] The Sanskrit words can, however, be understood as "He who sees the Self as other than it is . . . is a thief who steals the Self," and the commentators use the verse in this sense.

Nīlakaṇṭha, however, has his own opinion. Toward the end of the seventeenth century he wrote a commentary on the *Mahābhārata,* including the *Bhagavadgītā* which is incorporated in the *Mahābhārata.* He is a monist, close to the school of Śaṅkara but often with views of his own. He first explains in the traditional way that 'not to harm the self' means to see the mystical unity and so preserve the Self or Lord from the torments of rebirth. But he then adds a second possible interpretation: "Because he sees that the Self is but one, he does not harm another, just as he does not harm himself; that is, he has compassion for all."[43] Is this the *tat tvam asi* ethic? Nīlakaṇṭha does not say that the self of another is in itself my own self, as Schopenhauer and Deussen teach, but looks first at the universal self and concludes from its universality that it is in another as well as in me. There is still a difference.

It must be noted that this interpretation is found only in one late commentator, and even then only as a second possibility. It is clearly a new departure which does not depend on any tradition. This is clear from Dhanapati's commentary. Dhanapati repeats Nīlakaṇṭha's two explanations verbatim, but adds after the second: "This explanation was not taught by the masters."[44]

Our investigation, which has necessarily been rather long, has thus shown that we cannot say, as Schopenhauer does, that his "ethical metaphysics was the basis of Indian wisdom thousands of years ago."[45] There was in early medieval Hinduism a metaphysical, or rather theological, basis for ethics, but this was characteristically different from the *tat tvam asi* ethic. It is stated concisely in *Gītā* 6, 31–32, not in 13, 27–28; it is expressed negatively in 16, 18. It appears again in a more developed form in the legend of Prahlāda in the *Viṣṇu Purāṇa.*

3. Prahlāda In the *Viṣṇu Purāṇa,* a legend is told about Prahlāda, the asura's, or demon's, son who is devoted to Viṣṇu and is tormented for it by his demon father, but remains true to Viṣṇu throughout his tribulations.[46] This legend is full of enthusiasm for benevolence, which is probably influenced by the Buddhist ethic of compassion; it is questionable, however, whether such influence should also be traced in the *Bhagavadgītā.* In the legend of Prahlāda the injunction to benevolence is not based, as in Buddhism, on the ascetic way to salvation, but on a theistic monism; what is hinted at in the *Gītā* is here expressed more explicitly and emphatically, and is demonstrated in Prahlāda's behavior.

Prahlāda's relationship to Viṣṇu is a monism which varies with different situations His ethical attitude is expressed in the idea that "Viṣṇu is in everyone and everything"; his desire for deliverance—whether deliverance from extreme danger or the ultimate deliverance from rebirth—is expressed in the idea that "Viṣṇu is all."

Because Viṣṇu is in every being, he is directly honored by benevolent treatment of all beings; this, in brief, is Prahlāda's theological basis for benevolence. In the *Bhagavadgītā* the behavior of the wise or virtuous man toward his fellow man is chiefly represented as impartiality, in which no difference is seen between friend and foe. That is asceticism, not ethics. Prahlāda knows this type of behavior also, but he teaches further that one should have the same feeling toward all beings as the devotee of Viṣṇu has toward his God, namely *bhakti,* devotion, reverent love. That is ethics. The emphasis, however, as in the *Gītā,* is less on actively doing good to fellowmen or living beings (though of course this is not excluded) than on refraining from harming them, and on mental attitudes: wishing them well or thinking of them favorably and compassionately. It is appropriate here to use the term 'ethic of thoughts' *(Gedankenethik)* which Albert Schweitzer aptly coined for the characteristic feature of Buddhist ethics.[47]

Here, however, as in Hinduism in general, the ethical attitude takes second place to direct striving for salvation through meditation on the statement 'Viṣṇu is all.' It is hoped that by thinking this thought one will realize its meaning and reach an intimate relationship, if not identity, with God.

Prahlāda's ethic, formed perhaps around 500 C.E., seems to have fallen into oblivion during the rest of the middle ages. The Prahlāda legend was reworked many times, but it is only in the oldest of these later versions, dating perhaps from the seventh or eighth century and included in the *Bhāgavata Purāṇa,* that the ethic makes one last appearance, though even here it is already receding into the background and included among the numerous practices of *bhakti.* In the later versions the ethic has disappeared. It is not yet known whether a foundation of ethics such as Prahlāda teaches in the *Viṣṇu Purāṇa* is given by any of the systematic philosophers or theologians.

4. Bankim Candra Caṭṭopādhyāya Prahlāda is one of the great forms in which mythological thought has portrayed the ideals of Hinduism. Usually he has been seen merely as a *bhakta,* a devotee, rather than as a pattern of altruistic behavior. However, a thinker and novelist of the modern period, Bankim Candra Caṭṭopādhyāya (anglicized Chatterjee), who lived from 1838 to 1894 and was one of the first to attempt to vindicate and consciously modernize Hinduism, saw in Prahlāda the ideal of both love for God and love for man. In Chapter 21 of his *Principles of Religion*[48] of 1888, he uses the *Bhagavadgītā,* and even more the Prahlāda legend of the *Viṣṇu Purāṇa,* to present a basis for ethics.

Bankim, like the legend itself, uses several formulations of the idea of the unity of God and the world (i.e., man and living beings). Besides the idea that "God is in everything and in everyone," which predominates in Prahlāda's bhakti, he also stresses, more strongly than Prahlāda, the idea that "the world is in God." He also sometimes identifies, more or less fully, the world with God, but only in the realm of ethics, while Prahlāda's more emphatic identification is supra-ethical.

Bankim writes:

> The God of the Hindus . . . is [a God] who pervades all beings *(sarvabhūtamaya).* It is he who is the inner Self *(antarātmā)* of all beings. He is not the material world *(jaṛā jagat),* he is different [or "separate," *pṛthak*] from the world, but the world is in him. The world is in him as pearls in a necklace or the wind in space. No man is without him; he is present in everything. He is present in me. If I love myself, I love him. If I do not love him, I do not love myself. If I love him, I love all men. Anyone who does not love all men does not love God, and does not love himself. That is: if love does not include the whole world, there is no love at all. So long as I cannot perceive that I am the whole world, so long as I cannot perceive that there is no difference *(abheda)* between the whole world and myself, I have no knowledge, no religion *(dharma),* no

> devotion *(bhakti),* no love [of man] *(prīti).* Universal love *(jāgatika prīti)* is therefore the basis of the Hindu religion.

Bankim then quotes two verses of the *Bhagavadgītā,* including one of those which we have used in our exposition of the expression "harm the self by the self": "He who, with his self absorbed in yoga, sees the Self in all things and all things in the Self, seeing the same in all; he who sees me in everything, I am not lost to him, and he is not lost to me" (*Gītā* 6, 29–30).

The *Principles of Religion* is in the form of a dialogue; these words are spoken by the teacher.[49] After further instruction, the pupil sums up as follows:[50]

> Having perceived the nature of God, one should gradually understand that he and we are not different from the world. When one has followed the practice of regarding the whole world in the same way as oneself, love will reach its full development. I see where this love leads. Love of self cannot contradict it, since the whole world is filled with one's own self. Therefore it leads not simply to love of country *(deśa-vātsalya)* but to love of the whole world *(sarvaloka-vātsalya).*

In Bankim, as in the *Gītā* and in the Prahlāda legend, ethical reflection starts from three principles—God, one's fellow man, and oneself—not from two principles, as in the *tat tvam asi* ethic. He does indeed speak of nonseparateness *(abheda, abhinnatva),* but he cannot mean identity of being. For it is also stressed that God and the world are *in* one another and that God is *in* the self of man; further, Bankim says that one should learn or practice seeing the whole world (that is, all men, *sarvaloka*) *in the same way as* oneself *(āpnār mata),* not *as being* oneself. The phrase 'the whole world is full of the self' *(ātmamaya haïyā jāy)* cannot therefore have a strictly ontological meaning here. It is modeled on the Upaniṣadic statement 'all things have become his own self,'[51] but in the contexts in which it occurs, that statement has a different meaning. In its oldest context it is meant to explain the idea that after death there is no object of consciousness; a later Upaniṣad takes it over to show how the released person stands above the world. That is ontological monism, and the practical stance corresponding to it is ethically neutral. In Bankim, on the other hand, we can only speak of an ethical equation of the world with oneself, and ethics is his primary concern.

Bankim, then, did not know the *tat tvam asi* ethic. He does not even quote *Bhagavadgītā* 13, 27–28, the verses which have characterized that ethic since Schopenhauer. However, his thinking, prompted by Prahlāda, comes very close to it, and a world view to which Bankim's ideas contributed could find no difficulty in adopting the *tat tvam asi* ethic once it had been introduced. For Bankim had already applied Hindu monism, which was originally ethically neutral, to the teaching of ethics.

But how did Bankim come to bring Prahlāda's ethic out of oblivion? Obviously it was not just because he was familiar with the Purāṇas. Two motives are clearly recognizable in his work. First, he was repelled by the crude utilitarianism of the English philosophy which prevailed in his time, the principle of "the greatest good of the greatest number." He would and could find something better and deeper in the Hindu tradition to set against it. Second, he clearly wanted to set up a Hindu ideal to outdo and supplant the religious and ethical message of Christianity.

We have already seen how he uses the genuinely Hindu ideas that "God is in everyone and in everything" and that "all is in God" as sources for his "universal love" and contrasts it with the love of but one nation which he finds among Christian Europeans and represents as characteristic of them. He then goes on: "In short, for Hinduism love of God includes love of man; without love of man there is no love of God; love of God *(bhakti)* and love of man *(prīti)* are inseparable in the Hindu religion . . ."[52]

Bankim appropriates these ideas for Hinduism with these vigorous words: "I think this already shows the superiority of Hinduism over all religions."[53] Here he shows what his motive is. Even in the Prahlāda legend, the above idea does not appear as explicitly as in Bankim, and in other Hindu texts it does not appear at all. On the other hand, it appears just as explicitly elsewhere, in the New Testament: "If anyone says, 'I love God,' and hates his brother, he is a liar . . . And this commandment we have from him, that he who loves God should love his brother also" (I John, 4, 20–21). Bankim must have learned the idea from this source, whether directly or indirectly, before he could have derived it from Prahlāda's ethic. True, the idea is somewhat different in the context in which Bankim places it from what it is in the New Testament, but for this very reason the formal correspondence cannot be accidental. Bankim must have known that this idea is the core of Christian ethics, and we can thus easily understand why he wanted to claim it for his own religion, which he was trying to vindicate.

A few lines later, Bankim expresses the idea that "God is love." This, too, could hardly have been without Christian influence (I John, 4, 16), even though Bankim makes the one statement into two, since he distinguishes between reverent love *(bhakti)* and love of man *(prīti),* and even though he gives the idea a completely Hindu basis: "God himself is love, God himself is devotion; as supporter [or 'foundation'] of the world he dwells in the hearts of men in the form of psychic forces *(vṛtti).*"

The criterion for religious evaluation of ethical behavior contained in the statement 'without love of man there is no love of God' is not found in the Hindu tradition, but it can be built onto Prahlāda's ethic without logical difficulty. This enabled Bankim to recommend to his contemporaries not only Prahlāda's devotion to God but also Prahlāda's ethic. For here he found an idea which answered the interest in ethics aroused in him by contact with Christianity and Western philosophy, while also enabling him to effectively counter Christian teachings, since here were Hindu ideas from which the very core of Christian ethics could be derived. It is clear from many passages in Bankim's theological writing that such an apologetic against Christianity, culminating in a demonstration of the superiority of Hinduism, was one of his chief concerns.

5. Vivekananda

Just as many features of the Prahlāda legend make it seem unique in medieval India, so too in the modern period, the attempt to design a Hindu theological basis for ethics using ideas from that legend does not seem to have been followed up. Bankim's achievement lay more in the field of literature than in that of religious and philosophical thought. The reorientation of the Hindu world view in general, and of Hindu ethics in particular, received a far more lasting and far-reaching impulse from the writings and lectures of another Bengali, Swami Vivekananda (1863–1902). A disciple of the mystic Rāmakṛṣṇa (or Ramakrishna, 1836–88), Vivekananda contributed more than almost any other Indian to the modernization of the religious consciousness of the Hindus and the uplift of their self-awareness from a deep depression. He sought to build a new philosophical and religious outlook, at once genuinely Hindu and universal, on the foundation of the ancient, strongly monistic Vedānta metaphysics, and to show that an active approach to the problems of modern life was a necessary consequence of that metaphysics. Understandably, then, he took a lively interest in ethics.

Vivekananda does not seem to have seen the significance of the Prahlāda legend, and the ideas in the *Bhagavadgītā* which underly it, for a foundation of ethics. A verse in the legend reads: "Then the wise, seeing Hari (i.e., Viṣṇu) subsisting in all beings, must practice unswerving devotion *(bhakti)* toward all beings."[55] Vivekananda quotes this verse in his work *Bhakti-Yoga,*[56] but only in order to show that *bhakti* at its most intense level leads the mystic to revere every living being as a "manifestation of God." He has thus, quite in accordance with the Indian tradition, allowed Prahlāda's ethic to disappear into *bhakti* in such a way as to leave no sign of ethics as such.

I can give only a small sampling of the evidence for Vivekananda's ethical ideas. In his "Notes taken down in Madras, 1892–93,"[57] he writes:

> Morality is a relative term . . . Every man, in every age, in every country is under peculiar circumstances. If the circumstances change, ideas also must change. Virtue is that which tends to our improvement, and vice to our degeneration. Man is made up of three qualities: brutal, human, and godly. That which tends to increase the divinity in you is virtue, and that which tends to increase brutality in you is vice. You must kill the brutal nature and become human, that is, loving and charitable.

These sentences contain a typically Neo-Hindu combination of three elements. Vivekananda starts from the very Western idea that morality is relative, varying according to time and place. With this he skillfully combines the very different moral relativism of ancient Vedānta, according to which ethical behavior has no value in itself, serving only as a preparation for the knowledge which alone brings salvation. But he also expresses positively what ancient Vedānta states negatively; he speaks of "increasing the divinity," whereas traditional Vedānta would speak or purifying the mind *(cittaśuddhi).* Finally, and rather artificially, he adds to his genuinely Hindu individualism the Christian idea of active love for one's neighbor: "You must . . . become . . . loving and charitable." The connection between the two kinds of relativism is also artificial. For while the first depends on the laws of the development of nature and society, the second depends on the laws of the individual's spiritual development, which culminates in a lone, quietistic salvation.

The idea that morality is relative appears a few times in Vivekananda's later writings also.[58] So does the idea that ethical behavior is a means for spiritual progress, an exercise,[59] which is essentially the ancient Vedāntic ethical relativism. Vivekananda maintains this relativism so strongly that on occasion (1895) he even rejects compassion[60]—that compassion which, according to Schopenhauer and Deussen, is essential to ethical behavior. This clearly shows that up to 1895 he cannot have known the *tat tvam asi* ethic, in which any disparagement of compassion is unthinkable.

On May 31, 1893, Vivekananda sailed from Bombay to America, where he arrived at the end of July and took part in the Parliament of Religions at the World's Fair in Chicago in September. During the next two years he lectured at various places in the United States In August, 1895, he traveled via Paris to England; in December he returned to America, where he remained until April, 1896. During his stay in the United States he wrote and published *Bhakti-Yoga,* mentioned above, and also *Karma-Yoga,* which is considered his chief work.[61]

Karma-Yoga is particularly concerned with ethics. Here Vivekananda relies especially on the *Bhagavadgītā*. That is understandable, for the *Gītā,* more than any other Hindu text, makes action a religious necessity and gives it a positive value—not only cultic action, but also worldly action as prescribed by Hindu social norms. Vivekananda says nothing at all about those passages in the *Gītā* which point to the idea that "God is in all" as a basis for ethics. He illustrates the concepts of action *(karman)* and duty from the Hindu tradition; he teaches that one should do work for its own sake, selflessly and without thought of one's own advantage, and offer its fruits to God. He emphasizes that such action is just as valuable as renunciation.[62] But action has no value in itself. Action is good because it can lead to renunciation.[63] In *Karma-Yoga,* Vivekananda has adopted the ancient Vedāntic moral relativism in an acute form:

> Why should we do good to the world? Apparently to help the world, but really to help ourselves. We should always try to help the world, that should be the highest motive in us; but if we consider well, we find that the world does not require our help at all . . . The only help is that we get moral exercise . . . All good acts tend to make us pure and perfect . . . Let us give up all this foolish talk of doing good to the world . . . We must work and constantly do good, because it is a blessing to ourselves. That is the only way we can become perfect . . . Be grateful to the man you help, think of him as God. Is it not a great privilege to be allowed to worship God by helping our fellow men? . . . The world is a grand moral gymnasium wherein we have all to take exercise so as to become stronger and stronger spiritually.[64]

The idea that one worships God by doing good to others is not central here, as it is for Prahlāda. It could not be central, because in

Vedāntic monism the idea that "I am Brahman (God)" is no ecstatic exaggeration, but a fundamental truth. To worship God in another is here the same as to make manifest one's own metaphysical self. Vivekananda therefore teaches, exactly as traditional Hindu monism does, that in the end the value of moral behavior lies in spiritual self-perfection. It is in this sense that the doer is helping himself, not in the sense that the recognition of one's own self in the self of another is a motive for doing good to him. These passages are further evidence that it is impossible for a philosophy based on traditional Vedānta to know or discover the *tat tvam asi* ethic. In Vivekananda's works published up to the middle of 1896, some sentences taken out of context can sound like expressions of an ethic based on a theistic monism or a monism of will, but as soon as they are examined in context, fundamental differences appear.

Nevertheless, Vivekananda became the first Indian exponent of the pseudo-Vedāntic *tat tvam asi* ethic. It happened as follows. On April 15, 1896, Vivekananda left America.[65] During the next few months he stayed in England and in Switzerland. On August 9, he learned that Paul Deussen would be pleased if he would visit him.[66] Vivekananda went to Germany and was Deussen's guest in Kiel on September 9.[67] Three days later he went with Deussen to England; he was accompanied throughout his European tour by his admirer Mrs. Sevier and her husband Captain Sevier.

There are two accounts of these events: one by Deussen in his memoirs,[68] and another by Mrs. Sevier. Extracts from the latter are given in the anonymous *Life of Swami Vivekananda by his Eastern and Western Disciples,* published by the Ramakrishna Mission, and in an article by Romain Rolland in the Fifteenth Yearbook of the Schopenhauer Society.[69] There are also several remarks in Vivekananda's letters about his visit to Deussen and the time he spent with him, and he published an article on Deussen in an Indian periodical.[70]

Vivekananda was obviously very pleased at his new acquaintance with the German professor. In letters to friends he calls him a "warring Advaitist" and "the greatest living German philosopher,"[71] he says several times how pleasantly his visit went,[72] and later reports that he and Deussen have become great friends.[73] He has, he says, discussed Vedānta with the professor,[74] who has taken the opportunity to converse in Sanskrit.[75] In his article on Deussen he writes: "Deussen, unhampered by any philological leanings and possessing the training of a philosopher singularly well versed in the speculations of ancient Greece and modern

Germany . . . plunged deep into the metaphysical depths of the Upanishads, found them to be fully safe and satisfying, and then—equally boldly declared that fact before the whole world." He also expresses the hope that Deussen will equally boldly show the Indians the "defects" and "later corruptions" of their thought-systems.[76]

From these remarks we may infer that the Swami was ready to learn from the professor.[77] Deussen, for his part, indicates in his memoirs that he found nothing of significance in Vivekananda. The tone of his account suggests that he viewed his guest almost as a curiosity; his general impression of him was obviously not particularly favorable.[78] However, it seems that as a result of the Swami's visit, Deussen accompanied him to England. Was it merely for the opportunity of hearing and speaking Sanskrit for a few more days? We can assume that this was a powerful motive for Deussen, since his autobiography shows that he was always very pleased to be able to make use of foreign languages, and naturally Sanskrit had more attraction for him than any other. But since he does not mention in his memoirs that he discussed Vedanta extensively with Vivekananda, we may perhaps conclude that he attached little importance to the contents of his conversations with him.

That he did discuss Vedānta is, however, vouched for both by Vivekananda's letters and by Mrs. Sevier's account. She tells us:

> After a few preliminary inquiries regarding the travels and plans of Swamiji, I noticed the Professor directing his eyes to some volumes lying open on the table . . . he soon turned the conversation on books. . . . He considered the system of the Vedanta as founded on the Upanishads and Vedanta Sutras, with Shankaracharya's commentaries, some of the most majestic structures and valuable products of the genius of man in his search for truth, and that the highest and purest morality is the immediate consequence of the Vedanta. He quoted from an address he delivered before the Bombay Branch of the Royal Asiatic Society on the 25th February, 1893, on which occasion he concluded with the following advice to his audience: *'And so the Vedanta, in its unfalsified form, is the strongest support of pure morality, is the greatest consolation in the sufferings of life and death. Indians, keep to it!'*[79]

The fact that Mrs. Sevier quoted from Deussen's lecture shows that she had a copy of it; probably she had obtained one from Deussen. We may assume that Vivekananda, too, after his visit to Deussen, was able to make use of the text of the lecture, which in fact he did. He allowed himself to learn from Deussen. The Bombay lecture contains among other things a concise statement of the *tat tvam asi* ethic; Vivekananda did not miss the opportunity to appropriate an apparently genuine Hindu idea which enabled moral behavior to be judged not merely by its value for spiritual progress, but as an end in itself.

A few days after his arrival in England, Vivekananda gave a lecture in a private house in Wimbledon, perhaps in Deussen's presence, on "Vedānta as a factor in civilization."[80] Among other things, it included a presentation of the pseudo-Vedāntic ethic, based on ideas in Deussen's Bombay lecture. I give first the relevant sentences of Deussen's lecture:

> People have often reproached the Vedānta with being defective in morals, and indeed, the Indian genius is too contemplative to speak much of deeds, but the fact is, nevertheless, that the highest and purest morality is the immediate consequence of the Vedānta. The Gospels fix quite correctly as the highest law of morality: "love your neighbors as yourselves." But why should I do so, since by the order of nature I feel pain and pleasure only in myself, not in my neighbor? The answer is not in the Bible . . . but it is in the Veda, is in the great formula *'tat tvam asi,'* which gives in three words metaphysics and morals altogether. You shall love your neighbor as yourselves, because you are your neighbor, and mere illusion makes you believe that your neighbor is something different from yourselves. Or in the words of the Bhagavadgita: he, who knows himself in everything and everything in himself, will not injure himself by himself, *na hinasti ātmanā ātmānam.* This is the sum and tenor of all morality, and this is the standpoint of a man knowing himself as Brahman. He feels himself everything, so he will not desire anything, for he has whatever can be had; he feels himself everything, so he will not injure anything, for nobody injures himself. He lives in the world . . . but he knows that there is only one being, Brahman, the Ātman, his own Self, and he verifies it by his deeds of pure disinterested morality.[81]

Vivekananda's Wimbledon lecture contains these words:

> The Vedānta philosophers . . . discovered the basis of ethics. Though all religions have taught ethical precepts, such as, "Do not kill, do not injure; love your neighbor as yourself," etc., yet none of these

> has given the reason. Why should I not injure my neighbor? To this question there was no satisfactory or conclusive answer forthcoming, until it was evolved by the metaphysical speculations of the Hindus who could not rest satisfied with mere dogmas. So the Hindus say that this Atman is absolute and all-pervading, therefore infinite. There cannot be two infinites, for they would limit each other and would become finite. Also each individual soul is a part and parcel of that Universal Soul, which is infinite. Therefore in injuring his neighbor, the individual actually injures himself. This is the basic metaphysical truth underlying all ethical codes.[82]

The main ideas in this passage come unmistakeably from Deussen's Bombay lecture. There is even an allusion to the passage in the *Bhagavadgītā,* which is part of the foundation of the *tat tvam asi* ethic. Vivekananda claims this ethic as Hindu, and his words resound with pride that it was the Hindus who, in his view, discovered the metaphysical foundation of ethics.

From the spring of 1896 onwards, when he spoke about ethics in India, Europe, or America, Vivekananda habitually presented the Schopenhauer-Deussen pseudo-Vedānta, though without abandoning his earlier ethical ideas. While he occasionally modified or added to it, for instance by bringing it closer to a Prahlāda ethic, he always left clear traces of his dependence on Deussen. He does not, however, explain that this doctrine is not contained in traditional Vedānta, nor that it can only be derived from it if the traditional monism of consciousness is transformed into Schopenhauer's monism of the will to live.

Although not all Vivekananda's writings are dated, the above facts should be enough to lead to the conclusion that he learned the pseudo-Vedāntic ethic during his conversations with Paul Deussen and from Deussen's Bombay lecture, of which he probably had a copy. Among those dated works which contain the *tat tvam asi* ethic, none is dated earlier than September, 1896. Another decisive consideration is that in his principal work on ethics, *Karma-Yoga,* composed in late 1895, he would surely not have missed the opportunity to derive an ethical principle from Vedānta if he had had a suitable line of argument when he wrote the book.

The introduction of the *tat tvam asi* ethic into Hinduism can therefore be dated. The first date is Sunday, February 25, 1893, when Deussen gave his lecture "On the Philosophy of the Vedānta" in Bombay, which was immediately printed in India. The lecture gave, among other things, a brief presentation of the *tat tvam asi* theory of the foundation of ethics. This lecture, together with other writings of Deussen and Schopenhauer, influenced subsequent Neo-Hindu thinking, at least in the case of B. G. Tilak, as we shall see in the next section.

The second date is Wednesday, September 9, 1896. It represents a precisely traceable, effective, and enduring influence in the personal encounter of Vivekananda, the most influential Neo-Hindu propagandist of his time, with Paul Deussen of Kiel, the exponent of Schopenhauer and Vedānta.

6. Twentieth-Century Hindus

The formation of a national self-consciousness was sought in India not through political ideas, as in other countries, but through philosophy. Hence there was a need for a philosophical foundation for ethics that used indigenous concepts. In the nineteenth century and the beginning of the twentieth, Hinduism was in a state of paralysis and apathy. Hindu spirituality was felt to be powerless and inferior, and this condition was thought to be unalterable. Bankim Candra greatly deplored this state;[83] Vivekananda attacked it by calling for self-confidence; Radhakrishnan, the best-known living Indian philosopher, tells us that he himself succumbed to this spiritual paralysis in his youth.[84] Leading thinkers of the period saw the urgent necessity of finding the way out of resigned inactivity[85] into action—in social life, in education, and in politics. But the necessary impetus and self-confidence could only be gained when it was seen that Hinduism, that precious national inheritance, had been wrongly interpreted as quietism. It was the notion of the fatal quietism of the Hindu mind that contributed most to the apathy that had to be overcome. Hence the search for a genuinely Hindu ethic, already in Bankim Candra. Hence too the sensitivity with which Radhakrishnan, as late as January, 1939, reacted polemically to the reproach that Hinduism lacked a genuine ethic.[86]

The *tat tvam asi* ethic seemed to be the remedy for this painfully perceived defect. Even Vivekananda's *Karma-Yoga* had regarded action as a mere exercise to prepare for the individual's spiritual advancement. Ethics had yet to be anchored in metaphysics. Vivekananda could even say that it was ultimately "foolish talk" to speak of "doing good to the world." Despite all emphatic appeals, the impression remained that action as such was meaningless. Resignation remained supreme, even if this was not expressly stated. But the *tat tvam asi* ethic related action directly to the central concept of the most widespread and respected

Hindu metaphysical system. It taught that the true Vedāntin proved his perfect realization not by resignation and quietism, but by the very fact that he was active in the service of his fellow human beings. Action thus acquired a value, an intrinsic value, that it had never had before in Hinduism.

It is understandable, then, that the pseudo-Vedāntic ethic became widespread. It is also understandable that in the urgency of the situation no one should have paused to consider whether this ethic was traceable in historical Vedānta, and whether it fitted the nature of Vedānta as a monism of consciousness.

We can assume that the *tat tvam asi* ethic was propagated above all by the Ramakrishna Mission. This organization carries on the work of its founder Vivekananda; it sees its task as the propagation of Vedānta, including missions in America and Europe, and the adaptation of this philosophy to modern thought and modern needs, and it has extensive social and philanthropic activities in India. These activities would never have occurred to a Vedāntin of the old school, and in order to bring such activity into harmony with Vedāntic monism it is indispensable to establish the value of good action in the manner of the *tat tvam asi* ethic. It is to be expected, therefore, that writers belonging to the Ramakrishna Order would refer or allude either to *tat tvam asi* or to *Bhagavadgītā* 13, 28, the verse which since Schopenhauer has been associated with the *tat tvam asi* ethic, using the Schopenhauer-Deussen interpretation. This expectation is borne out by an examination of the writings of the Ramakrishna monks. We find such passages, for instance, in the works of Svāmī Abhedānanda, who lived from 1866 to 1939; he carried on Vivekananda's work in America from 1897, worked as a Hindu missionary until 1921, mainly in the United States, and became one of the most significant writers of the Ramakrishna-Vivekananda movement.[87] We find them again in Svāmī Akhilānanda, who is at present active in the Neo-Vedāntic movement in America.[88]

But the Ramakrishna Mission appears not to have been the only force to transplant this apparently Indian growth into Indian soil. The pseudo-Vedāntic ethic is expounded at greater length in Bāl Gangādhar Tilak's magnum opus than in any work of Vivekananda's, though Tilak hardly seems to have had any connection with the Ramakrishna Mission. He lived from 1856 to 1920, was the leader of Indian nationalism before the arrival of M. K. Gandhi, and between November, 1910, and March, 1911, while he was a prisoner in Mandalay, wrote a very prolix commentary on the *Bhagavadgītā* entitled "The Secret of the Glorious *Gītā* or the

System of Karma-yoga."[89] Again we find the word *karma-yoga,* which we have already met with in Vivekananda, and which may roughly be translated 'spiritual practice of action.' A considerable part of the *Gītā* does indeed treat of such an active spirituality. But Tilak tries to represent the doctrine of action as *the* doctrine of the poem, to which he subordinates all the rest of its contents. In the interests of the nationalist political program, he needed a clear call to action for himself and his associates, and to enable Hindus to act with a clear conscience, a basis for action had to be found in Hindu metaphysics. Tilak chose the monistic metaphysic but utterly rejected its traditional consequences of renunciation and quietism. But he was equally unhappy with the prevailing English ethical philosophy, with its maxim of "the greatest good of the greatest number," which had already repelled Bankim Candra Caṭṭopādhyāya. He cast around for support from Western philosophers who thought differently, and found it in Kant and in the English Kantian Thomas Hill Green,[90] but most of all in Schopenhauer, whose *World as Will and Idea* was known to him, and in Paul Deussen. He cites Deussen's Bombay lecture of 1893, his *Elements of Metaphysics,* and his *Philosophy of the Upanishads,* the latter two in English translation. When we consider that *The Elements of Metaphysics* was first published in English translation in London in 1894, and *The Philosophy of the Upanishads* in Edinburgh in 1906, while the lecture *On the Philosophy of the Vedānta* was published in Bombay in 1893, we can assume that Tilak, like Vivekananda, first became aware of the *tat tvam asi* ethic through this lecture, and afterwards, prompted by it, read the other works of Deussen and Schopenhauer that were available in English.

It is a feature of Tilak's monistic ethic that his dealings with the texts are more thorough, and philologically sounder, than Vivekananda's method. He quotes *tat tvam asi* in connection with his exposition of metaphysics[91] and without mentioning an ethical application of it. He knew that no such application had existed, and he probably considered it impossible. He does indeed give an ethical content to the text 'he does not harm the self by the self' (*Bhagavadgītā* 13, 28), but in a quite different sense from Schopenhauer, Deussen, and Vivekananda. He gives the meaning of the sentence a positive turn, and says it means: "[he] of his own accord, takes to the path of virtue."[92] Here again we have the view that Schopenhauer's reading of the text is impossible. The candor shown here can be noticed elsewhere in Tilak's work. He is emphatic that his view, that the doctrine of action was the true intention of the *Gītā,* differs from all traditional interpretations. He leaves the reader in no doubt that the monistic ethic was taught by Schopenhauer and Deussen.[93]

If Tilak was obviously of the opinion that the textual foundation that Schopenhauer and Deussen had given to their ethic was unable to carry the structure they built on it, he was, on the other hand, convinced that this structure was not only correct but was erected according to the principles of Hindu monistic metaphysics. He therefore gave it a new textual foundation in the form of a concept which was again to be found in a verse of the *Bhagavadgītā,* but also in other Indian texts, and indeed in much non-Indian literature. This concept is indicated by the Sanskrit expression *ātmaupamyena,* to be found in *Gītā* 6, 32, which we have already discussed on p. 283. This expression means literally "in such a way that one's own self is a likeness [of something named in the sentence]," or "in comparison with one's own self," or simply "like one's own self." But Tilak interprets it in the sense of "*as being* one's own self," "because [what is named in the sentence] is identical with one's own self." Admittedly he does not do so in his Marathi translation of the *Bhagavadgītā,* where he retains the meaning of 'like': "Whoever has begun to see others everywhere equally *by comparison with* himself, be it pleasure or pain, with such an *(ātmaupamya-)* eye . . ."[94] But he does do so in his exposition of ethics. There, he interprets the widely known maxim 'Treat others as you would treat yourself' as containing a declaration of the insight that one's own self is metaphysically identical with the self of the other. Tilak refers to this insight with the expression *ātmaupamyabuddhi,* which as he understands it may be translated: "insight into the sameness [not comparability] of the self."[95]

He explains:

> No ethical principle can more satisfactorily justify worldly [that is, relevant to everyday life] morality *(vyāvahārika nītidharma),* than the principle of considering that there is only one Ātman in all created beings, or of Self-identification *(ātmaupamyabuddhi).* For example, let us take the doctrine of charity *(paropakāradharma),* which has been given an important place in all countries and according to all codes of Ethics. This doctrine can be justified by no Materialistic principle *(ādhibhautika vāda),* as satisfactorily as by the Metaphysical principle *(adhyātmatattva)* that "the Ātman of the other man is the same as my Ātman."[96]

By "materialistic" theories of ethics, Tilak means principles such as "the greatest good of the greatest number."

Tilak has thus retained the philosophical content of the *tat tvam asi* ethic, but abandoned its textual basis and given it a new one. This has the distinct advantage over Schopenhauer's that the chosen verse really is about ethics. But Tilak failed to see what kind of foundation for ethics is implied, if not actually set out, in the text. He was unable to see it because he had learned his fundamental ethical principle from Schopenhauer and Deussen, not from Indian texts. So when he went back to the texts to look for this principle, he took up the first phrase that came to hand: "like one's own self." He translated it correctly, but interpreted it philosophically as if it meant "*as being* one's own self." He overlooked the reason why the yogin sees all beings as "like his own self," indicated in *Bhagavadgītā* 6, 31–2: the yogin sees and worships *God* in all beings.

Tilak states most emphatically that the monistic ethic belongs to the knower, the perfected one *(siddha),* and that it is he, because he recognizes the metaphysical basis of ethics, who would be driven to worldly action. Tilak's rejection of quietism is substantially more radical than that of Vivekananda and his followers.

Although Tilak's ethic agrees closely with the *tat tvam asi* ethic in its philosophical basis, it is better not to refer to it by this term, since Tilak does not refer to *tat tvam asi* in an ethical context. If we wish to describe it in one word that refers to its textual basis, we should call it the *ātmaupamya* ethic.

Vivekananda and Tilak have thus introduced the pseudo-Vedāntic ethic into Neo-Hinduism. (Whether other Indians have also done the same must remain an open question for the present.) They have been so successful that there are some leading personalities in Indian thought today who believe that this ethic is genuinely ancient Indian. As an example, I shall take Pandurang Vaman Kane. He is a man of stupendous learning in Sanskrit, and his works on the history of Indian poetics, and especially on the history of Indian law and custom, have earned him outstanding merit. In a work published in 1941, he wrote:

> The reason given for cultivating such virtues as *dayā* [compassion], *ahiṃsā* [nonviolence] is based upon the philosophical doctrine of the one Self being immanent in every individual, as said in the words *tat tvam asi.* This is the highest point reached in Indian metaphysics and combines morality and metaphysics. That doctrine requires us to regard the goodness or badness of one's actions from the standpoint of other individuals who will be affected by such actions. Dakṣa (III, 22) [the mythical author of a law-book] declares "one who desires happiness should look upon another just as he looks upon himself."[97]

We can see that the *tat tvam asi* ethic and the *ātmaupamya* ethic have been fused together here, and that no difference is seen between 'like one's own self' and 'as being one's own self.'

However, there are other Hindus who are aware that *tat tvam asi* is not a suitable basis for ethics, but nevertheless consider it useful or desirable to combine ethics with spiritual monism. An example of this is M. Hiriyanna (1871–1950). While he did not publish as much as many Indians who are better known but are not his intellectual equals, he was one of the best textual scholars as well as one of the most acute Vedāntic thinkers of his time. In an essay on "The Ethics of Advaita," first published in 1942, he writes:

> Some, no doubt, have held, both in the East and in the West, that the highest aim of life is to reach this negative ideal, and that morality therefore consists wholly in repressing one's desires and appetites. But the Advaita, though it recognizes self-conquest as a necessary stage in life's discipline, maintans that, owing to its negative character, it cannot stand for the ultimate purpose of human life. Life, according to this school, must have a positive aim, and we find it given to us in the character of the final truth which Māyā conceals from man. That truth is the *jīva's* [the individual self's] fundamental identity with Brahman, as taught in the Upaniṣadic formula 'That thou art' *(Tat tvam asi)*. Man is therefore more than the finite or narrow self which he ordinarily takes himself to be. He is really the universal self, but only hidden behind a finite guise. It is the grasping of this wider significance of the self that forms the positive aim of Advaita. But by 'grasping' here, if it should become a living influence on everyday conduct, we must understand not merely an intellectual acceptance of the truth about the self but also a ratification of it by one's own experience. Such a consummation, however, is within the reach of but a few, particularly on account of the arduous nature of the intellectual (including *yogic*) discipline necessary for it. Ethical conduct does not permit of any such restriction [to the few], and whether or not a person feels himself fit to strive for the highest, he has to live a morally worthy life. Hence it is necessary to restate the Upaniṣadic truth in a form which shows clearly its direct bearing on such a life. If every individual self is at bottom the same as Brahman, it follows that the selves cannot, in the end, be different from one another. This way of stating the truth discloses to us at once that there is no basis whatsoever in actual

> fact for any discrimination in our attitude toward others, and that we should therefore cherish the same kindly feeling, or bear equal love, for all.[98]

In this passage, Hiriyanna completely leaves aside the question whether a *tat tvam asi* ethic existed in historical Vedāntic monism. He obviously means to carry further the lines of thought indicated by traditional Vedānta, which were related to a particular situation. There must be a way, he says, by which the majority of mankind, who are unable to undergo the severe discipline required for the experiential realization of the doctrine of Vedānta, can translate into life what he holds to be the ultimate truth. He finds that this is possible if we bear in mind that Advaita Vedānta is ultimately concerned with something positive. There must, therefore, be a positive way of living out Vedānta, even for those who live a worldly life. Vedānta, Hiriyanna expressly says, must be restated to make this possible, and this is what the *tat tvam asi* ethic does.

In this essay, which incidentally was first published in a periodical of the Ramakrishna Mission, the *Vedānta Kesari,* Hiriyanna thus attempts among other things to rethink the *tat tvam asi* ethic, and to do so in such a way that its functional, pragmatic, and also relative character remains clear. That, after all, was perhaps the only way in which this ethic could be philosophically retrieved. But there remains the doubt that surrounds any philosophical system that contains a double theory of truth.

Finally, the *tat tvam asi* ethic has been taken up as a weapon in a polemic. Albert Schweitzer had characterized Hindu mysticism as ethically neutral, as "supra-ethical"[99] S. Radhakrishnan, the best-known in the West of living Hindu philosophical writers, has thoroughly criticized this contention. In this critique, which takes up a whole chapter of Radhakrishnan's book *Eastern Religions and Western Thought,*[100] we find the following argument among others.

> Schweitzer forgets that the great text 'That art Thou' *(Tat tvam asi)* is bound up with an ethic of active service. He writes: "Easy as it would be to turn the doctrine of *tat tvam asi* in an ethical direction, they nevertheless neglect to do it."[101] At the end of his Indian tour, Dr. Paul Deussen said to a gathering at Bombay: "The Gospels quite correctly establish as the highest law of morality, 'Love your neighbor as yourselves.' But why should I do so since by the order of nature I feel pain and pleasure only in myself, not in my neighbor? The answer is not in the Bible . . . but in the Veda, in the great

> formula 'That art Thou,' which gives in three words the combined sum of metaphysics and morals. You should love your neighbor as yourselves because you are your neighbor." In the words of the *Bhagavadgītā:* "He who knows himself in everything and everything in himself will not injure himself by himself."

Without expressly stating it, Radhakrishnan gives the impression here that in his opinion *historical* Hinduism—for this is what the polemic against Schweitzer is about—does put *tat tvam asi* to ethical use. Again without expressly stating it, he also implies, through his selection and juxtaposition of quotations, that Deussen had a different view on this question from Schweitzer's. In fact, Deussen's writings were Schweitzer's source, and Deussen himself declares that the Vedānta system lacks a "true morality" (cf. above, note 11). But, of course, Radhakrishnan himself knew that *tat tvam asi* was not put to ethical use in historical Hinduism. It is not Schweitzer who "forgets"; it is Radhakrishnan who "forgets" to inform his readers of the original contexts in which the passages he quotes appear. His argumentation using *tat tvam asi* deserves to be brought to light here, if only because it is in the above passage that a Western reader interested in India is most likely to come across the *tat tvam asi* ethic today.

7. Toward an Assessment of Neo-Hindu Thought

From the historical point of view, the *tat tvam asi* ethic appears as a curiosity in the history of ideas: a European philosopher imputes an association of ideas to the ancient Indians; his posthumous disciple tries to justify his master's notion, and presents his version of it to Indians in general and to a Hindu monk in particular; the European philosopher's idea becomes widely accepted in India, so much so that many Indians today take it to be actually Hindu.

From the philosophical point of view, to base the *tat tvam asi* ethic on the foundation of the Vedāntic monism of consciousness is a logical impossibility. But even on the basis of a monism of will, if this is understood in a strictly ontological sense, it does not survive close examination. Ethical behavior presupposes an interpersonal relationship, which loses its metaphysical justification if individual personhood has no ultimate reality. Accordingly, even for Schopenhauer, as we noticed at the outset, morality is "not the ultimate end"; this means not that ethics are subordinated to metaphysics or theology, but that they are, in the end, simply abolished.

Relations between persons cannot be reduced to an egoism of the universal One, as the ethics of the monism of will ultimately does. Whether ethical behavior is only a remote preparation for the pure quietistic state in which the universal One is experienced (as in the monism of consciousness), or whether it is a part of the realization of the universal One itself (as in the monism of will), the idea that ultimate reality is a universal One is always supra-ethical in the end. In the case of the monism of will, this feature is only superficially disguised by placing ethical behavior in the realm of true Being. For the monist of will means to *break through* the *"principium individuationis"* as through a "veil of Māyā," as Schopenhauer puts it.[102] This aim he shares with the monist of cognition or consciousness. Besides, whether the principle of individuality starts from space, time, and causality, as in Schopenhauer, or from metaphysical "unknowing," as in Vedāntic monism, in either case individuality must be annulled, either forever or temporarily. But personality presupposes individuality, and the possibility of ethical behavior presupposes the existence of persons.

Neither the monism of will nor the monism of consciousness or spirit has a real place for the concept of person. But when this concept is not taken seriously, ethics remains on a naturalistic level; that is, there is no true ethics, good and evil have no truly metaphysical relevance, and ultimately there are only ways of realizing or veiling the impersonal universal One. Thus the Neo-Hindu attempt to base ethics on monism would remain inadequate, even if the monistic foundation were transferred from a monism of consciousness to a monism of will or of life. There is no sense in which an identification of a 'that' with a 'thou,' such as we have in *tat tvam asi,* can explain why good and bad behavior exist. Interpersonal relationship is not identity, and it is certainly not identity of a person with an impersonal being.

This was seen by Radhakrishnan's younger contemporary, P. T. Raju. Raju is a more independent thinker than Vivekananda and Radhakrishnan, whose louder voices have become more audible in the West, and although he is close to Vedānta and also interested in ethics, he has not accepted such a logical monstrosity as the *tat tvam asi* ethic. He writes:

> The first act of positing or the act of self-externalization of the Absolute Self should . . . be understood as of the form, 'I and Thou,' and not merely as the Āgamas [the traditional Hindu texts] main-

> tain, of the form, 'I and That.' If the split is into 'I and That,' there would be no morality. The world would only be the world of the animal and its food, not of man and his ethical environment, though both may be *bhogya* or objects of enjoyment. There can be love, not between the I and the That, but between the I and the Thou. Both the Upanishads and the Āgamas are indifferent to this distinction . . . Here I feel Indian Philosophy is left undeveloped, and here is scope for further development. It is not a mere speculative consideration, but a consideration for a philosophy of life. The mere neutral That, unless it develops into a personal Thou, cannot offer itself as an object for moral activity . . . [103]

Raju is right when he coolly declares that ancient and medieval Indian philosophy did not discover the interpersonal relationship. However, it should be added that even if interpersonal relations in the human sphere were not thought about, some consideration was given to the personal relation between man and God. And it is only where that happened that we can observe the beginnings of a genuine ethic in Hinduism, less indeed in the "systems" *(darśana)* themselves than in the more poetical theology of the *Bhagavadgītā* and the legend of Prahlāda. There the interpersonal I-Thou relationship is reduced to the man-God relationship, since God is believed to be present in the Thou of one's fellow-being. Thus Hindu ethics, where it really existed, could only operate with *three* quantities: I, God, the world. I do not know whether any modern Hindu thinkers are developing these ideas further. If so, they may remain closer to an Indian tradition than does the monstrous *tat tvam asi* ethic.

At any rate, Neo-Hindu thought does not as yet give the impression of having started any potentially fruitful projects, or of having produced any achievements worth discussing, whether in ethics or in any other field. The acceptance of the *tat tvam asi* ethic, Bankim Candra's proof of the superiority of Hinduism, and Radhakrishnan's polemic against Albert Schweitzer's assertion that Hindu mysticism is nonethical, all give an impression of tendentious evasion, nervous haste, and failure to think things through; this impression has unfortunately not yet been removed.[104] In general—except perhaps Aurobindo Ghose and a few other, less well known thinkers—no one has succeeded in bringing the Indian tradition, Western and Christian influences, and the demands of the contemporary situation into a unity of thought. We can even state it as a rule that up till now the essential impulses and influential elements of Neo-Hindu thought have always come from the West or from Christianity, in such a way that an idea coming from those sources appears so powerful in a particular situation that its adoption is inevitable; that these impulses and elements are then hastily attached to inherited ideas or identified with them at the price of logical incongruity and even a kind of dissimulation; and that on the other hand—in typical Neo-Hinduism, as opposed to surviving traditional Hinduism—ideas inherited from the Hindu tradition hardly ever become significant or effective as such.

We can see this also in the realm of language. Literary Hindi nearly always uses Western concepts, and yet uses hardly any loanwords; instead, it uses Sanskrit words as shells in which the Western concepts are inserted. In the realm of political ethics, we should remember that the duty of nonviolence, which Tilak, and Aurobindo in his political period, did not recognize, but which has now become a universally binding ideal, was first discovered by Gandhi in Leo Tolstoy's writings before he attached it to the traditional Indian idea of *ahiṃsā*. The Neo-Hindu dogma of the equality of all religions, however much it can be supported by certain Hindu traditions, emerged originally at the beginning of the nineteenth century, probably from the ideology of the European Enlightenment. The Neo-Hindu concept of dharma was clearly prompted by the philosophy of Auguste Comte and John Stuart Mill,[105] but was then expressed in completely Indian terms. In Bankim's ethic of love,[106] and in Vivekananda's amalgamation of the Western and Indian forms of ethical relativism,[107] there is an attempt to fuse inherited Hindu ideas with concepts taken from Christianity or from Western philosophy, which provide the impulse for this attempt, and to fuse them in such a way that the result appears to be genuinely Hindu. Tilak looked for a text which would serve as a foundation for ethics, and found in *Bhagavadgītā* 6, 32 a text which could indeed be used for this purpose; but instead of bringing out what the verse implied, he read into it what he had learned from Schopenhauer and Deussen.

These examples could easily be multiplied. In each case some kind of impulse from a Western philosophical system or concept, or from Christianity and its theology, causes something in Hinduism to be recognized as valuable, and to appear notable, worth propagating, useful for solving a current problem, or suitable for use in apologetics.

It is to be hoped that Indian thought will soon outlive the memory of the colonial period and the deep wound which it left in the Indian mind, and regain a greater tranquillity and composure, so that it can attempt to sift through the various forces and impulses that are still clashing together in the world of Indian thought today in a more dispassionate and clear-sighted spirit, and find a new orientation.

Notes

[In these notes, square brackets enclose matter inserted by the translator. In the main text, square brackets enclose Hacker's own additions to quotations.]

1. Arthur Schopenhauer, *Die Welt as Wille und Vorstellung,* Book 4, section 66 (*Sämtliche Werke,* vol. I, ed. Paul Deussen. Munich, 1911, pp. 440ff.) [quoted here from Schopenhauer, *The World as Will and Idea,* tr. R. B. Haldane and J. Kemp (5th ed., London, 1906), vol. I, p. 481; cf. also *The World as Will and Representation,* tr. E. F.J. Payne (Indian Hills, Col., 1958), vol. I, p. 372].

2. Ibid., pp. 420, 442 [*The World as Will and Idea,* vol. I, pp. 459, 483; cf. the translation by Payne, vol. I, pp. 355, 374].

3. Schopenhauer, *Die Grundlage der Moral,* section 22 (*Sämtliche Werke,* vol. III (1912), p. 741) [For another translation, see *On the Basis of Morality,* tr. E. F.J. Payne (Indianapolis, 1965), p. 210].

4. Ibid., p. 744 [cf. *On the Basis of Morality,* tr. Payne, pp. 213f.]. Schopenhauer quotes the text in August Wilhelm von Schlegel's Latin translation:

> Eundem in omnibus animantibus consistentem summum dominum, istis pereuntibus haud pereuntem qui cernit, is vere cernit. Eundem vero cernens ubique praesentem dominum, non violat semet ipsum sua ipsius culpa: exinde pergit ad summum iter.

5. *Jahrbuch der Schopenhauer-Gesellschaft,* vol. 15 (Heidelberg, 1928), pp. 133–52. The quotation is on p. 151 [given here from *The World as Will and Idea,* tr. Haldane and Kemp, vol. III, p. 426; cf. Payne's translation (cited in n. 1), vol. II, p. 608].

6. Schopenhauer, *Die Welt als Wille und Vorstellung,* Book 2, chap. 48 (*Sämtliche Werke,* vol. II, p. 696) [quoted here from *The World as Will and Idea,* vol. III, p. 426; cf. Payne, vol. II, p. 608].

7. [*Chāndogya Upaniṣad* 6, 8–16].

8. One such exposition is described in Paul Hacker, *Untersuchungen über Texte des frühen Advaitavāda, 1: Die Schüler Śaṅkaras* (Mainz: Akademie, 1950), pp. 73–85; 95–8. Cf. further Paul Deussen, *Allgemeine Geschichte der Philosophie,* vol. I, Pt. 3 (3rd ed., Leipzig 1920), pp. 632–34; 658–63.

9. Albert Schweitzer, *Die Weltanschauung der indischen Denker* (Munich, 1935), p. 28 [A. Schweitzer, *Indian Thought and Its Development,* London, 1936, p. 43].

10. P. Deussen, *Allgemeine Geschichte der Philosophie,* vol. I, Pt. 2 (4th ed., Leipzig, 1920), p. 325.

11. P. Deussen, *Das System des Vedānta* (Leipzig, 1883), p. 61 [differently—and badly—translated in P. Deussen, *The System of the Vedānta,* tr. Charles Johnston, Chicago, 1912, pp. 58f].

12. P. Deussen, *Allgemeine Geschichte der Philosophie,* vol. I, Pt. 2, pp. 45f, and *Sechzig Upanishad's des Veda* (4th ed., Leipzig, 1921), p. x. [The substance of the last three sentences is also repeated in Deussen's lecture in Bombay, quoted below, p. 296].

13. Deussen places the two verses as an epigraph at the beginning of his book *Elemente der Metaphysik* (4th ed., Leipzig, 1907), in Sanskrit and in a Latin translation of his own in two couplets.

14. L. von Schröder, R. Otto and F. Edgerton have incorporated Schopenhauer's and Deussen's interpretation in their works on the *Bhagavadgītā.*

15. In the surrounding verses, the terms used for the highest spiritual being are *kṣetrajña* (field-knower), *puruṣa* and *paramātman,* not *īśvara* and *parameśvara* as in 13 and 27–28. These two verses are also marked out from their surroundings by their contents.

16. *samaṃ paśyan hi sarvatra samavasthitam īśvaram*
na hinasty ātmanātmānaṃ tato yāti parāṃ gatim.

17. 2, 55; 3, 43; 6, 5; 6, 6; 6, 20; 10, 15; 13, 24; 13, 28. The frequency of these forms is a characteristic of the *Gītā.* In the older and middle Upaniṣads they occur only in the following places: *Bṛhadāraṇyaka Upaniṣad* 4, 4, 23 (*ātmany evātmānaṃ paśyati;* this could have been the origin of the forms in the *Gītā*), *Mahānārāyaṇa Upaniṣad* (ed. Varenne, Paris, 1960), 1, 64 (*ātmanātmānam abhisaṃbabhūva,* occurring also in three other Vedic passages), and *Maitrī Upaniṣad* 6, 20 *ātmanātmānaṃ paśyati.* Further occurrences: *Gauḍapāda-Kārikā* 2, 12; Manu 12, 125 [further M. B. Emeneau, "Bhagavadgītā notes," *Mélanges d'indianisme à la mémoire de Louis Renou* (Paris, 1968), pp. 269–78; see pp. 272–76].

18. Compare *Bhagavadgītā* 2, 55; *ātmany evātmanā tuṣṭaḥ,* with 3, 17 *ātmany eva saṃtuṣṭaḥ* [both meaning 'contented with himself'].

19. *trividhaṃ narakasyedaṃ dvāraṃ nāśanam ātmanaḥ*
kāmaḥ krodhas tathā lobhas tasmād etat trayaṃ tyajet.

20. *yatra caivātmanātmānam paśyann ātmani tuṣyati.*

21. *yo māṃ paśyati sarvatra sarvaṃ ca mayi paśyati*
tasyāhaṃ na praṇaśyāmi sa ca me na praṇaśyati.

22. E.g., *Śvetāśvatara Upaniṣad* 2, 14; 3, 20; 6, 12.

23. *1. īśāvāsyam idaṃ sarvaṃ yat kiṃ ca jagatyāṃ jagat*
tena tyaktena bhuñjīthā mā gṛdhaḥ kasya svid dhanam.

3. *asuryā nāma te lokā andhena tamasāvṛtāḥ*
tāṃs te pretyābhigacchanti ye ke cātmahano janāḥ.

6. *yas tu sarvāṇi bhūtāni ātmany evānupaśyati*
sarva-bhūteṣu cātmānaṃ tato na vijugupsate [variant: vicikitsati].

7. *yasmin sarvāṇi bhūtāni ātmaivābhūd vijānataḥ*
tatra ko mohaḥ kaḥ śoka ekatvam anupaśyataḥ.

Verses 2, 4, and 5, omitted here, are not significant for the comparison with *Bhagavadgītā* 13, 28. Verses 4 and 5 also interrupt the sequence of 3 and 6, which fit well together, especially with the connecting *tu.*

24. Louis Renou, *Isa Upanishad* (Paris, 1943), translates: "Veuille jouir de ce qui est concédé par lui." But before this translation can be accepted, we need to establish that *tyaj* can be used in the sense of "concede."

25. The meaning of these words is unclear—like so many expressions in the *Īśā Upaniṣad* and in other Upaniṣads. I prefer to assume that they mean that he does not shrink from the dark, demonic worlds, because he has no need to fear them. Or do they mean that he does not shrink from living beings? Renou (see note 24) translates the variant *vicikitsati* as 'il ne veut plus distraire de là sa pensée.' It is most unlikely that this is meant.

26. *Īś* in the Upaniṣad, *īśvara* in the *Gītā.*

27. *Bhagavadgītā* 5, 25; 12, 4; 12, 13f.

28. *31. sarva-bhūta-sthitaṃ yo māṃ bhajaty ekatvam āsthitaḥ*
sarvathā vartamāno 'pi sa yogī mayi vartate.

32. ātmaupamyena sarvatra samaṃ paśyati yo 'rjuna
sukhaṃ vā yadi vā duḥkhaṃ sa yogī paramo mataḥ.

29. [In Hacker's original German, the difference is expressed in the two words *als,* implying identification, and *wie,* implying similarity. English uses *as* for both (as in *she introduced him as her son* and *she treated him as her son*). I have avoided the possibility of ambiguity by using phrases, as here, for *als* and *wie* whenever the argument turns on this difference. It is possible that some of the English-reading modern Hindus described in Section 6 may have overlooked the ambiguity.]

30. *karśayantaḥ śarīra-sthaṃ bhūta-grāmam acetasaḥ*
māṃ caivāntaḥ-śarīra-sthaṃ tān viddhy āsura-niścayān.

31. *ahaṃkāraṃ balaṃ darpaṃ kāmaṃ krodhaṃ ca saṃśritāḥ*
mām ātma-para-deheṣu pradviṣanto 'bhyasūyakāḥ.

32. This exemplifies the urgent necessity for a thorough philological interpretation before and during the process of examining ancient Indian texts from the point of view of the history of philosophy. Franklin Edgerton's work on the *Bhagavadgītā* (Cambridge, Mass., 1952, Harvard Oriental Series 38–9) is somewhat disappointing. The commentary should have dealt much more fully with philology and the history of ideas.

33. *91. sarva-bhūteṣu cātmānaṃ sarva-bhūtāni cātmani*
samaṃ paśyann ātma-yājī svārājyam adhigacchati.

118. sarvam ātmani saṃpaśyet sac cāsac ca samāhitaḥ
sarvaṃ hy ātmani saṃpaśyan nādharme kurute manaḥ.

125. evaṃ yaḥsarva-bhūteṣu paśyaty ātmānam ātmanā
sa sarva-samatām etya brahmābhyeti paraṃ padam.

34. They are contained in the following editions:
The Bhagavad-Gītā with Eleven Commentaries, ed. Shastri Gajanana Shambhu Sadhale (Bombay: Gujarati Press, 1935–38).

Śrīmadbhagavadgītā with the Commentaries Śrīmat-Śaṅkarabhāṣya with Ānandagiri; Nīlakaṇṭhī; Bhāṣyotkarṣadīpikā of Dhanapati; Śrīdharī; Gītārthasaṅgraha of Abhinavaguptāchārya; and Gūḍhārthadīpikā of Madhusūdana with Gūḍhārthatattvāloka of Śrīdharmadattaśarmā, ed. Wāsudev Laxmaṇ Shāstrī Paṇśīkar (2nd ed., Bombay: Nirṇaya-Sāgar Press, 1936).

Śrīmadbhagavadgītā with Sarvāloka of Rājānaka Rāmakaṇṭha, ed. T. R. Chintamani (Madras University Sanskrit Series, 14; Madras, 1941).

Śrīmad-Bhagavadgītā with the 'Jñānakarmasamuccaya' commentary of Ānanda (vardhana), ed. S. K. Belvalkar (Poona: Bilvakuñja Publishing House, 1941).

Bhagavadgītārthaprakāśikā of Śrī Upaniṣad-Brahma-Yogin (Adyar: The Adyar Library, 1941).

35. Ānandagiri (14th century); Madhusūdana (15th century).

36. Rājānaka Rāmakaṇṭha, Abhinavagupta and Ānanda.

37. Rāmānuja, Vedāntadeśika, Veṅkaṭanātha (perhaps not identical with Vedāntadeśika), Śrīdhara.

38. Vallabha and Puruṣottama.

39. Rājānaka Rāmakaṇṭha belongs to the 9th century C.E.

40. Ānanda completed his commentary in 1680; Upaniṣad-Brahma-Yogin is quite modern.

41. Veṅkaṭanātha, Śrīdhara, Madhusūdana and Dhanapati.

42. *yo 'nyathā-santam ātmānam anyathā pratipadyate*
kiṃ tena na kṛtaṃ pāpaṃ caureṇātmāpahāriṇā (*Mahābhārata* 1, 74, 27).

Quoted by Rājānaka Rāmakaṇṭha, Veṅkaṭanātha, Madhusūdana, Vallabha, Puruṣottama and Dhanapati.

43. *yad vā: aikyātma-darśitvāt svātmānam ivānyam apy ātmānaṃ na hinasti. sarvatra dayālur bhavatīti.*

A similar view is found in the syncretic monist text *Yoga-vāsiṣṭha* (9th century C.E. or later), where the sameness of the self in all human beings leads not to the ethical attitude of compassion, but to the ascetic attitude of freedom from feelings of friendship or enmity:

ekatve vidyamānasya sarvagasya kilātmanaḥ
ayaṃ bandhuḥ paraś cāyam ity asau kalanā kutaḥ.

44. *iti vyākhyānam ācāryair na pradarśitam.*

45. A. Schopenhauer, *Die Grundlage der Moral,* section 22, end (*Sämtliche Werke,* ed. P. Deussen, vol. III, p. 744).

46. For a fuller study of the legend and its doctrines, see Paul Hacker, *Prahlāda, Werden und Wandlungen einer Idealgestalt* (Abhandlungen der Akademie der Wissenschaften und der Literatur Mainz, Geistes- und sozialwissenschaftliche Klasse, 1959, No. 9), pp. 60–97; on ethics, see pp. 88–92.

47. Albert Schweitzer, *Die Weltanschauung der indischen Denker* (Munich, 1935), p. 79; 'Gedanken-Mitleid' p. 93 [*Indian Thought and Its Development,* London, 1936, p. 104; 'compassion in theory' p. 116].

48. *Dharmatattva.* I have used the edition in *Baṅkim-śatavarṣika saṃskaraṇa* [Bankim centenary edition] in Bengali (2nd ed., Kalikātā [Calcutta], 1351 Bengali era [1944 C.E.]).

49. *Dharmatattva,* p. 107.

50. *Dharmatattva,* p. 108.

51. *sarvam ātmaivābhūt—Bṛhadāraṇyaka Upaniṣad* 2, 4, 14 = 4, 5, 15; *sarvāṇi bhūtāni ātmaivābhūt—Īśā Upaniṣad* 7. The latter text is quoted by Bankim in a footnote on the passage under discussion.

52. *Dharmatattva,* p. 108.

53. *sakala dharmer ūpar Hindudharmer śreṣṭhatā,* ibid.

54. In the original, the birthdates for Vivekananda and Ramakrishna are erroneously given as 1862 and 1835 (editor's note).

55. *Viṣṇu Purāṇa* 1, 19, 9.

56. I use the Mayavati Memorial Edition of *The Complete Works of Swami Vivekananda* (cited hereafter as *Works*), published by the Advaita Ashrama Mayavati, Almora (vol. I, 8th ed., 1950; vol. II, 7th ed., 1948; vol. III, 6th ed., 1948; vol. IV, 6th ed., 1948; vol. V, 6th ed., 1954; vol. VI, 5th ed., 1951; vol. VII, 4th ed., 1953; vol. VIII, 1st ed., 1951). *Bhakti-Yoga* is in vol. III, the passage referred to here is on p. 82. Unfortunately the writings of Vivekananda are not arranged in order in the *Works,* and most of them are undated. Many of them can be dated from the anonymous *Life of Swami Vivekananda by his Eastern and Western Disciples* (cited hereafter as *Life*), but uncertainties often remain. [The pagination also differs with different editions. I have inserted page numbers in the more recent edition available to me, where they differ from the ones given by Hacker, and added references to additional material included in the later editions]. See also Romain Rolland, *La vie de Vivekananda,* 2 vols. (Paris, 1930).

57. Part of "Notes of Class-Talks and Lectures" *Works,* vol. VI. The passages quoted are on pp. 75 and 78 [10th ed., 1978, pp. 109, 112].

58. E.g., *Karma-Yoga* (1895–96), in *Works,* vol. I, pp. 34, 35, 108 [15th ed., 1977, pp. 36, 37, 110].

59. *Karma-Yoga* in *Works,* vol. I, pp. 73, 75, 78 [15th ed., 1977, pp. 75, 76f., 80]; "Inspired Talks" in *Works,* vol. VII, p. 67 [8th ed., 1972, p. 68] (25th July 1895); "The Absolute and Manifestation" (October–November 1896, cf. *Life,* p. 489) in *Works,* vol. II, p. 137 [13th ed., 1976, p. 141].

60. *Works,* vol. VII, p. 67 [8th ed., 1972, p. 69].

61. Cf. *Life,* pp. 393, 395, 398; Romain Rolland, op. cit. (note 55), vol. I, p. 94. *Karma-Yoga* and *Bhakti-Yoga* seem both to have appeared in print at the beginning of 1896.

62. *Works,* vol. I, pp. 45–49 [15th ed., 1977, pp. 47–51]. For the ideas in the preceding sentence, see *Karma-Yoga* (*Works,* vol. I), passim.

63. *Works,* vol. I, p. 38 [15th ed., 1977, p. 40].

64. *Works,* vol. I, pp. 73, 74, 75, 78 [15th ed., 1977, pp. 75, 76, 77, 80].

65. *Works,* vol. V, p. 82 [10th ed., 1973, p. 107]; vol. VIII, p. 384 [6th ed., 1977, p. 376].

66. *Works,* vol. VIII, pp. 393f. [6th ed., 1977, p. 387]; cf. vol. V, p. 86 [10th ed., 1973, pp. 112, 114]; vol. VI, p. 333 [10th ed., 1978, p. 370]. It is not clear from Vivekananda's letters who initiated this visit. The statement in *Life,* p. 433, that Deussen was interested in Vivekananda's philosophy, and therefore sent an 'urgent letter' inviting him, is hard to reconcile with Deussen's account in his autobiography; see below, note 77.

67. *Works,* vol. VIII, p. 396 [6th ed., 1977, pp. 387, 388, 391].

68. Paul Deussen, *Mein Leben,* ed. Erika Rosenthal-Deussen (Leipzig, 1922), pp. 305ff.

69. In the 4th ed. of *Life* which is used here, the parts of Mrs. Sevier's account which are most important for our investigation are omitted. However, they are reprinted, from the 1st edition of *Life* (1915), in the appendix to Romain Rolland's article 'Vivekananda et Paul Deussen,' *Jahrbuch der Schopenhauer-Gesellschaft,* vol. 15 (Heidelberg, 1928), pp. 158f.

70. *Works,* vol. IV, pp. 218ff. [11th ed., 1978, pp. 272–77].

71. *Works,* vol. VIII, p. 396; pp. 399f. [6th ed., 1977, p. 388; pp. 391f.]

72. *Works,* vol. VIII, p. 396; p. 399 [6th ed., 1977, p. 388; 391]; vol. VI, p. 337 [10th ed., 1978, p. 374]; Vol V, p. 89 [10th ed., 1973, p. 115].

73. *Works,* vol. V, p. 89 [10th ed., 1973, p. 115]; vol. VI, p. 338 [10th ed., 1978, p. 376].

74. *Works,* vol. VIII, p. 396 [6th ed., 1977, p. 388].

75. *Works,* vol. VIII, p. 400 [6th ed., 1977, p. 392].

76. *Works,* vol. IV, pp. 222f. [11th ed., 1978, pp. 276f.].

77. In view of this clearly discernible attitude of the Swami on the one hand, and of Deussen's somewhat belittling judgment of him (quoted in the next note) on the other, there is little reason to believe the claim in *Life,* pp. 438f., that it was Deussen who gained from Vivekananda "a much clearer insight into the whole body of Vedānta thought," and that "as he came to know the Swami more intimately, he understood that one must become de-Occidentalized, as it were, in order to master the spirit of the Hindu philosophical systems . . ."

78. This Swami had been summoned to the Chicago exhibition as a specimen of an Indian saint. Two friends of India, Miss Müller and Mr. Sturdy, had prevailed upon him to go from Chicago to London and give some lectures on Vedānta. They had then sent him to Switzerland for his health, and from there he came to Kiel with Mr. and Mrs. Sevier on the 9th of September, having first enquired whether I would be at home. I showed them the sights of Kiel, and persuaded them to spend one day in Hamburg, after which I met them again in Bremen so that we could travel together to London . . . Since I could hardly have changed hotels with all my luggage, I decided, for better or worse, to share a room with the brown brother from the East—not without hesitation, for my Indian tour had made me familiar with the habits of Indians. When I had retired to my room with the holy man and was ready for bed, the first thing he did was to light up his stubby English pipe, and I was obliged to fling open the door and windows and give him a brief lecture on the ill-effects of sleeping in a smoke-filled room. He spoke very good Sanskrit, and equally good English, was of a lively, agile, somewhat impetuous disposition, a young man, bursting with health, with full, rosy cheeks, very different from our usual idea of a saint. Anyway, these Indian saints are above all the rules of caste, and eat meat and drink wine; and when we went to a restaurant the next day, while the rest of us contented ourselves with single portions because of the exorbitant prices, he took double, all of which was paid for by the English couple since as a holy man he could not have any money. "What a holy man you are!" I said to him once; "you eat well, you drink well, you smoke all day, and deny yourself nothing." He replied in Sanskrit, "I keep my vow." "And what does your vow consist of?," I asked him. "It requires only kāma-kañcana-viraha—abstention from love and gold." Now he could easily abstain from gold, since others paid everything for him; and as for love, I allow him this—that, like many a healthy young Catholic priest, he honestly strove to put up a valiant struggle against flesh and blood, although on our evening stroll in the Kälberstraße he showed a rather disturbing interest in the sylphs who were hovering around us with inviting smiles.

—Deussen, *Mein Leben,* pp. 305f. Deussen's account of Vivekananda is thus quite detailed, but as far as intellectual matters are concerned it tells us more about the author, his time, and his attitudes than about the Indian he is describing.

79. See *Jahrbuch der Schopenhauer-Gesellschaft,* vol. 15 (1928), pp. 158f. Deussen's Bombay lecture is also reprinted in Paul Deussen, *Erinnerungen an Indien* (Kiel and Leipzig, 1904) pp. 243–451 [also in *The Philosophy of the Vedānta by Paul Deussen and The Vedāntasāra of Sadānanda Yogendra translated with annotations by G. A. Jacob,* Calcutta, 1957, pp. 21–30]. In the last sentence the *Jahrbuch der Schopenhauer-Gesellschaft* reads 'unfalsified forms'; but in Deussen's *Erinnerungen an Indien* [and in the reprint cited above] we find 'form.'

80. *Works,* vol. I, pp. 382ff. [15th ed., 1977, pp. 383–86]. For dating, see *Life,* p. 437.

81. Deussen, "On the Philosophy of the Vedānta," in Deussen, *Erinnerungen an Indien,* pp. 250f. [*Philosophy of the Vedānta* (see note 79), pp. 29f.].

82. *Works,* I, pp. 383 f. [15th ed., 1977, pp. 384f.].

83. Cf. R. Antoine in *Indica: The Indian Historical Research Institute Silver Jubilee Commemoration Volume* (Bombay, 1953), pp. 8f.

84. Radhakrishnan writes of his student days at Madras Christian College:

> I was strongly persuaded of the inferiority of the Hindu religion to which I attributed to political downfall of India . . . I remember the cold sense of reality, the depressing feeling of defeat that crept over me, as a causal relation between the anaemic Hindu religion and our political failure forced itself on my mind during those years ("The Spirit in Man," in *Contemporary Indian Philosophy,* ed. S. Radhakrishnan and J. H. Muirhead, 2nd ed., London, 1952, pp. 475ff.).—Editor's note: Radhakrishnan (born 1888) died in 1975, more than a decade after the publication of Hacker's article.

85. In Hindi, *akarmaṇyatā;* cf. Premcand, *Sevāsadan* (Varanasi: Sarasvatī Press, n.d.), p. 246 (in Hindi).

86. See below, pp. 304 f.

87.
> Standing on the rock of the spiritual oneness of the universe, Vedānta explains the basis of Ethics. If we injure, hate, or cheat others, we injure, hate, or cheat ourselves first. For this spiritual oneness we should love our neighbors as ourselves.

—Abhedānanda, "Hindu Philosophy in India," in *Contemporary Indian Philosophy,* ed. S. Radhakrishnan and J. H. Muirhead (2nd ed., London, 1952), p. 62 (1st ed.: 1936). The same idea, in almost the same words, in Abhedānanda, *Philosophy and Religion* (Calcutta, 1951), p. 32. See also:

> When we begin to feel for others in the same way as we do for ourselves, we commence to rise above the limitations of this narrow self... When we begin to cherish all living creatures as we cherish ourselves, we have reached the state of development where the sense of 'I,' 'Me,' and 'Mine,' vanishes; where we see all creation as one on the spiritual plane. Therefore it is said in the Bhagavad Gītā: "He who sees the same divine Self equally abiding in all, doth not kill himself by his Self and so attaineth the supreme goal."

In: Abhedānanda, *Doctrine of Karma* (3rd ed., Calcutta, 1947), pp. 116f.

88. "Because the Godhead is within each one of us, Vedanta teaches not merely the brotherhood, but the identity of man with man. It says, 'Thou art that.' Every soul is your own soul. Every creature is yourself. If you harm anyone, you harm yourself."

In: Akhilānanda, *Hindu Psychology: Its Meaning for the West* (2nd ed., London, 1953), p. 226 (foreword dated 'Vedanta Society, Boston, Massachusetts, November 12, 1945').

89. The original is in Marathi, with the title *Śrīmadbhagavadgītārahasya athavā karmayogaśāstra,* and was published in Pune (Poona) in 1915. English translation by Bhalchandra Sitaram Sukthankar: B. G. Tilak, *Śrīmad Bhagavadgītā Rahasya or Karma-Yoga-Śāstra,* 2 vols. (Poona, 1935–36).

90. T. H. Green, *Prolegomena to Ethics,* first published 1883.

91. P. 225 of the original; p. 313 of the English translation.

92. *āpaṇa hoūna-ca cāgalyā mārgalā lāgato* (p. 792 of the original; p. 1121 of the English translation).

93. Cf. p. 480 of the original; p. 681 of the English translation.

94. *sukha aso vā duḥkha aso, āpalyāpramāṇe itarānā aśā (ātmaupamya-) dṛṣṭīne jo sarvatra sārakh pāhū lāgalā* ... (p. 705). [The translation above follows Hacker's translation of Tilak's Marathi translation of *Bhagavad-Gītā* 6, 32; Sukthankar's English version of Tilak's book (p. 999) reads:

> who has begun to look everywhere with a (Self-Identifying-) Vision according to which, others are the same as himself...]

95. Sukthankar accordingly translates *ātmaupamya* as 'self-identification.'

96. P. 382 of the original; pp. 534f. of the English translation. [This translation is followed here; it includes the slanted rendering 'self-identification' mentioned in note 94. The Sanskrit words in brackets are those used in the original Marathi and supplied by Hacker.]

97. P. V. Kane, *History of Dharmaśāstra,* Vol. II, Pt. 1 (Pune, 1941), p. 7.

98. M. Hiriyanna, *Popular Essays in Indian Philosophy* (Mysore, 1952), pp. 85f.

99. See above, note 9.

100. 2nd ed., London, 1940 (1st ed.: 1939). The passage quoted is on p. 101. A very faulty German translation by F. Thierfelder was published in Darmstadt and Geneva in 1952; its title *Die Gemeinschaft des Geistes* ['the community of the spirit'] does not correctly indicate the contents of the book. The relevant passage is on p. 116.—Editor's note: On Radhakrishnan as "living" writer, see above, note 84.

101. A. Schweitzer, [*Indian Thought and Its Development,* tr. Mrs. C. E. B. Russell (London, 1936), p. 43. This is the source quoted by Radhakrishnan; Hacker quotes the original German:] *Die Weltanschauung der indischen Denker* (Munich, 1935), p. 28.

102. [*The World as Will and Idea,* tr. Haldane and Kemp, vol. I, pp. 481f.]

103. P. T. Raju, "The Inward Absolute and the Activism of the Finite Self"; in: *Contemporary Indian Philosophy,* ed. S. Radhakrishnan and J. H. Muirhead, 2nd ed. (London, 1952), pp. 509–34; quotation from pp. 532ff.

104. Cf. also P. Hacker, "Der Dharmabegriff des Neuhinduismus." ZMR 42 (1958) pp. 1–15 (*Kl. Schr.,* pp. 510–524); for an English translation, see Chapter 12 in this volume.

105. See the essay cited in note 104.

106. See above, pp. 288 ff.

107. See above, pp. 291 ff.

14

Vivekananda's Religious Nationalism

Narendra Nath Datta (this was Vivekananda's name before he adopted the life-style of a Hindu ascetic) was born on January 12, 1863, in Calcutta. By caste, he was a kāyastha. The scribes of the princes used to be members of this caste. Accordingly, the kāyasthas view themselves as a subcaste of the nobility, the kṣatriyas, although some accord them only the status of śūdras. Later on, Vivekananda himself defended with passion his kṣatriya descent and rejected the claim that he was a śūdra.[1]

Narendra, who was to become Vivekananda, studied at Presidency College and the Scottish Church College in Calcutta and was awarded the degree of B.A. in 1884.[2] He also acquired a good traditional training in Sanskrit, partly under the guidance of pandits.[3] His youthful theistic faith in God, which was influenced by the reform group of the Brahma Samāj, collapsed after he became acquainted with the philosophers of European positivism.[4] He studied the positivists John Stuart Mill and Auguste Comte,[5] also the skeptic Hume and the agnostic Herbert Spencer.[6] But the world view designed by one of his friends saved him from becoming engulfed in skepticism and agnosticism; in this world view, the faith in reason characteristic of the European age of enlightenment was combined with Hindu spiritual monism.[7] In Vivekananda's later thought, the influence of positivism[8] is still quite alive, as well as strong rationalistic tendencies. As a matter of fact, these philosophical tendencies have molded the style and content of his thought at least as much as the great religious experience of his adolescence, which was to determine his path up to his early death (he died on July 4, 1902).

This experience was the encounter with Ramakrishna. Ramakrishna lived from 1836 to 1886. He was a temple priest, a devotee of the goddess Kālī, and an ecstatic mystic. He tried to demonstrate in an experiential fashion (and this makes his procedure remarkable in the history of religions) that all religions, in particular Hinduism, Islam, and Christianity, constitute equal paths to God. In doing so, he identified emotionally with each one of the three religions in succession through strongly emotional contemplation. In each of these cases, this led to a vision, and this was for Ramakrishna the proof for the equality of the religions.[9] Narendra (Vivekananda) did not try to repeat these experiences of his master for himself, but he remained theoretically committed to the doctrine of the equality of religions, as derived from Ramakrishna's experiences.[10] But this doctrine was not the most decisive spiritual inspiration which he owed to Ramakrishna; rather, it was mystical immersion as such. Through such immersion, i.e., through mystical experience, Narendra learned that there was, indeed, religious experience in the form of direct experience of the religious object as something real. This was for him the final conquest of positivistic skepticism. The dogmatic system to which he committed himself was that of Advaita Vedānta, of spiritual monism. In mystical experience, he was certain of the identity of God and the soul.

Narendra is said to have been Ramakrishna's favorite disciple;[11] Ramakrishna, we are told, bequeathed to him his spiritual power.[12] However, he shared the emotional disposition of his master's religiosity only while he was a young man; as an adult, he distanced himself from it and sometimes rejected emotional enthusiasm as a weakness. His preaching did not appeal to feeling, but to the intellect and will power.[13]

In Vivekananda's divided soul, an emotional, trustful theistic Hindu piety always coexisted with his philosophical monism and rationalism, and with his nationalism and altruistic activism;[14] this was the living continuation of what had developed in him during his association with his master Ramakrishna, Ramakrishna was the true center of Vivekananda's *religion*. Vivekananda's thought, as well as his practical life, was completely permeated by a religious fervor which had been kindled by the personality of the master. He worshipped Ramakrishna like a God, or even *as* God, and prayed to him.[15] He believed that the dead master was active through him.[16] He wanted to see Ramakrishna being worshipped and his teachings being disseminated.[17] Vivekananda taught that Ramakrishna was the living commentary to all the sacred scriptures of the Hindus,[18] and that he combined within himself the results of thousands of years of Hindu religious life.[19] With his birth the Golden Age, the "Age of Truth," had once again dawned.[20]

For Vivekananda, Ramakrishna's greatest significance was not to be found in a reproducible doctrine but in the general inspiration which he felt was emanating from the personality and the life of the master. In his own activities he did not always stay within the framework of what Ramakrishna had done and said. Indeed, one has to admit that Vivekananda's own project (i.e., the foundation of the Ramakrishna Order for the propagation of Hinduism in India and abroad, for popular education, and for philanthropic work) was in no way directly inspired by Ramakrishna's ideas. Some of the other disciples of the master held this expressly against him. This is what he had to say against such charges: "Shri Ramakrishna is far greater than his disciples understand him to be. He is the embodiment of infinite spiritual ideas capable of development in infinite ways. . . . One gracious glance of his eyes can create a hundred thousand Vivekananadas at this instant! If he chooses now instead to work through me, making me his instrument, I can only bow to his will."[21]

His adoration of Ramakrishna was deification of the guru in the genuine Hindu sense. Vivekananda knew himself at one with the eternal spirit of his guru, even if he did not follow the tradition of his spoken words in a strict sense. By using the traditional guru cult, he justified, in his own Hindu manner, that which was untraditional and new in his teaching and practice. In one essential sense, this new element can be described as "religious nationalism." I want to deal with it in greater detail. Vivekananda believed that Ramakrishna's spirit, and with it the spirit of all the millennia of the Hindu religion, was alive in himself, and that his thought and action were directed by this spirit. Therefore, he was convinced that his plans and activities were nothing foreign and new, but only an unfolding of the original spirit of Hinduism.

For some time after the death of Ramakrishna, Narendra lived with other disciples of the master in a small monastery; at other times, he wandered around the country in the manner of Hindu itinerant monks. A few letters are the only indubitable documents for his inner development during that time, i.e., in the years from 1886 to 1893, between his twenty-third and his thirtieth year. These letters reveal his zeal for learning, his serious craving for philosophical knowledge and religious experience, and his ardent devotion to the deceased master. They do not yet reveal those traits which are characteristic of the later Vivekananda—the man whom we may call one of the fathers of Neo-Hinduism. However, later documents, for instance Vivekananda's letter of March 19, 1894,[22] ascribe to the end of that seven-year period an experience and an idea which already breathe the spirit of the last nine years of his life. The experience was the shock caused by the humiliation and poverty of the Indian people, and this led to his determination to improve the condition of his people. Such thoughts constitute a major change in his inner life. Only four years earlier, in 1890,[23] Narendra had felt inadequate because he caught himself constantly thinking of the interests and the well-being of others instead of his own ultimate salvation. This was still the traditional attitude typical of a Hindu ascetic—to care for oneself and not for others. Even years later, after his views had changed, Vivekananda could still be gripped, in a period of exhaustion, by the notion that his drive to help others was only māyā, the play of the great cosmic illusion,[24] just as in March, 1890, Narendra had seen his inclination to care for the well-being of others as an aberration. Nonetheless, the letter of March, 1890, foretells that altruistic activism which became so characteristic of Vivekananda after 1893. The Narendra of 1890 is still different from the Vivekananda of 1893–1894; but looking back from his later years to the earlier statement, one recognizes what was to come; on the other hand, the old Hindu-style soteriological individualism had occasional revivals even in his later years.

After his encounter with Ramakrishna, the second great event in Vivekananda's life was his exposure to the Western way of life, i.e., the United States of America and Europe. In connection with a World Fair, a meeting of representatives of all world religions was held in Chicago in 1893; it was called "Parliament of Religions." Narendra (since about 1893 he called himself Vivekananda)[25] heard of the project of this "Parliament" and decided to travel to America and to represent Hinduism. Friends provided him with the necessary financial resources. He traveled to Chicago and delivered his speech at the "Parliament of Religions." He stayed in the West until 1896, mostly in the United States, with interim journeys to Europe, especially England. In the years 1899 and 1900, he was again in the United States and in Europe, where he attended the international congress for the history of religion in Paris. During his first stay in the West, he established himself as the Vivekananda who made history as the most influential shaper and propagator of the Neo-Hindu spirit.

Why did Vivekananda travel to America? To answer this question, we have to rely on the most authentic documents, the extant letters of Vivekananda. On September 20, 1892, i.e., eight months before his departure, he wrote: "We must travel, we must go to foreign parts. We must see how the engine of society works in other countries, and keep free and open communication with what is going on in the minds of other nations, if we really want to be a nation again."[26]

The idea of how to achieve nationhood thus emerges in the mind of the 29-year old Vivekananda. This idea continued to accompany him for the remaining ten years of his life. How does a group of humans who coexist in the same geographical region become a nation? The passage from the letter just quoted mentions the communication with foreign nations as a condition for becoming a nation. But according to Vivekananda, the essence of nationhood does not simply consist in the exchange with foreign nations. The people of a country, so he says, form a nation when "civilization and education" have permeated the masses.[27] This is the case in the Western countries, but not yet in India. Therefore, the people of those countries form nations, but not the Indians. In Vivekananda's view, this is the reason why it was so easy for the British to conquer India; they were a nation, while the Indians were not. In 1897 he wrote: "The chief cause of India's ruin has been the monopolizing of the whole education and intelligence of the land, by dint of pride and royal authority, among a handful of men. If we are to rise again, we shall have to do it in the same way [as the Western nations], i.e., by spreading education among the masses."[28] In March, 1894, he declared: "We, as a nation, have lost our individuality, and that is the cause of all mischief in India. We have to give back to the nation its lost individuality and *raise the masses.*"[29]

This is the motto which emerges again and again in Vivekananda's letters and speeches: uplift of the masses. In a letter from Yokohama dated July 10, 1893, while on his journey to America, he had already stated the following demands: ". . . to struggle unto life and death to bring about a new state of things—sympathy for the poor and bread to their hungry mouths, enlightenment to the people at large—and struggle unto death to make men of them who have been brought to the level of beasts by the tyranny of your forefathers."[30]

Vivekananda understood the uplift of the masses primarily in an intellectual sense. Accordingly, popular education, religious as well as secular, constitutes for him the most important means for reaching this goal. In several letters from the West, he explained the motive and the purpose of his journey as follows: he had gone to America to acquire the financial resources necessary to help the oppressed masses of India.[31]

After his return to India, he said in 1897 in one of his speeches: "In Europe, political ideas form the national unity. In Asia (Vivekananda means, of course, India in particular), religious ideals form the national unity."[32] This was an idea which had to generate its own reality. When it was first uttered, there was hardly any reality corresponding to it. It would simply be anachronistic to speak of an Indian *nation* or of an Indian *national consciousness* prior to the time of European influence; as a matter of fact, Vivekananda himself deplored that there was no nation and no national consciousness in nineteenth-century India. However, this idea soon *became* reality, and in an eminent sense this was due to Vivekananda's work. Indeed, the Indian nationalism to which Vivekananda contributed so energetically is different from all other types of nationalism in the world insofar as it is not inspired by *political* recollections and *political* ideologies but by cultural ones. In a country where the Hindus constitute the predominant religious group, this means: by the religious ideas of Hinduism.

For India to become a nation, Hinduism should, according to Vivekananda's postulate, forget its inner tensions and conflicts, and it should understand itself as a unity.[33] Such ideas reveal clearly that nationalism is the origin and the driving force of the Neo-Hindu conception of unity. After all, the Hindu group of religions is little more than a geographical unity. Within it we find many common denominators, but even more antagonism, rivalry, and division. Hinduism, according to Vivekandana's demand, should understand itself as a unity so that India can become a nation. However, this idea of unity can be maintained only insofar as *one* of the Hindu systems, i.e., the monistic Vedānta system, is considered to be universally superior; all other types of religion found within Hinduism are recognized as its preliminary stages and as having a relative validity only. In short, Vivekananda's idea of the unity of Hinduism amounts to the proclamation of the superior and universal authority of Advaita Vedānta. And this authority has to prevail for the sake of nationhood.

For Vivekananda, religion and nation are one. Therefore, he says: "Our vigor, our strength, nay, our national life is in our religion."[34] Therefore he considers it necessary for the genesis of the nation that Hinduism be reformed.[35]

Some reformers had held the view that religion, i.e., Hinduism, was the cause of India's national breakdown. Vivekananda rejects this view passionately.[36] "Religion therefore is not to blame, but men."[37] "With all their faults the Hindus are head and shoulders above all other nations in morality and spirituality."[38] Notice that Vivekananda says "head and shoulders above all other *nations*," not "*religions!*" Against the earlier reform movements, especially the Brāhma Samāj and the Ārya Samāj, Vivekananda raised the charge that they had been insufficiently national. They were, he says, "useless mixtures; they were only voices of apology to our English masters to allow us to live! We have started a *new India*," he wrote proudly in October, 1899. "The test of truth for this Brahmo Samaj is 'what our masters approve'; with us, what the Indian reasoning and experience approves."[39] Prior to his first journey to America in 1892–1893, he had already stated as a rule: "Everything that comes from India take as true until you find cogent reasons for disbelieving it. Everything that comes from Europe take as false until you find cogent reasons for believing it."[40] Vivekananda thus initiated a way of thinking which is still alive today and which has, in extreme cases, produced the tendency to elevate the geographical and national concepts of East and West almost to the level of metaphysical categories.

Such religious and nationalistic ideas sound highly political, and insofar as their practical consequences are concerned, they are, indeed, political, even if their original and immediate intent was not political. However, Vivekananda always rejected direct political action; likewise, he was not interested in any social reforms that were isolated from the spiritual dimension.[41] It is a sign of his greatness that he saw the pivotal point for any reform in the spiritual sphere; for him as a Hindu this meant in religion.[42]

The reform out of the sources of his own tradition which Vivekananda tried to bring about does not amount to self-isolation. On the contrary, in his view, contact with foreign nations is indispensable for the genesis of nationhood and for an awareness of one's own identity; this is what we have already seen in his letter of September, 1892. Elsewhere he emphasizes time and again that the Hindus have to learn from the others,[43] but that on the other hand external expansion is necessary to activate and invigorate one's own vitality.[44]

What should the Hindus learn from the West? They should adopt the spirit of the Western social order, the spirit of equality and liberty, of work and energy, and they should combine these attributes with Hindu religiosity.[45] They should acquire the capacity of organization and cooperation.[46] They should combine "some of the active and heroic elements of the West with the calm virtues of the Hindus."[47] They should learn the natural sciences of the West.[48] Vivekananda was particularly impressed by the solidarity and public charity which he found to be highly developed in America. On the other hand, he complained bitterly that the Indians only knew how to lament their poverty but were unable to move toward practical improvement and did not even develop any compassion "for the two hundred millions of men and women sunken forever in poverty and ignorance."[49]

For anyone who reads how Vivekananda combines his praise of the American social structure with bitter criticism of the Indian life, it will be evident that he has learned important lessons in America. It was, above all, his contact with America which turned him into an altruistic activist and an organizer of philanthropy and popular education; as such, he was a phenomenon without precedent in the history of Hinduism. From America he constantly admonished his friends at home with urgent requests, trying to shake them up, full of intense fervor, imploring them, often in a harsh tone, sometimes sharply reprimanding them. They should work incessantly, overcome the national temptations of inertia and jealousy, and recruit more fellow-ascetics. The itinerant monks should not only preach Ramakrishna's religious ideas but also lecture about secular knowledge.[50] They should start journals and establish centers of preaching and training for sannyāsins. In April, 1896, his plans crystallized and produced a detailed outline for the organization and structure of such a center.[51]

As we have heard, the second objective of making contact with foreign nations is external expansion. In theory and when the occasion seems right, Vivekananda sometimes advocates the idea of the equality and community of all religions;[52] in practice, however, he was interested in and pursued concerted missionary activities in America and England. In part, this was obviously meant to counteract the Christian mission. In July, 1895, he wrote to the Mahārāja of Khetri: "The more the Christian priests oppose me, the more I am determined to leave a permanent mark on their country."[53] For years he himself preached Vedānta in the United States and England. The Indian religious centers which he planned and established were supposed to send preachers into every country of the world.[54] "Half the United States can be conquered in ten years," he stated in 1896.[55] In 1899, he wrote with proud irony: "I am going to deluge your Yankee land with idolatrous missionaries."[56] "England we shall conquer, England we shall possess, through the power of spirituality . . . Conquest of England, Europe, and America—this should be our one supreme Mantra at present, in it lies the well-being of the country"—thus in 1897.[57]

"Within fifty years the educated of the world will come to believe in the eternity of both soul and creation, and in God as our highest and perfect nature, as taught in our holy Vedas"—this is his proud prediction to the Mahārāja of Mysore in 1894.[58] "My idea is the conquest of the whole world by the Hindu race . . . Up, India, and conquer the world with your spirituality! . . . The only condition of national life, of awakened and vigorous national life, is the conquest of the world by Indian thought."[59] These are statements from one of the speeches which Vivekananda gave in 1897, after his return from the West. In an interview in 1899, he stated that conversions to Hinduism were possible and welcome, even if the convert or his ancestors had not previously been part of Hinduism.[60]

The kind of Hinduism for which Vivekananda wants to "conquer" the world is the Vedānta. Hinduism and Vedānta are for him almost synonyms,[61] and the culmination of all the trends in Vedānta is the absolute monism of Advaita.[62] Theoretically, and in accordance with the way of thinking of his master Ramakrishna, Vivekananda held the view that Hinduism does not make a distinction between true and false religion, but only between stages of truth.[63] In practice, however, he claims that Vedānta is the universal human religion,[64] and he proclaims vigorously and repeatedly: "Ours is the true religion."[65]

What makes, according to Vivekananda, this religion so well suited not only to serve the national resurrection of India, but also to fulfil the aspirations of mankind? In 1892–1893, prior to his journey to America, he still held the view that ultimate Advaitism could not be brought down to the level of practical life.[66] This is in accordance with the original and traditional understanding of the Vedānta philosophy, because in its essence Advaita Vedānta is the most world-negating world view which we find in the world. But in four different ways, Vivekananda proceeded to give a worldly, practical application to this most unworldly of all philosophies and to provide it with the capacity to be the national religion he was looking for and, moreover, the expanding universal religion of which his national pride was dreaming.

First of all, he applied the Vedānta doctrine to individual life, the self-education of the individual person. Advaita Vedānta teaches the identity of the individual with the highest self, of the soul with God. In its basic intention, this doctrine is entirely metaphysical, unworldly, and abstract. But to derive practical benefit from it, Vivekananda draws it into the psychological and worldly realm. He concludes: If in my own innermost essence I am God, and if I become so well-versed in this awareness that it permeates me completely, then this must give me an irresistible self-confidence, a faith in myself which will produce an enormous strength for great achievements. To make this source of strength accessible, Vivekananda preached incessantly the doctrine of the divine essence of man, and he always emphasized as its practical consequence that this teaching justifies an unlimited faith of man in himself, and that it unlocks strength for practical action. He taught: "You can do anything and everything, you are almighty." "The Vedanta teaches men to have faith in themselves first." "The old religions said that he was an atheist who did not believe in God. The new religion says that he is an atheist who does not believe in himself." Vivekananda adds: "But it is not a selfish faith, because the Vedanta, again, is the doctrine of oneness. It means faith in all, because you are all."[67] I shall return soon to this altruistic extension.

According to Vivekananda, anybody can experience the divinity of man, or God in man.[68] The influence of the school of Ramakrishna may be found in this view. Vivekananda wants to make the content of this mysticism of identity accessible to everybody. Through appropriate education, the faith of man in himself is awakened, and through such faith the absolute brahman which is dormant in man.[69] Vivekananda deplores bitterly that the Hindus, who discovered the divinity of the self, completely forgot this doctrine in their practical life. Nations that do not believe in it practice it better than the Hindus. I quote some statements from speeches which Vivekananda gave in 1897 after his return from the West:

> What our country now wants are muscles of iron and nerves of steel, gigantic wills which nothing can resist . . . and that can only be created, established, and strengthened by understanding and realizing the ideal of the Advaita, that ideal of the oneness of all. Faith, faith, faith in ourselves, faith, faith in God—this is the secret of greatness. If you have faith in all the three hundred and thirty millions of your mythological gods, and in all the gods which foreigners have now and again introduced into your midst, and still have no faith in yourselves, there is no salvation for you. Have faith in yourselves, and stand up on that faith and be strong; that is what we need. Why is it that we three hundred and thirty millions of people have been ruled for the last one thousand years by any and every handful of foreigners who chose to walk over our prostrate bodies? Because they had faith in themselves and we had not . . . I saw that inside the national hearts of both Europe and America

resides the tremendous power of the men's faith in themselves . . . We have lost faith in ourselves. Therefore to preach the Advaita aspect of the Vedanta is necessary to rouse up the hearts of men, to show them the glory of their souls."[70] "Stand up, assert yourself, proclaim the God within you, do not deny Him!"[71] "The Englishman believes in himself and you do not. He believes in his being an Englishman, and he can do anything. That brings out the God within him, and he can do anything he likes. . . . What we want is strength, so believe in yourselves. . . . We have wept long enough . . . stand on your feet and be men. It is a man-making religion that we want. It is man-making theories that we want. It is man-making education all round that we want."[72] "We are weak, very weak. . . . We are lazy, we cannot work; we cannot combine, we do not love each other; we are intensely selfish, not three of us can come together without hating each other, without being jealous of each other. . . . What is the cause of that? Physical weakness. . . . Be strong, my young friends: that is my advice to you. . . . Feel that you are great and you become great. . . . You have no faith in yourselves! Centuries and centuries, a thousand years of crushing tyranny of castes and kings and foreigners and your own people have taken out all your strength, my brethren. Your backbone is broken . . . Who will give you strength? Let me tell you, strength, strength is what we want. And the first step in getting strength is to uphold the Upanishads, and believe—'I am the Soul' . . . I am the Omnipotent, I am the Omniscient."[73]

Thus Vivekananda derives from the Upaniṣads a nationalistic, even an almost political religion. The Vedānta of the Upaniṣads, which had been meant in a very different sense, is supposed to be put to use for the rise of India, simply in the following manner: the metaphysical monism, the identification of God and the soul, is supposed to yield a faith of man in himself, a psychological attitude which lets man expect great things, or indeed everything, of himself, and thus gives him great mental and physical strength. Education and self-education are supposed to build up and cultivate this attitude.

This educational goal also requires negative demarcations—not only against the vices of laziness, cowardice, selfishness, ingratitude, slavishness, and especially jealousy (in his letters and speeches Vivekananda criticizes these character flaws innumerable times with relentless harshness and rigor) but also against humility, which Vivekananda does not recognize as a virtue,[74] and against the Christian doctrine that man is sinful. He states sharply: "The Vedanta recognizes no sin, it only recognizes error. And the greatest error, says the Vedanta, is to say that you are weak, that you are a sinner."[75]

A second practical application of Vedāntic monism relates to community life and reveals clearly the influence of European positivism. Positivism *substitutes* mankind for God; Vivekananda *identifies* God with the totality of human souls or with mankind. Thus he says: "Ishwara is the sum total of individuals; yet He Himself is also an individual . . . Samashti or the Collective is God."[76] For Vivekananda, just as for positivism, divine service becomes service to mankind: ". . . worship the Living God, the Man-God—every being that wears a human form—God in His universal as well as individual aspect. The universal aspect of God means this world, and worshipping it means serving it—this indeed is work, not indulging in ceremonials. . . . preach this worship of the universal aspect of the Godhead."[77] ". . . the only God I believe in, the sum total of all souls—and above all, my God the wicked, my God the miserable, my God the poor of all races, of all species, is the special object of my worship."[78]

According to Vivekananda, the identification of the *totality* of human souls thus leads to altruistic *service* to *mankind;* the identification of the *individual* soul with God is supposed to produce an invigorating *faith* of man *in himself.* It seems that the altruism of Vivekananda cannot be traced back to Christian influence, certainly not with regard to its philosophical justification, because this justification shows unmistakable traces of that *secularization* of Christianity which was systematized in positivism.

The notion that mankind is God took a somewhat different turn with Vivekananda after he became acquainted with Schopenhauer's and Deussen's ethical application of the Upaniṣadic sentence *tat tvam asi.* This is his third adjustment of the Vedānta metaphysics to the practical philosophy which he needed. Unlike the positivistic reinterpretation of the Vedāntic monism, it does not look at mankind as a collective, but at the other as an individual, or at the others as individuals, and then establishes the ethical imperative as follows: Do good to the other, because the other is in reality yourself. Vivekananda taught this foundation of ethics, which is seemingly Hindu-monistic but in reality Schopenhauerian, side by side with the positivistic-monistic one. At this point, I don't want to enlarge on this foundation. I have dealt with it in my article "Schopenhauer und die Ethik des Hinduismus" in the journal

Saeculum (1961), I would just like to note that I, when I wrote that article, had not yet recognized the *apposition* of Schopenhauer's foundation of morality with Vivekananda's positivistic ethic and the imperative of believing in one's own self.[79]

Finally, a fourth practical application of Advaita Vedānta proclaims it to be the modern religion of mankind. According to Vivekananda, the Vedāntic monism is the only religion which is in accordance with the thought of modern natural science. Vivekananda states that every (natural) science tries to find a unitary and single principle from which everything else can be derived. But Hinduism has possessed such a principle all along in the Vedānta system.[80] Thus Vedāntism alone can hold out against the claims of the natural sciences.[81] Four years prior to his American journey, young Narendra already saw a kind of Advaitism in the doctrine of evolution produced by European science.[82] According to Vivekananda, Vedānta also agrees with modern scientific thought in that it does not demand faith, but is instead based on experience, i.e., on a spiritual experiment, just as the sciences are based on material experiments.[83] Here, Vivekananda forgets that Vedānta, even if it promises a gnosis as its goal, first requires devotion and faith from its disciples.[84] Vivekananda thinks that Vedānta alone, because it does not demand faith, is destined to be the future religion of the educated part of mankind.[85] But here, we have to note the reason why Vivekananda's version of Vedānta seemed to agree so well with that rationalism which had turned science into a surrogate religion: he himself had already filtered the Vedānta in a positivistic and rationalistic sense.

The religious nationalism which I have tried to describe is not the totality of Vivekananda's thought. In my introduction, I have referred to another, genuinely religious force in his personality: the inspiration which he received from his master Ramakrishna. Many interesting observations could be made if we were to draw a complete picture of Vivekananda's thought and practical work. We could, for instance, investigate in a more comprehensive manner how Vivekananda interpreted and popularized ideas of traditional Hindu philosophy. We could also present in detail the events relating to the foundation of his organization, the Ramakrishna Mission. My present investigation was only meant to illustrate *one* of the essential motivating forces in Vivekananda's thought and practice. His historical position and his accomplishment can be assessed realistically only if we recognize the crucial importance of his religious nationalism.

This religious nationalism has had an extraordinary effect. Together with other movements, for instance the Theosophical movement, the spiritual current generated by Vivekananda has contributed significantly to raising the national self-awareness of the Indians and thus, ultimately, also to the political liberation of the country. This is a historical achievement that has to be recognized quite apart from any evaluation of its justifications and motivations. Another lasting accomplishment is Vivekananda's vigorous opposition to the *mleccha* ideology,[86] i.e., that attitude which does not deem the mleccha or non-Indian worthy of any attention. Vivekananda, the philosophical nationalist, has at the same time effectively promoted India's intellectual relations with the world abroad. There was yet another courageous achievement of great significance: within Hinduism and against an all-powerful individualistic tradition, Vivekananda propagated the religious relevance of the spirit of community, the service to one's neighbor, and he promoted it by creating philanthropic organizations. This remains remarkable quite apart from the positivistic and monistic doctrine through which Vivekananda tried to justify the idea of service to mankind.

On the other hand, we cannot refrain from stating the limits of our recognition. There is more than one element in Vivekananda's religious nationalism that reminds us in an unpleasant manner of an ideological nationalism which we have experienced in our own country and which we do not want back. The slogan "religion out of blood and soil" ("Religion aus Blut und Boden") already suggests a distressing analogy. Some very questionable elements may also be found in Vivekananda's ideas concerning the intellectual and spiritual contact with the non-Hindu world. In an essential sense, this contact is represented by the encounter between Hinduism and Christianity. In principle and in theory, Vivekananda advocated the unity or equality of all religions. But the primacy of Hinduism in its Vedāntic form was always taken for granted. In an address at the Vedānta center Kumbhakonam, he declared emphatically: "Ours is the true religion."[87] Just as a medieval Vedāntin could view all other religious and philosophical systems of *Hinduism* as imperfect preliminary stages of his own system,[88] so Vivekananda regarded *all religions of the world,* especially Christianity, as preliminary stages of Advaita Vedānta. He maintained that the Christians did not yet understand their own religion; they would understand it properly only in the light of the Vedānta.[89] Thus he could refer quite casually to a conquest of the Christian countries for Hinduism. His idea of the equality of all religions, which he adopted in theory, is—to say the least—very ambiguous. Moreover, it seems that he never made an effort to learn about Christian doctrine and spirituality thoroughly and patiently. His statements on

Christianity remain at the surface; they are often distorted and sometimes on a rather low level.[90]

In large part, these defects are historically understandable if we consider the fact that Vivekananda's defense of Hinduism, under the skilful formula of the equality of all religions, was a reaction to the colonialism of that time, during which the Christian missionaries on their part did not make any effort to study Hinduism thoroughly. But for this very reason Vivekananda's method is as obsolete today as that missionary practice. What is needed today in the encounter between Christianity and Hinduism is careful attention to the position of the other and an exchange of thoughts conducted in mutual human recognition, but without concealing contradictions and without simulating concordance, an exchange which is free, objective, and committed to truth. Vivekananda has not conducted such a dialogue. As his letters show, his dialogue partners were always such Americans and Europeans who were ready to accept his ideas.

Notes

In the notes, the following works are cited in abbreviated references:

Only volume and page numbers (for instance, vol. VI, p. 184) are given for *The Complete Works of Vivekananda.* Mayavati Memorial Edition, Calcutta; vol. I, 8th ed., 1950; vol. II, 7th ed., 1948; vol. III, 6th ed., 1948; vol. IV, 6th ed., 1948; vol. V, 6th ed., 1954; vol. VI, 5th ed., 1951; vol. VII, 4th ed., 1953; vol. VIII, 1st ed., 1951. The references are not exhaustive. [The pagination differs with different editions. The page numbers given by Hacker do not necessarily apply to the later editions of the *Works.* As an illustration of the discrepancies, occasional references to other editions have been added to Hacker's own references.]

The Life of Vivekananda, by his Eastern and Western Disciples. Calcutta, 4th ed., 1949, is quoted as *Life.* [Here, too, the pagination may differ.] The present article is largely identical with a lecture which I have given at various places in 1963.

1. Vol. III, pp. 211 f.

2. *Life,* pp. 88 f.

3. See, for instance, vol. VI, pp. 179–83.

4. *Life,* p. 77.

5. *Life,* p. 72.

6. *Life,* p. 77.

7. *Life,* pp. 78 f.

8. See vol. VI, p. 184.

9. See J. N. Farquhar, *Modern Religious Movements in India* (New York, 1915), pp. 192 ff.; D. S. Sarma, *The Renaissance of Hinduism* (Benares, 1944), p. 239.

10. See vol. VI, p. 83.

11. *Life,* p. 43 ff.

12. *Life,* p. 148.

13. See, for instance, vol. III, pp. 237; 241 ff.; vol. V, pp. 260; 304; against enthusiasm: vol. VIII, p. 533.

14. See vol. VI, p. 268.

15. Vol. VI, p. 201.

16. Vol. VI, 297.

17. Vol. VI, pp. 159; 209; 245 f.; 253; 260; 281; 300; 302 f.

18. Vol. V, p. 41.

19. Vol. IV, p. 227; vol. VI, p. 276.

20. Vol. VI, pp. 287; 302.

21. *Life,* p. 515 [ed. 1965, p. 505].

22. Vol. VI, p. 225.

23. Vol. VI, p. 198.

24. Vol. VI, p. 264.

25. See D. S. Sarma, *The Renaissance of Hinduism,* p. 263.

26. Vol. V, p. 2 [10th ed.: p. 5].

27. Vol. VIII, p. 314; cf. vol. IV, p. 415.

28. [Hacker gives no reference for this quote. It is found in vol. IV, seventh impression, 1955, p. 482, in a letter to Sarala Ghosal on "The Education that India Needs."]

29. Vol. VI, pp. 225 f. [6th ed.: p. 255; this reference combines Hacker's notes 28 and 29].

30. Vol. V, pp. 8 f. [10th ed.: p. 11].

31. See, for instance, vol. V, p. 23; vol. VI, p. 226 (but cf. also pp. 216 f.); vol. VII, p. 411; vol. VIII, pp. 314; 317; 331.

32. Vol. III, pp. 286 f.

33. Vol. III, pp. 287 f.

34. Vol. III, p. 289.

35. Vol. V, p. 37; vol. VI, p. 226; vol. VIII, p. 316.

36. See, for instance, vol. V, p. 19.

37. Vol. VI, p. 226 [6th ed.: p. 255]; cf. vol. V, p. 37.

38. Vol. VIII, p. 331.

39. Vol. VIII, p. 485 [5th ed.: pp. 477 f.].

40. Vol. VI, p. 89 [9th ed.: p. 123].

41. Vol. IV, p. 415; vol. V, pp. 59; 145.

42. See, for instance, vol. V, p. 59.

43. Vol. III, p. 272; vol. V, p. 26; VIII, pp. 331 f.

44. Vol. III, pp. 272 f.; 277; vol. IV, pp. 310 f.; 419.

45. Vol. V, p. 26; vol. IV, p. 313.

46. See, for instance, vol. VIII, p. 336; cf. also vol. VI, p. 266.

47. Vol. VIII, pp. 331 f [5th ed.: p. 322].

48. Vol. III, p. 443.

49. Vol. V, pp. 23; 45 [10th ed.: p. 58].

50. Vol. III, p. 223; vol. VIII, p. 316.

51. Vol. VII, pp. 421 ff.

52. See, for instance, vol. IV, p. 176 (from a lecture in New York); vol. V, p. 121 (from an interview for the *Sunday Times*).

53. Vol. V, p. 69 [10th ed.: p. 91].

54. Vol. V, p. 92.

55. Vol. V, p. 87 [10th ed.: p. 117].

56. Vol. VIII, p. 470 [5th ed.: p. 462].

57. Vol. IV, p. 419 [10th ed.: p. 486].

58. Vol. IV, p. 308 [10th ed.: p. 362].

59. Vol. III, pp. 276 f.

60. Vol. V, p. 163 ("born aliens").

61. Vol. III, pp. 229; 323 f.

62. See, for instance, vol. V, p. 64.

63. Vol. I, p. 15; vol. II, pp. 360 ff.; vol. VI, p. 69.

64. See, for instance, vol. III, p. 182.

65. For instance, vol. III, p. 180.

66. Vol. VI, p. 88.

67. Vol. II, pp. 298; 292; 299 [11th ed.: pp. 292ff.].

68. See, for instance, vol. I, pp. 126 ff.; vol. II, pp. 162–74; vol. III, pp. 283 f.

69. Vol. IV, p. 416.

70. Vol. III, pp. 190 f.

71. Vol. III, p. 193.

72. Vol. III, p. 224.

73. Vol. III, pp. 241–44.

74. See, for instance, vol. V, p. 56; vol. VI, p. 276.

75. Vol. II, p. 293 [12th ed.: p. 295]; cf. p. 237.

76. Vol. VIII, p. 392 [5th ed.: p. 385].

77. Vol. VI, p. 279 [6th ed.: p. 265].

78. Vol. V, p. 106 [10th ed.: p. 137].

79. [In: *Kl. Schr.*, pp. 531–64; English trans. in the present volume, pp. 273–318].

80. See, for instance, vol. VII, p. 48.

81. Vol. I, pp. 373; 375.

82. Vol. VI, p. 184.

83. See, for instance, vol. I, pp. 128 ff.

84. Cf. Śaṅkara, *Brahmasūtrabhāṣya* I, 1,1; also my article "Über den Glauben in der Religionsphilosophie des Hinduismus." *ZMR* 38 (1954), pp. 51–66 [in: *Kl. Schr.*, pp. 360–75].

85. See, for instance, vol. I, pp. 370 ff.

86. For instance, vol. V, p. 40.

87. Vol. III, p. 180.

88. See, for instance, Madhusūdana Sarasvatī, *Prasthānabheda*.

89. Vol. I, p. 319.

90. Vol. III, p. 275; vol. V, pp. 344–439; vol. VI, p. 351.

15

A Prasthānatraya Commentary of Neo-Hinduism:

Remarks on the Work of Radhakrishnan

"In India the threefold canon of religion, *prasthāna-traya,* consists of the *Upaniṣads,* the *Bhagavadgītā,* and the *Brahma Sūtra* . . . I have written on the *Upaniṣads* and the *Bhagavadgītā,* and this study of the *Brahma Sūtra* may be a small contribution to the development of solidarity in thought to which the modern world is committed." These are statements from Radhakrishnan's preface (pp. 10 f.) to his annotated translation of the *Brahmasūtras.*[1] The prefaces to the annotated translations of the *Bhagavadgītā*[2] and a collection of eighteen *Upaniṣads,*[3] which Radhakrishnan published earlier, do not make it clear that he was already planning at that time to comment on all three basic texts. These texts certainly do not constitute the "canon of religion" in India, but they are basic texts for those religions or schools of Hinduism which purport to be Vedāntic.

The preface of the *Bhagavadgītā* commentary, published in 1948, places this work in the situation in which it originated; in a perilous postwar situation, so we are told, the Gītā is capable of providing valuable spiritual help. In his *Upaniṣad* commentary, Radhakrishnan even mentions a different trinity of basic texts: *Vedas* with *Upaniṣads, Bhagavadgītā,* and *Dhammapada* (p. 9). In the meantime, he had published an annotated translation of the *Dhammapada.*[4] It is characteristic of the Neo-Hindu that he wants to include Buddhism, too, in the "national" heritage. Yet it would not be quite appropriate to say that the old *prasthānatraya* has been turned into a *prasthānacatuṣṭaya.* In his introduction to the *Dhammapada,* Radhakrishnan distances himself in part from the specifically Buddhist doctrines, and in the preface to his version of the *Brahmasūtras,* he does not mention the *Dhammapada* at all. Thus we can speak of a Neo-Hindu *prasthānatraya* commentary. This designation is suggested by Radhakrishnan's words quoted at the beginning of this article, and even more so by his statement that "the *Upaniṣads,* the *Bhagavadgītā,* and the *Brahma Sūtra* are said to have unity of purpose and meaning, *aikārthya,*" and that it was his desire to explain this "general purport" in his Brahmasūtra commentary (p. 12). At the time when he wrote these words, i.e., in 1959, it was Radhakrishnan's obvious intention to resume the old *prasthānatraya* tradition.

Proposing this designation calls for comparative and differentiating reflections; in fact, it has meaning only insofar as it evokes such reflections. The similarity between the medieval *prasthānatraya* commentaries and those works by Radhakrishnan for which the same term might be used does not go very far. If we compare the case of a modern Hindu commenting on the old *prasthānatraya* with the commentaries on this trinity of basic texts produced in earlier centuries, then it becomes evident what is new and special in Neo-Hinduism.

We assess neither Radhakrishnan's history of philosophy[5] nor his translations and explanations of Hindu scripture properly if we equate them with products of philological and historical research. Radhakrishnan recognizes that he has derived benefit from the results of this research (*The Principal Upaniṣads,* p. 7). But in the first sentence of the preface to his Brahmasūtra commentary, he emphasizes: "This book is not a product of purely scholarly interests." Also, if we judge his philosophizing in terms of a strictly theoretical philosophizing, we miss its essence (this applies also to other modern Indian thinkers).[6] To be sure, Radhakrishnan says: ". . . my interest is philosophical" (*The Principal Upaniṣads,* p. 7). But here the word "philosophy" has a special meaning.

Radhakrishnan says of his annotated translation of the *Brahmasūtras*: "It has grown out of vital urges and under the pressure of a concrete historical situation." These words seem significant for understanding not only the book in whose preface they appear, but also Radhakrishnan's work in its entirety. The situation which afflicts him is primarily an Indian one. From a distance of approximately thirty years, he described how he had experienced this situation in his youth, as a student at Madras Christian College (1905–1909): "I was strongly persuaded of the inefficiency of the Hindu religion to which I attributed the political downfall of India . . . I remember the cold sense of reality, the depressing feeling of defeat that crept over me, as a causal relation between the anaemic Hindu religion and our political failure forced itself on my mind during those years."[7]

The situation which in those days gave him his "depressing feeling of defeat" was defined by the atmosphere of the Christian College. But the Indian situation in general was certainly similar. Centuries ago, conquering Islam had raised its absolutistic claims in India much more rigorously than the conquering Christians of the nineteenth century. Yet, by and large, Hinduism had remained unshaken. But now, there was this paralysis, this sense of spiritual defeat. At the same time, it was impossible not to think of the foreign religion. As it had happened earlier to Vivekananda (1863–1902), the debate with Christianity runs through Radhakrishnan's entire work. In addition, there is, of course, his response to Western intellectual culture and to Western forms of public life.

In all his books, Radhakrishnan refers time and again to his own situation. Now he views it from an Indian angle, now in a global perspective. In his descriptions of the situation, he speaks of "faith" which is "shaken," "venerable structures" which are "attacked," "customs of long centuries" which are being uprooted, "standards, aims and institutions" which are "challenged," "unstable equilibrium," "restlessness," "dissolution," "breakdown," "confusion," "gloomy moments in history," "fateful hour," "crises," "contradictions," "menace," "immense dangers," "insecurity."[8]

But the paralysis and dejection of his youth was transformed into positive and active responses. Assertion of the Hindu heritage, hope for the future, and the effort to contribute to the spiritual formation of this future: perhaps we may use these three notions to describe in a most general fashion the content of Radhakrishnan's work.

Others who were, like Radhakrishnan, suffering from the "depressing feeling" of the "inefficiency" of Hinduism, had paved the way for a reassessment of the Hindu heritage; the Neo-Vedāntin Vivekananda was one of the first among them. *Indian Philosophy* (1923–1927) and *The Hindu View of Life* (1927) are among Radhakrishnan's early works. They attempt a reinterpretation of the philosophical and religious heritage.

Indian Philosophy is a brilliant arrangement of report, selection, emphasis, critical assessment, and reinterpretation. *The Hindu View* is a fascinating idealization as well as a skilful reinterpretation. Since 1948, Radhakrishnan, in the four annotated translations mentioned earlier, made further contributions to the preservation and actualization of the heritage. The image of an idealized Hinduism emerges, time and again, also in his other books. Radhakrishnan does not overlook grievances and a "lack of vitality" in contemporary traditionalistic Hinduism. But he believes that the ideal as he sees it is a spiritual power which has kept Hinduism alive until now.[9] Glorifications of the value and continuity of the Hindu view of the world are not uncommon in Radhakrishnan's work.[10] When a contemporary thinker confronts him with a harsh formulation of a Christian viewpoint, he goes on the offensive.[11] At Madras Christian College, Hinduism had been criticized as "ethically unsound."[12] The claim that Hinduism did not have an ethics in the proper sense touched a nerve in Radhakrishnan and made him write the most detailed polemics ever produced by him.[13]

For Radhakrishnan, hope grows directly out of his consideration of a desperate situation.[14] It does not have a very definite content. It consists essentially in the prospect of a "religion of the spirit," which is supposed to unite mankind in "a fundamental unity with a free differentiation."[15] Radhakrishnan wants to contribute through his work to the realization of this goal. Therefore, he presents the spiritual achievements of the past in such a manner that they can become significant for the present. He presents his world view in a relatively systematic fashion in *An Idealist View of Life* (lectures delivered in 1929; published in 1932). In *Eastern Religions and Western Thought* (1939), he tries to observe religion as reality, doctrine, and ideal in a global perspective and throughout the course of history. Basically, this is an attempt to demonstrate the superiority of Hinduism by stating or insinuating that what is valuable in "Western" religions and philosophies owes such value to its affinity with an idealized spiritual Hinduism. In all his books, Radhakrishnan tries to show, through an effective use of quotations, that the spiritual, mystical essence of Hinduism is related to or identical with what is essential in all religions, especially in Christianity.[16] Time and again, he rejects absolutistic claims and religious propaganda. But he expects, for instance, Christians to give up what is essential for Christianity from its very origin,[17] in order to pave the way for an indefinite future. Doesn't this imply that he is soliciting recognition of the absolutistic claims of his own ideology? Most of his writings have, either in part or in their entirety, the character of an appeal. He is committed to a renewal of religion out of mysticism or "spiritual experience"; he assumes that religious experience is essentially the same in all religions, and it is his goal to initiate a "solidarity" or "interreligious friendship."

The extraordinary sensitivity with which Radhakrishnan responds to the Indian as well as global situation, and the exceptional alertness which lets him perceive inherent spiritual and intellectual forces, make him far superior to most of his Western critics and admirers. Apart from his brilliant style, these attributes seem to be a reason for the fascination emanating from his discourse. One cannot be indifferent toward someone who endures a situation of spiritual breakdown, insecurity, and indecision with such clear awareness, and who responds to it so vividly. Radhakrishnan compels our human sympathy, even if we find much to criticize in his work, and if we regard the direction of his search for new paths as wrong.

Radhakrishnan does not deal from a scholarly distance with the problems which disturb him, neither in the sense of a conceptual and argumentative nor of a speculative procedure. Literary style is the only means to gain that distance which is necessary for reflection; evocative and floating formulations stylize the problems; they do not solve them. His ideas combine indictment, defense, and appeal; it seems that his thought is always involved in and always responds to an actual situation. With versatility and open-mindedness he absorbs new ideas and suggestions, responds to them, uses them to exemplify and corroborate his judgments and proclamations, or integrates them in a vague synthesis. It is fascinating to find in the indices which have been added to most of his books, always more new names. The total number of thinkers and scholars with whom he debates in his writings is enormous. He is not so much concerned with what a particular writer meant to say with a particular statement in a given systematic context; he is always primarily interested in what their thoughts can contribute, in a positive or negative sense, to his own concerns, and how they can be utilized to illustrate, define, corroborate, and proclaim these concerns.

The religious figures, thinkers, and scholars of whom Radhakrishnan takes note and with whom he deals, as well as the events and conditions of his time, constitute the concrete characteristics of the situation whose "pressure" he feels. To identify and describe these characteristics, partly constant, partly variable, and to examine the means which Radhakrishnan employs to cope with them, would be a significant task not only with regard to the exploration of Radhakrishnan's work, but also with reference to an understanding of contemporary Indian spiritual and intellectual life in general. After all, the fact that he is one of its leading representatives seems to be an essential aspect of Radhakrishnan's importance.

With our preceding observations, we have already indicated essential departures from the internal structure of the old *prasthānatraya* commentaries. Rigorous argumentation is missing in Radhakrishnan's interpretation of the texts; also, the effort to demarcate truth against error, indispensable for all living metaphysics and theology, is missing. Radhakrishnan thinks that truth as such can never be adequately formulated, and that in today's world the distinction between different viewpoints is insignificant vis-à-vis the common necessity to affirm the spiritual. But this may appear as an impossible attempt to evade inescapable laws of thought. In his Brahmasūtra commentary, Radhakrishnan juxtaposes the views of the medieval commentators. In some passages, he adds his own thoughts and, as is his habit, quotations from Western philosophers and scientists, from mystics, the Bible, Christian theologians, Indian texts, etc. He does not weigh the different views, nor does he offer an opinion or decision.

Radhakrishnan says: "The Vedas . . . speak to men in their concrete situations" (*The Brahma Sūtra,* p. 113; this is probably an idea borrowed from Christian theologians). How do the Vedas, through the summary of their metaphysical doctrines in the Brahmasūtras, speak to him under the "pressure of a concrete historical situation" in which he finds himself?

An explicit commentary with Radhakrishnan's own thoughts is provided only for the first four Sūtras. Beginning with Sūtra I,1,5, pieces which one could call Radhakrishnan's own commentary are very rare. For the most part, his notes on the Sūtras consist of references to the views of the Indian commentators. Altogether, he considers twelve of them. (This makes his book valuable even for the historian of Indian philosophy. However, what was said by Śaṅkara himself, whom Radhakrishnan follows in most instances, cannot always be clearly distinguished from Radhakrishnan's interpretation.) It seems, then, that most Sūtras have not spoken to him in a direct fashion.

Let us review briefly his ideas concerning the first four Sūtras. His concluding remark on the first Sūtra is: "The main emphasis of this *sūtra* is that a candidate for spiritual knowledge and life should be morally pure" (p. 234). This is certainly in accordance with the Indian tradition, but at the same time, it reflects Radhakrishnan's interest in ethics, which is a product of the contemporary predicament.

The second Sūtra teaches that *brahman* is the cause of the world. Radhakrishnan notes: "In this *sūtra* we exclude the appeal to religious experience and take into account facts which are firmly established and universally acknowledged. The world tells its own story and offers its own suggestions" (p. 238). The style is harmonious, vague, and floating. Radhakrishnan strings views of the old Brahmasūtra commentaries together with those of the Bible, the Koran, Christian theologians, Western thinkers and scientists, and finally with pessimistic and atheistic views. Then he says: "This *sūtra* asks us to take a more universal and dispassionate view. The world moves . . . It is a perfecting process . . . The future is open. When we face disaster, we begin to doubt and despair . . . We are afraid that mankind will destroy itself. There is no inevitability about it. It will yet become a family. For the laws of nature and God co-operate with one another and the darkness we now are in is a herald not of death but of the dawn of a new era" (p. 240). It is not evident how these thoughts are connected with the sūtra, *janmādy asya yataḥ,* i.e., "[*brahman* is that] from which this [world] has its origin, [duration and destruction]." A connection could have been made by stating with determination and confidence: "*Brahman* preserves the world." But such determination is missing. Instead, modern anxiety about the world and hope for progress are expressed, even against the meaning of the Sūtra, which indicates preservation and destruction of the world but no "perfecting process."

The third Sūtra *(śāstrayonitvāt)* teaches that *brahman* is the source of the Veda, or that the Veda is the source of the knowledge of *brahman.* Here, Radhakrishnan presents his views concerning the knowledge of God; this has to be supplemented by the chapter "Reason and Revelation" in his introduction (pp. 103–118). In a formal sense, this topic and the Sūtra are well matched. The first and last criterion in Radhakrishnan's theology is inner experience. "Spiritual experience offers a valid proof for the experience of God" (p. 242). Similar statements are found in other works by Radhakrishnan. Surrendering to creative intuition constitutes faith (p. 116). Already in *The Hindu View of Life* (p. 16), Radhakrishnan (adding a symptomatic reference to Wesley, the founder of Methodism) derived *faith* from *experience;* he does so again in *The Brahma Sūtra.* He distinguishes (in the introduction, not in his commentary on Sūtra I,1,3) between *faith* and *belief.* Unlike faith, belief is not based on experience but on the acceptance of traditional doctrines. It corresponds to *śravaṇa,* the first level of Vedāntic instruction; it has to be elevated to the experience of *ātmadarśana* by means of reflection *(manana)* and meditation *(nididhyāsana).* In traditional terminology, the sacred texts of the Indian tradition are the "testimony of reliable witnesses" *(āptavacana).* In Radhakrishnan's interpretation, this means that they are "records of the experiences of the great seers" (pp. 113 and 250; cf. also p. 242: "spiritual experience which is registered in the *Śāstras*"); this alone accounts for their authority, not the assumption that they are the word of God. They come out of experience, and they are meant to guide us to experience.

With these thoughts, formally affiliated with the Hindu tradition, Radhakrishnan's concept of faith combines borrowings from most recent Western theology: "(Faith) is the response of the whole man, which includes assent of intellect and energy of will" (p. 245). That this idea, as far as its origin is concerned, is hardly compatible with the idea of *spiritual experience* is no problem for Radhakrishnan. Faith which originates from spiritual experience, or even consists in it, is, according to Radhakrishnan, not contrary to reason. To be sure, "the inadequacy of rational knowledge is accepted by all knowers of God." (In this connection, Radhakrishnan quotes a passage from the Bible,[18] which is, as often, not appropriate: "For the wisdom of the world is foolishness to God"; i.e., 1 *Corinthians* 3, 19). But "faith seeks understanding" (here, he quotes Anselm of Canterbury). "The seers of the Upaniṣads and the Buddha, Plato and Plotinus point to the validity of mystical experience on grounds of logical thought . . . Logical scrutiny is the one safeguard against mere caprice" (p. 246). The reader may think: if only Radhakrishnan himself had followed this sound rule. There is too much irritating logical (and historical) "caprice" in his work. But a more rigorous method would have forced him to revise his dogma of adogmatism, and it would have seriously jeopardized his method of harmonization. Harmonization *(samanvaya)* is the topic of Brahmasūtra I,1,4. Concerning this topic, Radhakrishnan notes: "Today this *samanvaya* or harmonization has to be extended to the living faiths of mankind" (p. 249). But the method of harmonization in the Brahmasūtras and its medieval commentators is certainly very different from the one which Radhakrishnan employs in all his works, and one cannot help saying that it is far more scientific, because it is more systematic.

Radhakrishnan's procedure is most simple; he juxtaposes everything he wants to consider as the expression of an inner experience. Attempts such as those made by the medieval Vedānta scholars to reconcile divergent texts on the basis of certain basic premises are missing. There is only a rudimentary kind of hermeneutics; it consists in the idea that the texts reflect spiritual experiences. But a systematic development of this principle is not to be found, neither in an explicit presentation nor implied in the interpretation. Philological questions are not asked—for instance the question whether a sentence, taken in its original context, really has the meaning one would like to express through its citation. Moreover, it seems that historical perspectives, such as the assumption that one should clarify the meaning of a statement in its own time and situation before translating it into the context of another time, does not concern Radhakrishnan.

If a "harmonization" of the type presented by Radhakrishnan were to become part of general education, its consequences would be bad. It does not teach how to think logically or historically; nor does it teach taking the words of a text seriously. It is conducive to an undisciplined rambling of the spirit in the realm of evocative ideals. The magnificent discipline which distinguishes ancient and medieval Indian thought seems lost. Radhakrishnan's method appears as a symptom of that "dissolution of old norms" which troubles him, and hardly as the beginning of a conquest of his distressful situation. To do justice to him, it is advisable to assess his work from the angle of the situation. It documents an inner reflection of the external situation. Therefore, the diagnosis of logical unbalance, argumentative weakness, and methodological deficiency is not a final value judgment, but part of a description of this very situation. Radhakrishnan's thought is a mobile and moving search for the possibility of new ways; it is not in itself a new way, nor is it the continuance of an old one.

In a sense, even the Neo-Hindu method of identifying juxtaposition, or indiscriminate coordination, has its precedents in an Indian tradition. In the history of Hindu thought, an identifying coordination of Gods and religions has occurred for various reasons; the details still require further exploration. In the late Vedic period, specifically among brahminical ascetic mystics who had secluded themselves from the groups of Aryan society,[19] such equalization may have been used as follows: it may have been a means to supersede the old polytheism as well as the impersonalism of the speculation about *brahman* and, moreover, the rivalry among theistic groups. But Radhakrishnan's equating cannot be affiliated with this, nor with the practice of Advaitic illusionists, for whom Gods were identical with each other because they viewed everything personal, even in the case of Gods, as an illusion. Radhakrishnan is not an illusionist, and he does not want to be one. Above all, the Neo-Hindu practice of identifying coordination cannot refer to the great theologians and philosophers of Hinduism and Buddhism. They had honest conflicts about distinctions which Neo-Hinduism ignores, and if they made identifications, they did so in accordance with explicit methodical principles. However, in Purāṇic and similar texts, we find at times an inclusivism which is very close to the thought of Radhakrishnan and other Neo-Hindus. In such texts, just as in Neo-Hinduism, foreign religions or systems per se do not appear as adversaries; only their exclusivistic claims are opposed. If we explore the circumstances, then it turns out to be highly probable that here, too, the proposal of a religious "solidarity" or an "interreligious friendship" was often an attempt to get away from the "pressure of a concrete historical situation."[20] What the two cases have in common is the presence of the "pressure of a concrete situation" as such; the content of the situation and the kind of pressure are, of course, completely different.

On the one hand, the coordination and identification of Gods and religions in historical Hinduism is meant to assert one's own absolutistic claims; as is still being done by the Neo-Vedāntic Ramakrishna Mission today, other religions are presented as relatively valuable but inferior forms whose content of truth converges with one's own metaphysics. On the other hand, it is done with a view to holding one's own ground against the absolutist claims of another religion; in this case, the claim is made that the foreign God who is presented as the absolute one by his devotees is in reality identical with the God of one's own religion. That kind of internal unity, and, above all, the awareness of such unity, which Radhakrishnan would like to see in Hinduism,[21] has not been there in traditional, historical Hinduism;[22] in this connection, it seems appropriate to recall that the word 'Hinduism,' as a collective label, was first coined by Western scholarship. To be sure, there was rivalry and cleavage, victory and defeat, defense and propagation, stimulation, assimilation, exchange, and reconciliation in one and the same geographical region. Radhakrishnan's practice of equating is proclamation and appeal rather than a structure of thought. Similarly, the sentence 'Viṣṇu and Śiva are one,' which is so common in Śaivite Purāṇas, is not only meant to be a theological statement, but also an appeal to the Vaiṣṇavas. That Radhakrishnan also wants to appeal to the non-Hindus, especially the Christians, is made evident by the fact that the great majority of his books were published in Europe.

In *The Principal Upaniṣads,* and even more so in *The Bhagavadgītā,* the notes on the translation express Radhakrishnan's own views more frequently than in *The Brahma Sūtra.* This may have to do with the fact that so far Neo-Hinduism has not developed a very lively relationship to the rather didactic Brahmasūtras, in contrast to the Bhagavadgītā, for which we already have a certain tradition of modern exegesis, and to some Upaniṣadic texts, for instance the *Īśā Upaniṣad,* which Radhakrishnan supplied with an especially detailed commentary. In all three books, Radhakrishnan's own doctrine is found primarily in the introductions. The ratio of the number of pages in the introduction to that in the text is 68:305 for the *Bhagavadgītā,* 129:790 for *The Principal Upaniṣads,* and 205:338 for *The Brahma Sūtra.* These proportions, especially the (by comparison) massive extent of the introduction to *The Brahma Sūtra,* corroborate what can also be demonstrated with regard to many details: Neo-Hindu thinking has not primarily emerged from an encounter with the texts of the old tradition, but has been motivated by the present, i.e., the contemporary Indian situation and the encounter with Western and Christian thought. In a secondary manner, and in association with those motivating factors, it was then affiliated with the Hindu tradition. Therefore, only a small segment of the Neo-Hindu ideas can be expressed in the form of a commentary to the old basic texts; there is no choice but to present them separately it in the form of an Introduction.

In his commentaries, Radhakrishnan shows "great respect for the traditional interpretations" (*The Brahma Sūtra,* p. 12); at the end of *The Brahma Sūtra* (pp. 563 f.), he says:

> This great work Brahma Sūtra is capable of answering the main problems of the philosophy of religion, though many of its detailed references may be outdated. It deals with the problems of religious experience and scriptural authority, *mokṣa* as union with the Godhead, and worship as the confrontation of the human individual and the Divine Reality, the destiny of the individual, ethics, and spiritual life. We have inherited a priceless trust which must be fostered until, as the Arabs say, the stars grow old, the sun grows old, and the leaves of the judgment book unfold.

But it does not seem that this "trust" or entrusted wealth is still a living force for him. The preface articulates his program "[to] re-establish it [i.e., the Brahmasūtra] in the minds and hearts of the people" and "to present a reasoned faith which deals justly with the old Indian tradition and the demands of modern thought." "The classics should be not only guardians of the past but heralds of the future . . . Any system of thought should satisfy two basic requirements; it should state the truth and interpret it for each new generation" (p. 11).

But for a credible attempt to interpret the text for a "new generation" and thereby to present it as a "herald of the future" and "re-establish it in the minds and hearts of the people," the following would have been necessary: to demonstrate in detail, i.e., in commenting on specific relevant Sūtras, how the themes of the text listed in Radhakrishnan's concluding remarks can be translated into "modern thought," and to show which references are "outdated," what has remained valid, and how it is still valid. This has not been accomplished. Can it be accomplished at all? One can treat the old texts with great reverence and yet present those ideas which really move our contemporary world apart from these texts.

Notes

1. S. Radhakrishnan, *The Brahma Sūtra. The Philosophy of Spiritual Life.* Trans. with an introduction and notes (London: Allen and Unwin, 1960; 606 pages).

2. S. Radhakrishnan, *The Bhagavadgītā.* With an introductory essay, Sanskrit text, English translation and notes (London: Allen and Unwin, 1948; 388 pages).

3. S. Radhakrishnan, *The Principal Upaniṣads.* Ed. with introduction, text, translation and notes (London: Allen and Unwin, 1953; 958 pages).

4. S. Radhakrishnan, *The Dhammapada.* With introductory essays, Pāli text, English translation and notes (London: Oxford University Press, 1950; reprinted 1954; 1958; vii, 194 pages).

5. S. Radhakrishnan, *Indian Philosophy.* 2 vols. (London: Allen and Unwin; New York: Macmillan, 1923–27; 7th impression, 1956; 738, 807 pages).

6. Such a judgment has been attempted by Icilio Vecchiotti, *Pensatori dell' India contemporanea* (Rome, 1959; see P. Hacker's review, *Kl. Schr.,* pp. 752–56).

7. *Contemporary Indian Philosophy,* ed. by S. Radhakrishnan and J. H. Muirhead (London, 2nd ed., 1952), pp. 475 f. [1st ed.: 1936].

8. With reference to India—1926: "We feel that our society is in a condition of unstable equilibrium" (*The Hindu View of Life,* p. 130); 1926: "The assimilation of a different culture . . . has shaken the faith in the traditional solutions . . . It is a bewildering phenomenon that, just when India is ceasing to appear grotesque to Western eyes, she is beginning to appear so to the eyes of some of her own sons" (*Indian Philosophy,* vol. 2, pp. 773; 779); 1929; ". . . venerable structures built by the patience and effort of unnumbered generations are attacked from all sides. Religion is set down as the cause of our intellectual and national bondage, of our failure and lack of vitality" (*An Idealist View of Life,* p. 49); 1942: "In this fateful hour, when our society has become a pathless jungle . . ." (*Religion and Society,* p. 117); 1951: "When an old binding culture is being broken,

when ethical standards are dissolving, when we are being aroused out of apathy . . . when there is in the air general ferment, inward stirring, cultural crisis, then a high tide of spiritual agitation sweeps over peoples, and we sense in the horizon something novel, something unprecedented, the beginnings of a spiritual renaissance" (*The Principal Upaniṣads,* p. 9).—With reference to the world—1928: "The slow dissolution of traditional codes of social customs and beliefs, the steady breakdown of inherited sanctions of religion and law, the confusion in regard to social ethics, and the principles of government are some of the most striking features of our age" (*The Religion We Need,* p. 1); 1929: "Civilization today seems to be passing through one of its periodic crises . . . Standards, aims and institutions which were generally accepted even a generation ago are now challenged and changing" (*Kalki,* p. 5); 1929: "The world is a chaos today" (*East and West in Religion,* p. 77); 1939: "Modern civilization . . . is uprooting the world over the customs of long centuries and creating a ferment of restlessness . . . We are at a gloomy moment in history" (*Eastern Religions and Western Thought,* pp. vii; 383); 1949: "There is a startling relaxing of traditions, of restraints and of established law and order" (*Religion and Society,* p. 10); 1955: "Whether in the East or in the West, we have unresolved contradictions . . ." (*East and West,* p. 13); 1955/56: ". . . when other civilizations collapsed, the attack came mainly from without; today the menace is from within . . . The contemporary situation is pregnant with great possibilities, immense dangers or immeasurable rewards . . . the sense of insecurity, of impending doom . . ." (*Recovery of Faith,* pp. 3 f.); 1959: "We are in the midst of one of the great crises in human history . . ." (*The Brahma Sūtra,* p. 7).

9. *The Hindu View of Life,* p. 128.

10. See, for instance, *The Brahma Sūtra,* p. 7: "Hindu thought, whether or not we agree with its transcendental claims, has survived the storms of the world for over three thousand years. It has seen empires come and go, has watched economic and political systems flourish and fade . . . Recent events have ruffled but not diverted the march of India's history. The culture of India has changed a great deal and yet has remained the same for over three millennia. Fresh springs bubble up, fresh streams cut their own channels through the landscape, but sooner or later each rivulet, each stream merges into one of the great rivers which has been nourishing the Indian soil for centuries" (*The Brahma Sūtra,* p. 7).

11. See his polemics against Karl Barth in *Eastern Religions and Western Thought,* pp. 283–87; 297–304; 341–43.

12. *Contemporary Indian Philosophy,* 2nd ed., p. 475.

13. See his polemics against Albert Schweitzer in *Eastern Religions and Western Thought,* chapter 3.

14. See the quotations from *The Principal Upaniṣads* and *Recovery of Faith* in n. 8.

15. *Recovery of Faith,* p. 199.

16. See, for instance, *Recovery of Faith,* chapter 5.

17. See, for instance, *Recovery of Faith,* pp. 126; 185 f.; and especially p. 197.

18. From the context of the first letter to the Corinthians, it is evident that the Corinthians prided themselves on a certain "spiritual experience." But just this, as well as other "spiritual experience," to the extent that it deviates from the Christian message, is meant when Paul speaks of the "wisdom of the world" which is "foolishness to God." The idea that rational knowledge is inadequate is not at all under discussion in *1 Corinthians* 3, 19. It is obvious that the "wisdom of the world" is "foolishness to God" not because it is rational, but because, as Paul himself says in 1,21, "God decided to save those, who have faith (in it), through the 'foolishness' of his message (κήρυγμα)." This is only one of countless cases where Radhakrishnan makes an incorrect use of quotes he has divorced from their context.

19. See J. Varenne, *La Mahā Nārāyaṇa Upaniṣad* (Paris, 1960; Publications de l'Institut de Civilization Indienne, vols. 11 and 13); esp. vol. 2, pp. 43–50 [see also P. Hacker's review, *Kl. Schr.,* pp. 776–79; on "serial identifications," see above, Chapter 4, section IV B].

20. See P. Hacker, *Prahlāda* (Mainz: Ak.Wiss.Lit., 1959), pp. 182–85; 196–98.

21. See *The Brahma Sūtra,* p. 269 (concluding statements on the first *pāda* of the first *adhyāya*): ". . . the great structure of Hinduism. Regarded from the outside, it may have the appearance of a confused mass of conflicting ideas, a congeries of contradictory elements, a complex of varied forces. There is, however, an identity, not mechanical but organic."

22. Works such as Madhusūdana's *Prasthānabheda* cannot be cited as evidence for an awareness of the unity of Hinduism. They demonstrate invariably nothing but the absolutistic claims, furnished with inclusivistic arguments, of particular groups (often, Advaita Vedānta) within Hinduism.

Bibliographical Notes on the Texts and Translations

The fifteen articles assembled in this volume constitute an almost complete collection of Hacker's articles on classical and modern Vedānta, as found in his *Kleine Schriften* (ed. by Lambert Schmithausen. Wiesbaden, 1978). One very early and one relatively late contribution were omitted: "Vedānta-Studien. 1: Bemerkungen zum Idealismus Śaṅkaras." *Die Welt des Orients* 3 (1948), pp. 240–49 (*Kl. Schr.*, pp. 59–68): "Notes on the Māṇḍūkyopaniṣad and Śaṅkara's Āgamaśāstravivaraṇa." *India Major* (Leiden, 1972; Festschrift J. Gonda), pp. 115–32 (*Kl. Schr.*, pp. 252–69). In addition to his articles, Hacker published two monographs on Advaita Vedānta: *Untersuchungen über Texte des frühen Advaitavāda. 1: Die Schüler Śaṅkaras* (Wiesbaden, 1951; Ak. Wiss. Lit. Mainz, 1950); *Vivarta, Studien zur Geschichte der illusionistischen Kosmologie und Erkenntnistheorie der Inder* (Wiesbaden, 1953; Ak. Wiss. Lit. Mainz, 1953). An English translation of these two pioneering studies, which would certainly be fully justified, would require a separate volume. This might also include Hacker's investigations on Vimuktātman, which still await editing and publishing in their original German version. Hacker's articles on "inclusivism," which contain significant references to Vedāntic thought, have been discussed in *India and Europe* (pp. 403–18).

The nucleus of this volume is found in Chapter 5, i.e., Jarava Lal Mehta's translation "Śaṅkara the Yogin and Śaṅkara the Advaitin" (*Kl. Schr.*, pp. 213–42). More than a decade ago, J. L. Mehta (1912–1988) told me about the existence of this translation, which he had made at the request of T. M. P. Mahadevan and used in some of his classes at the Harvard Center for the Study of World Religions. He provided me with a copy of his translation, as well as with the only other piece he had translated, i.e., a short, yet significant section "On Śaṅkara and Advaita

Vedānta" (Chapter 1 in this volume), which is found in Hacker's review article "Zur Geschichte und Beurteilung des Hinduismus. Kritik einiger verbreiteter Ansichten" (*Kl. Schr.*, pp. 476–483; especially pp. 478–80). It was at this time that the idea of publishing a collection of Hacker's Vedānta studies in English took shape. A few years later, I learned that two other articles by Hacker were available in unpublished English translations: "The Concept of Dharma in Neo-Hinduism" (Chapter 12) and the major part of "Schopenhauer and Hindu Ethics" (Chapter 13), both by Dermot Killingley (University of Newcastle upon Tyne). Dr. Killingley was kind enough to complete his translation of the Schopenhauer article (certainly one of Hacker's most intriguing and provocative studies) specifically for this volume. At my request, my colleagues and friends John Taber (University of New Mexico, Albuquerque) and Hugh van Skyhawk (University of Heidelberg) joined in the effort. Dr. Taber translated "Distinctive Features of the Doctrine and Terminology of Śaṅkara" (Chapter 4) and "The Theory of Degrees of Reality in Advaita Vedānta" (Chapter 6); Dr. van Skyhawk worked on "The Idea of the Person in the Thinking of Vedānta Philosophers" (Chapter 7). I added my own translations of "Being and Spirit in Vedānta" (Chapter 9), "Vivekananda's Religious Nationalism" (Chapter 14), and "A Prasthānatraya Commentary of Neo-Hinduism" (Chapter 15), as well as five articles which Hacker himself had written and published in English (Chapter 2, 3, 8, 10, and 11).

With the exception of "The Idea of the Person in the Thinking of Vedānta Philosophers" (a very personal, passionate, and somewhat idiosyncratic statement of a convert, which posed special problems and called for a collaborative effort), my own editorial revisions of the contributions I received were minimal. Because of the different styles and backgrounds of the translators and because of changes and variations in Hacker's own presentations, complete homogeneity and consistency were neither possible nor even desirable. Some adjustments were, of course, made in the area of bibliographical and other conventions. Brief additions and explanations were occasionally added to Hacker's notes, either by the translators or the editor. They appear in "[]" or are otherwise characterized as such. A few minor stylistic changes were made in Hacker's English texts.

The articles span the period from 1947 (Chapter 3) to 1976 (Chapter 10; presented in 1976; first published in 1978). In a footnote in *Kleine Schriften* (p. 41), Hacker says about the first of these two articles ("Śaṅkarācārya and Śaṅkarabhagavatpāda") that it was printed in *New Indian Antiquary* 9 (1947), pp. 1–12, but that this volume of the journal "actually appeared only about 1950." He adds: "The author had received no proofsheets. The result was an intolerably large number of misprints, one of which even distorted the sense of a passage to the contrary of what the author had intended to say." Not only the misprints were corrected for the republication of the article in *Kl. Schr.* (pp. 41–58): "On this occasion, the author has made, especially on the last pages, a few changes which no longer reflect the views he held at the time when he first wrote the paper but correspond to the stage of development his scholarly views had reached by the time of the compilation of the present volume" (i.e., 1978). The second of the two papers, "Cit and Noûs," was originally presented at a conference on "Neoplatonism and Indian Thought," held in 1976 in St. Catharines, Canada. After its first publication in *Kl. Schr.* (pp. 320–37), it appeared also in *Neoplatonism and Indian Thought,* ed. by R. B. Harris (Albany, 1982), pp. 161–80.

The remaining thirteen articles in our volume come from a variety of Indological, theological and philological sources. "On Śaṅkara and Advaitism" (Chapter 1) represents one section of Hacker's review article "Zur Geschichte und Beurteilung des Hinduismus. Kritik einiger verbreiteter Ansichten" ("On the History and Assessment of Hinduism. Critique of Some Common Views": *Orientalistische Literaturzeitung* 59, 1964, cols. 231–45; *Kl. Schr.,* pp. 476–83; especially pp. 478–80). Chapter 2 ("Relations of Early Advaitins to Vaiṣṇavism"; *Kl. Schr.,* pp. 205–12) has its origin in a presentation at the meeting of the Deutsche Morgenländische Gesellschaft (German Oriental Society) in 1949; it was first published in WZKSO 9 (1965), pp. 147–54. The original German text of Chapter 4 ("Eigentümlichkeiten der Lehre und Terminologie Śaṅkaras"; *Kl. Schr.,* pp. 69–109) appeared in ZDMG 100 (1950), pp. 246–86, that of Chapter 5 ("Śaṅkara der Yogin und Śaṅkara der Advaitin"; *Kl. Schr.,* pp. 213–42) in WZKSO 12–13 (1968: Festschrift E. Frauwallner), pp. 119–48. Chapter 6 is based on an article commissioned by the editors of the *Zeitschrift für Missionswissenschaft und Religionswissenschaft* (see the editorial note to "Die Lehre von den Realitätsgraden im Advaita-Vedānta," *Kl. Schr.,* p. 120); it was meant for the instruction of Christian readers and was first published in ZMR 36 (1952), pp. 277–93. Chapter 7 ("Die Idee der Person im Denken von Vedānta-Philosophen"; *Kl. Schr.,* pp. 270–92) is a more committed, more polemical statement; it was first published in the Vatican journal *Studia Missionalia* 13 (1963), pp. 30–52 and reflects Hacker's conversion to Catholicism. Chapter 8 ("Śaṅkara's Conception of Man"; *Kl. Schr.,* pp. 243–51) appeared in the same journal, vol. 19 (1970), pp. 123–31; under the title "A Note on Śaṅkara's Conception of Man," it was also published in *German Scholars on India,* ed. by the Cultural Department of the Embassy of the Federal Republic of Germany, New Delhi. Vol. 1 (Benares, 1973), pp. 99–106. Chapter 9 was first published in an Italian translation ("Essere e spirito nel Vedānta." *Filosofia e vita* 10, 1969, pp. 26–46); the original German text ("Sein und Geist im Vedānta") appeared in *Kl. Schr.,* pp. 293–319. Chapter 11 ("Aspects of Neo-Hinduism as Contrasted with Surviving Traditional Hinduism") was presented as a lecture at the University of London in 1970 and again in 1976 at the University of Pennsylvania; it was first published in *Kl. Schr.,* pp. 580–608. Chapter 12 ("Der Dharmabegriff des Neuhinduismus"; *Kl. Schr.,* pp. 510–24) appeared once again in the Catholic missionary journal ZMR (vol. 42, 1958, pp. 1–15), while Chapter 14 ("Der religiöse Nationalismus Vivekanandas"; *Kl. Schr.,* pp. 565–79) was published in its Protestant counterpart *Evangelische Missionszeitschrift* (vol. 28, 1971, pp. 1–15). Chapter 13 ("Schopenhauer und die Ethik des Hinduismus"; *Kl. Schr.,* pp. 531–64) appeared in *Saeculum* 4 (1961), pp. 365–99. The review article "Ein Prasthānatraya-Kommentar des Neuhinduismus" (*Kl. Schr.,* pp. 525–30), which appears as the last Chapter in our collection, was first published in *Orientalistische Literaturzeitung* 56 (1961), cols. 565–76, i.e., in the same journal from which our first chapter was taken.

To all my co-translators, I am most grateful. In addition, I want to thank all those who accompanied the preparation and completion of this volume with their encouragement, advice, and good wishes. Paul Hacker's family was very supportive of the project. The publishers of the original edition of his *Kleine Schriften,* Franz Steiner Verlag (Stuttgart), as represented by Vincent Sieveking, agreed most willingly to the publication of this volume in English. To the editor, Lambert Schmithausen (Hamburg), I am indebted for his "Foreword." It is to be hoped that this compilation of Hacker's studies of traditional and modern Vedānta will serve as an incentive to consult the original edition of his *Kleine Schriften* and to make use of the superb analytical index provided by Professor Schmithausen.

Above all, I feel indebted to Jarava Lal Mehta (1912–1988) and to Paul Hacker (1913–1979) himself. This volume is a small sign of gratitude for the extraordinary academic inspiration and the generous personal encouragement I received from both of them.

Abbreviations

Hacker's explanations of specific abbreviations used for individual articles can be found in these articles themselves. In this volume, such lists appear usually between the text and the notes of an article, although Hacker himself preferred to present them at the very beginning of his texts. In some cases, explanations of abbreviations appear within the notes (see, for instance, Chapter 4, notes 8 and 18). The following brief list supplements this with some additional or more general abbreviations.

Ak. Wiss. Lit.	Akademie der Wissenschaften und der Literatur.
IIJ	*Indo-Iranian Journal.*
India and Europe	W. Halbfass, *India and Europe: An Essay in Understanding* (Albany, 1988).
JAOS	*Journal of the American Oriental Society.*
Kl. Schr.	P. Hacker, *Kleine Schriften,* ed. L. Schmithausen (Wiesbaden, 1978; Glasenapp-Stiftung, vol. 15).
l.	line.
n.	note.
tr., trans.	translated (by), translator.
v.	verse.
WZKS(O)	*Wiener Zeitschrift für die Kunde Südasiens* (formerly: *Süd- und Ostasiens*).
ZDMG	*Zeitschrift der Deutschen Morgenländischen Gesellschaft.*
ZMR	*Zeitschrift für Missionswissenschaft und Religionswissenschaft.*

Other abbreviations are self-explanatory.

Index

The index lists proper names and a selection of relevant terms from the text of the book. With the exception of important anonymous works, titles of works are usually not listed. Names and concepts from the notes appear only if they are of thematic relevance and go beyond the information provided by the text. Entries do not necessarily appear in the form in which they occur in the text. Some teminological entries refer to exemplary usages only. Subheadings have been generally avoided. All references, if not marked otherwise, are page references. Loriliai Biernacki, Ph.D. candidate in the Department of Religious Studies, University of Pennsylvania, deserves special recognition for her contribution to this index.